MW00355850

# GRAPHIC NOVELS
## for
## CHILDREN AND
## YOUNG ADULTS

# GRAPHIC NOVELS for CHILDREN AND YOUNG ADULTS

## A Collection of Critical Essays

### Edited by Michelle Ann Abate & Gwen Athene Tarbox

University Press of Mississippi | Jackson

Children's Literature Association Series

www.upress.state.ms.us

The University Press of Mississippi is a member of
the Association of American University Presses.

Copyright © 2017 by University Press of Mississippi
All rights reserved
Manufactured in the United States of America

First printing 2017

∞

Library of Congress Cataloging-in-Publication Data available

LCCN 2016055428
ISBN 978-1-4968-1167-7 (hardcover)
ISBN 978-1-4968-1168-4 (epub single)
ISBN 978-1-4968-1169-1 (epub institutional)
ISBN 978-1-4968-1170-7 (pdf single)
ISBN 978-1-4968-1171-4 (pdf institutional)

British Library Cataloging-in-Publication Data available

# CONTENTS

## GRAPHIC NOVELS AS COMICS STORYTELLING: WORD AND IMAGE, FORM AND GENRE

## HYBRID COMICS, TRANSMEDIAL STORYTELLING, AND GRAPHIC NOVELS IN ADAPTATION

## THE PEDAGOGY OF THE PANEL: COMICS STORYTELLING IN THE CLASSROOM

## REPRESENTING GENDER AND SEXUALITY IN THE COMICS MEDIUM

# ACKNOWLEDGMENTS

Over the last decade, scholars in literary studies, visual theory, library and information science, and education have developed a serious interest in children's and YA comics. At national conferences and in leading journals, experts such as Charles Hatfield, Philip Nel, Joe Sutliff Sanders, and John Schumacher have helped to define the medium in relation to young readers. We are extremely grateful for their contributions to the field, as well as those of comics theorists such as Thierry Groensteen, Scott McCloud, Jared Gardner, Barbara Postema, and Hillary L. Chute, whose scholarship has helped to inform many of the essays included in this volume. We also want to acknowledge the work of the Comic Book Legal Defense Fund; their website includes a number of resources related to children's comics, including Meryl Jaffe's *Raising a Reader! How Comics & Graphic Novels Can Help Your Kids Love To Read!*, which has introduced scholars and school children alike to the value of reading children's and YA comics.

As we worked to assemble this collection and write the introduction, we were aided in our research efforts by librarians at a number of institutions, including the Billy Ireland Museum at The Ohio State University, Dwight B. Waldo Library at Western Michigan University, and the Belgian Comic Strip Center in Brussels. In the last few years, we both attended informative conference panels sponsored by the Modern Language Association, the Children's Literature Association, the International Comic Arts Forum, the National Council of Teachers of English, and perhaps most memorably, a series of talks at the First International Conference on Comics and Graphic Novels: Sites of Visual and Textual Innovation, sponsored by the Instituto Franklin at the Universidad de Alcalá in Alcalá de Henares, Spain. It was at that conference that we had the pleasure of meeting many international scholars who were engaged in the study of children's comics, and we are grateful for their generosity and support.

At the University Press of Mississippi, we began this project with Vijay Shah, who helped usher us through the proposal stage before handing the project off to Katie Keene, who has worked with us closely throughout the manuscript-editing process. We appreciate their encouragement, advice, and unwavering support of this project. We also want to thank Valerie Jones and Robert Norrell for their editorial help. We want to thank the Children's Literature Association Publications Committee for their review of the proposal and the subsequent readers of the manuscript. Their helpful comments and advice enabled us to develop what we hope is a substantive and timely collection.

The initial call for essays for this project solicited proposals from over fifty scholars, an indication of the growing interest in children's and YA comics. We want to thank everyone who participated in this initial phase. We wish we could have included all of your fine scholarship in this volume—and we hope that you will continue to research, write, and publish your excellent work about comics and graphic novels for young people in other venues. We owe a special thanks to those scholars whose work appears in these pages. They adroitly engaged with numerous rounds of editorial feedback, and they delivered quality chapters in a timely fashion. We thank you for your unfailing professionalism, your intellectual diligence, and, of course, your marvelous essays.

Michelle wishes to thank, first and foremost, her coeditor, Gwen. Your intellectual input, editorial hard work, and myriad logistical efforts were tremendous assets to this project. In addition, your lively conversation, buoyant personality, and general good cheer made the long and often arduous process of putting together a volume of this nature pleasurable. Michelle is equally indebted to her colleagues and students at The Ohio State University. Caroline Clark, Sandra Stroot, Pat Enciso, Mollie Blackburn, Jenny Robb, Caitlin McGurk, and Karly Marie Grice provided not simply the intellectual camaraderie but also the material support that helped to make research projects like this one possible. Finally, Michelle owes a special debt to Annette Wannamaker for her wisdom, her good humor, and her patience. I value your friendship, both personally and professionally, more than I can express.

Gwen would like to thank her coeditor, Michelle Ann Abate, for bringing her extensive expertise in children's and YA literature to bear on this collaboration, and for her enthusiasm about the comics medium in general. Gwen would also like to thank Alex Enyedi, former dean of the College of Arts and Sciences at Western Michigan University, as well as Jonathan Bush, former department chair in English, and Nicolas Witschi, current department chair, for their support of this project from the outset. They helped her to secure travel and research funds as she worked to further her understanding of comics studies, and along with her department colleagues, provided a wonderful home base from which to conduct scholarship. Gwen is also grateful to colleagues in comics studies, including Charles Hatfield, Aaron Kashtan, Joe Sutliff Sanders, Philip Nel, Barbara Postema, Pascal Lefèvre, Ian Hague, Paul Gravett, Hillary L. Chute, and Greice Schneider, who introduced her to advanced comics theory.

In Fall 2012 and Spring 2014, Gwen had the privilege of teaching two upper-division courses in comics studies at Western Michigan University; in each instance, her students proved themselves to be exceptionally gifted at comics interpretation and often served as sounding boards for her ideas. Among this group of talented students, Gwen wants to extend a special note of thanks to Traci Brimhall, her teaching assistant for ENGL 5970, Introduction to Comics Studies, whose expertise in poetics helped further some of her ideas about comics structure.

Gwen's comics family has grown in the last couple of years to include Derek Royal and Andy Kunka, the Two Guys with PhDs Talking About Comics, whose Comics Alternative podcasts reflect the very best ideas, trends, and concepts in the field. In 2015, Derek and Andy invited Gwen to co-host a podcast devoted to children's and YA comics, along with Andy Wolverton, a librarian in the Anne Arundel County Public Library system in Maryland. Gwen's work on children's comics has been greatly enhanced by this collaboration, and she is grateful to all three guys for their help and support.

Finally, Gwen would like to thank her dear friends in the Children's Literature Association for their willingness to talk about all things comics, as well as her mom, Nan Tarbox, who read the funny pages with her father, Joe Jordan, and her sister, Kay McCall, when she was a little girl, who loved *Wonder Woman* comics as a teen, and who introduced Gwen to their local comics store back in Flint, Michigan. She even bought Gwen *The Peanuts Cook Book* that she loved as much for the recipes as for the Charles Schulz images that accompanied them.

Art Spiegelman, the American cartoonist who created such well-known graphic texts as *Maus* and *Little Lit*, once commented, "I'm interested in comics. Sometimes I'm interested in making them, sometimes I'm interested in looking at them, sometimes I'm interested in thinking about and writing what it is that I'm understanding about them" (240). *Graphic Novels for Children and Young Adults: A Collection of Critical Essays* was created according to this same ethos: by a group of individuals who are interested in looking at, thinking about, writing on, understanding more concerning, and even making, comics. We hope you enjoy reading this volume as much as we have enjoyed assembling it.

## Works Cited

Spiegelman, Art. *Conversations: Art Spiegelman.* Ed. Joseph Witek. Jackson: University Press of Mississippi, 2007.

# INTRODUCTION

## Gwen Athene Tarbox and Michelle Ann Abate

### The Varied Landscape of Contemporary Children's and YA Comics

The closing decades of the twentieth century and the opening years of the new millennium witnessed an array of profound transformations in children's and young adult literature. From the worldwide craze over the *Harry Potter* series and the meteoric rise of dystopian YA fiction to the exponential increase in cinematic adaptations of children's texts and the advent of digital storytelling, the field underwent profound literary, artistic, and commercial changes. Arguably one of the most significant transformations that took place in the realm of literature for children and young adults during this period was the resurgence of comics geared toward a youth readership.

Matthew Holm, who, along with his sister, children's author Jennifer Holm, draws the popular children's graphic novel series *Babymouse* (2005–2015), reflected on this phenomenon in a recent interview. Looking back over the trajectory of his own experience as a comics reader and as a comics creator, Holm remembers a relatively barren landscape for young readers of comics during his childhood in the 1970s and early 1980s. The meteoric popularity of adult-oriented graphic novels such as *Watchmen* (1986) and *Batman: The Dark Knight Returns* (1986), combined with the decades-old Comics Code restrictions, diminished the quality of comic book offerings for children and sent the message that, in Holm's words, "comics [were] not for kids" (Smith).

The phenomenon that Holm describes can be traced back to the early 1950s, when the rise of popular culture artifacts marketed specifically to young people, including films, television programs, record albums, teen magazines, and comic books, created a concern among parents and educators that children's minds and bodies were being harmed by over-exposure to lowbrow influences. The publication in 1954 of Fredric Wertham's *Seduction of the Innocent*, which provided proportedly scientific proof of the dangers of comics reading, fueled a national crusade against comics that included adult-sponsored book burnings and US Senate hearings that attempted to prove that reading comics caused juvenile delinquency (Tilley 402). In an attempt to salvage their industry, comics publishers established the Comics Magazine Association of American (CMAA), an organization that profoundly restricted content by ensuring that any comic bearing its seal would be "free of offensive content such as poor grammar, excessive violence, and supernatural beings" (Tilley 385).

Once the Comics Code was in place, artists who wanted the freedom to express controversial ideas or to depict a broad range of protagonists and experiences turned to writing comics for adults. Compounding this situation was the fact that the overwhelming majority of comics were sold outside the traditional bookstore environment frequented by children and their parents; comic book specialty stores operated on the subscription model whereby customers signed up in advance to receive serialized comics every week, and most of these venues had long ceased catering to a child clientele (Lopes 73). In response to questions regarding their early influences, contemporary children's comics artists such as Holm, Raina Telgemeier, and Jeff Kinney recall reading Sunday comic strips and printed collections of *Peanuts* or *Calvin and Hobbes* comics that they purchased at bookstores, before moving directly to more high-art comics such as Art Spiegelman's *Maus* (1986) or Neil Gaiman's *Sandman* series (1989).

A powerful impetus for North American publishers to reinvest in children's comics had its origin in the successful importation of Japanese anime and manga to English speaking audiences during the late 1980s and early 1990s. Both the *Pokémon* and *Sailor Moon* series, which were only two of hundreds of child-oriented comics and cartoons produced in Japan during this era, were broadcast on North American television and set the stage for entrepreneurs such as Dark Horse Comics and VIZ Media to collect popular manga serials into graphic novels and offer them for sale, relying on word of mouth and the growing presence of manga and anime booths and cosplay events at comics conventions to attract a preteen and teenage following. This strategy was enhanced by Tokyopop, a US-based producer of original English-language (OEL) manga, which began publishing numerous successful titles in the late 1990s. Run by Stu Levy, the company aggressively pursued a child demographic, "publishing manga in a diversity of genres, and helping to establish comics in general bookstores" (Reid). Moreover, industry analyst Calvin Reid has credited Levy's primary focus "on shoujo manga, or Japanese comics targeting young girls—for helping to attract millions of American girls, long ignored by U.S. comics publishers, into reading comics and going to general bookstores to buy them" (Reid).

North American book publishers were initially unprepared to meet the growing demand for manga, but by the mid-2000s they had transformed their distribution and editorial practices when it came to getting graphic novels into the hands of child readers. Diamond, which handles the distribution of DC and Marvel comics, established Diamond Kids in 2006 in order to connect traditional comic book stores with a younger demographic. Random House,

Scholastic, and Harper Collins support comics imprints for children; independent comics publisher Fantagraphics regularly reaches child readers through a distribution agreement with W. W. Norton; and Macmillan has bolstered its presence in the teen market by acquiring First Second Books, the publishers of Gene Luen Yang's blockbusters *American Born Chinese* (2007) and *Boxers & Saints* (2013), as well as Vera Brosgol's *Anya's Ghost* (2011).

Even a cursory examination of book sales and publishing trends reveals the extensive scope of the contemporary children's and YA graphic novel phenomenon: the Holms' *Babymouse* books have sold two million copies since their debut in 2005; Jeff Smith's *Bone* (1991–2004) has gone through no fewer than thirteen editions; Bryan Lee O'Malley's *Scott Pilgrim* series (2004–2010) has sold a million copies in North America, and the series has been translated into thirteen languages (MacDonald "Scott Pilgrim's Finest Sales Chart"); and finally and perhaps most persuasively, Jeff Kinney's *The Diary of a Wimpy Kid* series (2007–2014) boasts more than sixty million copies in print. Not surprisingly, given these figures, *Publisher's Weekly* reported in its 2013 survey that the sales of children's and YA graphic novels continue to outpace the overall comics market. In 2015, ICv2, a consulting firm that publishes an annual white paper on the comics industry, noted that children's comics production had reached its highest point in history, with over 400 new titles entering the market and a 35 percent sales increased in the children's category for the first 8 months of 2015 (Griepp). Prizing committees have also taken notice of the genre: Gene Luen Yang's *American Born Chinese* became the first graphic novel to win a major American Library Association prize, the Michael L. Printz Award for Young Adult Literature, in 2007. By 2012, the Will Eisner Awards offered three categories to honor children's and young adult comics: the Best Publication for Early Readers (up to age 7), the Best Publication for Kids (ages 8–12), and the Best Publication for Teens (ages 13–17).

Far from simply replicating manga in terms of style, content, or form, contemporary children's comics have benefited from a heightened appreciation for generic and artistic experimentation that has characterized children's and YA literature as a whole. Today, both in text-only and in comics narratives, children's book authors are likely to employ child focalizers, provide indeterminate endings, and foster other forms of postmodern ideation, including deviations in terms of narrative coherence and a furtherance of the expectation that readers need to be challenged to fill in interpretative gaps on their own. In this atmosphere of experimentation, hybridity has come to the fore. The most popular children's comics over the last decade, Shaun Tan's *The Arrival* (2006), Kinney's *Diary of a Wimpy Kid* series (2007–2014), and Brian Selznick's Caldecott Medal-winning *The Invention of Hugo Cabret* (2007) all depart from the traditional comics format of sequential panels.

Contemporary children's and YA comics possess a multifaceted lineage and boast a group of creators whose backgrounds, stylistic allegiances, and varied levels of engagement with traditional children's book publishing combine to offer a plethora of choices for young readers. For instance, buoyed by the mainstream success of high-art, long-form comics such as Alison Bechdel's *Fun Home: A Family Tragicomedy* (2006) and Marjane Satrapi's *Persepolis* (2007), comics creators such as Hope Larson and Barry Deutsch have begun to develop children's comics in addition to their work on adult-focused projects. Larson's adaptation of Madeleine L'Engle's *A Wrinkle in Time* has been praised for its stark aesthetic that places the text in a long tradition of adult high-art comics, and Deutsch's Hereville series includes a technical economy of line and story pacing that reflects his years as a political cartoonist. Other comics creators, including Faith Erin Hicks, Dav Pilkey, and Raina Telgemeier, have chosen to work exclusively in children's and YA comics and will often incorporate narration techniques (such as first person focalization) and tropes (including the absence of adult authority) that are prevalent in text-only books for children.

The field is also enhanced by partnerships between established children's and YA authors and comics creators, providing another venue for comics creation. While Kate DiCamillo and K. G. Campbell's Newbery Award-winning hybrid comic/text *Flora and Ulysses: The Illuminated Adventures* (2014) emerged out of a more traditional arrangement in which Campbell and the art director at Candlewick Press developed the comics that appear in the novel (Mandel), Sherman Alexie's collaboration on *The Absolutely True Diary of a Part-Time Indian* (2007) with artist Ellen Forney was a close partnership. As Alexie has noted, working with Forney sparked his own visual creativity, enabling him to make a significant contribution to the look and the content of comics that appear in the novel:

> When I started writing [*The Absolutely True Diary*] as a novel, for some reason in the first paragraph, I made [Arnold] a cartoonist. I sent Ellen Forney, who is a friend of mine, about a page, I think, and I said, "Can you draw a cartoon of this?" About five minutes later, it came back over the e-mail. So she was a part of this five minutes into its creation. (Dunnewind)

Alexie went on to observe that contrary to what early reviewers of the the novel might have thought regarding his motivation for creating a hybrid comic/text novel, he was involved throughout the process, explaining that while Forney completed a third of the images on her own, "some of them I dictated, some of them we did together," establishing a process in which Alexie was able to highlight his skills as a comics script writer while also benefiting from Forney's experience as an artist (Dunnewind).

Comics adaptations are another popular segment of the children's and YA comics market, ranging from graphic novel renderings of children's classics, such as Hope Larson's highly acclaimed version of Madeleine L'Engle's *A Wrinkle in Time* (2012) to illustrated comics versions of high school English classics such as *The Great Gatsby* by Nicki Greenberg (2008). Children's texts that originated as text-only narratives have been adapted into graphic novels, and in some instances, those same artifacts have been made into films, including Neil Gaiman and P. Craig Russell's *Coraline* (2008) and Eric Shanower and Skottie Young's *The Wizard of Oz* (2010). In this instance, the ability to experience a story line across three forms of media provides child readers with the ability to practice comparative analysis. Rounding out the resurgence of the field of children's and YA comics was the recent decision by DC and Marvel Comics to reboot popular series with young child readers in mind. Laura Hudson, a journalist who writes on comics trends, explains that "although the most popular superheroes tend to be white guys created decades ago, legacy heroes who pass their familiar names to new characters are one way publishers like Marvel and DC Comics have brought greater diversity to their fictional worlds" ("First Look"). Marvel's *Ultimate Comics: Spider-Man*, which debuted in 2011, features Miles Morales, a middle grade student of African American and Latinx heritage, and the 2014 iteration of the Ms. Marvel series focuses on a sixteen-year-old Pakistani American character, Kamala Khan. Both of these reboots, and others like them, are bringing young readers back to reading serial comics written specially for a young audience.

Another factor that has contributed to the increased public presence, readerly popularity, and critical esteem of children's and YA comics involves the support of K-12 and community librarians. At their annual conference in 2002, the American Library Association (ALA) hosted an event to acknowledge the growing significance of North American comics for children and young adults. Bearing the provocative title "Get Graphic @ Your Library," the session also provided guidance for how the genre would develop in the new millennium. The Young Adult Library Services Association preconference session on comics brought together nearly two hundred fifty youth services librarians to learn about the history, format, and content of comics from what was then a relatively small cadre of authors and artists who were interested in the genre. Neil Gaiman, one of the comics authors in attendance, told an interviewer:

> I went [to ALA] expecting to be talking to the 250 comics fans who had grown up to be librarians; I couldn't have been more wrong: the librarians were getting pressure from their readers. The librarians knew that graphic novels . . . were popular, and they wanted to know what they were. So they got [us] to tell them what we though they should know. And the libraries . . . started ordering the books. (quoted in Serchay)

Gaiman was far from alone in this assessment. In a comprehensive study of graphic novel circulation in US public libraries conducted in 2013, researcher Edward Schneider revealed that 98.1 percent of libraries now house a graphic novel collection, and that children under the age of eighteen represent over half of all graphic novel borrowing statistics (74). This pattern is replicated in many school libraries, where graphic novels represent a majority of check-outs, even in collections where the graphic novels holdings are relatively small (Schneider 76).

Young people are likewise connecting with graphic novels in the classroom. In 2011, the Toronto District School Board hired the owners of The Beguiling comic book store to serve as consultants in their effort to integrate graphic novels into the K-12 curriculum, and in the US, Diamond Kids has launched an annual list of over a hundred graphic novels that meet specific guidelines in the Common Core State Standards Initiative. The Comic Book Legal Defense Fund publishes a helpful PDF guide for parents, educators, and students entitled *Raising a Reader! How Comics & Graphic Novels Can Help Your Kids Love To Read!*, authored by Meryl Jaffe and illustrated by Matt Holm and Raina Telgemeier. *Raising a Reader* includes a primer on basic comics grammar, a list of recommended texts, and a description of the literacy benefits of reading comics.

The career trajectory of Raina Telgemeier, author of the highly popular and award-winning graphic novels *Smile* (2010), *Drama* (2012), *Sisters* (2014), and *Ghosts* (2016), exemplifies another key trend that has enabled authors to reach young readers in greater numbers: *Smile* originated as a web comic series before transitioning to print format. Telgemeier told an interviewer in 2010: "Thanks to the instant feedback I got each week, I was also able to gauge which storylines resonated with my readers" (Dueben). Akin to Matthew Holm and Raina Telgemeier, many comics creators have been bolstered not only by online reader reactions to their work, but by the in-person response from young people at comics conferences, book signings, and library visits. Jeff Kinney, author of the popular series *The Diary of a Wimpy Kid*, for example, sold out the Sydney Opera House during a recent world tour. Meanwhile, media specialists struggle to keep up with reader demand (MacDonald). Esther Keller, a librarian in the New York Public School system, explains that maintaining a middle school comics collection can be daunting, both because of the volume of new releases and the breadth of subject matter that interests her students:

> I have some students who watch Anime at home and want to continue the experience by reading Manga. They'll read whatever they can get their hands on. It's difficult because of the narrow age group I work with (11–14), it's hard to find enough age appropriate titles or just keeping up with the sheer number of

volumes in ongoing series make it impossible to keep up. Then there are the kids who love anything super hero and finally I have the group of kids who discovered a title like Raina Telgemeier's *Smile*.... From there, they've grown to Faith Erin Hicks and other titles that speak to teenagers. (Keller)

## Scholarship on Children's and YA Comics

Given the popularity and influence that children's and YA graphic novels enjoy, contemporary developments in the genre have received surprisingly scant critical attention. In 2006, writing in the periodical *The Lion and the Unicorn*, comics scholar Charles Hatfield argued that for too long, academics have viewed graphic novels for young people as lowbrow artifacts unworthy of study alongside award-winning prose novels: "Rhetorically, the 'comic book' has traditionally served, and to an extent still continues to serve, as a kind of last glaring example of the unassimilated and unassimilable, a marker of the boundary between literature and mere 'reading'" (365). Calling for a greater rapprochement between the fields of literary criticism and comics studies, Hatfield guest edited the 2007 publication of a special issue of the online scholarly journal *ImageTexT* focused on children's comics; but for the most part, key scholarship, such as Bradford Wright's *Comic Book Nation: The Transformation of Youth Culture in America* (2003), Dan Hadju's *The Ten-Cent Plague: The Great Comic-Book Scare and How It Changed America* (2008), and Jean-Paul Gabillliet's *Of Comics and Men: A Cultural History of Comic Books* (2010), has largely limited itself to historical overviews of children's comics written before 2000.[1] *Graphic Novels for Children and Young Adults: A Collection of Critical Essays*, which treats over twenty-five graphic novels written for young people since 2000, embraces Hatfield's call for scholarship that applies a variety of critical lenses to this growing and vibrant genre.

## Methodology and Organization

Any book concerning comics storytelling needs to address the question of the terminology that is used to describe these works. It is common practice to refer to texts such as Yang's *American Born Chinese* or Telgemeier's *Smile* as everything from simply "comics" or, somewhat more accurately, "long-form comics," to the more general "graphic narratives," or most pervasively as "graphic novels." The medium of comics refers to sequential art, though many scholars consider individual panels such as those created by Bil and Jeff Keane for their long running comic strip *Family Circus* to be part of the comics medium as well. Will Eisner, a prolific US comics artist, is commonly credited with coining the term "graphic novel" in the 1970s to refer to long-form comics that feature compelling narratives, such as his 1978 classic text, *A Contract with God*, though the term actually first appeared in an article by Richard Kyle in his comics magazine *Wonderworld* (Sanders). Many comics creators and academics have gravitated towards the term "graphic novel," in part to try to distinguish high art comics from serial comic books. The phrase "graphic narrative" serves a similar function. We have left it up to the collection's authors to determine which term they prefer, but use of "graphic novel" in the collection's title is meant to encourage the interest of the broadest readership possible, keeping in mind that the American Library Association often uses this term on its website and in the titles of its recommended lists, and most major publishers have followed suit. While the collection's authors hale from a variety of disciplines, including literary studies, pedagogy, and library science, all of them take into account the inherently visual and tactile nature of comics. This common vision creates a necessary cohesion, especially for work in a field that is still defining its purview, terms, and methodologies.

The essays in this volume have been separated into five thematic sections. Part I, which is titled "Graphic Novels as Comics Storytelling: Word and Image, Form and Content," contains essays that explore the structural and narratological elements that make comics a distinct and unique literary genre. The essays collected in Part II discuss titles that engage in transmedia storytelling, embody examples of a hybrid comics, or represent graphic novels in adaptation. By contrast, Part III shifts the focus of consideration from comics to their flesh-and-blood audiences, especially students; accordingly, this section spotlights what we call "The Pedagogy of the Panel: Youth Readers and Comics in the Classroom." Part IV features chapters that focus on the representation of gender and sexuality in comics for young readers. Finally, Part V engages with comics that explore questions of identity in general, and the way in which identity is refracted through a text's engagement with history, culture, and politics in particular. The purpose of this organizational plan is twofold. First, and most pragmatically, it allows scholars, students, and teachers to quickly and easily locate essays of interest. Second, and more theoretically, these groupings reflect some of the most important critical issues and recurring topics in comics scholarship.

In Part I, "Graphic Novels as Comics Storytelling: Word and Image, Form and Genre," the first chapter, Annette Wannamaker's "This Is a Well-Loved Book": Weighing (in on) Jeff Smith's *Bone*," chronicles the production history of the 1,332-page epic *Bone*, a comics text that has been published in multiple editions designed to appeal to both children and adult readers. Wannamaker asks whether a comic's aesthetic and material form influences how it is read and who is interested in reading it. This overview of comics format is followed up by three essays that focus on "the grammar of comics" itself, the way that artists and authors use various techniques to create meaning. In chapter 2, Karly Marie Grice introduces the idea of visual repetition as part of her analysis of Gene Luen Yang's two-part epic *Boxers & Saints*. In addition to "drawing on the work of Thierry Groensteen and his idea of 'braiding,'" Grice reviews "panel permeation, emphasizing postmodern and metafictional alterations to structural elements and color alteration, supported by theories of various visual analysis including picture books and multimodality" in order to uncover which of the many competing narratives that appear in Yang's diptych are meant to have the most sway with the reader.

The coming-of-age narrative, which is a feature of many YA comics, becomes the focus of essays by Sarah Thaller and Catherine Kyle. In chapter 3, "Comics, Adolescents, and the Language of Mental Illness: David Heatley's 'Overpeck' and Nate Powell's *Swallow Me Whole*," Thaller explores the manner in which visual imagery, rather than traditional prose narration, provides comics creators with an effective way to depict mental illness, noting that Heatley and Powell's comics "have the potential to combat the misinformation and damaging portrayals so commonly presented in YA literature and change the way mental illness is perceived and presented."

In chapter 4, "Not Haunted, Just Empty: Figurative Representation in Sarah Oleksyk's *Ivy*," Catherine Kyle looks at issues of emotional distress in *Ivy*, a comic that depicts the coming-of-age of an artist whose monstrous drawings offer clues to the state of her emotional and creative development. Kyle claims that the inclusion of imagery in the longstanding genre of the *Künstlerroman* "opens up vast possibilities for the depiction of the coming-of-age artist" and her "ability to represent metaphoric, symbolic, and figurative content visually on the page."

In Part II, "Hybrid Comics, Transmedial Storytelling, and Graphic Novels in Adaptation," Rachel L. Rickard Rebellino's "'Are You an Artist like Me?!' Do-It-Yourself Diary Books, Critical Reading, and Reader Interaction within the Worlds of the *Diary of a Wimpy Kid* and *Dork Diaries* Series" examines both the extraordinary popularity of text/image hybrid comics diaries created by Jeff Kinney and Rachel Renee Russell, as well as the companion texts that have been developed to encourage young readers to generate hybrid diaries of their own. Along the same lines, in chapter 6, "Parodic Potty Humor and Superheroic Potentiality in Dav Pilkey's *The Adventures of Captain Underpants*," Joseph Michael Sommers traces how Pilkey takes traumatic scenarios from his own childhood that could not be discussed or written into twentieth-century comic book heroics, and "reinvigorates them in the present moment where such discussions are not only realizable but encouraged" by creating the popular and complex *Captain Underpants* texts.

Both Aaron Kashtan's "Multimodality Is Magic: *My Little Pony* and Transmedia Strategies in Children's Comics" and Meghann Meeusen's "Framing Agency: Comics Adaptations of *Coraline* and *City of Ember*" focus on the properties of comics that do and do not translate well into other media. In chapter 7, Kashtan argues that of all the print, visual, and interactive versions in the *My Little Pony* franchise, the comics series is best placed "to promote the use of techniques for encouraging reflexive thinking about media that are difficult to implement in television, such as expressive typography." In chapter 8, Meeusen demonstrates how graphic novel adaptations of *Coraline* and *City of Ember* traverse the "line between childhood and adolescent quests in ways unique from either their source texts or film counterparts," noting that young people's power and agency are situated with more clarity in the comics medium.

Part III, "The Pedagogy of the Panel: Comics Storytelling in the Classroom," shifts the focus to the way that comics are being shared in a variety of educational settings. In chapter 9, Gwen Athene Tarbox draws on her experience integrating graphic novels into university-level children's literature courses, with a particular emphasis on how the comics medium pairs well with such established forms as illustrated novels, picture books, and films. In chapter 10, "Looking beyond the Scenes: Spatial Storytelling and Masking in Shaun Tan's *The Arrival*," Christiane Buuck and Cathy Ryan discuss how introducing comics theorist Thierry Groensteen's ideas about visual repetition enriched their university students' ability to interpret the medium. First introduced in his 1999 classic *The System of Comics* and reinforced in his 2012 text *Comics and Narration*, Groensteen's term "braiding" refers to a repeated element in a comic that draws the reader's attention to a particular idea or theme using images rather than words. The repeated element can be a page layout, the layout of an image in a panel, the repetition of a design, the figural placement of characters or objects on the page, but the key is that the braid requires the reader to be an active agent in the interpretative process (*Comics and Narration* 35). Buuck and Ryan demonstrate that many of the repeated elements—what they term "visual metaphors"—in Shaun Tan's *The Arrival* "offer opportunities for readers to superimpose their own lived experiences and cultural perspectives on the book's visual landscapes."

Rounding out Part III, Michael L. Kersulov, Mary Beth Hines, and Rebecca Rupert describe their use of the comics medium in a high school environment, sharing the results of a series of writing workshops in which ninth and tenth grade students read Sherman Alexie and Ellen Forney's award-winning *The Absolutely True Diary of a Part-Time Indian* and utilized the comics medium to create personal narratives that touched on trauma and its expression in meaningful ways.

The essays that comprise Part IV, "Representing Gender and Sexuality in the Comics Medium," underscore the complex and often controversial ways that gender identity, gender expression, and sexual orientation manifest themselves in a medium that is heavily image-centric. In chapter 12, "'Unbalanced on the Brink': Adolescent Girls and the Discovery of the Self in *Skim* and *This One Summer* by Mariko Tamaki and Jillian Tamaki," Marni Stanley traces the Tamaki cousins' depiction of coming-of-age as a gradual process of disillusionment paired with hope, a combination that is visualized in the graphic novels *Skim* and *This One Summer* via the connection of small objects (doodles, scrapbook pages, fragments of drawings) to the larger themes of "depression, racism, class hierarchies, sexualities, and the politics of women's bodies."

In chapter 13, "The Drama of Coming Out: Censorship and *Drama* by Raina Telgemeier," Eti Berland, a librarian and scholar of censorship, focuses on the importance of including LGBTQ friendly comics such as Telgemeier's *Drama* in school and community libraries. Noting that Telgemeier's text "has provided a new model for the coming out narrative that better portrays the realities of modern youth" Berland utilizes new constructions about genderqueer identity and nonheteronormative sexualities in the analysis of comic.

In her chapter on the Eisner-award winning comic book series *Lumberjanes*, Rachel Dean-Ruzicka suggests that the series "presents new forms of feminist identity by working outside of the neoliberal frameworks that often, as well as unfortunately, characterized third-wave feminist discourse, especially in the 'Girl Power' movement." Noting that "one of the most important aspects of *Lumberjanes* is how it employs collectivism," Dean-Ruzicka explores how intersectionality informs the series's core value.

Chapter 15, Rebecca Brown's "Engendering Friendship: Exploring Jewish and Vampiric Boyhood in Joann Sfar's *Little Vampire*," and chapter 16, Krystal Howard's "Gothic Excess and the Body in Vera Brosgol's *Anya's Ghost*," consider the way Romantic and Victorian-era literary forms affect the themes and images prevalent in a subgenre of middle school and YA comics focused on Gothic themes. As Brown points out, Joann Sfar's *Little Vampire* reworks Victorian and Edwardian ideas regarding the purported monstrous nature of non-normative subjectivity, thus making "the interconnections between Jews and vampires visible" and capable of serving as an argument in favor of marginalized selves. Howard takes up this theme as well, demonstrating that the titular protagonist of Brosgol's *Anya's Ghost* comes to terms with her status as an immigrant and works through her anxieties about her body via interactions with a ghost whose own difficulties serve as an object lesson.

The essays in Part V, "Drawing on Identity: History, Politics, Culture," concern the relationship between ideology and comics. Lance Weldy's chapter 17,

"Graphically/Ubiquitously Separate: The Sanctified Littering of Jack T. Chick's Fundy-Queer Comics," chronicles Chick's career as the purveyor of morally didactic comic tracts that feature "fundamentalist ('fundy' for short)" takes on "a wide range of topics such as abortion, Catholicism, communism, evolution, homosexuality, Islam, and rock music." In addition to detailing the history of the Chick Tract, Weldy sets out to show how these comics "explicitly indoctrinate children through visual literacy while serving a political purpose by means of categorical religious xenophobia."

Both David Low's chapter 18, "Waiting for Spider-Man: Representations of Urban School 'Reform' in Marvel Comics' Miles Morales Series," and Joanna Davis-McElligatt's chapter 19, "'Walk Together, Children': The Function and Interplay of Comics, History, and Memory in *Martin Luther King and the Montgomery Story* and John Lewis's *March: Book One*," are equally interested in the way that graphic novels can become the catalyst for the discussion of civil rights issues. Low's examination of the way that academic opportunity is quite literally raffled off in school districts that serve under represented groups includes a fascinating glimpse at how the exceptionalism usually associated with superhero comics is complicated by discourses that demonstrate how luck often plays a large role in whether or not children gain access to competent schooling. And in "'Walk Together, Children,'" Davis-McElligatt suggests that the structure of noted civil rights activist John Lewis's graphic autobiography underscores the importance of informing today's young readers about the history of civil rights while also demonstrating how such advocacy can—and must—play a role in their daily lives.

In the final chapter in Part V, "*Sita's Ramayana*'s Negotiation with an Indian Epic Picture Storytelling Tradition," Anuja Madan explains how the 2011 graphic novel version of the popular Indian epic *Ramayana* is strikingly different visually from the other myriad picture books and comic book adaptations of the tale, because of its use of the centuries-old *patua* folk art form. Central to Madan's analysis are these questions: "What gets gained/lost/changed when an oral performative tradition of the epic is translated into Western modes of representation?" and "Do the interpretive possibilities of the *patua* storytelling tradition get somewhat diluted in its new avatar?"

Many of the graphic novels featured in this collection are available in electronic formats. Accordingly, the coda reflects on the future of children's and YA digital comics. Noting that many comics written for adults have been developed to include elements of interactivity, Joe Sutliff Sanders observes that "while digital comics for adults and even digital picture books (including revisions of classics such as *The Monster at the End of This Book* and *Don't Let the Pigeon Drive the Bus*) have shown significant innovation and reaped financial success, digital comics for children have shown little enthusiasm for experimentation."

In addition to speculating on why e-comics creators and electronic publishers have been slow to develop a truly significant presence in children's and YA comics, Sanders speculates on the future of the digitized comics medium.

In a talk given at the 2015 New York Comic Con, industry analyst Milton Griepp reported that "comics and graphic novel properties have the highest profile they've had since the early 50s," especially among young readers. He pointed to a 35 percent increase in the sales of children's graphic novels in 2015 as an indicator of future growth, and echoing Sanders, he speculated that digitalization has the potential to broaden the readership for comics and to expand the children's market even further (Griepp). Of course, the sustained success enjoyed by children's and YA comics has brought a renewed scrutiny to the medium. Three graphic novels or graphic novel hybrids—Sherman Alexie's *The Absolutely True Diary of a Part-time Indian*, Marjane Satrapi's *Persepolis*, and Raina Telgemeier's *Drama*—were among the ten most challenged books in 2015 ("Frequently"), and as librarian Robin Brenner explains, "the more popular something is, the more press you can get by challenging it" (Alverson). The essays featured in the pages that follow join the discussion about the comics medium, while they simultaneously push it in new directions. As the first book-length collection of critical essays about this subject, *Graphic Novels for Children and Young Adults* will be of interest to scholars, teachers, librarians, readers, and comics fans alike.

## Notes

1. *Comic Books and American Cultural History: An Anthology*, edited by Matthew Pustz, does break from this trend. The final two sections contain essays that examine millennial-era comics and graphic novels, including the work of Gene Luen Yang. However, the overall critical focus of the essays in Pustz' volume is not on comics for young readers.

## Works Cited

Alverson, Brigid. "Why All the Drama About *Drama*?" *School Library Journal*. 20 April 2015: np. Web. 6 September 2015.

Dueben, Alex. "Raina Telgemeier Opens Up About *Smile*." *Comic Book Resources*. 12 Feburary 2010: np. Web. 4 April 2015.

"Despite Early Sales Slump, Comics Retailers Remain Upbeat." *Publishers Weekly* 261.12 (2014): np. Web. 6 September 2015.

Dunnewind, Stephanie. "Sherman Alexie Captures the Voice, Chaos and Humor of a Teenager." *The Seattle Times*. 8 September 2007, np. Web. 2 November 2015.

"Frequently Challenged Books." *American Library Association*. 11 October 2015: np. Web. 6 September 2015.

Granata, Kassondra. "Graphic Novels as Common Core-Aligned Teaching Tools." *Education World*. 29 December 2014: np. Web. 6 September 2015.

Groensteen, Thierry. *Comics and Narration*. Jackson, MS: University Press of Mississippi, 2011. Print.

Griepp, Milton. "ICv2 Presents White Paper at New York Comic Con." *ICv2: The Business of Geek Culture*. 9 October 2015: np. Web. 15 October 2015.

Hatfield Charles. "Comic Art, Children's Literature, and the New Comic Studies." *The Lion and the Unicorn* 30.3 (2006): 360–82. Web. 4 April 2015.

———. "Introduction: Comics and Childhood." *ImageTexT: Interdisciplinary Comics Studies* 3.3 (2007). Web. 4 April 2015.

Hudson, Laura. "First Look at the New Ms. Marvel, a 16 Year-Old Muslim." *Wired*. 7 January 2014: np. Web. 6 September 2015.

Keller, Esther. Personal Interview with Gwen Athene Tarbox. 22 August 2015.

Kim, Ann, and Michael Rogers. "Librarians Out Front at Comic Con." *Library Journal* 132.6 (2007): 15. Web. 6 September 2015.

Lopes, Paul. Demanding Respect: The Evolution of the American Comic Book. Philadelpia: Temple University Press, 2009. Web. 4 April 2015.

MacDonald, Heidi. "ALA 2015: Comics: Not Just for Kids." *Publishers Weekly*. 12 June 2015: np. Web. 6 September 2015.

———. "Scott Pilgrim's Finest Sales Chart: 1 Million in Print." *Comicsbeat*. 17 September 2010: np. Web. 29 September 2016.

Mandel, Ronna. "An Interview with Kate DiCamillo." *Good Reads With Ronna*. 18 October 2013. Web. 2 November 2015.

Murray, Noel. "'Superhero Girl': Faith Erin Hicks harnesses the power of the Web." *Los Angeles Times*. 10 April 2013: np. Web. 4 April 2015.

Pustz, Matthew, ed. *Comic Books and American Cultural History*. London: Bloomsbury, 2012. Print.

Reid, Calvin. "Stu Levy and the Rise and Fall of Tokyopop." *Publisher's Weekly*. 8 March 2011: np. Web. 4 April 2015.

Sanders, Joe Sutliff. Personal interview. 20 January 2016.

Schneider, Edward Francis. "A Survey of Graphic Novel Collection and Use in American Public Libraries." *Evidence Based Library and Information Practice* 9.3 (2014): 68–79. Web. 4 April 2015.

Smith, Zack. "Talking *Babymouse* with Matthew & Jennifer Holm." *Newsarama*. 3 November 2008: np. Web. 4 April 2015.

Tilley, Carol. "Seducing the Innocent: Fredric Wertham and the Falsifications That Helped Condemn Comics." *Information & Culture: A Journal of History* 47.4 (2012): 383–413. Print.

PART ONE

GRAPHIC NOVELS as COMICS STORYTELLING

WORD and IMAGE, FORM and GENRE

# 1

## "This Is a Well-Loved Book": Weighing (in on) Jeff Smith's *Bone*

### Annette Wannamaker

> Books are not only reading machines, they are talismans. They bring with them the profound penumbra of all that books have represented to all of us who value them. Here touch and feel and binding do matter. The physical stuff of the book carries a profound electrical charge.
> —**Richard Lanham**, *The Economics of Attention: Style and Substance in the Age of Information*

> It [*Bone*] is a wonderful thing to just drop on the table and listen to the thunder as it falls.
> —**Scott McCloud**, *The Cartoonist*

When my son, Will, was eleven years old, we took him on a road trip to Columbus, Ohio, to see the author of his favorite book and the premiere of *The Cartoonist*, a documentary about the creation and impact of Jeff Smith's *Bone* series. We stood in a long, winding line for the book signing, which was equally composed of kids around Will's age and their parents, and men in their thirties and forties, clutching piles of flimsy comic books carefully protected within plastic covers. When we finally reached Mr. Smith, Will plunked his beloved, four-pound behemoth of a comic—the 1,344-page *Bone: The Complete Cartoon Epic in One Volume*—onto the signing table. Mr. Smith looked at him and asked, "Have you read all of this?" Will grinned and replied, "Yeah, three times!" Then, Smith looked down at our dog-eared, stained, and torn copy of his epic work, smiled, and said, "I can tell. This is a well-loved book." That comment made me an even bigger fan of Smith's, partially because he was being really nice to my kid, but also because that is precisely how I feel about books as tactile objects, which are meant to be loved, used and re-used, and perhaps a little abused.

I share this anecdote because this chapter is in part about books as objects, as *things* that engage senses beyond just sight when we feel their weight in our hands and the texture of the page on our fingertips, when we smell that musty book smell, when we curl up with them in bed contorting our bodies and their spines so that we can flip pages under the covers, or when, as Scott McCloud said, we drop them on a table to hear and feel their bulk. Reading and writing are bodily activities, and the shape, size, weight, binding, and texture of the cover and the pages influence the ways that a book embodies us, the physical ways in which we interact with it. These physical features also carry cultural weight, marking the taste, class, and age of the object's reader, or endowing a book with that magical thingness that makes it a fetish object, a collectable item, a thing of worth, a sacred talisman, or an object of ridicule. Books are also objects that are mass-produced, marketed, branded, and sold as commodities in a transnational economy; they are products, accessories, status symbols, home décor, and clutter.

Smith's epic comic, *Bone*, further complicates these intricate relationships between narrative and object because it is available in a wide variety of forms, shapes, and sizes. Smith has said that he created the Bone characters when he was doodling as a five year old boy and that bits of the narrative that eventually become *Bone* were first published as a daily comic strip in The Ohio State University's student newspaper. Two decades after the Bone characters first appeared in print, the compiled epic narrative was published as *Bone: The Complete Cartoon Epic in One Volume*, which weighs in at almost four pounds and is a mighty two-and-half-inch-thick tome of black and white illustrations. This weighty volume is a bound compilation of the entire *Bone* series, texts that were initially released as thin comic books that were published, sporadically, in fifty-five issues over a thirteen-year period, from July 1991 to June 2004. Diana Schutz explains, "In addition to the comics, Bone has been collected in book form: first, in the three paperback volumes of *The Complete Bone Adventures*. In 1995, Smith decided to rearrange the collections around the story arcs instead, so he relaunched with *Bone: Volume One: Out from Boneville*, in both hardcover and soft, culminating in 2004 with *Bone: Volume Nine: Crown of Horns*" (13). Starting in 2005, these nine volumes were transformed by Scholastic Books into squat, colored editions marketed directly to elementary and middle school children and their parents; and then, in 2011, the complete *Bone* narrative was released in a full-color, hardbound, one-volume edition. Each physical form of this narrative—comic strips, comic books, bound graphic novels, children's graphic novels printed in color, and an epic novel printed in both black and white and in color, in both soft and hard cover—is aimed at a slightly different audience (though avid comics fans and collectors often acquire their favorite comics in multiple forms). For instance, the backs of the earlier bound collections geared more toward adult readers feature quotes from *Publishers Weekly* and *Spin Magazine* reviews that praise *Bone*'s "masterful story-telling" and call it a "sprawling, mythic comic," while the back covers on the Scholastic versions marketed to children cites a brief one-line blurb from *Publishers Weekly* characterizing the books as "first-class kid lit."

Smith, who has said he did not initially think of the *Bone* series as a work for child readers, always intended for *Bone* to be a big book, an epic and weighty narrative akin to *The Lord of the Rings*, *Star Wars*, or *Moby-Dick*. In *The Cartoonist*, he says, "Even as a kid, I looked everywhere for that book, for that Uncle Scrooge story that was eleven hundred pages long" (Mills). This odd juxtaposition of a Donald Duck character and epic, classic literature is part of what gives *Bone* its eclectic shapes as multiple series of objects, and also as a narrative that challenges expectations of genre and medium. The comic is filled with sight gags and one-liners, physical humor and silliness, but it also contains well-developed characters, a fully created secondary world, allusions to *Moby-Dick*, hints of Australian Aboriginal mythology, and the structure of a hero narrative. When it begins, we get to know the Bone cousins—Smiley Bone, Phoncible P. "Phoney" Bone, and Fone Bone—who are lost in the desert and wander into The Valley, a secondary world filled with dragons, talking animals, voracious rat creatures, menacing locusts, and a dethroned princess named Thorn. As the narrative slowly unfolds, Thorn emerges as its hero, her grandmother (Rose) is revealed to be the Queen Mother and a fierce warrior, and we learn her great aunt (Briar) is a powerful villain who betrayed her family in order to serve the amorphous Lord of the Locusts. Commenting on his text, Smith has said, "I like fantasy because you can use metaphor, you can use symbols. You can talk about things with a slight, oblique angle on them, giving yourself distance" (Mills). Interestingly, Smith also has said that, "I actually kind of wanted to hide the fact that it was a big, epic fantasy for as long as I could" (Mills). This narrative subterfuge may have worked when *Bone* was initially issued in comic book or even bound graphic novel formats, but the bigness of the narrative is boldly on display and impossible to ignore in *Bone: The Complete Cartoon Epic in One Volume*, a text that challenges the later Harry Potter novels and even Samuel Richardson's *Clarissa* for heavy weight status.

Scholars writing about comics or picture books have discussed illustrated books as tactile objects that rely on physical interactions (page turns, the weight and feel of the page and binding, the shape and size of the book) for at least some of their meaning. In *Words About Pictures: The Narrative Art of Children's Picture Books*, Perry Nodelman explains that, in addition to learning to read symbols and images, children just entering literacy must also learn to interact with books as distinct physical objects that "must be held in a certain direction" and read in a particular order, "from front to back and turning only one page at a time" (22). Although these physical interactions become automatic, so much so that we rarely stop to think about them, they have a significant impact on the ways we make meaning from a narrative and on the meanings we attach to that text as an object. For example, Lawrence Sipe and other scholars who have studied the effect of page turns in picture books focus on the ways that the physical placement of portions of a narrative influence its meaning: "There is not only a pause as we turn the page; there is likely to be a gap or indeterminacy (Iser, 1974) in the narrative" (Sipe 243). In this way, page turns in illustrated texts encourage readers to contemplate and fill in narrative gaps in ways that most novels do not. Similarly, Ian Hague writes that comics are a visual medium that need also to be considered as physical objects: "At the most basic level, the feel of a comic book in our hands can assure us of its existence, its reality, and perhaps if we are collectors the authenticity of the object in our possession" (99). Hague also points out the ways in which senses other than sight (smell, touch, and hearing) affect our comics reading experiences.

*Bone* is an especially fruitful set of texts to use when considering the materiality of the comic book because the same narrative has been published in a variety of formats, each aimed at different audiences. Comparing various forms of the narrative, as well as their production and cultural context, creates an opportunity to think carefully about the ways in which the materiality of the comic book, as physical object, influences our processes of meaning making. In other words, does the weight of a book change the ways in which it is read? How do books, and comic books in particular, embody a reader? In what ways is the physical form that a book takes influenced by genre expectations and experimentation, and the publishing industry and market forces? And most relevant for this collection, focused on children's comics, in what ways do these physical differences mark a comic as being "for adults," "for children," or, as one reviewer of the *Bone* books phrased it in the *Comics Journal*, "that rarest of all clichés: fun for the whole family"? (*Out from Boneville*, back cover).

The physical form a book takes is influenced by, among other factors, creative impulses, genre expectations, and market forces. While Smith's creative impulses seem unflinching—he created the *Bone* characters as a child (inspired by his love of comics and of the Fonebone characters in *Mad Magazine*), made them the main focus of his college newspaper comic strip, and then made them part of a larger comic book narrative that was thirteen years in the making—he was creating these various texts at a time when both the comics industry and the genre expectations of comics were undergoing dramatic fluctuations. Very briefly, the Comics Code that pushed innovative and "adult" comics underground in the mid- and late twentieth century also helped to spawn a comic-book-store culture and market. Stephen Weiner explains that these comic book stores created enough of a market for small, independent comics publishers to stay in business alongside larger publishers, and that bound collections of comics started to be published regularly and sold in comic book stores in the 1980s. "Readers were interested in bound comic book collections, whether they were called phone books, comic book novels, albums, or graphic novels" (27–28). The critical acclaim that greeted Frank Miller's *Batman: The Dark Knight Returns*, Art Spiegelman's *Maus*, and Alan Moore and Dave Gibbons's *Watchmen* in the late 1980s demonstrated that comics could be serious, literary, and "adult." Additionally, the comic book collecting craze of the early 1990s demonstrated that comics could also be valuable, but it almost crippled the industry. While comic book stores fostered a market for comics, the niche market of rare collectables discouraged long shelflives for editions and discouraged reprints of popular titles, which would make valuable titles less rare and therefore less valuable. These factors created a marketplace that was not sustainable over the long term.

Jean-Paul Gabilliet points out that "the number of comic book stores grew from around twenty-five hundred at the end of the 1980s to over nine thousand in 1993" (148). But then the crisis hit: "The crisis, whose first victims were the retailers, resulted from the effect of a shift in market focus from comic book stores to collector-speculators" (148). As a result, the number of stores shrunk to 6,000 in 1995, to 4,500 in 1996, and down to 2,300 in 2002 (148). Significantly, this was precisely the time period during which Smith was successfully publishing and selling his *Bone* series. It was also in this context that Smith quit his job as a successful animator and, with his wife, Vijaya Iyer, founded his own publishing company, Cartoon Books, which published and distributed the *Bone* comic books and, shortly after, bound collections of the comics.

Smith's choice to self-publish and then to republish the *Bone* comics in collected editions during a crisis in the comic book industry turned out to be serendipitous. Weiner explains that Cartoon Books' decision to publish bound collections in the mid 1990s was at direct odds with the rare-comic collecting frenzy of the time:

> The buying and selling of rare comic books (the "collector's" market) was one of the economic realities of the comic book marketplace. Collecting a popular comic book series like *Bone* minimized the importance of buying back issues, and would cause the prices of back issues to drop. But the impulse behind the decision by Cartoon Books to collect the series was unrelated to the collecting of comics. It was done to keep the entire *Bone* series in print, exactly what any small publisher would do. Reprinting the books in this way made it easy for new readers to jump right into the story. It also encouraged readers uncomfortable with comic books to give the series a try. (45)

In the case of the *Bone* series, then, the physical forms of the books were directly related to the shape of the marketplace at the time they were published. Smith, who was in the process of creating a work that straddles various genres, also thought carefully about the marketing, production, and distribution of his work in ways that straddle various publishing categories. Randy Duncan and Matthew Smith write, "Smith believed that comics deserved to have a longer shelf life than the monthly turnaround on comics racks. 'When bookstores sell out of any other kind of book, they restock it with more copies,' he explains" (210). Smith, able to reimagine his work as part of a larger publishing landscape, had a keen understanding of all aspects of creating and selling his work because he was a sort of one-man band of comics publishing. His bound collections, which were carefully organized around story arcs so that each text resembles a graphic novel, were at the forefront of a significant shift in the comics business. "The rest of the [the 1990s] saw large and small publishers treat comic books as the prepublication form for books destined for long-term profitability in opposition to the short-term profitability that pamphlets had traditionally represented" (Gabilliet 100). Indeed, the *Bone* series was so successful that Smith soon became overwhelmed with the workload. Before he convinced his wife to become his business partner, he was not only writing, drawing, and lettering, he was also taking and filling orders for his comics, packing boxes, putting boxes on UPS trucks, and answering letters until, he said, "I was starting to screw up . . . not drawing, not getting orders fulfilled" (Mills). Once his wife, who left a steady and well-paying job to become his business manager, took over the business side of Cartoon Books, sales rose, deliveries were on time, and Smith was able to focus again on drawing and writing.

This hands-on history of the *Bone* series is central to the various forms it has taken and is visible in everything from the publication information included in the various editions, to Smith's website and his public persona, to the comic's illustrations, characters, and narrative structure. For example, our 1996 version of *Bone: Volume Two: The Great Cow Race* finishes with an end page that lists the other books in the series and various ways to acquire them: "You just finished the latest adventure in the award winning Bone saga! You can join in the adventures of the Bone cousins and their friends in the next book, *BONE, Volume Three: Eyes of the Storm*" (144). Readers are advised to go to their local comic book store, to write to Cartoon Books at a PO box in Columbus, Ohio, or to call 1-800-SMILEY-2 to order the next book in the series. The page is punctuated with two tiny illustrations of Ted, a character from the series who is a talking bug and is represented by an iconic crescent shape with three stick legs. Ted would be unrecognizable as a character outside of the context of the narrative, but in this case he moves beyond the fictional space of the book to become a sort of logo for Cartoon Books in the front matter and end pages of various collected editions and on www.boneville.com, where he is subtly sitting in the top right corner of each page. This simply drawn stick figure gives the various editions and even the website graphics a feel of being homemade.

Although they are mass-produced reproductions, the lines of all the *Bone* comics retain the feel of being hand-drawn illustrations. In the black and white versions especially, Smith's careful and distinct use of line makes visible the hand of the artist in its creation. In his essay "Mise en Scène and Framing: Visual Storytelling in *Lone Wolf and Cub*," Pascal Lefèvre explains that the handmade drawings used to illustrate most comics often call attention to themselves in particular ways, specifically in the way that lines are prominent and visible as lines: "Drawings in comics are static and strongly stylized, so the spectator becomes aware of their hand-made quality" (73). Additionally, Hillary L. Chute writes that when a comic is handwritten and when "the same hand is responsible for both the drawing and the writing" that an "intriguing aesthetic intimacy" (6) between author and reader is created: "[Art] Spiegelman points out that James Joyce and Jacqueline Susann can both be set in Times New Roman; I suggest, then, that what feels so intimate about comics is that *it looks like what it is*; handwriting is an irreducible part of its instantiation" (11). Because Smith wrote, drew, and lettered *Bone* (work typically done by several different people at a large publisher such as Marvel or DC) the entire text carries with it remnants of his physical interactions with each page. These bodily, performative qualities are especially prominent in *Bone: The Complete Cartoon Epic in One Volume* because, even though it is reprinted and mass produced, and therefore not an "original" work of art, the lengthy text nonetheless represents physical evidence of thirteen years of handwriting and drawing accumulated on page after page. Smith, who is often shown in photographs wearing a wrist brace, developed a severe case of carpal tunnel syndrome from writing and drawing sometimes twenty hours a day. The complete collection, assembled as one narrative, feels like a contemporary version of an illuminated manuscript because it is a text where one is continuously made aware of its creator and of the years of physical, creative, hands-on labor that went into crafting the comic.

These bodily interactions with the text are further enhanced by Smith's choice of illustrative style, which is strongly influenced by Walt Kelly's Pogo comics. The Bone cousins are minimally drawn icons, but the residents of The Valley and the setting are drawn realistically and based on places and landscapes that carry significant personal meaning for the artist. In *Understanding Comics,* McCloud argues that comics that combine characters depicted in iconic ways with detailed backgrounds help readers to insert themselves more easily into the narrative: "This combination allows readers to mask themselves in a character and safely enter a sensually stimulating world. One set of lines to see. Another set of lines to be" (43). The simpler a visually iconic character is, the more it becomes a blank slate onto which the reader can project her or himself. The Bone cousins, who are drawn to look like big-nosed versions of Casper the Friendly Ghost and who are from a world much like ours, are illustrated with very simple thick lines that are in sharp contrast with the more realistic characters drawn with thinner lines and much more detail. McCloud argues that readers must work to fill in the details missing from iconic depictions, explaining that "icons demand our participation to make them work. There is no life here except that which you give it" (59).

McCloud focuses a great deal in *Understanding Comics* on the gaps in comics that readers must actively work to fill in as they read: gaps in meaning created through linguistic indeterminacy, gaps created by missing information, and physical gaps on the page that readers must traverse as they move across white space from panel to panel. In a special forum on comics and picture books published in the winter 2012 issue of *Children's Literature Association Quarterly*, Michael Joseph expands on claims that comics require active participation from their readers in ways that non-illustrated texts do not, writing, "Readers of comics are not only compelled to participate more in the creation of narrative coherence (Hatfield, *Alternative* xiv), but also must examine more of the book object and ponder its physical operations and cultural history" (455–56). Furthermore, Joseph argues, when a book highlights the ways in which it is an object, this also encourages readers to consider the ways in which "they, themselves, are a material reality" (455).

The various sizes and shapes of the *Bone* narrative embody the reader in various ways by asking her or him to hold, read, and interact with each text differently. The four-pound complete epic, for example, is nearly impossible to read while lying in bed and makes my wrist hurt when I hold it up for too long in one hand (perhaps Smith's karmic revenge for his case of carpel tunnel syndrome). Joseph explains that oddly shaped books require readers to "abandon conventional reading postures, and engage their own physicality as well as the book's" (460). So, the bigness of the complete collection, as an object, calls attention not only to Smith's physical labor but also to the physical act of reading. Additionally, the bigness of the book calls attention to the narrative as a whole, assembled in one mighty tome, creating a tangible, material sense of place in the storyline so that readers can feel the weight and thickness of being one third through the narrative or of still having eight hundred pages left to finish. While Smith always intended the *Bone* series to be one complete narrative, this physical relationship between reading time and space and narrative time and space is not as pronounced, present, or performative in the thin comic books or even in the nine bound volumes. Interestingly, Smith often equates narrative with space, saying, for instance, that he felt limited by drawing a short daily comic strip, but once he began to think of *Bone* as a long, epic adventure akin to his favorite book *Moby-Dick*, he "loved having the space to expand" (Mills). Indeed, he says that some fans of the original comic books would get annoyed with him because he "would have one scene that would take two or three issues to get through" (Mills). This thwarting of genre expectations—that each comic book should depict a self-contained scene—is another example of the ways that Smith reimagined the comics medium and market.

Smith has explained his formal experiments by describing his work as a mash-up of seemingly disparate texts: "Bugs Bunny meets *The Lord of the Rings*" (Mills) and "I wanted to create something in comics that up until that time I had only seen in prose: an epic on the scale of *War and Peace*, with a real beginning, middle, and end" (quoted in Weiner, 45). Interestingly, three disparate types of books that inspired Smith's genre bending are represented in the narrative when Smith uses them to characterize each of the Bone cousins. When Fone Bone and Thorn are getting to know one another, he tells her about the reading material he has brought along with him in his backpack:

> BONE: When me an' my cousins got run out of Boneville, I packed some stuff for us to read....
>
> THORN: I love Books! OOH! What are these?
>
> BONE: Just some comic books. I brought those for Smiley Bone.
>
> THORN: I've never seen one before.
>
> BONE: You haven't? You must've had a deprived childhood. These I brought for Phoney Bone . . . They're financial magazines.
>
> THORN: Didn't you bring anything for yourself?
>
> BONE: Sure! This is Moby Dick! It's my favorite book. I've read it three times!
> (*Out from Boneville* 61–62)

A recurring joke in the narrative is Fone Bone's love of *Moby-Dick*, which he is often depicted holding or reading. He tries several times to read it aloud to the other characters, who immediately glaze over or fall asleep. But *Moby-Dick* is also used to represent Fone Bone as the most earnest of the three cousins and as a heroic character, through whom much of the story is focalized. In his dreams, he is Ishmael floating on an open ocean atop a coffin, witness to and participant in events much larger than himself, and a survivor. In Fone Bone's *Moby-Dick* dreams, his cousin Phoney Bone becomes Ahab, a fitting stand-in for a character who, akin to Uncle Scrooge, is obsessed with one goal: making money. While Phoney Bone often provides comic relief and is often thwarted in his get-rich-quick schemes, especially when they are at the expense of others, he is also depicted as a sympathetic character because he feels financially responsible for his family. "When we were kids, Phoney was the oldest and he took care of us," explains Fone Bone. "I always figured that was WHY he got so resourceful and stingy" (*Complete Cartoon Epic* 794). If Fone Bone's novel represents the literary influences on the *Bone* narrative, then Phoney's financial magazines represent the reality of having to create work that is financially viable, marketable, and that supports oneself and one's family. Finally, it is telling that Smiley's favorite books are "just" comic books, a third influence on the narrative, and that when Thorn says she's never seen one, Fone Bone responds, "You must have had a deprived childhood."

Smith links comics reading to childhood, but simultaneously distances the creation of the *Bone* comics from an audience of child readers. For example, Smith has said that his earliest memories as a reader involve wanting to understand what was happening in the newspaper funny pages. "I learned to read because I wanted to know what was going on in *Peanuts*" (Mills). In a short comic titled "A Personal Appreciation of Walt Kelly" that was published in 2001, he explains that reading Kelly's *Prehysterical Pogo* at the age of nine inspired him to become a comics artist. "Even though I'm forty-one now, I think the cartoonist part of me is still nine" (Schutz 16–17). Despite his profound childhood experiences with comics, Smith has said many times that he did not initially imagine the Bone series as texts that would interest child readers:

> *Bone* was never intended for children. It was always written mainly for me and, second, for other cartoon heads. I never dreamed that it would have a huge audience of children around the world because comics in the early 1990s, when I started, were primarily sold in comic book shops and all the customers in comic book stores were like me, namely, 30 year old guys. (Mills)

*Bone*'s transition from being a text mostly read by adult "cartoon heads" to one also enjoyed by children and young adults was fueled largely by school and public librarians. As Stephen Weiner notes, "In the mid-1990s, *Bone* was embraced by the public library community" (46). Indeed, our used copy of *Bone: Volume Two: The Great Cow Race*, which was published in 1996, was originally owned by the Cuyahoga County Public Library in Parma, Ohio. Affixed to the spine are two stickers that read "Graphic Novels" and "Teen," which make me think the book, which came out years before the Scholastic editions targeted at younger readers, was most likely shelved in a section for teen readers. Commenting on the influence of librarians upon the success of the *Bone* series, Smith has said, "The librarians got it. The librarians understand it as reading" (Mills).

The idea that comics reading might actually *be reading* is becoming more widely accepted, though many still do not think of comics as texts that aid in literacy acquisition or as texts with literary merit. Also, although children read comics, there are very different associations attached to illustrated books written expressly for child readers versus comic books. Charles Hatfield and Craig Svonkin argue that although comic books and picture books share many formal elements—they are "dominantly visual" and "sometimes also tactile and multisensory" (431)—these similarities "have been obscured by different ideological frameworks: picture books are generally seen as empowering young readers to take part in a social structure that prizes official literacy, while comics, in contrast, are often seen as fugitive reading competing with or even obstructing that literacy" (431). A number of scholars, teachers, and librarians are beginning to understand, though, that many children (like Smith and like me) came to literacy by reading the Sunday funnies, *Mad Magazine*, and Archie comic books, and that both comics and picture books are complex texts worthy of careful scholarly attention.

Simultaneously, comics scholars, creators, and fans who spent decades arguing for the legitimacy of comics by distancing the medium from child readers ("Comics are serious and sophisticated; they are not for children") have allowed the medium to expand over the past twenty years to include a greater variety of genres and forms—including children's literature—that appeal to a broader reading public. Whether this was his intention or not, Smith was one of the comics creators who helped to open up the comics field to new generations of readers, who, once introduced to comics as child readers, might grow up to become adult comics fans. "There was actually a prevailing thought in comics in the 90s that kids were lost, that kids just don't read comics," Smith has said. "But I think we've seen, with manga and with the Scholastic books, that kids are reading comics by the millions; that they like them. . . . It's changing. In the last ten years you see kids going to comic book stores" (Mills). Smith's series, I would argue, is one important factor responsible for this change in comics readership.

While Smith was initially resistant to including colored illustrations in the distinctively black and white Bone books, the Scholastic editions colored by Steve Hamaker created yet another form of the narrative that changes the ways in which the comic is read and to whom it is marketed, and may be helping to foster a next generation of comics fans and creators. Furthermore, because they are marketed by Scholastic and often sold at book fairs in schools, the *Bone* series is helping to legitimize comics as texts that can aid in literacy instruction. For example, our copy of *Bone: Eyes of the Storm,* features the familiar Scholastic logo in several spots, has a prominent "3" on the spine to mark it (as is the case with many children's texts) as belonging to a series, and has a table of contents page that gives the book the feel of a children's chapter book. Parents and teachers, who might not ordinarily shop in a comic book store, eagerly buy these legitimized Scholastic versions for child readers, and may indeed (as I did) become hooked themselves in a narrative that appeals to children, teens, and adults.

The blending of disparate genres, mediums, narratives, conventions, and illustrative styles that characterizes *Bone*—telling an epic narrative in the comics medium; Smith's use of his training as an animator to create perfectly timed gags on paper instead of film; interspersing slapstick comedy with a dark adventure narrative and meditations on dreams and dreaming; making a pretty girl an epic hero, her grandmother a warrior, and her great aunt a powerful villain in a literary form long dominated by male heroes who are often preserving the honor of princesses in need of rescue or protection; and Smith's use of iconic figures instead of realistically drawn characters to tell a serious story—is what allows *Bone* to take several different physical forms and to attract a broad audience of readers from different age groups. It is indeed a "well-loved book."

## Works Cited

"Boneville: Comics by Jeff Smith." Cartoon Books. 2013. Web. 16 August 2014.

Chute, Hillary L. *Graphic Women: Life Narrative and Contemporary Comics.* New York, NY: Columbia UP, 2010. Print.

Duncan, Randy, and Matthew J. Smith. *The Power of Comics: History, Form, and Culture.* New York: Continuum, 2009. Print.

Gabilliet, Jean-Paul. *Of Comics and Men: A Cultural History of American Comic Books.* Trans. Bart Beaty and Nick Nguyen. Jackson: University Press of Mississippi, 2010. Print.

Hague, Ian. "Beyond the visual—the roles of the senses in contemporary comics." *Scandinavian Journal of Comic Art* 1.1 (2012): 96–110. Web. 12 May 2015.

Hatfield, Charles, and Craig Svonkin. "Why Comics Are and Are Not Picture Books: Introduction." *Children's Literature Association Quarterly* 37.4 (2012): 429–35. Web. 19 May 2014.

Joseph, Michael. "Seeing the Visible Book: How Graphic Novels Resist Reading." *Children's Literature Association Quarterly* 37.4 (2012) 454–67. Web. 19 May 2014.

Lanham, Richard. *The Economics of Attention: Style and Substance in the Age of Information.* Chicago: University of Chicago Press, 2006. Print.

LeFèvre, Pascal. "Mise en Scène and Framing: Visual Storytelling in *Lone Wolf and Cub.*" *Critical Approaches to Comics: Theories and Methods.* Eds. Matthew J. Smith and Randy Duncan. New York: Routledge, 2011. 71–83. Print.

McCloud, Scott. *Understanding Comics: The Invisible Art.* New York, NY: Harper Perennial, 1993. Print.

Mills, Ken. director. *The Cartoonist: Jeff Smith, Bone, and the Changing Face of Comics.* 2009. DVD.

Nodelman, Perry. *Words About Pictures: The Narrative Art of Children's Picture Books.* Athens: University of Georgia Press, 1988. Print.

Schutz, Diana. Ed. *The Art of* Bone. Dark Horse Books: China, 2007. Print.

Sipe, Lawrence R. "The Art of the Picturebook." *Handbook of Research on Children's and Young Adult Literature.* Eds. Shelby A. Wolf, et al. New York: Routledge, 2011. Print.

Smith, Jeff. *Bone Volume Two: The Great Cow Race*. Columbus, Ohio: Cartoon Books, 1996.
    Print.

——. *Bone Volume One: Out from Boneville*. Columbus, Ohio: Cartoon Books, 2003. Print.

——. *Bone: The Complete Cartoon Epic in One Volume*. Columbus, Ohio: Cartoon Books,
    2004. Print.

——. *Bone: Eyes of the Storm*. New York, NY: Scholastic, 2006. Print.

Weiner, Stephen. *Faster Than a Speeding Bullet: The Rise of the Graphic Novel*. New York: Nantier,
    Beall and Minoustchine Publishing, 2003. Print.

# 2

## "What Is China but a People and Their (Visual) Stories?" The Synthetic in Narratives of Contest in Gene Luen Yang's *Boxers & Saints*

*Karly Marie Grice*

In Gene Luen Yang's graphic novel[1] diptych *Boxers & Saints*,[2] the fierce yet compassionate female warrior Mei-wen asks Boxer Rebellion leader Little Bao, "What is China but a people and their stories?" (*Boxers* 312). Within the plurality of Mei-wen's rhetorical question is the implication of a multitude of stories, leading the words to be a self-referential gesture to the dual narratives of *Boxers & Saints* itself. If Jerome Bruner's "narrative identity thesis"—described by James Phelan as "the idea that the very conception of selfhood depends on having *a* narrative of one's life" ("Narratives" 166; italics added)—is true, then competing historical narratives of ancestral origin complicate one's selfhood. For a Chinese Catholic, the narrative of the introduction of Catholicism to China competes with that of the Chinese nationals who resisted colonization during what came to be known as the Boxer Rebellion. As a Chinese American Catholic and an author who frequently explores identity in his texts, this very complication prompted Yang's interest in telling the multiple stories of the Boxer Rebellion (Mayer). But how can these competing narratives exist together unless one comes out as the victor? Phelan would say that attentiveness to this issue is part of the "new twist in the [narrative] turn, a twist in the direction of locating the analysis of individual narratives within a larger, often implicit contest among alternative narratives" ("Narratives" 166). Yet instead of leaving the contesting narratives implicit, Yang displays them in explicit opposition and juxtaposition in *Boxers & Saints*. I believe Yang's rhetorical intention with his diptych is to use the synthetic component as a hermeneutic for the purpose of revealing this narrative contest and locating the dialectic "truth" in the gaps between. I will first explore Phelan's concept of narratives of contest before looking into examples of how Yang structures the narrative to highlight the synthetic component in aid of his authorial purpose. I will then reflect on the complication of Yang's choice to conclude the narrative in epilogue. I will close by returning to Yang's rhetorical purpose and situating it, as well as Phelan's contest of narratives, in connection to dialectics.

Phelan explains that "every story is potentially contestable by multiple alternatives" ("Narratives" 168). If narratives are rhetorical designs, constructed a certain way to serve "a purposive communicative act" (Phelan, "Rhetoric/ Ethics" 203), then it stands to reason that each narrative constructed to tell a certain story for a certain purpose could have a counter narrative constructed to serve an antithetical purpose (Phelan, "Narratives" 168). Acknowledging that this contest even exists also concedes the rhetorical intention of the counter narrative's design—that authors are "likely to construct their tales at least partly in response to or anticipation of one or more possible alternatives" (Phelan, "Narratives" 168). This means that rhetorical strategy is often designed around knowing the opposition and weaving elements into the narrative for either defense or attack against the alternative narrative. Phelan argues that an author's "purpose situates him in the contest among alternative narratives" ("Narratives" 172). If an author's purpose is to undermine the counter narrative and undergird her own, the narrative will include elements intended for this specific purpose.

Phelan admits that not all contests are equal or "carried out on a level playing field": "Some narratives acquire a sacred status in a given culture or subculture (religions are often founded on such narratives), and some narratives, while clearly not sacred, have the strong endorsement of culturally powerful groups" ("Narratives" 168). Challenging such privileged narratives is precisely that: a challenge. The Catholic missionary/European colonial narrative opposing the Boxer narrative has been historically positioned as more powerful. If Yang's purpose in the contest were to position himself on the Boxer Rebellion side opposing this privileged narrative, his rhetorical strategy would necessitate flipping the imbalance of narrative power. From an initial analysis of materiality and publication, one could presume that this is Yang's purpose, to challenge the Catholic narrative and promote the Chinese national—or Boxer—narrative. Materially, *Boxers* is twice the size of *Saints*, with the former coming in at 325 pages and the latter at 162[3]. This length differential could serve both a postmodern and a postcolonial purpose to Yang's text by telling the often hidden stories of the colonized voices of the Boxer Rebellion, working against the otherwise sacred narrative. Yet the materiality of his diptych gestures towards a purpose beyond solely the success of the previously silenced contesting narrative. The interconnected covers further express a postmodern principle of fragmentation, but one that foregrounds the fragmentation of characters and multiple narratives in order to battle the presumption of a completely whole hero in a completely right narrative. Each cover displays its respective protagonist looking forward but with only half of their faces displayed. Through this figural placement, Yang suggests that each protagonist is complicated, wounded, and lacking. This visual also connects to the kind of incomplete narration any reader can expect to see in a first person point of view narrative, precisely the kind that awaits them within the pages of the books. When the covers are aligned beside one another, the fragmented face of one completes the face of the other, reminding the reader that no single narrative is complete without considering the whole narrative contest in which it exists.

Yang displays what could be potentially another preference for the Boxer narrative in choosing to make it the first readers experience. With its first person narration by and focalization on Little Bao, the leader of the Boxer Rebellion, this move could possibly serve to create a primary association between the reader and the Boxers' cause prior to the Catholic narrative, thus forcing the latter to dig itself out of the hole created by the negative first impression from the former. This effect of publishing would possibly be even weightier had Yang's original idea of publishing the texts separately been carried out, with *Boxers* coming first and *Saints* being released later (Mayer). Without being aware of the protagonist of *Saints* while reading *Boxers*, what might have been the difference in rhetorical effect or ethical reader response when Little Bao kills his narrative successor? While these actions of forwardly positioning and intending to primarily publish *Boxers* might not overcome the imbalanced history behind the narratives themselves, as rhetorical choices they could signal author purpose and preference, and they do at least work towards "leveling the playing field" that Phelan references.

Even taking into account the materiality and publication as a sign of authorial intention, what might be more important to consider is that "comics exploit *format* as a signifier in itself" (Hatfield 52, emphasis in text). One such signification of the comics format is the very nature of any narrative contest composed in the medium, represented through its structural form as the "art of tensions" (Hatfield 36). This inherent tension primes comics to be the perfect medium for presenting narratives of contest as the form itself insinuates an opposition and omission that must be overcome. The greatest structural element of comics implicated in this tension is the gutter, or the empty space between panels. Scott McCloud posits this convention as being critical to the form, crediting it as the location of the "magic and mystery" of comics (66). McCloud's description of the gutter's power implies that comics require the reader to attend to the construction of the narrative, and likewise its position in the contest, due to the gutter's role in forcing the hand of the reader into becoming co-conspirator. The tension developed through such a convention leads other scholars also to comment on the unique reader reaction to such a form. Discussing the potential of the comics form in connection to the gutter as well as other medium specific narrative conventions, Charles Hatfield

writes, "From a reader's viewpoint, comics would seem to be radically fragmented and unstable. I submit that this is their great strength: comic art is
composed of several kinds of tension, in which various ways of reading—various interpretive options and potentialities—must be played against each other"
(36). Perry Nodelman refers to a "disorientation" he felt as a reader approaching comics for the first time, but explains that "the extreme fragmentation and
instability of the sequence seems revelatory of a *deliberately unsettled world
view inherently full of new possibilities*" (444, 440–41, italics added). McCloud,
Hatfield, and Nodelman all gesture towards not only the elevated efficacy of
comics at tackling narrative contests and their inherent tension, but also the
possibility that through this form the authors and readers may explore new
possibilities with the narratives.

What new possibilities might Yang bring to the Boxer Rebellion contest of
narratives? Given that Yang's text is composed in the comics medium, it carries with it an implicit signification of tension that must be resolved with some
form of closure during the reading act. It's possible that the compilation of
various tensions could, as Hatfield describes it, "interact to create a yet more
complex tension, soliciting the reader's active efforts at resolution" (48). Just as
Yang himself discusses the diptych's construction as part of his own grappling
with the tension of narratives within the history of a Chinese Catholic identity,
he is asking his audience to do the same through the act of reading. Yang does
not just locate his narrative in "a contest among alternative accounts" through
the medium itself, though (Phelan, "Narrative" 172). He compiles the narratives
and compounds the tension by telling both sides of the narrative contest and
by choosing to do so in separate books, utilizing the physical space between
the two separate objects as an even greater metaphorical gutter that must be
closed in the reading of *Boxers & Saints*. What awaits readers in that gutter is
the driving force of the contest of these narratives: a definition of heroism.

In order to discuss how Yang uses each narrative to construct the contest of
heroism narratives, it's important to note he does so rhetorically through the
synthetic component in order to emphasize the actual contest itself. Phelan
explains the synthetic component as "[involving] an audience's interest in
and attention to the characters and to the larger narrative as a made object"
("Rhetoric/Ethics" 210). The synthetic component's use in a text works to
remind the reader that the hand of the author is always present in the construction of the text that is being read. While Yang does not structure *Boxers &
Saints* entirely—or even mainly—in the synthetic mode, when he does employ
it he does so for the purpose of highlighting the constructedness not just of the
text as text but of the narrative as a rhetorically created narrative for participation in a contest of narratives. Yang includes many moments and methods of
the synthetic component, but for the purposes of this exploration I will limit

my examples to the following three visual narrative structural elements: visual repetition, panel permeation, and color alteration.

The first method of the synthetic component, visual repetition, is inherently connected to the graphic narrative aspect known as braiding. Braiding refers to "the way panels (more specifically, the images in the panels) can be linked in a series (continuous or discontinuous) through non-narrative correspondences, be it iconic or other means" (Groensteen ix). Braiding is a key element that serves Thierry Groensteen's overall idea of arthrology, "the study of the relations between panels, whether linear . . . or distant" (ix). Craig Fischer and Charles Hatfield explain that braiding itself can occur through "recurring images, panels, or symbols, whether adjacent or widely separated across the work" (82). As such repetition draws attention to "the network" that is the nature of comics (Groensteen 147), it serves to highlight a text's constructedness and thus its synthetic format. Yang uses this braiding not just within the confines of the separate narratives but across both physical texts to further the conversation between the contesting narratives and to aid the reader in performing the necessary closure.

The most overt form of visual repetition, or braiding, occurs during the narrative present across the separate texts where Little Bao, the narrator/focalizer of *Boxers*, and Vibiana, the narrator/focalizer of *Saints*, first physically cross paths. This point occurs early in both narratives when Little Bao sees Vibiana (then named Four-Girl) going with her mother to the acupuncturist to fix her devil-like face. The basic components of the plot are repeated visually in both texts: Vibiana and her mother walking, Vibiana scowling at Little Bao, and Little Bao looking at her with surprise. The strongest evidence of braiding here occurs with the almost exactly duplicated panel of Vibiana's face (*Boxers* 8.4; *Saints* 22.3). Having these panels and this portion of the story occur twice serves as visual repetition to connect the stories, characters, and overall contests. Even though Vibiana's panel is almost completely reproduced, alterations in narration and color reflect a shifting both in style and, concurrently, focalization in the narrative, factors I'll further address shortly. Yet even had Yang employed exact replication of the panels, Groensteen explains that "[repetition] without modification" is impossible in comics: "The second occurrence of the panel is already different from the first by the sole fact of the citation effect that is attached. The repetition raises the memory of the first occurrence, if it is a matter of a rhyme (distant repetition), or manifests a singular insistence, if the two occurrences are contiguous" (148). This panel as it occurs in *Saints* is automatically linked to its previous appearance. The effect is an inextricable connection between the two characters. The echo of the former narrative's interactions between the two characters provides a heaviness that floods the reader of the latter narrative with memories.

Another stark repetition occurs when Little Bao saves and then successively kills Vibiana (*Boxers* 242–45; *Saints* 150–62). The length of time spent in each scene is altered through variety in panel numbers to extend or truncate the narrative time as well as the emphasis on the internal thoughts of the focalizer for the respective scenes. Even with the sobering silence and narrative deceleration conveyed through three large, horizontally stacked panels opposite his last interaction with Vibiana, *Boxers* implies the scene goes rather quickly, concluding in less than three pages. It appears that the interaction has failed to alter Little Bao's course as he immediately goes on to burn down a church containing women and children (245). However, *Saints* extends their face to face conversation ten more pages, interrupted by a one on one conversation between Vibiana and Jesus before she teaches Little Bao how to pray. This alteration of the repetition through extension of narrative time and interaction signifies that, at least according to the *Saints* narrative, the scene had a great impact on both.

This same scene, in connection to another from *Boxers*, shows how Yang utilizes braiding to concatenate religious iconography from both narratives, simultaneously undermining the opposition of the contest as it highlights religious coexistence through synthetic components. In two large, single-panel pages, both narratives display religious figures of compassion and salvation: Guan Yin, the Buddhist Goddess of Compassion, emerging from the heart of the lotus, and Jesus Christ, the Christian Son of God, emerging from the heart of the tomb (*Boxers* 282; *Saints* 158). Both figures are centrally positioned on the page and visually facing the reader. This braiding through composition links together these figures from the two opposing sides' religions. Yang uses even more explicit repetition of iconography reminiscent of the hamsa, an open palm with an eye in the center, a symbol of protection that is thought to predate both Judaism and Islam (Afshar and Ahmadi 779). The choice to interject this iconography into both visuals that isn't otherwise directly related to their stories but that does have a history of crossing over various religions creates a message of parallel beliefs and spiritual harmony in Yang's narratives. This repeated icon acts as a symbol to both braid the narratives of *Boxers &* *Saints* as well as reference a larger unity predating the narratives of contest.

The final visual repetition is one of less direct braiding than repeated panels or iconography but is nonetheless powerful for its method; the emphasis is in the more implicit symbolic repetition that comes from placing the focalizers in reminiscent visual constructs. The result is a subtle one, almost of déjà vu, but is effective enough to braid together the contesting narratives through the positioning of their focalizers despite all their differences in similar fates. The panels in reference are the concluding visuals of the seemingly mortal wounds for both Little Bao and Vibiana (*Boxers* 322.1; *Saints* 162). Both characters are viewed from an aerial perspective, with the focalization looking down on their suffering, sprawled bodies. From the placement of the pool of blood, each appears to be similarly wounded in the heart. But the strongest braiding is through the lines Yang uses to illustrate their bodies: the same angled, spread legs and curved backs, both bending in a way to continue the visual line projection off to the bottom right corner of the panel. Such a strong repetition unites their narratives' conclusions, as if to suggest that even with the contest between their narratives and all their opposing objectives, their fates are intertwined.

The second method of synthetic component Yang employs is panel permeation, or the moment when the otherwise complete panel is crossed by an icon. Michael Joseph describes this technique writing, "Alternative comics contravene the design norms of the ideal book, fashioning a complex, ideologically permeable aesthetic that also adapts and revitalizes traditional comic tropes" (461). Joseph's observation about this method implies that by quite literally drawing outside the box, the comics illustrator is imploring the audience to also think outside the box. Such frame-breaking and invasion of the space outside the panels is often employed in postmodern visual narratives (Kiefer and Tyson 69), serving as a visual metafictive device in tune with the objectives of postmodernism, emphasizing the synthetic component as an element of narratives. This frequently occurs in the text in connection to Yang's inclusion of embedded narratives, furthering the reader's awareness of the constructedness of stories. During moments when the focalizers are listening to another character tell a story or watching the performance of a play, the focalizer is placed outside of the image crossing through the panel (*Boxers* 4–5, 265–66, 277–82; *Saints* 34–35, 38, 158). For example, as Vibiana listens to Dr. Won read gospel stories, the story she hears plays out in a traditional panel in the background (*Saints* 34–35). Vibiana, however, is not encapsulated in any panel but is instead positioned in front of the panel, giving it the appearance that she has crossed over or through the panel frame. From this, the reader is able to visualize the layers of the narration as the embedded narrative plays out, Vibiana listens, and the reader sees it all.

This illustrative move emphasizes the synthetic nature of the text by reminding the reader of the previously un-emphasized panels, highlighting the borders of the story that are meant to be overlooked when the reader is enveloped in the tale. Yang's choice to do this suggests he wants his readers to be more aware and critical of the story that they're consuming. Furthermore, this synthetic component visually represents the positioning of the various audiences occurring at these moments. When the protagonists who are normally both narrator and focalizer in Yang's texts split, making a side character the narrator and the focalizer the narratee, the actual reader is further removed—or at least reminded of this new intermediary audience—having been previously the directly receiving narratee of the first person narrator/ focalizer. By placing the narratee outside of the panel and bleeding off of the page, Yang visually constructs the tiers of the narrative audience and reminds the reader of his art in composing the story as a whole.

The third and final method of the synthetic component I will explore is color alteration. McCloud refers to color in comics as "a formidable ally" and even goes on to list several comics artists who utilize color skillfully to define their style (185). Jan Baetans also values color usage in comics highly, referring to it as a "crucial factor" for understanding the narrative world (117). Fischer and Hatfield argue that visual style elements like color serve the same narratological purposes as other linguistic narrative devices that would convey the likes of tone and mood (78), and more than one comics and visual design scholar has suggested that color can be used to imply mood or other semiotic messages in visually based narratives (McCloud 190; Lefevre 20; Kress and van Leeuwen 225–38). In the beginning of the diptych with *Boxers*, the colors are bold and bright, reminiscent of the comics history of primary-color-clad superheroes that precedes Yang's text (McCloud 188). Such a stylistic choice directly connects Little Bao's narrative with heroes and heroism. Yang develops Little Bao's "beliefs, desires, motivations, and biases" or altogether composite "subjectivity through pictures" (Fischer and Hatfield 77). His use of bold colors to illustrate the Gods of the Opera, who become the Boxers' alter egos during battle, creates intertextuality between the narrative of Little Bao and the caped crusaders of comics yore ("How"; "Boxers"). In the brightly colored narrative of *Boxers*, Little Bao and the Boxers are heroes, fighting evil, standing for justice, and bringing peace to China.

Color might play less of a role in Yang's diptych if it were not for his choice to vary the color styles across narratives. When stylistic devices or choices are altered in a text, the narrative "shifts in tone, focus, and implicit meaning" (Fischer and Hatfield 76). Pascal Lefevre argues the importance of being attuned to such visual shifts in narrative as he posits that "style implies a particular ontology, and consequently will suggest to the reader a particular way of interpreting the storyworld" (31). In *Saints*, Yang makes a strong contrasting choice to paint Vibiana's life and narrative as monochromatic. Her life and narrative are both drained of color, visually representing the emotional emptiness that leads her within ten pages of the opening to run off to the woods and pray for death (*Saints* 10). This color choice would not feel like such a strong value signifier if it were not for the juxtaposition against the bright colors of the previous narrative. The only color in Vibiana's life comes in the form of magical[4] encounters with Joan of Arc, whose overall presence and storyline exude a golden glow. After an initial hesitance towards the glowing apparition,

Vibiana is drawn to Joan and views her as a mentor—an empowering yet ulti-mately tragic choice of life model as any success would imply an early, violent martyrdom. Such stylistic color choices could imply that while Little Bao views his life as brightened by his mission of heroism to save China, Vibiana views her life as dull and hopeless until it is brightened by Christianity. Her aspira-tion to become a hero like Joan is what colors her life, much like the Gods of the Opera color Little Bao's. Similar to how the choice of primary colors intro-duces intertextuality to the *Boxers* narrative, Yang's decision to color Vibiana's mentor gold leads to external searches for meaning. Drawing on poetic refer-ences to the attractive yet ephemeral nature of gold, namely that described by Robert Frost as "nothing gold can stay," the reader who has become attentive to the synthetic nature of Yang's work and his use of intertextuality is left critical of the golden ghost and curious if and when Vibiana's life will lose this newly acquired shine. But just as Frost incorporates paradoxes into his poem that the reader must struggle to reconcile, so does Yang ask the reader of *Boxers & Saints* to make sense of the oppositions and tensions of the contest of narra-tives surrounding the Boxer Rebellion.

While Yang does not make another stylistic shift in color, he does make a shift in narration and focalization as he maintains the color scheme of *Saints*. Yang ends the central narrative at Vibiana's death, but the story doesn't close there. Instead of continuing the narrative with an otherwise uninterrupted shift in focalization, Yang chooses to conclude the central narrative of *Saints* with Vibiana's death. The text continues instead with a break and then an epi-logue, a textual element described by Mike Cadden as "post-narrative despite being narrative" (344). Yang extends past Vibiana's death and reintroduces the still-alive Little Bao as the final narrator and focalizer. He chooses to maintain the monochromatic color style of illustrations that characterized the *Saints* narrative despite shifting back to Bao whose world had previously been delin-eated—defined, even—by color. This color choice implies that while some Chinese nationals found hope and color through Christianity, others, like Little Bao, were instead drained by the religious colonization. As her last living act, Vibiana teaches Little Bao how to pray. After Little Bao's narrative resurrec-tion, the European soldiers spot him, identify him as a Boxer, and prepare to kill him. With the gun pointed at his head, Little Bao kneels and prays an "Our Father" as an act of desperation (*Saints* 167). Hearing him, the foreign soldiers worry that if they kill a Christian they'll be sent to Purgatory. With this act, Little Bao finds a physical salvation through Christianity, but not a spiritual one. All the cultural color that had defined his life, that he and the Boxers had been fighting for, is washed away. The closing scene of *Boxers* foreshadows this future draining of color as the seemingly dying Little Bao watches the "bits of vivid color" that represent the Gods of the Opera "disappear into the blue"

(323). For Little Bao and the surviving Boxers, Christianity was acquiescence and assimilation, not affirmation and ascension.

Choosing to end in epilogue rather than merely continuing the narrative seems at first unnecessary. Yang's enactment of disnarration, previously employed to provide the reader with information on Vibiana's experiences in *Boxers*, about which Little Bao could not have known (218–23), would have worked just as aptly to switch focalization on her death. But since he has chosen to present the ending in this fashion, and as his authorial strategy has been stressed through his use of the synthetic component throughout his work, this move must be taken as rhetorical strategy. Cadden argues that the inclusion of an epilogue speaks to the implied audience and what the author thinks that audience needs (344). Often in children's literature this strategy is used to provide the completion of the story for a young audience that needs a happily ever after. Ends are tied up nicely and large leaps are made in time to show that the solution of the conclusion in the central narrative is maintained. Yet Yang does not write an epilogue that provides this unquestioned happiness and solution. Instead, he gives his readers a complicated "closure" without "completion"— two ideas Cadden pulls from Phelan as differing between merely an end to the narrative and a resolution to the complications (344). Vibiana is dead, Peking is burned to the ground, and Little Bao has sacrificed his values in order to live, resulting in a bleak future and bloody past. Yang's decision reflects his understanding of the implied audience of *Boxers & Saints* as not the same youthful audience of which Cadden writes, but an older young adult audience that is often characterized in texts by its burgeoning understanding of the world as it really is, which means facing the fact that not all stories have happy endings.

Taking into consideration the effect of genre on Yang's rhetoric and ultimate purpose, I suggest that his decision to end in epilogue also serves a valuable role for a postmodern application of historical fiction. Together with his use of the synthetic component, it reminds the reader that all written histories are constructed. Their closures are chosen for effect, but real completion is nonexistent, as all moments in history have stories that continue afterwards. When Yang chooses to conclude both narratives with his protagonists' apparent deaths, he is working towards his authorial purpose of stressing the bleakness of the Boxer Rebellion and the similarity in the narratives of contest, emphasized by his use of braiding. The epilogue then becomes both a tool for further highlighting the synthetic components as well as questioning neat conclusions in historical fiction, both moves that will lend the text to facilitating a more critical audience of readers.

Yang doesn't stop at questioning the synthetic nature of conclusions in history. Just as all histories are constructed, so too is the historical definition of what makes a hero. Yang has commented that Little Bao "would probably be labeled a terrorist if he were real and alive today" (quoted in Mayer). Similarly, the Chinese government feels that the canonization of Chinese saints from the Boxer Rebellion is the Catholic approval of "traitors" (Mayer). Yang's diptych then becomes one that reveals the fine line between being a hero and being a terrorist or traitor. Where a person stands on either side of that line is drawn in large part by whoever has the most privileged narrative. Taking this into consideration, Yang is performing his own act of narrative rebellion by repositioning both narratives as simultaneously tales of heroes and terrorists/traitors, implicating his readers in the contest of narratives and forcing them to think for themselves about these definitions.

Through his utilization of graphic narrative elements that emphasize the synthetic component, Yang uncovers for his readers the assembly of competing narratives surrounding the Boxer Rebellion. The importance of this rhetorical move is to make his readers attend to both sides of the narrative contest. Phelan wraps up his exploration of narratives of contest by proposing, "The larger point here is that the contest among alternatives does not have to be a death match, from which only one narrative emerges alive" ("Narratives" 172). Phelan argues the importance of delaying narrative interpellation and exploring varying, contradictory narratives. "[E]ven then," he explains, "we do not have ultimately to choose, because *we may well decide that there are no fixed answers* to the questions these narratives address. At that point, the contest among alternatives becomes less of a competition and more of a never-ending dialogue ("Narratives" 174, italics added). Such a description recalls dialectics, which posits: "All the oppositions that are assumed as fixed . . . are not in contradiction through, say, an external connection; on the contrary, as an examination of their nature has shown, they are in and for themselves a transition; the synthesis and the subject in which they appear is the product of their concept's own activity of conceptual reflection" (Hegel 647). Phelan seems to suggest exploring the expanses of a contest of narratives as postmodern in its denial of an ultimate truth or answer, an eternal dialectic for the truth that doesn't exist. It's in this rhetorical vein that I believe Yang ultimately positions his diptych. He hopes to make readers see that there isn't a single answer, and even if there were it would have to be located in the dialectic that occurs from attending to multiple narratives. Coming to such a conclusion, I return to the way Mei-wen places the identity of a people in its *stories*—plural—and believes in this ideal so much that she runs into a burning library, potentially sacrificing her life in an effort to save the books. Her model serves to remind us of the importance of attending comprehensively to the contest of narratives, all the while remembering that the contest isn't about who wins. This is why Yang named his work *Boxers & Saints*, not *Boxers vs. Saints*.

# Notes

1. I am aware of the debate surrounding the usage of the term "graphic novel" and have chosen to use this term over "graphic narrative," as *Boxers & Saints* is part of the historical fiction genre and is referred to on the book flap as a "novel." This choice has also been made to minimize the use of the term "narrative" and reserve the word for reference to elements of narrative theory.

2. For the purposes of this paper, I will refer to *Boxers & Saints* as a single text with distinct materiality but not as two different publications. I want to highlight how they work together and the effects of their being published/sold concurrently. For clarity in reference, I will cite them individually.

3. *Saints* is 170 pages, but Vibiana's narrative ends on 162. The remaining pages are separated and entitled "Epilogue," distinguishing it as post-narrative, a choice I address later.

4. I choose "magical" to refer to these events so as to avoid making a judgment about their reality, something that could not be wrestled with without also facing both the magical elements of *Boxers* and the history of magical elements in Yang's previous texts (Jin transforming into Danny and the Monkey King transforming into Chin-Kee in *American Born Chinese*, and three small angels caring for Dennis while he attends medical school in *Level Up*).

# Works Cited

Afshar, Ahmadreza, and Aziz Ahmadi. "The Hand in Art: Hamsa Hand." *Journal of Hand Surgery* 38.4 (2013): 779–80. Web. 15 May 2014.

Baetens, Jan. "From Black & White to Color and Back: What Does It Mean (not) to Use Color." *College Literature* 38.3 (2011): 111–28. Web. 20 May 2014.

Cadden, Mike. "All Is Well: The Epilogue in Children's Fantasy Fiction." *Narrative* 20.3 (2012): 343–56. Web. 15 May 2014.

Fischer, Craig, and Charles Hatfield. "Teeth, Sticks, and Bricks: Calligraphy, Graphic Focalization, and Narrative Braiding in Eddie Campbell's *Alec*." *SubStance* 124.40.1 (2011): 3–13. Print.

Frost, Robert. "Nothing Gold Can Stay." Poets.org. American Academy of Poets. Web. 15 May 2014.

Groensteen, Thierry. *The System of Comics*. Trans. Bart Beaty and Nick Nguyen. Jackson: University Press of Mississippi, 2007. Print.

Hatfield, Charles. *Alternative Comics: An Emerging Literature*. Jackson: University Press of Mississippi, 2005. Print.

Hegel, G. W. F. "Dialectics." *Literary Theory: An Anthology*. Eds. Julie Rivkin and Michael Ryan. 2nd ed. Malden: Blackwell, 2004. 647–49. Print.

Joseph, Michael. "Seeing the Visible Book: How Graphic Novels Resist Reading." *Children's Literature Association Quarterly* 37.4 (2012): 454–67. Print.

Kiefer, Barbara, and Cynthia Tyson. *Charlotte Huck's Children's Literature: A Brief Guide*. 2nd ed. New York: McGraw Hill, 2013. Print.

Kress, Gunter, and Theo van Leeuwen. *Reading Images: The Grammar of Visual Design*. 2nd ed. London: Routledge, 2006. Print.

Lefevre, Pascal. "Some Medium-Specific Qualities of Graphic Sequences." *SubStance* 124.40.1 (2011): 14–33. Print.

Mayer, Petra. "*Boxers & Saints* & Compassion: Questions for Gene Luen Yang." NPR. 22 October 2013. Web. 23 March 2014.

McCloud, Scott. *Understanding Comics: The Invisible Art*. New York: William Morrow, 1993. Print.

Nodelman, Perry. "Picture Book Guy Looks at Comics: Structural Differences in Two Kinds of Visual Narrative." *Children's Literature Association Quarterly* 37.4 (2012): 436–44. Print.

Phelan, James. "Narratives in Contest; or, Another Twist in the Narrative Turn." *PMLA* 123.1 (2008): 166–75. Print.

———. "Rhetoric/Ethics." *The Cambridge Companion to Narrative*. Ed. David Herman. Cambridge: Cambridge UP, 2007. 203–16. Print.

Yang, Gene Luen. *Boxers*. New York: First Second, 2013. Print.

———. "The Boxers and the Power of Pop Culture." GeneYang.com. 20 Febuary 2013. Web. 25 March 2014.

———. "How Chinese Opera and American Comics Are Alike." GeneYang.com. 27 Febuary 2013. Web. 25 March 2014.

———. *Saints*. New York: First Second, 2013. Print.

# 3

## Comics, Adolescents, and the Language of Mental Illness: David Heatley's "Overpeck" and Nate Powell's *Swallow Me Whole*

### *Sarah Thaller*

Recent studies reveal that approximately 50 million people in the United States, including children and adolescents, live with some form of mental illness ("Mental Health"). Young adult literature is aimed directly at adolescent readers and generally attempts to address the real-life concerns and issues of that population. However, despite the fact that many adolescents live with mental illness, there are very few examples of YA literature that present accurate representations of the experience of living with a mental illness. Part of the issue is that not every narrative can be fully conveyed in traditional written text.

One form of mental illness that seems to be beyond the scope of traditional written language is post-traumatic stress disorder. In *Trauma and Recovery: The Aftermath of Violence—from Domestic Abuse to Political Terror*, Judith Herman explains that "certain violations . . . are too terrible to utter aloud: this is the meaning of the word *unspeakable*" (1). People who have lived with PTSD attest to the "frozen and wordless quality" of their experiences and traumatic memories (37). Herman posits that there is a lack of clear "verbal and narrative context" to such experiences, which are instead "encoded in the form of vivid sensations and images" (38). According to Cathy Caruth, PTSD "resists simple comprehension" and demands a "new mode of reading and listening" (6, 9).

Similarly, in the effort to write their personal narratives, authors with schizophrenia have described the difficulty of conveying in words the experience of living with their disease. In her memoir about living with schizophrenia in adolescence, Elyn Saks explains that while she can describe some of the individual aspects or emotions involved, the overall experience is indescribable. Throughout *The Center Cannot Hold: My Journey Through Madness*, she mentions the complexity when reality and delusion are so tangled and blurred that it is difficult to distinguish, much less describe, the difference. Additionally, the experience of schizophrenia is outside of "normal" comprehension, and authors struggle to find avenues to bridge this gap. Saks elaborates on attempting to relate to emotions or experiences that people without schizophrenia can understand: "This experience is much harder, and weirder, to describe than extreme fear or terror. Most people know what it is like to be seriously afraid. . . . But explaining what I've come to call 'disorganization' is a different challenge altogether" (13).

Authors with schizophrenia describe their hallucinations and psychosis as dreamlike, all-consuming, and a part of their physical reality. The challenge is describing experiences outside of the realm of "normal" psychological experience with "normal" written text. The medium necessary to transcend the barriers of indescribable and incomprehensible experience is one that bridges the gap between conventional written narratives and wordlessness.

## Comics: Transcending the Barrier

In "So Long as They Grow Out of It: Comics, the Discourse of Development, Normalcy, and Disability," Susan Squire describes the ability of comics to confront issues of disability in a unique and authentic way. She argues that comics allow the combination of "verbal and gestural expression," that comics "can convey the complex social impact of a physical or mental impairment, as well as the way the body registers social and institutional constraints" (74). Squire claims that comics allow a person with a disability to fully narrate his or her experience because they include "pre-verbal components: the gestural, embodied physicality of disabled alterity in its precise . . . specificity" (86). In comics, the combination of text and image allows for the describable and indescribable to function together to form a more comprehensive narrative (Groensteen 124). Squire explains the function of image to the disability narrative: "Not only do these illustrations reveal the social processes that disable him, but they also suggest the impairment produced by this epilepsy: multiple distortions in his own sense of himself" (Squire 77). Authors do not have to tell the reader about the experience of living with a disability or mental illness because the comic form utilizes the "symbols that 'show' and symbols that 'tell'" (Hatfield 134).

Squire further explains that comics have the power to move readers "into a genuine encounter with the experience of disability" (86). And while this is true, comics are an apt medium for narratives about mental illness because of the way that the process of reading a comic forces readers to adjust their thought processes as they move from panel to panel and from page to page. The logistics of reading traditional books, for example, reading top to bottom, left to right, do not always apply to the reading of a comic. A comic may direct the reader to read in unexpected directions and to incorporate images, page layouts, and panels in order to follow the plot. Additionally, a comic requires a reader to interpret images in order to form meaning. And as interpretation is based on subjective experience and understanding, readers may end up with different interpretations of the text. In this way, comics are able to raise questions about the existence of an objective reality.

Comics, while generally presented in familiar, established patterns, can also challenge traditional reading paths by violating panels and borders, creating a free-flowing page with no discernible pattern, or by using formats that are open to interpretation and nonlinear reading (Kannenberg 316). Methods such as these allow the reader to explore and establish individualized reading paths. The comic is open to subjective interpretation and challenges the notion of there being only one acceptable perspective or pathway. Reading the page "backwards" at times, going from right to left, can have an unsettling effect for Western readers. This practice contributes to the overall effectiveness of comics in forcing readers to confront unfamiliar experiences, challenge what is "normal," and reconsider how they interpret a text.

The relationship between image and text is crucial for conveying the narrative, but comics also rely on the reader to make sense of this relationship and adjust according to the individual comic. In "Beyond Comparison," W. J. T. Mitchell explains that there is a "normal" relationship between image and text that follows "traditional formulas involving the clear subordination and suturing of one medium to the other, often with a straightforward division of labor" (117). Comics can manipulate this relationship to confuse the reader. In comics about mental illness, the relation between text and image can shift from one panel to the next, leaving readers questioning what is real and what is imagined. Comics about mental illness can also feature images that are simultaneously figurative and literal. The process of reading becomes completely unfamiliar and uncertain. In this way, comics require parts of the brain that function differently, "the part that reads, and the part that looks," to make meaning together (Kannenberg 309). This complex system allows verbal and visual symbols to retain traditional function while affecting each other in complex ways—where no meaning is lost, and there is only room for gain (Kannenberg 308). Because of this, there are ample opportunities for subjective interpretations depending on how one chooses to read the comic, that has the potential to create more complicated, personalized understanding of mental illness.

A recent literary project that addresses "the intersection of the medium of comics and the discourse of healthcare" is the *Graphic Medicine Manifesto*, written by MK Czerwiec, Ian Williams, Susan Squire, Michael Green, Kimberly Myers, and Scott Smith (1). This project argues that comics allow "a more inclusive perspective of medicine, illness, disability, caregiving, and being cared for" and provide "a voice to those who are often not heard" (Czerwiec, et al. 2). Through a series of individual comic analyses, the *Graphic Medicine Manifesto* aims to demonstrate that "comics are a powerful medium for presenting different ways of seeing and thinking about our views, perception and values" (Czerwiec, et al. 8). This is very much tied to the notion that traditional written text is not accessible for all authors or all readers. And while the writers of the *Graphic Medicine Manifesto* maintain that "those best positioned to represent illness and caregiving are those living with it," it seems clear that comics as a medium provide a venue where the opportunities for representation and authenticity are available for any authors and illustrators with awareness, sensitivity, and insight (Czerwiec, et al. 20).

To demonstrate the ability of comics to transcend the limitations of language in narratives about mental illness, this analysis will focus first on David Heatley's three-part comic, "Overpeck," which tells the story of a young girl, Sadie Grace, who lives with PTSD, a complex mental disorder that occurs as a result of trauma, and second on Nate Powell's *Swallow Me Whole*, a long-form comic that brilliantly uses the combination of text and image to convey the experience of two teenage siblings with schizophrenia. While neither of these texts is directly marketed as YA fiction, both feature adolescent protagonists with experiences that are relatable and understandable for young readers who would benefit greatly from such authentic depictions of mental illness. *Swallow Me Whole* has been widely received and recognized as a YA graphic novel. It has been reviewed by Brigid Alverson on teenreads.com and by the *School Library Journal*, which listed it as being appropriate for readers in grade ten and higher. Additionally, the Young Adult Library Services Association (YALSA) included the text in their list of "great graphic novels for teens." "Overpeck," on the other hand, was originally featured in MOME, a seasonal collection of independent comics published through Fantagraphic Books. Fantagraphic Books publishes a wide variety of comics, including several YA books. Because so few comics about mental illness are now aimed at young audiences, "Overpeck" and *Swallow Me Whole* have the potential to enrich the discussion of mental illness affecting children and adolescents by communicating with both youth and adult readers. Particularly evident in their use of full-page panels, both Heatley and Powell utilize comic form to transcend the silences and the indescribable nature of mental illness in order to tell stories of young people experiencing mental illness.

## Comics and PTSD: David Heatley's "Overpeck"

David Heatley's three-part comic "Overpeck" is the story of a child struggling with the psychological aftermath of severe trauma. Conveyed as a permanent aura surrounding Sadie's naked, exposed body, PTSD becomes a physical burden for her to bear. She cannot shake it off, she cannot forget its presence, and no one can deny the impact it has on her existence. Numerous critical studies and personal accounts explain that PTSD is a difficult subject to portray, particularly because the traumatic experience, as Anne Whitehead explains, "overwhelms the individual and resists language or representation" (3). Through symbolism, violation of traditional reading patterns, and the combination of text and image, Heatley allows readers to understand the lasting repercussions of PTSD, how trauma affects external relationships and behaviors, and more importantly, how it changes her very identity.

A full-page panel that demonstrates comics' unique ability to convey the experience of PTSD is what I refer to as "the Walking Page," found on page 100 of the comic. This page is so effective that it is braided throughout the three parts of the comic, which means that its recurring presence allows the reader to make complex connections across the many separate panels and parts (*The System of Comics* 159). At first glance, this page appears to be a tangled web of image and text, leaving the reader feeling lost and somewhat overwhelmed as to how to digest and process the page properly. Searching for some sort of anchor, the reader will eventually note the square panel at the top, left-hand corner of the page. In this panel, Sadie moves from being the subject of others' conversations and gossip to moving into the forefront of her own story. From this location, Sadie walks a distinct path that winds back and forth across and down the page, revisiting the location and memory of her trauma, and attempting to find relief from post-traumatic stress. In this process, she weaves in and out of the form of a duck, shows specifics about the traumatic event, and demonstrates a desperate need for psychological escape (100).

Images of Sadie's violent rape are in the center of the page (100). Even if the reader tries to resist the narrative path, the trauma is an inescapable truth in Sadie's life and the reader's experience. Additionally, the layout of this page helps to clarify an aspect of living with PTSD: no matter the approach, no matter the resistance, the trauma is inescapable. According to Dori Laub in *Testimony: Crises of Witnessing in Literature, Psychoanalysis and History*:

> The traumatic event . . . took place outside the parameters of 'normal' reality, such as causality, sequence, place and time. The trauma is thus an event that has no beginning, no ending, no before, no during and no after . . . Trauma survivors live not with memories of the past, but with an event that could not and did not proceed through to its completion, has no ending, attained no closure, and therefore, as far as its survivors are concerned, continues into the present and is current in every respect. (69)

Heatley's choice to place Sadie's rape in the center of a page that is dominated by chaos enables him to convey this break with linear time and reinforce the enormity and centrality of trauma for those with PTSD. Sadie's trauma is not in her past, nor is it in her future, but it exists in her continual present.

On "The Walking Page," the symbol of the duck is crucial for understanding Sadie's psychological need to part with reality. During her assault, Sadie needed to escape and because she could not literally change what happened or walk away from it, she metaphorically flies away from her battered body as a duck (100). Like many people with PTSD, she cannot accept or cope with what has happened and clings to the fantasy of having the power to take flight and abandon her trauma. That this process is conveyed through an image rather than through a written description allows the reader to witness the constant fluctuation in her psychological state.

Herman explains this transcendence into a nonhuman form: "Traumatized people feel utterly abandoned, utterly alone, cast out of the human and divine systems of care and protection that sustain life" (52). Sadie attempts to escape from her trauma but, as the bottom series of panels clarifies, transformation and avoidance are not sustainable. As she walks through the page, passing and reliving her trauma as though it were a physical landmark in her journey, her heart begins to pound and she attempts to distance herself from pain. She tells herself to be calm and immediately transforms into the duck (100). According to Herman, such a response is common in children and adolescents with PTSD who attempt to run away or hide from reliving trauma (100).

But the reality of PTSD is that Sadie cannot avoid her traumatic past or the impact on her psychological and physical wellbeing. She tries to cling to the duck-form but painfully and grotesquely morphs into her human self, passing through phases where she is neither human nor animal but something existing outside of normality completely: a person who suffers the lifelong consequences of profound trauma. In the second part of the comic, Sadie wakes up as a duck and feels relief to be away from the horrors of human cruelty (68). Immediately, she is bombarded with imagined scenarios of violence such as a wolf attacking and decapitating a duck, a chef chasing and devouring a duck, and a second duck beating her duck form and raping her corpse while calling her a "stupid bitch" (69). Herman explains that "although dissociative alterations in consciousness . . . may be adaptive at the moment of total helplessness, they become maladaptive once the danger is past" (45). And because people with PTSD may attempt to keep themselves and their trauma away from their ordinary consciousness, "they prevent the integration necessary for healing" (45). Sadie cannot survive as a duck/human hybrid nor can she escape PTSD no matter her physical form.

From her first appearance in the comic, Sadie is completely nude surrounded by a colorful aura. Demonstrated on "The Walking Page," the aura only appears after the trauma has occurred and then becomes a physical burden for her to bear (100). The aura, combined with her nudity, functions as a beacon, a scarlet letter, so to speak, for the shame she now bears. According to Herman, rape survivors, in addition to PTSD and emotional and physical damage, have the added burden of social judgment (Herman 67). Sadie is exposed: everyone knows what has happened to her, everyone knows her trauma, everyone knows about a very private and personal violation. Her aura, with its vibrant colors, draws attention to her naked body. Because the aura is a physical reality for her, one only complicated upon closer inspection, the reader is to understand that the aura represents the physicality and longevity of PTSD.

In the third part of the comic, another walking page appears that furthers this notion of public stigma and perception. In this version, much like the first, Sadie walks a nonlinear path that invites a multitude of possible readings. At the top of the panel, her face is nothing more than a blank outline, and slowly comes into focus as she moves towards the bottom corner (55). Her body, however, remains perfectly visible and detailed, with different sexualized parts of her body highlighted at each step in her pathway. The entire page centers on the external gaze. Unnamed characters move through the page and make comments and judgments. Sadie is defined in this gaze by her sexuality, but more importantly, as a spectacle. Her trauma, mental health, and identity are inconsequential, as demonstrated when an unnamed character says of her: "I heard about her. Most people can't even see her" (55). Given the representation issue of invisibility, this seems an obvious commentary on Western culture's tendency to ignore or deny the presence of mental illness, and in this instance, Sadie's nudity is presented as a mark of shame and inspiration for social torment and isolation. It also draws a gaze that sexualizes her, trivializes her trauma, and distracts others from acknowledging her as an individual, compassion, and the larger issue at hand. By focusing on her physical body, others ignore the reality that a child was the victim of rape, incest, and profound sexual abuse.

As with the original walking page, there is no definitive or correct way to move through the page, and interpretation is complicated by interspersed, disconnected commentary about Sadie. Depending on how the reader chooses to form a path, she can transform from a sexualized object of the neighborhood boy's desire, to someone he is genuinely interested in learning about. Or, conversely, she can go from being a sexualized spectacle to a humanized and empathetic person, yet quickly revert to being cast as hyper-sexualized and trivialized. If one were to follow the Western reading pattern, Heatley makes a powerful point. The bottom right of the panel features a clear image of Sadie's face with absolutely no hint of her naked body, yet the text is centered on the boy's interest in whether or not she would have sex with him (55). Sadie, and others with PTSD, are humanized through narratives that tell their individual experiences and convey what it is like to live with mental illness, but if the focus remains on externalities and not on the unspeakable experiences, she will remain only a spectacle.

"Overpeck" also demonstrates the power of comics to convey the interior and personal experience of trauma and PTSD. At the bottom of "The Walking Page," as Sadie mutates from the duck to her human body, the colors of the aura shift from calming blues to bright red, orange, and yellow: colors that suggest imminent danger. Once she has failed at maintaining the duck façade and returns to her human form, she appears in a tall panel, extending the entire height of the page, showing her in the midst of an intrusive panic attack (101). Because Sadie experiences the terror and pain of the event on a continual basis in the present, "the traumatic moment becomes so encoded in an abnormal form of memory, which breaks spontaneously into consciousness, both as flashbacks during waking states and as traumatic nightmares during sleep" (Herman 37).

Heatley's depiction of the panic attack emphasizes the most vulnerable regions of Sadie's body: her breasts, vagina, spine, and the sides of her torso are fully exposed (101). The entire image is covered in red scratches, resembling panicked cuts or scratches that a person might make on her body in a moment of severe distress or in an attempt to cause self-harm.
The scratches convey Sadie's emotional state, without attempting to define each response individually and sequentially. Instead, the combination of images, marks, and colors allows the reader to understand the essence of that moment.

At this point in the comic, the true significance of Sadie's aura is revealed. In the close up image, the reader now sees that her aura is the embodiment of her emotional and psychological distress, which has become a physical part of her being. The aura contains confusion, guilt, hate, stigma, self-blame, and anger at herself and at her perpetrator. The aura, in tiny handwriting, features vulgar and harsh language that demonstrates how the traumatic event has burrowed into her consciousness, identity, and ability to function. Her aura features phrases such as: "Stupid ugly cunt . . . I hate your fucking guts bitch . . . you fat little piece of meat . . . submit, bow down, and treat me as your king" (101). The physical presence of this internalized aura reinforces that PTSD is an illness, just like any other medical condition, that she cannot ignore or deny.
"Overpeck" is able to address PTSD recovery without being overly instructive, didactic, or aggressive. In the third part, Sadie meets Robert the Wise, who is guarded by several armed men (Part 3 64). One might expect a respected elder or prominent sage to appear before her, but Robert the Wise is a child who went missing years before. He is bloody, wearing only his underwear, covered in bandages, relying on crutches, and, like Sadie, surrounded by an aura (64).

His aura is drastically different in color and the reader understands him to be part of the community of children with PTSD. Despite being victimized years before, his trauma freezes him in time. He is able to speak to her as a peer, relating to her without the text needing to dictate their mutual understanding and similarities. Robert tells her that she is standing in the way of her own healing and demands that she take ownership of her recovery (65).

The comic ends with Sadie finally putting herself on the literal road to recovery (Part 3 67). The last hyper-panel (the page in its entirety) of the series features her doing cartwheels, relieved of her aura, expressing her hope for healing. She remains nude, reminding the reader of her vulnerability and that she will most likely always have to battle social perception. The text of her final monologue reads: "Everything looks so perfect today! So rich and full of life. Each thing exactly where it should be. And I'm one of those things! If I can just maintain this attitude . . . (and why shouldn't I be able to now that I see the truth?) . . . I'll never be unhappy again!" (67). Sadie walks down train tracks with full ownership and authority over herself and her recovery. Interestingly, there is a hand-drawn author's note in the bottom corner of the panel that this is part three of four. But the fact that this fourth part was never published only further contributes to the comic's depiction of PTSD. Trauma recovery is not easy, nor is it quick. More than likely, it is a condition that Sadie will live with for the rest of her life, with severity and symptoms wavering and changing with age and new life experiences (Herman, Caruth). Had the comic ended with finality with Sadie being cured, the overall depiction would be unrealistic. Yet if it had ended with her being inundated by PTSD symptoms, the depiction would still not represent an authentic experience of lifelong struggle, of ups and downs, and of the hope that is so crucial in the path to recovery.

## Comics and Schizophrenia: Nate Powell's *Swallow Me Whole*

Like Heatley, Nate Powell effectively uses full-page manifestations of characters' struggles with mental illness. *Swallow Me Whole* is Powell's long-form comic about teenaged step-siblings, Ruth and Perry, who are experiencing the onset of schizophrenia. The siblings have different symptoms, but are united in their hallucinations and the inability to distinguish between reality and hallucinatory experiences. Ruth is diagnosed with schizophrenia, while Perry, who also hallucinates, but whose symptoms do not inhibit his ability to function socially, is diagnosed as having excessive stress. *Swallow Me Whole* presents schizophrenia as individualized but also as a community experience where the step-siblings are connected through shared understanding. Powell utilizes incredibly creative methods in order to convey a personalized narrative of mental illness that not only grant readers insight into schizophrenia as a disease, but also into the experience of living with profound mental illness.

*Swallow Me Whole* is able to capture authentic onset of mental illness by depicting schizophrenia and hallucinations as concrete objects. In her memoir about experiencing the onset of schizophrenia in her teens, Sandra Yuen MacKay describe the illness as being deceptive: "It slips into the conscious mind, drawing one into an alternate world. The line between reality and dreams bends and blurs. My delusions became concrete beliefs I could not shake" (56). In the comic, mental illness become visual and tangible, hallucinations become reality. Through this method, readers are able to better understand the impact and confusion involved when the boundary between reality and psychosis blur.

While Perry experiences hallucinations of a wizard pen commanding him to draw different images, the narrative centers on Ruth's schizophrenia as it first enters and then consumes her life. As her illness begins to manifest itself, Ruth experiences hallucinations related to her collection of cicada specimens that she keeps in jars in her bedroom (13). They remain her private possession and completely under her control. She can monitor them, organize them, and keep them distinct from her daily life. Soon, living cicadas begin crawling and falling through the vent in her ceiling and it becomes clear that she can no longer control or maintain them (17–18).

The cicadas are a real-life, concrete reference point for readers who may not be able to empathize with the experience of schizophrenic hallucinations. Authors with schizophrenia have described visual hallucinations as being in the corner of their eyes, but also sometimes completely solid and tangible (Schiller 225). Lori Schiller explains the frustration she experienced when people would talk about her voices and hallucinations as being imagined, because, for her, they were just as real as the people telling her that they were not (90). Powell's method features no stylistic difference between hallucinations and real people, conversations, or moments. In this way, *Swallow Me Whole* is able to present schizophrenia as described by those who live with it.

Powell's choice to use cicadas, a swarming insect, brilliantly captures how authors with schizophrenia describe the onset and escalation of their condition: where delusions slowly swallow reality and become their whole life (MacKay 62). While the cicadas are contained at the beginning of the narrative, they slowly grow in number until they are uncontrollable swarms. Much like the actual insects with vegetation, they eventually overwhelm individual panels and pages and then completely take over. The incessant buzzing overwhelms any written text and the blackness of the swarm consumes all other images. At some points, the cicadas cover Ruth's entire face and overwhelm her very identity and existence, while other characters become nothing more than vague outlines who are defined by the shape of the swarm around them (57–61). This symbol is effective because psychosis and actual cicadas follow similar patterns: intensity fluctuates, at times with few remaining insects, but she is able to function through the ebb and flow (65). However, once the cicadas enter Ruth's life, they are always present to some extent, underscoring the chronic nature of schizophrenia.

At the end of the comic, the swarm's intensity is extreme and Ruth is carried through a window and into the neighborhood (173). As she floats, the cicadas grow in numbers and the amount of white space in each panel is slowly consumed. Eventually, they cling desperately to her, become a physical part of her, and seem to form every shape around her. The swarm has taken over her world completely (173–97). The swarm not only allows a concrete visual example of the experience of being overwhelmed by something outside of one's control and the physical reality of hallucinations, but because cicadas are natural entities that operate according to natural cycles, their presence also reinforces mental illness (specifically schizophrenia) as a natural or biological force.

This symbolism is complicated and enriched by the presence of a frog that Ruth steals from the museum. She hides the frog in her room and it seems to watch her and her advancing condition. Once she is subsumed by the cicadas, she climbs into the frog's massive mouth perhaps seeking refuge or perhaps because she has become a cicada, which would be natural food for the frog. Later, in an attempt to rescue his sister, Perry slowly feeds the frog the cicadas. The frog devours them with a winding, violently eager tongue (201). As he feeds it, the outline of his grandmother appears behind him and warns him to be careful because the frog will "swallow you whole" (205). Slowly, as the frog feasts on Ruth's cicadas, the giant frog changes shape so that it is Ruth's body with a frog head (203–8). There are then several pages of blackness to end the comic. Because of the subjective nature of images in comics, this can be interpreted a variety of ways. The frog could be commentary on the mental health field and how it feeds off of people for profit or it could be a reference to natural order and systems of consumption. Perhaps Perry's actions demonstrate the lifelong struggle the two will face in order to manage their mental illness, or perhaps Ruth has committed suicide and the scene represents this loss. Just as in "Overpeck," *Swallow Me Whole* invites this openness, and the opportunity to create subjective meaning allows readers to form connections and reactions on a personal level.

Even though Perry and Ruth are not blood-related, they share in the experience of mental illness. Because the characters are teens, they hesitate to reveal the truth of their conditions to anyone else but are able to confide in one another. Interestingly, despite the completely subjective experience of psychosis, the siblings share delusions. They express being aware that other people cannot see or hear what they do, and this further strengthens their bond (47–48). Toward the end of the comic, after Ruth has experienced a major schizophrenia break, symbolized by her abduction by the cicadas, Perry is able to sense that something is wrong without any outward indication. Rather than seeing innocuous trees, as the reader does, he is aware of the cicadas lurking in the black shapes of the trees (173–97). The next panels show the swarm creating utter chaos around him, drowning out his screams to his sister, and making it nearly impossible to decipher what is happening (173–97). After she vanishes into the frog's mouth, there are three pages of blackness until Perry digs through the cicada corpses and allows white light to break up the darkness (197). The siblings' ability to share in each other's delusions demonstrates the need for community, particularly with adolescents who often feel afraid and shameful admitting to adults that they may be experiencing possible symptoms of mental illness (MacKay, Snyder, Schiller). *Swallow Me Whole* communicates the importance of peer communities for adolescents with mental illness and also reinforces that healing occurs in the context of relationships rather than total isolation. Perry seeks his sister, faces the barriers and obstacles of her psychosis, and demonstrates that treatment and recovery require support, patience, and physical effort (173–97).

*Swallow Me Whole* demonstrates the capacity of comics to convey realistic personal experiences with schizophrenia in allowing readers to share in the hallucinations. A barrier in attempting to convey personal narratives about mental illness is the inability of the reader to relate to experiences so disparate from "normal" experiences. Kurt Snyder, a mental health advocate who was diagnosed with schizophrenia as a teenager, explains: "The behavior of a person with schizophrenia often seems inexplicable to outside observers. But to a person who is ill, it makes complete sense in the context of his or her reality" (Snyder, et al. 41). In this comic, the reader sees what the protagonists see, only knows reality as it presented through that perspective, and has no way to determine what is real from what is not. In the midst of a chaotic swarm, Ruth's behavior makes perfect sense in the context of what the reader sees as her reality.

Even though many of the delusions are absurd in concept, such as a talking wizard pen or dead cicadas communicating from inside jars, the fact that they are depicted as concrete and just as real as anything else disorients the reader from reality because there is no other frame of reference (32, 35, 36). The reader is never certain of what is hallucinated and what is real. The swarming cicadas are Ruth's delusions but also seem to exist in the real world as part of a natural cycle (199). The question of witnessing and experience shifts so that the reader not only takes part in Ruth's hallucinations but also must question his or her own notion of reality.

💬 ✳ 🗨

As demonstrated in these brilliant full-page panels in "Overpeck" and *Swallow Me Whole*, the reader is not only able to see mental illness from a new perspective, but through the experience of the comic, he or she is able to form a personal connection. Such texts are crucial for YA readers in the effort to eliminate damaging stereotypes, but also for young people who are experiencing issues of mental illness and are searching for connection, information, insight, and guidance. Heatley and Powell's works are able to not just tell readers about what it is like to have mental illness, but to show and share the experience. "Overpeck" expresses the interiority and complexity of PTSD and *Swallow Me Whole* demonstrates the concrete, disorienting, overwhelming, and subjective nature of schizophrenic delusion. These two works demonstrate the ability of comics to transcend the barriers of the unspeakable and inexplicable in order to convey authentic representations of the experience of living with mental illness. Often, narrative authenticity becomes lost in translation, yet comics, unlike any other form of art or literature, provide a venue that communicates directly in the visual/verbal language of experience.

## Works Cited

Caruth, Cathy. *Unclaimed Experience: Trauma, Narrative, and History*. Baltimore: Johns Hopkins UP, 1996. Print.

Czerwiec, MK, Ian Williams, Susan Squier, Michael J. Green, Kimberly R. Myers, and Scott T. Smith. *Graphic Medicine Manifesto*. University Park, Pennsylvania: The Pennsylvania State University Press, 2015. Print.

Groensteen, Thierry. "The Impossible Definition." *A Comic Studies Reader*. Ed. Jeet Heer and Kent Worcester. Jackson: University Press of Mississippi, 2009. Print.

———. *The System of Comics*. Trans. Bart Beaty and Nick Nguyen. Jackson: University Press of Mississippi, 2007. Print.

Hatfield, Charles. "An Art of Tensions." *A Comic Studies Reader*. Eds. Jeet Heer and Kent Worcester. Jackson: University Press of Mississippi, 2009. Print.

Heatley, David. "Overpeck (Part 1)." *MOME* (Summer 2005): 99–108. Print.

———. "Overpeck (Part 2)." *MOME* (Fall 2005): 68–77. Print.

———. "Overpeck (Part 3)." *MOME* (Winter 2006): 53–67. Print.

Herman, Judith. *Trauma and Recovery: The Aftermath of Violence—from Domestic Abuse to Political Terror*. New York: Basic Books, 1992. Print.

Kannenberg, Gene, Jr. "The Comics of Chris Ware." *A Comic Studies Reader*. Ed. Jeet Heer and Kent Worcester. Jackson: University Press of Mississippi, 2009. Print.

Laub, Dori. "Bearing Witness or the Vicissitudes of Listening." *Testimony: Crises of Witnessing in Literature, Psychoanalysis, and History*. Ed. Shoshana Felman and Dori Laub. New York: Routledge, 1992. Print.

MacKay, Sandra Yuen. *My Schizophrenic Life: The Road to Recovery from Mental Illness*. Ontario, Canada: Bridgeross Communications, 2010. Print.

"Mental Health by the Numbers." *National Alliance on Mental Illness*. n.p. 2016. Web. 3 October 2016.

Mitchell, W. J. T. "Beyond Comparison." *A Comic Studies Reader*. Ed. Jeet Heer and Kent
    Worcester. Jackson: University Press of Mississippi, 2009. Print.
Powell, Nate. *Swallow Me Whole*. Marietta, GA: Top Shelf Productions, 2010. Print.
Riley, Charles A. *Disability and the Media: Prescriptions for Change*. Hanover, NH: University
    Press of New England, 2005. Print.
Saks, Elyn R., *The Center Cannot Hold: My Journey Through Madness*. New York: Hyperion,
    2007. Print.
Schiller, Lori, and Amanda Bennett. *The Quiet Room: A Journey Out of the Torment of Madness*.
    New York: Warner Books, 1994. Print.
Snyder, Kurt, Raquel Gur, and Linda Wasmer Andrews. *Me, Myself, and Them: A Firsthand
    Account of One Young Person's Experience with Schizophrenia*. New York: Oxford University
    Press, 2007. Print.
Squire, Susan M. "So Long as They Grow Out of It: Comics, The Discourse of Developmental
    Normalcy, and Disability." *Journal of Medical Humanities* 29.2 (2008): 71–88. Print.
Whitehead, Anne. *Trauma Fiction*. Edinburgh: Edinburgh UP, 2004. Print.

# 4

## Not Haunted, Just Empty:
## Figurative Representation in Sarah Oleksyk's *Ivy*

### Catherine Kyle

In Sarah Oleksyk's *Ivy*, monstrosity abounds. Teachers, parents, and adolescents, including the protagonist herself, are portrayed as malicious, aggressive, and sometimes downright dangerous. Alliances are unreliable, trust comes with a price, and violence both verbal and physical inundates Ivy's life. Douglas Wolk writes in his introduction to the collected version of the five unpaginated "mini-comics" (2) that Oleksyk self-published in Portland, Oregon, that "high schoolers can be horribly cruel to each other," adding that *Ivy* is "about that vicious bind" (1). He describes Ivy Stenova as "angry . . . mean, short-tempered, inattentive, deceitful" and "bitter" (1). Oleksyk herself refers to the character as an "anti-hero" (Long), "abrasive," and "a bit of a bully" (Dueben). The motif of monstrosity is most overtly expressed through Ivy's artwork, which features a range of corpses, demons, and gore. Yet as Wolk observes, "Oleksyk makes us root for her [Ivy] anyway" (1). Ivy is more than a short-tempered bully or a troubled, morbid painter. Her abrasiveness stems not from some sort of innate, pathological rancor but from a cultivated defensiveness vital to her survival. As Wolk states, "cruelty is often a kind of armor" (1), and for Ivy, this supposition holds true. She is more complicated than she knows, more vulnerable, and far more emotionally sensitive than she might first appear. Arguably, Ivy never fully accepts this reality, even at the end of the story. But Oleksyk, through her drawings as omniscient narrator/illustrator, makes Ivy's true nature clear to readers. Her use of visual metaphor exposes Ivy's vulnerability in moments when Ivy herself refuses to acknowledge it. The comic thus engages in a kind of double-speak—Oleksyk's visual metaphor complicates everything that Ivy draws, says, and does. A key insight emerges when the titular character expresses hesitation about spending the night in a rundown shack for fear that it is haunted and her boyfriend insists, "It's not haunted, it's just empty!" (164.3). In the pages that follow, I make a case that this line alludes to the greatest tension at the heart of the text. For all her bravado, Ivy is fighting her own sense of emptiness far more than any external monster, but this revelation comes only through the careful juxtaposition of the character's artwork and that of the omniscient narrator/illustrator.

## Art within Art: Branched Monstration

Clearly, all the artwork that appears within *Ivy* was drawn by Sarah Oleksyk. However, because the distinction between the images Oleksyk depicts as Ivy's art and the images unattributed to her is so central to this discussion, I will refer to anything that appears in Ivy's sketchbook or on her canvases as Ivy's and everything else as Oleksyk's. This need for clarification is indicative of another tension inherent in *Ivy* and other recent comics: the dual representation of characters' and narrators' separate subjectivities. Hillary Chute observes that in comics such as Alison Bechdel's *Fun Home: A Family Tragicomedy*, Lynda Barry's *One Hundred Demons!*, and Marjane Satrapi's *Persepolis*, the authors create "doubled narration" (Introduction) by providing a voice for characters' words and thoughts via speech and thought balloons and, concurrently, a voice for the narrators via separate rectangular panels or other means. She writes that this enables comics creators, particularly those producing memoirs, to "stage dialogues among versions of self" (Introduction)—in short, to speak as child-self and adult-self on the same page. *Ivy* is not a memoir (though Oleksyk states in an interview with Aaron Long that the comic is semi-autobiographical), and it does not utilize the "doubled narration" to which Chute refers—at least, not verbally. However, Oleksyk does accomplish a kind of doubled, and even tripled narration through her illustrations.

In *Comics and Narration*, Thierry Groensteen theorizes that comics' "enunciation," or methods of communication, can be divided into two areas of study: the recitation and the monstration (5.2.1). (He borrows the term "monstration" from film theorist André Gaudreault.) Groensteen explains that with regard to comics, recitation refers to the verbal aspects, while monstration refers to the visual aspects. Accordingly, the reciter is the verbal narrator, where one exists, and the monstrator is the visual equivalent, which Groensteen argues comics cannot exist without. The idea of the monstrator is key: it is essentially the visual narrator of the comic. Like a verbal narrator, the monstrator can occupy variable subjectivities: omniscient, third-person limited, first-person, unreliable, and so on. Just as it is important not to confuse the author with the narrator of a novel, it is important not to confuse the illustrator with the monstrator of a comic. As Groensteen writes, "Asserting the material existence of a monstrating instance within a narratological theory means isolating, in the process of comics creation, what pertains specifically to the drawing inasmuch as it is driven by a narrative intention and imbued with subjectivity" (5.2.1).

To clarify my argument, then, I see generative tensions between Ivy's art and Oleksyk's monstration that reveal new meanings of the text. I have termed this phenomenon, which occurs in other comics as well, *branched monstration*. Both Ivy's art and Oleksyk's monstration use visual metaphor—figurative representation—to comment on Ivy's emotional state. But their commentary differs, because they reflect different narrative perspectives.

### "If I Can Draw What I'm Feeling": Ivy's Art

Ivy's art, the first path of the text's branched monstration, reflects her conscious desires, emotions, and reactions to the events that befall her. They represent the means by which she translates these experiences into tactile, visible form—the products and evidence of her creative mind at work. As such, they shed light on that which Ivy is willing to admit to herself about the way she perceives her struggles and her world. Significantly, her art is predominantly monstrous. Though she does sketch a few realistic images, many of her drawings are of surreal, nightmarish ghouls or glowering demons. Her sketchbook, which appears on *Ivy*'s cover as well as in its pages, sports a sharp-toothed, horned, angry-looking creature. Because the monster has two speech balloons emitting from its mouth declaring the spiral notebook "Ivy Book" (27.9), it seems safe to assume that Ivy drew it. Her portfolio contains paintings of a fanged, clawed creature (33.2), a grimacing doglike monster (33.2), and a fish with the head of a woman wearing a pensive expression (39.4). In art class, she sketches one leering, humanlike creature with minimalistic features stabbing another with a spear (76.4). Similar humanlike creatures appear in her sketchbook and on a canvas in her bedroom: the sketchbook depicts a faceless, dark-haired, naked figure holding its knees to its chest (190.3), and the canvas shows a faceless, dark-haired woman hunching her shoulders and clenching her fists, as if preparing for a fight (213.7). In another scene, Ivy draws an enormous horned devil with charcoal on the underbelly of the railway overpass where she goes to collect her thoughts (116.3). The devil's gaping mouth is lined with jagged teeth, its eyes are narrowed, its brow is furrowed, and its sharp claws reach out as if to snatch passersby. Due to its implied scale within the narrative and its literal scale on the page (nearly all of it), this railway demon is arguably the most powerful example of Ivy's supernatural, monstrous art. While Rachel Gear observes that female visual artists can engage with monstrosity to subvert the historical conflation of women's bodies with abjection (322–23), I suggest that Ivy's intentions are less complex, given the context in which she creates. She is enraged in nearly all the aforementioned examples, a correlation that equates her monstrous drawings with her subjective take on reality rather than subversion or reclamation.

Even in some of Ivy's more realistic drawings, the content is remarkably violent. In one scene, she draws her math teacher being impaled by a giant stake (28.2). The old woman's head sits skewered at the top of the spike and her body hangs at the bottom. Blood jets out of both the decapitated head and the severed neck; coils of intestines spew out of the body. The lolling tongue and X-shaped eyes add a somewhat cartoonish note to the illustration, but the blood and detailed innards make it grisly nonetheless. Ivy also draws a glaring face with vacant eyes devoid of irises and pupils (52.7); a headless, emaciated body with its intestines spilling out (76.5); and her own gravestone bearing the words "Here lies Ivy Stenova / Much loved / Much hated" (76.6). It is true that Ivy draws and paints a few nonviolent images, including a still life of fruit (12.1), her crush Russ (28.1), her eventual boyfriend Josh (42.3; 58.9–58.10; 119.4; 170.2), and a smiling, nude woman spreading her arms as if in flight (157.5). However, these instances are in the minority, and none appear on the same scale as the railway demon. Taken in isolation, Ivy's array of artistic expressions aligns with Wolk's and Oleksyk's assessments of the character as abrasive and antiheroic. Ivy's obsession with violence and death may even raise concerns in readers or make her unsympathetic. However, Ivy's art is only one small piece of the psychological portrait provided by the text as a whole.

## "Surrounded by Monsters": Oleksyk's Literal Omniscient Monstration

Oleksyk's monstration works on three levels in the text: literal omniscient, figurative third-person limited (what I here refer to as the "cognitive" level), and figurative omniscient (what I here refer to as "psycho-monstration"). While the goal of this discussion is to focus primarily on the interactions between Ivy's use of figurative representation and that of Oleksyk, I will supply a brief overview of Oleksyk's use of nonfigurative monstration to give these interactions context. In short, Oleksyk uses literal omniscient monstration, along with some dialogue and other uses of language, to establish Ivy's school and home as legitimately monstrous settings.

Setting plays a major role in *Ivy*. Wolk praises Oleksyk's "knack for staging" and the way she "establishes a sense of place," opining that the railroad overpass, for instance, is "practically a character in itself" (2). Indeed, the environments Ivy inhabits understandably influence her impressions of life as a kind of horror story. The first word of the comic is "*Grrrr!!!*" (emphasis in original) and the first panel depicts Ivy's high school from the outside with a sign that includes the words "Home of the Fighting Quakers" (11.1). Immediately, this visceral growl and invocation of combat portray the school as a hostile setting. The fact that the high school's mascot is the "Fighting Quaker"—an oxymoron, as Quakers are well known for their pacifism—stresses the confrontational nature of the school to an even greater extent. In another example, a skeleton dominates the still life Ivy's art teacher sets up in class one day (56.3). Ivy's math teacher, who repeatedly humiliates Ivy publicly for failing to complete her homework, is drawn with a fixed grimace, facial warts, elongated nails, and knobbed, quivering hands (113.1; 113.4), making one student's declaration that she is a "witch" somewhat understandable (22.6). Yet another instance is a panel depicting Ivy crying openly in a school toilet stall, surrounded by profanity-filled graffiti. The wall behind her reads "Missy B. is a Bitch," "Fuck you," "A Dick," and "No shit!" (57.4). In English, profanity is often referred to as cursing, and in this image, Ivy appears simultaneously overburdened by and engulfed in the weight of these peripheral curses. Similar graffiti appears in other scenes as well. A drawing of a phallus inside a bathroom stall is accompanied by the words "Eat it!" followed by the retort, "Gross" (69.8). A drawing of a woman's naked torso is accompanied by the words "Angela R. fucks dogs" followed by the comeback, "Fuck you!" (70.1). It would be naïve to expect a high school restroom to contain cheerful messages of hope and inspiration, but Oleksyk's inclusion of these hostile phrases emphasizes the toxic nature of Ivy's academic and social setting. These multimodal exchanges, though seemingly superfluous to the story, also express something of Ivy's peers' attitudes toward sexuality. Nudity, as invoked by the phallus and the torso, are conflated with "Gross"-ness and bestiality. Sexuality hovers in the background, literally and figuratively, alluding to the contradictory blend of fascination and revulsion with which Ivy's peers regard it. In short, sexuality and even the human body are made monstrous. In this regard, *Ivy* follows in the footsteps of Charles Burns's graphic novel *Black Hole*, wherein a sexually transmitted disease causes horrific mutations in teens.

Oleksyk's juxtaposition of sexuality with discomfort and disgust emerges elsewhere in the text as well. As she walks down the hall at school, Ivy shoots a disapproving look at a couple engaged in open-mouthed kissing (14.4). The pair is surrounded by sound effect balloons that read "smeck," "gnuck," and "slarp!"—noises more associated with the creatures from the Black Lagoon than romantically entwined lovers. Between Ivy's gaze and the sound effects, the kissing is portrayed as a distasteful act. Later, on a walk near the railway overpass—which, incidentally, can only be reached via graveyard—Ivy stumbles on a pornographic magazine. At one point she thumbs through the images of women's bodies—all "cropped" (by Oleksyk's monstration, of course) to omit anything above the neck or below the knees—and exclaims, "God, they're so fucking bovine. . . . They don't even have *souls!*" (49.2–49.3, emphasis in original). Ivy's statement reveals her concern that sexuality is limited to the profane context of her high school's bathroom graffiti: bestial, headless, and "soulless." The compartmentalized images of body parts, detached from the whole and from any recognizable identity, are mirrored in the restroom and magazine. Both portray sex as something that divides, something that rends flesh and banishes soul—in short, something monstrous. Even in her "safe space," the railway overpass, Ivy is accosted by unsettling imagery. In a letter to Josh, she writes that she is "—nded by monsters" (112.7). The beginning of the first word is cut off by the edge of the panel, but the most likely completion is "surrounded." Ivy feels surrounded by monsters. If cruelty is armor, high school is a brutal, psychically violent coliseum.

Elements of the monstrous surround Ivy at home as well, primarily stemming from her mother. *Ivy* is, at its root, a *Künstlerroman*. As Wolk observes, the story takes place in "the moment when the spark and gifts in her [Ivy] can either flourish or be crushed" (1). Though she longs to attend an out-of-state art school and her potential is recognized by her art teacher and recruiters alike (13.6; 39.5), Ivy collides with two of the most common obstacles to artistic maturation: family disapproval (Trites) and low socioeconomic standing (Wallace 325). Her mother, who is alone in raising Ivy, repeatedly tries to discourage her daughter from pursuing a career in art. Her main concerns are economical, as is evidenced by statements such as, "I won't let you waste that mind of yours by getting some worthless art degree!" (18.5) and "I'm not shelling out 25 grand a year for you to play around and then come out *flipping burgers!!*" (132.7, emphasis in original). Her concerns are also personal, as she exposes by continually comparing Ivy to her "lying, deceitful" father, whom she despises for "running off to pursue his 'dreams' and leaving [her] behind" (133.5). Ivy grapples with both sets of accusations, addressing the economical by insisting, "I got a scholarship. I don't need your help," and the personal with the tearful protestations, "I'm nothing like Dad!" (133.5) and "I'm not him!!" (134.1). After she runs away from home, Ivy wanders alone, mimicking her mother, saying, "'You and Glenn. What a pair.' 'The apple never falls far from the tree,'" before finally realizing, "I ran out on her too" (183.1; 183.6). In this moment, Ivy encounters both her farther's antagonistic nature and her own. Thus, she is waging a war on two fronts: not only against the specter of her father, but also against the parts of herself she fears may resemble him.

The tensions created by Ivy's father's absence and her mother's financial anxieties cast the Stenova home as a monstrous setting. Ivy and her mother are not always at odds, but monstrosity lingers on the borders, always ready to encroach. Oleksyk makes this clear via literal omniscient monstration. Ivy's mother is depicted as consuming alcohol on several occasions (51; 110; 128.5; 136.2; 207.4), sometimes to the point of inebriation (51) and sometimes as a coping mechanism (136; 207). One telling example shows the mother emptying her wine glass into her mouth after Ivy storms out on her. Though she looks remorseful in the panel where Ivy slams her bedroom door, the next panel shows her with an angry expression draining the contents of her wine glass (51). Though the text does not imply that the mother is a full-blown alcoholic, these repeated representations suggest that alcohol may play a role in her generally inflammatory demeanor. Ivy's mother has moments of kindness and concern, but her bitterness about her own circumstances often manifests as sudden bursts of anger. Neutral situations quickly give way to close-up images of the mother scowling (18.4; 51.9; 110.4). María J. Oritz observes that size often corresponds with importance in images (1574), and in *Ivy*, this principle holds true. Oleksyk nearly always "zooms in" on the mother when she is upset, magnifying the anger's significance. Even in the panel depicting Ivy and her mother at their most harmonious, monstrosity looms in the background. Though the wordless panel depicts both characters smiling in their living room at Christmastime, complete with presents and decorated tree, an image of Dr. Seuss's Grinch leers eerily from the television screen (128.5). The Grinch is drawn in pale gray, in contrast to the well-defined, black lines of the rest of the comic. He is easily overlooked, and could be considered a mere detail serving to emphasize the time of year. However, given the way monstrosity is "braided," or incorporated as a visual motif (Groensteen, *The System*, Introduction) throughout the text, I suggest that his appearance is more purposeful.

Ivy's artwork may be violent and gruesome, but it is a direct product of her surroundings and her culture. Monstrosity surrounds her, from her nettlesome math teacher and the hostility literally bound in the walls of her school to her embittered mother and the ever-present specter of her absent father—a monster that she fears she may, in fact, resemble. Bombarded from all directions by monstrous people, words, concepts, and environments, Ivy translates her emotions into images that make sense to her: demons, acts of violence, and angry, looming faces. Susanne Langer argues that the visual arts are products of metaphoric thinking (Feinstein 45), and George Lakoff and Mark Johnson agree, concluding that metaphor "is pervasive in everyday life, not just in language but in thought" (3). As a blossoming artist, Ivy is assigning visual metaphors to her emotions. After her art teacher expresses concern over her violent illustrations, Ivy even articulates this herself, stating, "If I can draw what I'm feeling, then it gets it out of my head" (77.7). Oleksyk's literal omniscient monstration makes it clear where Ivy is gleaning inspiration for her monstrous creations. What is less clear is whether the act of drawing actually purges Ivy's feelings in the way she insists.

## Dreams, Imaginings, and Perceptions: Oleksyk's Cognitive Monstration

Though Ivy espouses the cathartic powers of drawing, her mere admission that her gruesome artwork represents her feelings testifies to those feelings' depth, potency, and prevalence. Does drawing monstrosity really "get it out of her head"? Or is she simply arguing this to put her teacher's mind at ease? The text suggests that the latter is the case. Like Ivy's art and Oleksyk's literal omniscient monstration, Ivy's dreams, imaginings, and perceptions contain several monstrous motifs, suggesting that these feelings are still very much *in* her head. As Sigmund Freud writes in *The Interpretation of Dreams*, the anxieties expressed symbolically in dreams are symptomatic of "neurotic anxiety in general"—in other words, anxiety experienced in waking life (90). Such figurative representations form another path of *Ivy*'s branched monstration.

Dreams, imaginings, and perceptions as depicted in comics pose a somewhat difficult question because it is not always clear to whom their figurative representation should be attributed. On the one hand, it is the character's mind that is presented as the originator of the metaphors. But at the same time, it is the monstrator who has control over the depiction of these metaphors. (As Derrida suggests, there may be a certain "doubleness" [Kavka para. 1] in play that allows both interpretations to exist simultaneously, or even dialectically.) Unlike Ivy's art, which is clearly Ivy's, and Oleksyk's literal omniscient monstration, which is, if not "objective," at least literal (i.e.,the Grinch is literally on TV, the graffiti is literally on the restroom stall, etc.), dreams, imaginings, and perceptions are figurative representations produced by a character's mind, but over which she may not have complete, voluntary control. Oleksyk's hand tells readers what Ivy's mind sees, much like an third-person limited narrator can tell readers what a character is thinking internally.

Ann Miller notes that comics can depict "purely subjective images" that reveal information about a character's frame of mind, such as a memory of violence being shown in pixels (110). Through the monstrator's decision to depict the memory in pixels, the reader gleans the information that the character's memory is fragmented, surreal, or hazy. It is unlikely that the monstrator is suggesting that the character "literally" remembers the scene in pixels—it is a figurative representation chosen by the illustrator. Silke Hostkotte and Nancy Pedri call this type of third-person figurative monstration "cognitive focalization" (334), "focalization" being simply the filtering of a narrative through a certain point of view (Niederhoff para. 2), and Kai Mikkonen writes that such forms of monstration can reveal "complex inner experience in the . . . protagonist's mind" (116). There are a few clear instances where Ivy uses her imagination consciously, as is indicated by traditionally shaped thought balloons, and these occurrences are generally positive in nature. To name a few examples, she imagines herself painting on large-scale canvases (17.2), having her work shown in a gallery (17.4), receiving money from adoring patrons (17.6), and hitching a ride on a train (28.6). But in supplemental instances of what I will call cognitive monstration (i.e., third-person limited monstration), monstrosity reemerges.

Ivy has only one dream sequence in the text, indicated by an image of her sleeping followed by an image of her walking down an unnaturally waving hallway (73.4). In the first panel of the dream, she gazes with a concerned expression at a group of unnamed high school students who turn their backs to her, staring over their shoulders and glaring uninvitingly. Even the few students whose bodies are oriented toward her display closed-off body language—one folds her arms, another places her hand on her hip. All wear irritated expressions. In the next panel—one that takes up nearly the full page—Ivy sees her friends Marisa and Brad through a fish-eye-lens-like window through which she cannot break. The sound effect "Bam bam" positioned near her fist shows that she is trying (74.1). Not only is Ivy trapped behind the window, so too is she silenced. "Marisa . . . ? . . . Can you hear me?" she calls, but neither friend turns on the other side of the glass (74.1). In the lower half of the panel, Ivy looks startled as she is grabbed around the waist from behind by a male figure that resembles Josh, but whose eyes and nose are obscured by his long, shaggy bangs. Directly adjacent, the Josh-creature holds Ivy at arm's length, and finally, in a third depiction, leans into her neck. Whether he is kissing her or biting her as a vampire might is unclear; the back of his head obscures his mouth's actions. Given his frighteningly oversized mouth in his first two depictions, the absence of any other facial features, and Ivy's alarmed expression in the first two depictions, I am inclined to read the action as a bite. However, Ivy's face in the depiction where he actually leans toward her neck could be interpreted as aroused, or at least accepting. In either case, the aforementioned conflation of sexuality with monstrosity is vividly reiterated in this scene. So too is the conflation of Ivy's high school and peer group with monstrosity. Overall, Ivy's unconscious (not to be confused with subconscious)[1] cognition produces something that is far more nightmare than dream. I draw a distinction between the unconscious and the subconscious here because Ivy's subconscious—that of which she is cognitively unaware—seems to be articulated in a separate path of branched monstration, as I will shortly discuss. Judging from her disgruntled expression upon waking up from the dream (74.2) and the fact that she immediately seeks her mother, perhaps to debrief (74.3), I believe that Ivy recalls her dream. Though its metaphoric content may be involuntary, Ivy's awareness of it distinguishes this form of cognition from what I will argue are her more truly subliminal emotions.

Outside of dreams, Ivy imagines and perceives several monstrous things as she interacts with others in her waking life. In one instance, her friend Brad shows up to school with a black eye (54). When Ivy demands, "What happened to you?" Brad responds, "I really don't want to talk about it." Ivy presses, "Who did that to you? Was it your dad?" Then, in a wordless image that maintains the sequence of panels on the page but lacks a frame itself (that is, it essentially floats in the gutter), a minimalistic humanlike figure wearing an angry expression clobbers another humanlike figure (54.6). This image is contained in a cloud shaped balloon shaded entirely gray, and the figures are drawn in a sketchy, loose line style. In the next panel, Ivy says, "He's a dead man." Marisa tells Ivy that it was indeed Brad's father who struck him, but this leaves some mystery about what is occurring in the gray balloon. In the panels where Ivy is clearly imagining something (having her work in a gallery, etc.), the small bubbles customarily seen in comics lead from her head to full-fledged thought balloons. Here, that is not the case. This ambiguity leaves a few possibilities. Perhaps Brad narrates the event, but the monstrator conceals his language with an image (Brad has said, after all, that he doesn't want to talk about it, and the image may serve as commentary on the unspeakability of child abuse). Alternatively, perhaps the image represents Ivy's imagined version of the violence. If this is the case, her mind has once again displayed its inclination toward monstrous metaphor: the minimalistic figure of the father does resemble those appearing in her sketchbook. This scenario would suggest that in both dreams and perception, Ivy's cognition is plagued by visions of monsters, which in turn would suggest that drawing does not necessarily free her to the extent she would like to believe.

This interpretation is bolstered by similar imaginings when Ivy and Josh meet near the railway overpass and Ivy "sees" soldiers on horseback running alongside her and Josh with the face of a wolf (92.4; 92.6). On a conscious and unconscious level, Ivy's mind translates her experiences and emotions into images of monstrosity. Again, this is not necessarily unwarranted—Oleksyk makes it clear that Ivy's setting is a hostile one, and in the scene where Ivy "sees" these visions, Josh is acting like a literal and figurative beast. Though Josh has only met Ivy once before and exchanged some letters with her, he pinches her (86.4; 89.9); kisses her even though she initially resists (88.5–89.2); painfully rips her hangnail off with his teeth (94.3); grabs her breasts, eliciting an uncomfortable look (95.7); makes unnerving "jokes" such as, "This is where I'll stash your body when I 'accidentally' kill you," (93.6) and "We can run off and breed a bunch of mutant kids"; and snarls and howls when Ivy suggests they should "become like the wolves to survive" beyond the bounds of society (91.7; 91.8). Though not all of these actions occur before Ivy "sees" Josh as the wolf, his monstrous nature is established by the time the "vision" emerges, and is only enforced by the actions that follow it. I use the words "sees" and "vision" in quotes because unlike the frameless image of Brad and his father, the images of the soldiers and the Josh-creature appear enclosed in panels, making them more concrete parts of the story. Also, unlike the Brad image, they are drawn in the same clear line style as the rest of the primary narrative. Furthermore, each panel is preceded by a panel showing Ivy gazing in a specific direction.

While the text does not suggest that Ivy is literally seeing these things, it does seem to suggest that her imagination is running away with her—that these are her metaphoric translations of her experience, what Wolk refers to as "impressionistic suggestions of what Ivy's feeling" (2). Oleksyk's cognitive monstration, like her literal omniscient monstration and Ivy's art, implies that Ivy's greatest conscious struggle is to defend herself from monsters—to keep up her armor against external foes. However, this cohesive narrative is disrupted when a final level of monstration is taken into account: that which exposes Ivy's subconscious emotions.

## "Just Empty": Oleksyk's Psycho-Monstration

In the scene where Ivy and Josh stroll near the railway overpass, one page stands out from the rest. The top tier shows the pair kissing, set against a cloudy sky and silhouetted fir trees (figure 4.1). By all standards, this top tier appears to be a normal instance of literal omniscient monstration. The characters are shown from the outside in a manner that could be observed by the naked eye. The second tier exhibits slightly more figurative monstration, depicting a close-up of Ivy's lower neck and chest with the words "Thump thump thump" emitting from her back (90.2), followed by a close-up of her heart muscle surrounded by motion lines and the same "thump" sound effects (90.3). Tier 3 shows blood vessels surging in a vein, still accompanied by "thump" sounds (90.4), followed by a sprawling network of veins from a more distant vantage point, devoid of sound effects (90.5). Tier 4 shows a set of almost completely barren branches with a leaf fluttering downward (90.6), followed by a close-up of Ivy's scarcely open eye looking at Josh, whose lips are still touching hers (90.7). His depicted eye is shut, and a single raindrop strikes Ivy's cheek directly below her eye.

This panel neither depicts literal omniscient monstration nor cognitive monstration. I suggest that instead, it displays what I will here call "psycho-monstration." This term is inspired by Dorrit Cohn's "psycho-narration," which Cohn defines as language that reveals "the narrator's superior knowledge of the character's inner life" and "superior ability to present and assess it" (29). Cohn writes: "This cognitive privilege enables him [the narrator] to manifest dimensions of a fictional character that the latter is unwilling or unable to betray" (29). She uses an example from James Joyce's *A Portrait of the Artist as a Young Man* to demonstrate psycho-narration: "He shook the sound out of his ears by an angry toss of his head and hurried on . . . his heart already bitten by an ache of loathing and bitterness . . . but, as he walked down the avenue . . . his soul was loosed of . . . miseries" (quoted in Cohn 30). Cohn points out that in this passage, the narrator "avoids prominent analytical or perceptual terms" such as "he thought" or "he knew," using instead "phrases

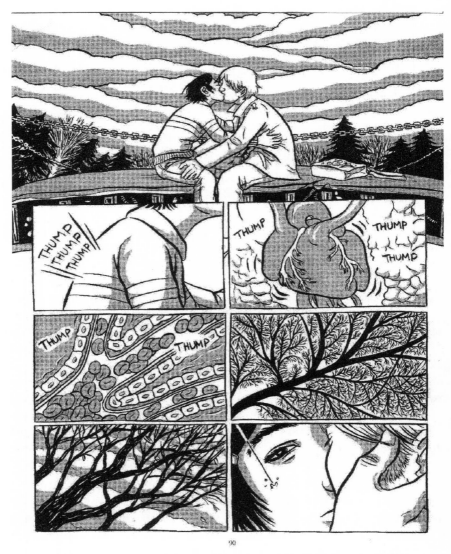

Fig. 4.1. Psycho-monstration in Ivy. In Sarah Oleksyk, *Ivy*. Portland: Oni Press, 2011. 90.

denoting inner happenings" (31). Summarizing a major tenet of affect theory, Emily Martin writes that "humans are corporeal creatures with important *subliminal* affective intensities and resonances that are decisive in the way we form opinions and beliefs" (S154, emphasis mine). This page of *Ivy* exposes such "subliminal affective intensities." Unlike in her artistic expressions, imaginative perceptions, and even recollected dreams, where Ivy has conscious recognition of, and even willpower over, the way her mind processes metaphor,

I suggest that in this instance of figurative monstration, Ivy is unaware of her "inner happenings." And significantly, Oleksyk's revelation of those inner happenings adds a new layer of complication to Ivy's character.

Oleksyk's psycho-monstration suggests that in addition to fighting external monsters, Ivy is grappling with a deep sense of emptiness. Consider, again, the page where she and Josh are kissing. Tiers 2 and 3 depict a series of panels that "zoom in" farther and farther, starting outside Ivy's body (90.2), penetrating her body (90.3), and even penetrating her veins (90.4). There is a shift halfway through Tier 3, though, as panel 90.5 depicts an abruptly "zoomed out" perspective of those very veins. In Tier 4, this morphs into an image of the empty branches, signaling a return to the world outside Ivy's body (90.5), and finally, to Ivy's more cognizant perception, as is indicated by her open eye (90.6). On a very straightforward level, this page is depicting processes Ivy cannot see; no one can see their own blood pumping. I suggest that this carries into the emotional, as well. Ultimately, Oleksyk's psycho-monstration zooms into the heart, the alleged center of emotion, where readers might reasonably expect to find a figurative representation of love. Yet its lens finds nothing at the center but barrenness, as is reflected by the bleak, leafless trees. Echoing Derridean notions of Deconstruction, there is no center at the center. Ivy is not fighting monsters; she is fighting the absence of them. In short, she is fighting her own sense of emptiness and her longing for something substantial.

The motif of emptiness appears twice more in the text. The first is when Ivy sees Russ, the boy for whom she had feelings before meeting Josh, in the arms of her most hated peer (126.4). The bottom tier of this page shows the outline of Ivy set against a black backdrop, all features but her eyes whited out as if by eraser (126.5), followed by a nearly identical image of her set against a gray backdrop (126.6), followed by, at last, a panel of nothing but whiteness (126.7). Ivy is figuratively erased from the universe, with not even her eyes left to perceive. The second appearance of this motif comes when Ivy and Josh have intercourse: Oleksyk's monstration of Josh goes from depicting him with obscured eyes (a reference, perhaps, to his monstrous appearance in Ivy's dream) (176.2) to depicting him from behind, drawn as a solid being (176.3) to depicting him more closely with looser, less detailed lines (176.4) to depicting him as all but an outline, completely filled with whiteness (176.5). Ivy gazes toward him with a sorrowful look (176.5), but on the next page she says the experience was "pretty fucking awesome" (177.5) and smiles. Because she does not seem to consciously grapple with the feeling of emptiness the sexual encounter elicited, nor the feeling of emptiness brought on by the sight of her crush in another girl's arms, I suggest that these are both other instances of psycho-monstration, wherein Oleksyk reveals the "inner happenings" Ivy cannot face. In the scene where Josh and Ivy encounter the "haunted" house, it seems that finding ghosts and goblins would have been preferable to Ivy. She may have the capacity to fight monsters with monsters, but the one thing she cannot fight is her own emptiness.

## "Imagined Parts": Conclusion

The ending of *Ivy* is bittersweet. Ivy goes through a violent falling out with Josh and remains ostracized by Marisa and Brad, who have treated her increasingly coldly since the start of the text. However, she reconciles with her mother, finds a new friend in a girl whom she had dismissed as a pretentious rival, and appears on course to attend an out-of-state art school once she graduates. The closing line of the book, which Ivy delivers after throwing her letters from Josh off the railway overpass, is, "I just imagined all the best parts of you . . . wish I could do that for myself" (217.1; 217.3). Imagination is a key aspect of *Ivy*, in terms of both protagonist and author/illustrator. While Ivy's richly creative and visually inclined imagination leads her to transform internal experiences into representations of monsters, Oleksyk's figurative monstration provides imaginative iterations of the complex interactions between conscious, unconscious, and subconscious mind. Expressing occasionally complimentary and occasionally contradictory themes through Ivy's art, literal omniscient monstration, cognitive monstration, and psycho-monstration, Oleksyk pushes the idea of "doubled narration" to a new and sophisticated level. While Ivy may not yet be able to "imagine the best parts" of herself, the text suggests that this dilemma is certainly not due to a dearth of metaphoric options, and that if Ivy ever does face her inner sense of emptiness, her imagination will be her most powerful armor.

## Notes

1. I am here referring to the unconscious as anything the character experiences when she is not conscious, i.e., awake, and the subconscious as the "hidden mental contents" (Miller *Unconscious* para. 2) frequently referenced in psychoanalysis.

## Works Cited

Chute, Hillary L. *Graphic Women: Life & Narrative in Contemporary Comics*. New York: Columbia University Press, 2010. Kindle file.

Cohn, Dorrit. *Transparent Minds: Narrative Modes for Presenting Consciousness in Fiction*. Princeton: Princeton University Press, 1978. Print.

Dueben, Alex. "Oleksyk Watches 'Ivy' Grow." *Comic Book Resources*. Comic Book Resources, 31 January 2011. Web.

Feinstein, Hermine. "Meaning and Visual Metaphor." *Studies in Art Education* 23.2 (1982): 45–55. Print.

Gear, Rachel. "All Those Nasty Womanly Things: Women Artists, Technology and the Monstrous-Feminine." *Women's Studies International Forum* 24.3/4 (May 2001): 321–33. Print.

Groensteen, Thierry. *Comics and Narration*. Trans. Ann Miller. Jackson: University Press of Mississippi, 2013. Kindle file.

———. *The System of Comics*. Trans. Bart Beaty and Nick Nyugen. Jackson: University Press of Mississippi, 2007. Print.

Hostkotte, Silke, and Nancy Pedri. "Focalization in Graphic Narrative." *Narrative* 19.3 (2011): 330–57. Print.

Kavka, Martin. "The Rationality of Derrida's 'Religion without Religion': A Phenomenological Gift for John D. Caputo." jrtc.org. n.p., 1999. Web.

Lakoff, George, and Mark Johnson. *Metaphors We Live By*. Chicago: University of Chicago Press, 1980. Print.

Long, Aaron. "Interview: Sarah Oleksyk Discusses Eisner-Nominated IVY." Comicosity.com, 4 July 2012. Web.

Martin, Emily. "The Potentiality of Ethnography and the Limits of Affect Theory." *Current Anthropology* 54.7 (October 2013): 149–58. Print.

Mikkonen, Kai. "Subjectivity and Style in Graphic Narratives." *From Comic Strips to Graphic Novels: Contributions to the Theory and History of Graphic Narrative*. Ed. Daniel Stein and Jan-Noël Thon. Berlin: De Gruyter, 2013. 101–23. Print.

Miller, Ann. *Reading Bande Dessinée: Critical Approaches to French-language Comic Strips*. Chicago: University of Chicago Press, 2007. Print.

Miller, Michael Craig. "Unconscious or Subconscious?" *Harvard Health Blog*. Harvard Health Publications, 6 August 2010. Web.

Niederhoff, Burkhard. "Focalization." *The Living Handbook of Narratology*. Interdisciplinary Center for Narratology, University of Hamburg, 11 August 2011. Web.

Oleksyk, Sarah. *Ivy*. Portland: Oni Press, 2011. Print.

Oritz, María J. "Primary Metaphors and Monomodal Visual Metaphors." *Journal of Pragmatics* 43 (2011): 1568–80. Print.

Trites, Roberta Seelinger. *Disturbing the Universe: Power and Repression in Adolescent Literature*. Iowa City: University of Iowa Press, 2000. Kindle file.

Wallace, Diana. "Ventriloquizing the Male: Two Portraits of the Artist as a Young Man by May Sinclair and Edith Wharton." *Men and Masculinities* 4.4 (2002): 322–33. Print.

Wolk, Douglas. Introduction. *Ivy*. By Sarah Oleksyk. Portland: Oni Press, 2011. 1–2. Print.

PART TWO

HYBRID COMICS, TRANSMEDIAL STORYTELLING,

and GRAPHIC NOVELS in ADAPTATION

# 5

## "Are You an Artist like Me?!" Do-It-Yourself Diary Books, Critical Reading, and Reader Interaction within the Worlds of the *Diary of a Wimpy Kid* and *Dork Diaries* Series

*Rachel L. Rickard Rebellino*

In late 2010, Scholastic released a list of the top trends in children's literature from that year. Together with acknowledging the wave of dystopian fiction and a continued expansion of paranormal romance, the popular children's publisher identified the following as the eighth most popular literary trend: "The rise of the diary and journal format" ("Scholastic Experts"). Examining the middle-grade section of any local bookstore reveals the continued strength of this genre. Hardcover books of lined, "handwritten" pages claiming to be the diary of someone, such as a "totally lame vampire," a "schoolyard bully," or just your average "wimpy kid" fill the shelves (Collins; Katz; Kinney). Of course, diary books are not new to children's literature; but this particular wave of diary books featuring writing alongside illustrations has become a fixture in North American middle-grade literature.

Two of the most prominent examples of this phenomenon are Jeff Kinney's *Diary of a Wimpy Kid* series and Rachel Renée Russell's *Dork Diaries* series. Both Greg Heffley, the *Wimpy Kid* protagonist, and Nikki Maxwell, the protagonist of *Dork Diaries*, attempt to navigate the uncertainties of middle school. The two series explore similar themes, looking at "popularity, mean girls/bullying, self-concept and self-esteem, friendship, and adult naiveté" (Taber and Woloshyn 227). And despite numerous differences between the narratives, there are core similarities. Both feature hardcover books with lined pages, "handwritten" font, and relatively simple black-and-white illustrations, and both the language of the written text and the style of the drawing suggest that the texts could have been composed by a flesh-and-blood middle school pupil (Shine 338).

*Wimpy Kid* and *Dork Diaries* have also attained similar levels of commercial success. Kinney's series is currently nine books long, and each new book is met with release parties at libraries and bookstores. In addition to the books, the *Wimpy Kid* empire has expanded to include three movies, *The Wimpy Kid Do-It-Yourself Book* (a journal where readers can mimic Greg's signature style), a board game, and an online interactive game. Meanwhile, the *Dork Diaries* series currently contains eight books, as well as two do-it-yourself style journals, a board game, a CD, and a vibrant online community, which includes a character blog, an advice column, and opportunities for fans to interact with each other and with the protagonist.

Greg and Nikki's stories are told through a combination of words and pictures, and the books' meanings would be significantly altered were the pictures removed. As Nancy Taber and Vera Woloshyn point out, *Dork Diaries* and *Diary of a Wimpy Kid*—as well as books like them—"are not as reliant on images as graphic novels, but do rely on images more than illustrated books" (229). Jeff Kinney, though, asserts that the *Wimpy Kid* books are comics at their core: "I think what I did was create a very particular format where the interaction of text and comics creates a rhythm, a call-and-response that's essential to the humor. The DNA of my books is in comics, not literature. In a sense, the books are long-form comics" (Cavna). Both the *Wimpy Kid* and *Dork Diaries* series are doubtlessly rooted in the graphic novel tradition, and, perhaps, this connection provides an interesting intersection between these extremely popular middle-grade fictional diaries and recent critically and commercially successful graphic life writing, such as Alison Bechdel's *Fun Home: A Family Tragicomedy* or Marjane Satrapi's *Persepolis*. Studies of graphic memoirs of childhood and adolescence like those of Bechdel and Satrapi have gained increasing attention in the field of children's literature, and critical discussion of comics and graphic novels for child and young adult audiences more generally has expanded; however, works like Kinney and Russell's have been largely ignored. This new genre—not early reader, comic, or illustrated novel, but some new, hybrid form—as well as its implications for middle grade readers also calls for critical attention. I believe these series deserve careful consideration, as the overwhelming popularity of the books is indicative of several issues in relation not only to children's literature but also to literacy, education, and composition.

The books themselves—like many other illustrated texts beyond the picture book level—are routinely identified as being for reluctant readers (Young and Ward 72; Juchniewicz 81; Risko, Walker-Dalhouse, Bridges, and Wilson 376–77; Hunt 205–6), and even Kinney has stated that his books are mainly directed toward this audience. In an interview where Kinney was asked whether his sons read the *Wimpy Kid* books, he responded that that his older son moved quickly past Kinney's own books to series like *Harry Potter*, because he "didn't need them" as he had become a "reader," implying, of course, that real "readers" would move from the *Wimpy Kid* books to other, and presumably more complex, texts ("Jeff Kinney: Diary of a Wimpy Kid"). Just as Kinney seems to devalue the literary quality of his own books, the *Wimpy Kid* narratives have been routinely criticized, sometimes quite vociferously, for their nonliterary qualities, especially the protagonists' behavior: Greg is often cruel to his friends, irresponsible, and disrespectful (McCabe); Nikki is materialistic and obsessed with social status and popularity. As a rule though, the books are accepted as literary junk food that will hopefully give readers an appetite for more intellectually nutritious literature. However, rather than being unnecessary literary fluff or destructive garbage, the books promote complex reader-book engagement through their multimodality and through the two series' do-it-yourself journals, which provide opportunities for students to develop critical literacy skills as they actually write alongside Nikki and Greg.

## The Multimodal Diary Book and Reader Engagement

Multimodal and multimodality have become buzzwords in the fields of literature, composition, and education, so defining precisely what I mean by this term is essential. In their breakdown of the terminology surrounding multimodality, Jeff Bezemer and Gunther Kress define a mode as "a socially and culturally shaped resource for making meaning" (171), and they posit that any text that relies on two or more of these resources can be considered multimodal. Within children's literature, not only graphic novels but also picture books fall into the larger category of multimodal literature because, as Charles Hatfield and Craig Svonkin argue in "Why Comics Are and Are Not Picture Books: Introduction," "both are popular forms of *imagetext* . . . which build narratives visually as well as, or sometimes instead of, verbally" (431). Further, it is worth noting that nearly any text can be considered multimodal as the act of interpreting a text brings in another mode, and the factor of time can also be considered a mode (Balzalgette and Buckingham 10). However, for the purposes of this essay, multimodality will be used when referring to multiple genres of communication through which meaning can be made.

In both the *Diary of a Wimpy Kid* and *Dork Diaries* series, the story is constructed—like the stories told in both comics and picture books—through at least two different modes (alphanumeric text and cartoon-like illustrations), and this multimodality complicates an easy reading of the books. In the words of Frank Serafini, a leading scholar in multimodality in children's literature, "the world shown is different from the world told" (86); the pictures—despite being purportedly drawn by the same narrator writing the diary entries—often show a scene that complicates the story that the narrator tells primarily through his or her words. The unique multimodality of these books, which is more reliant on pictures than illustrated novels but not quite as reliant on pictures as graphic novels, also complicates their categorization. Some bookstores shelve them alongside comics and graphic novels, while others house them with more traditional, text-based narratives. Even the cover of the first volume, *Diary of a Wimpy Kid*, hints at this difficulty in categorization with its pronouncement that the book is a "novel in cartoons," notably *not* a graphic novel. The cartoon images that accompany the books are different from those in most comics or graphic novels, both in terms of style and presentation. Panels are not used regularly in either series, and the images are rarely "sequential art" as comics are often defined (McCloud 5–9). The written diary entries are the predominant means of storytelling, and the way that images must be read in relation to the text changes throughout the books. At times, the pictures contradict the words, supplement the words, clarify the words, or work in a number of other ways, and the two series use other modes within the text including notes, newspaper and magazine articles, "photographs," and graphs and charts.

This type of multimodality changes the reading experience of the books as engaging with multimodal texts requires readers to reflect on which pieces of information are shown through which modes. Serafini states: "The semiotic resources used to create multimodal texts are different from the ones drawn upon to create printed texts, and bring with them different potentials for making meaning. This shift from a linguistic focus to a multimodal one requires readers to navigate, design, interpret, and analyze texts in new and more interactive ways" (86). As readers consume multimodal texts, they engage with the texts differently than alphanumeric texts. This interaction requires audiences to use analytical processes to understand, interpret, and discuss multimodality, which rely on more complex language and thought processes than the standard ones taught in language arts classrooms like visualization, summarization, and prediction. Readers must broaden their "interpretive repertoires to consider the perceptual, structural, and ideological perspectives" in order to "deal with the complexity inherent in multimodal texts (Serafini 101).

One of the key premises for the inclusion of multimodal texts in classroom environments is the belief that multimodal literacy is essential for the real-world writing and reading that children experience. The Common Core State Standards include objectives from Kindergarten onward that encourage students to "integrate and evaluate content provided in diverse media and formats, including visually and quantitatively, as well as in words" (Common Core State Standards Initiative 10), and studies have shown that writing multimodally can help to meet language arts standards, albeit in ways that are sometimes "untraditional and unexpected" (Bitz 584). Further, the reflectivity that multimodal composition requires allows writers to engage more critically with their own writing and to understand how they are making meaning, perhaps even allowing for more invention within that writing (Albers and Harste 15). Further, researchers like Kathy Mills have pointed out the necessity of the development of more nontraditional literacies: "This is an age of multimedia authoring where competency with written words is still vital, but is no longer all that is needed to participate meaningfully in the many spheres of life. Adolescents need fluency with an array of multimodal and digital literacies for different social purposes: critical inquiry, creativity, and communication" (36). Despite the attempt to move classrooms toward multimodality, diary books with multimodal and interactive elements like *Wimpy Kid* and *Dork Diaries* are still generally seen as "lightweight" books.

In reality, though, both *Diary of a Wimpy Kid* and *Dork Diaries* do the important work of facilitating the transition of multimodal readers into multimodal writers. The complexity of reader engagement with the *Dork Diaries* and *Diary of a Wimpy Kid* series is perhaps best evidenced in the interaction the series' readers have with the texts in spaces outside of the books that comprise the narrative series. According to Jen Curwood, paratexts, or texts that accompany or parallel (yet are distinct from) the primary texts on which they are based, "often serve as a way for readers to access schema, critically understand themes, construct knowledge, and engage in multimodal content creation" (423). Both the *Wimpy Kid* and *Dork Diaries* series have multiple paratexts that work alongside the narrative series, such as interactive online environments and do-it-yourself diary books. For the purposes of this essay, though, I will focus exclusively on the do-it-yourself diary books that encourage readers to turn into creators of their own diaries, just like Nikki and Greg, and to explore the act of composing multimodally. The first edition of *The Wimpy Kid Do-It-Yourself Book* was published in 2008, with an updated edition released in 2011. Similarly, Aladdin Books released *How to Dork Your Diary* in 2011 and another supplemental book, the *OMG! All About Me Diary!*, in 2013. For avid fans, these interactive texts shift the types of participation that the books expect from and even require of readers. Rather than giving their audience a traditional narrative to follow, the narratives produce what Henry Jenkins terms transmedia environments where multiple types of media converge, each offering its own "distinctive and valuable" contribution to the world of a text (109). In the case of the *Wimpy Kid* and *Dork Diaries* do-it-yourself diaries, the readers are able to turn into co-writers alongside Greg and Nikki and to become immersed in the modalities the two protagonists use.

## "This Is NOT a Diary": *The Wimpy Kid Do-It-Yourself Book*

From the title page of *The Wimpy Kid Do-It-Yourself Book*, the reader is placed immediately into the text along with Greg. This page features the title and, in the bottom right-hand corner, an illustration of Greg. In the bottom left-hand corner, there is the text "Your Picture Here" with an arrow pointing to a space for the reader to draw himself or herself into the narrative. The fact that the audience is encouraged to draw before he or she is even encouraged to write his or her name in the book—this comes on the next page—privileges drawing over writing. Like Greg, who is portrayed as an avid cartoonist across the *Wimpy Kid* series, this opening encourages the reader to immediately explore his or her artistic abilities—no matter how limited they may be.

The first page of the DIY book echoes the beginning of Greg's own first journal. In the opening pages of the first *Wimpy Kid* book, Greg clears up how he feels about the term "diary": "First of all, let me get something straight: This is JOURNAL, not a diary" (*Diary of a Wimpy Kid* 1). The first page of the do-it-yourself book parallels these words as Greg introduces the premise of the book to the readers, who have now become reader-writers: "But if you write anything in this journal, make sure you hold on to it. Because one day you're gonna want to show people what you were like back when you were a kid. Whatever you do, just make sure you don't write down your 'feelings' in here. Because one thing's for sure: This is NOT a diary" (*Do-It-Yourself Book* 1).

And it really is not. Most pages feature prompts that ask for a variety of sorts of writing, none of which exactly match Greg's diary entries in the series. Reader-writers are encouraged to make lists of what they would bring with them to a desert island, to answer "have you ever" questions, to draw their dream homes, to create a family tree, to tell a story of the worst nightmare they have ever had, to create their own greeting cards, and more. The book also contains a personality test, a version of the popular future-predicting game MASH (Mansion-Apartment-Shack-House), and lots of pieces that tie into Greg's various adventures throughout the *Wimpy Kid* series, such as an opportunity for reader-writers to design their own haunted house like Greg does in the first book. It does not ask its audience to describe their days or to finish certain entries on certain days. Instead, the many different prompts give opportunities for those with different creative strengths to explore the process of composing from various entry points. This variety, in turn, encourages composition as a complex undertaking, not a linear, one-size-fits-all process. The multiple activities and entry points allow writers to participate in what Jody Shipka calls an "activity-based multimodal framework," which places writers in a "position of considering the various ways in which, and conditions under which, a task might be accomplished," ultimately encouraging writers to work "differently," providing moments to learn by doing (49–51). Reader-writers are not passive observers of writing but active participants in their own learning.

At times, the writing prompts do veer toward instructional, with Greg modeling the action that the reader-writer is intended to emulate. For instance, one prompt features a comic Greg and his friend Rowley first come up with in the first *Wimpy Kid* book—entitled "Zoo-Wee Mama!"—complete with panels, illustrations, and filled in speech bubbles. The next page contains a different "Zoo-Wee Mama!" comic, whose panels feature an almost identical scenario with regard to characters and order of events, but with empty speech bubbles, asking the reader-writer to imitate this form. The page that directly follows asks reader-writers to make their own comics. This type of scaffolded composing experience mimics the instruction one might see in a classroom when a student receives a new writing assignment, allowing the reader-writer to experience an increasing amount of autonomy. Reader-writers are expected to not only understand Greg's comic as they must do while reading the *Wimpy Kid* books, they are called on to examine, understand, and interpret the skills necessary for composing the comic in order to reproduce it. Fitting with this expectation, although all other prompts in the book are distinct, blank boxes for comic creation occur repeatedly.

This repeated encouragement towards comic creation may feel didactic and even heavy-handed, but the use of comics to develop literacy skills has been lauded. In "The Comic Book Project," Michael Bitz and others from Columbia University launched an after-school program, which encouraged children throughout New York City to create comic representations of their lives with help from instructors, including artists from Dark Horse Comics. The researchers found that student writing had improved in regard to both large-scale concerns like structure and voice and lower-order issues such as grammar and mechanics. Students also reported having a better general understanding of the writing process, and Bitz notes that the project "seemed to have the most marked effect on children with limited English proficiency" whose comic books contained "more writing than they had produced in English class throughout the entire school year" (Bitz 584–85). Other research has noted that reading and then creating comics allows for increased understanding of genre conventions, development of writer confidence, and overall literacy growth (Hammond 28–29).

At the same time that Greg's examples in the *Wimpy Kid Do-It-Yourself Book* function as a type of scaffolding, they also offer a different view into his character, furthering audience interaction with and understanding of the texts. For instance, a prompt that asks the reader to divide what is in his or her brain (the things he or she thinks about most) also depicts Greg's brain similarly divided, with the largest portion dedicated, unsurprisingly to avid fans of the books, to video games (12–13). The text also offers prompts that allow readers to interact with other characters. A prompt from Greg's friend Rowley features questions such as "Do you believe in unicorns?" reinforcing Rowley's childlike nature (70). Meanwhile, a later question from reoccurring character Fregley posits ridiculous scenarios like "Do animals ever use their thoughts to talk to you?"—a query that calls attention to Fregley's haphazard and often disconcerting behavior (128). Another section by Greg's older brother and recurring antagonist Rodrick features impossible activities like a maze with no exit as an "Intelligence Tester" ("Do this maze and then check to see if you're dumb or smart." [52]). These pranks are similar to those that Rodrick pulls on Greg in the series, which are often aimed at making the central character look dumb—convincing him that his father is taking him to an orphanage, for instance (*Dog Days* 197–98). Rodrick's section also contains a piece on creating one's own band (Rodrick's band, Löded Diper, is prominent across the series), which includes crafting a name, identifying band members, writing a song, and designing a tour bus (*Do-It-Yourself Book* 82–93). The book ends with excerpts from Rowley's diary and a variety of full-color comics from various characters throughout the series, including Rowley and Fregley. Comics, written by Greg and by secondary characters, are highlighted throughout the series, but the DIY book is the only print opportunity readers have to see them in full color.

The inclusion of a variety of pieces of writing from multiple characters provides opportunities for the comparison of narrative styles. The various prompts do not just encourage writing; they also provide a complex narrative structure with text and pictures that reference not only other activities within the DIY book but also important moments throughout the series as a whole. One question from Greg, for example, asks readers if it "get[s] on [their] nerves when people skip," accompanied by an illustration of Greg staring disgustedly at Rowley as he skips along (27). Later, one of Rowley's questions for the readers asks if they have friends who are jealous that they are "a really good skipper," featuring a similar illustration in Rowley's childlike style with an arrow pointing to Greg explaining that he "can't skip" (71). These sidebars provide an opportunity for reader-writers to learn valuable skills about composition. Greg's journals in the main *Wimpy Kid* books provide only his perspective, but the DIY book includes pieces of writing—each with their own style of handwriting, tone, and content—that invite the audience to reflect on how style and point-of-view change from writer to writer. The variety of voices also alludes to skills that writers must develop to communicate effectively, such as the ability to alter one's tone or style to match a specific context or particular purpose. When the book depicts different viewpoints of the same incident, Greg's perspective is not necessarily given any more weight than those of other characters, allowing the audience to recognize the validity and importance of multiple perspectives. Additionally, the inclusion of multiple characters' viewpoints democratizes the practice writing. Greg is not the only one who writes; it is something everyone within the *Wimpy Kid* world—and presumably outside the *Wimpy Kid* world—can and should do.

The multiple narrators and resulting interwoven narrative allows readers to be immersed even more into the *Wimpy Kid* world, providing a prime example of what Henry Jenkins calls convergence culture and exemplifying the way "new" consumers read and respond to media:

> If old consumers were assumed to be passive, the new consumers are active. If old consumers were predictable and stayed where you told them to stay, then new consumers are migratory, showing a declining loyalty to networks or media. If old consumers were isolated individuals, the new consumers are more socially connected. If the work of media consumers was once silent and invisible, the new consumers are now noisy and public. (32)

This type of immersive, active participation within *Wimpy Kid* is encouraged through the published DIY book but is simultaneously mediated by Jeff Kinney and the *Wimpy Kid* editors and publishers. The multiple narrators and varied prompts in the DIY book inspire active, as well as different, reading. Because the narrative is not linear and features multiple narrators, it relies on readers' past knowledge of the various books in the series in order to fully comprehend the text's nuances. In this way, the DIY book rewards active reading and participation in *Wimpy Kid* fan culture.

While the opening of *The Wimpy Kid Do-It-Yourself Book* assures readerwriters that this book will not be a space to express their feelings and the book resists a typical "diary" form, it does consciously promote reflection. Many prompts ask reader-writers to consider what they would like to accomplish in the future as well as to process past events. Questions such as "What's something you wish you were brave enough to do?" imply that the act of writing can inspire change (66), although the text does not directly state this message. Such encouragement to consider the future includes subtle attempts to stimulate the development of literacy skills. For instance, a list of "Things you should do before you get old" includes "Mail someone a letter with a real stamp and everything" and "Read a whole book with no pictures in it" alongside other items like "Get in a food fight" and "Use a porta-potty" (44–45). With these recommendations Kinney's books attempt to provoke literacy development, pushing fans of the *Wimpy Kid* series to become active readers of texts outside of the books and strong writers who can communicate both in traditional modes and using multimodal methods. The type of literacy this list advocates for is not without its problems, though, as the suggestion to "read a whole book with no pictures in it" undermines the importance of texts with pictures in them. This encouragement to read something other than comics within a comics-based text is not new and is in many ways reminiscent of the book lists and reviews once included in serialized comics as a means of encouraging readers to engage in reading traditional books. As Carol Tilley points out in her article "Superman Says, 'Read!' National Comics and Reading Promotion," "between 1935 and 1946, through a series of adaptations, columns, campaigns, and reviews, National [Comics] pushed its readers—especially its younger ones—to broaden their sources of leisure reading and to make use of local libraries." These encouragements, however, "seemed to be arguing that 'real' reading was something different than comic book reading" (Tilley 252), just as the list item in the *Wimpy Kid Do-It-Yourself Book* appears to do. Ultimately, these prompts encouraging literacy development appear to be an attempt to appeal to the parents and institutions mediating children's reading material at the same time as they endeavor to built readers who are active participants in their own literacy development. Fitting with this, the final pages of the book provide ample blank, lined pages for the reader to "keep a daily journal, write a novel, draw comic strips, or tell [his or her] life story" (172), giving readers a variety of options and a safe space to continue to explore both multimodal and traditional writing.

## Embrace One's Inner Dork: *How to Dork Your Diary*

The first companion book in the *Dork Diaries* series, *How to Dork Your Diary*, initially appears to be somewhat similar to *The Wimpy Kid Do-It-Yourself Book*. However, the literary work that it attempts to perform for its readers is much different than that of what is attempted in the *Wimpy Kid* text.[1] The cover advertises the book as a place to "write the stuff you only say inside your head," both echoing one of Nikki's catchphrases and directly encouraging reader-writers to use the book for self-reflection. The *Dork Your Diary* book does not feature a series of many discrete prompts like *The Wimpy Kid Do-It-Yourself Book*; rather, it combines a new narrative about Nikki's life with relatively few prompts that allow for lengthy responses. The book is numbered 3½ in the series, and, unlike the other *Dork Diaries* books, contains journal entries that are dated with days of the week rather than dates of the year. The narrative takes place only over a couple of days following the loss of Nikki's diary, and fits into the series without actually taking up space in the internal chronology of the books. After much panicking over this loss ("I can't imagine NOT writing in my diary! It's like I'm addicted or something!" [3]), she decides to use her younger sister's doodle book to "write very specific instructions to [herself] about HOW to keep a diary" (13), a comment that leads to a whole series of subsequent prompts that invite the reader turned reader-writer to create a diary alongside her.

First, Nikki encourages her audience to "Discover Your Diary Identity"—a process that is accomplished through a quiz to determine what type of diary is best suited for an individual's specific personality. The eight-question quiz gives readers four options for each question, and each answer falls into one distinct category. For example, the quiz begins with a question concerning use of free time; reader-writers can choose tech-savvy "A" ("play an exciting round of your favorite computer or video game"), introverted "B" ("spend time relaxing by reading that new book your BFF has been raving about"), extroverted "C" ("check in with your friends via e-mail, text, or a social-networking site like Everloop."), or artsy "D" ("let your creative juices flow by drawing your favorite anime characters") (*How to Dork Your Diary* 16). The intended reader is clearly a heterosexual, gender-conforming girl given that, throughout the quiz, Nikki refers to the reader's crush as "him" and best friend as "her" and gives advice to "rush to the *girl's* bathroom" (17; emphasis added), while the *Wimpy Kid Do-It-Yourself Book* does not have any clear gender indicators about its intended readership—a feature that aligns with the readership of the series as a whole. The *Dork Diaries* series is marketed largely toward girls through feminine pronoun use in marketing, appearance (lots of pink and glitter), and content (much gushing about fashion and boys). Meanwhile, although Jeff Kinney has stated that his books appeal more to boys ("Jeff Kinney"), the marketing lacks gendered pronouns, and boys and girls appear to attend release parties for the books in fairly equal numbers. The quiz to determine diary type is itself problematic with its depiction of identity as fitting into easily defined categories— "smart and curious" A, "kind and sensitive" B, "friendly and outgoing" C, and "creative and independent" D. However, the advice that the text gives readers concerning choosing a medium for journaling gives attention to an often ignored aspect of the writing process.

Tech-savvy A-type girls might enjoy keeping a diary on a computer, while "kind and sensitive" Bs might like a paper journal. Outgoing Cs are encouraged to keep a blog where they can share their experiences publicly, and artistic Ds might want to get a sketchbook where they can combine "poetry, beautiful art, and hilarious doodles" (*How to Dork Your Diary* 25–26). However, Nikki encourages girls to try out both the forms suggested by the quiz results and other mediums to find the best fit. Although the quiz's attempt to place readers into narrow categories leaves much to be desired, the overarching concern for audience and publication method is worth attention. Considerations of how audience and medium may affect writing can be difficult for young writers to grasp, so the promotion of these moments as key to the writing process is positive.

At times, Nikki's advice on how to keep a diary veers very directly into the didactic: "It's always fun to write about things that make you happy. But did you know that writing about a bad experience or a disappointment can sometimes make you feel a lot better about the situation? If you're having a really cruddy day, remember to use your diary as a way to help you vent and work through your frustrations" (28–29). After this advice, the diary provides space for the reader to write about the best thing that ever happened to them and, even more notably, how they *felt* about it. The following page prompts the reader-writer to draw a picture about that moment, mimicking Nikki's signature style. This layout is repeated with prompts asking about the worst and most embarrassing experiences that ever happened to the reader. While the original *Dork Diaries* books model this type of engagement as Nikki routinely reflects through words and pictures, *Dork Your Diary* explicitly teaches that a diary is a tool for reflection.

The *Dork Diaries* series as a whole has received some criticism in both published book reviews and online forums because her "immature" behavior and language (Lawler 92; Green 53). Nikki isn't necessarily considered a strong role model for girls, especially with regard to her use of non-Standard English. She writes using lots of abbreviations, squeals, slang, and all-caps, and her entries focus on the types of problems which plague the lives of many middle school girls—her crush, her popularity, her friends, and her family. In short, much of the criticism seems to be a sign that Rachel Renée Russell is capturing what it means to be in middle school, something that Russell herself considers one of her strengths ("'Dork Diaries' Reveals"). Nikki's voice is unabashedly that of a middle schooler who, like most middle schoolers, doesn't speak in Standard English about deeply meaningful issues on a regular basis.

The *How to Dork Your Diary* book, though, changes Nikki's voice. The diary entries chronicling Nikki's attempts to find her diary are written in the same style as the other diary books: grammatically incorrect, emotionally charged, and resplendent with catchphrases. However, the places where Nikki attempts to tell her readers how to keep a diary are written differently. For instance, when Nikki discusses the mean-girl at her school potentially finding her diary, she is distressed:

> Even if at some point my diary IS turned in to the lost and found, there's a VERY good chance MacKenzie is going to intercept it, read it, and then plaster pages around the school—just to make my life more miserable than it already is. And there's nothing I can do about it. Except rush straight to the girls' bathroom and have a massive mental meltdown . . . AAAAAAHHH ☹!!" (46)

That said, pages later when addressing how the reader-writer ought to view keeping a diary, the tone changes. This time, Nikki writes: "Never let anyone tell you that keeping a diary is a silly or childish thing to do. Reflecting on your feelings and experiences is actually a very mature activity. If someone said something rude about you having a diary, what would your response be?" (50). The book as a whole repeatedly demonstrates this contrast between emotional middle-school Nikki and calm instructor Nikki, who sounds suspiciously like an adult providing writing advice to young people. Middle-school Nikki uses all-caps in the middle of sentences and smiley faces; instructor Nikki does not. Middle-school Nikki melodramatically bemoans that her life is going to be "more miserable than it already is" (46) instructor Nikki describes reflection as a "very mature activity" (50). Middle-school Nikki is often drawn as frazzled and screaming; instructor Nikki is drawn with a pointer stick in her hand. This difference in language and image repeats throughout the book. The text from instructor Nikki encourages girls to "discover" who they are, urging them to "be very comfortable with writing about YOU!" (58–59), and pushing readers to think about their future because "a diary can be a great place to figure out your future goals in life" (89). At times, the book even seems to mimic the language of textbooks as it clearly explains why a writing prompt exists before getting to the prompt itself. The repeated returns to Nikki's traditional voice in her hunt for her journal, though, do ground the book in the same middle-school style that has made the series so popular.

In keeping with the focus on multimodality in the *Dork Diaries* series, the prompts that appear in *Dork Your Diary* encourage reader-writers to do more than compose traditional narratives. *How to Dork Your Diary* Tip #7, "Release Your Inner Artist," is followed by an invitation to create a cartoon (78). In this scaffolded section, Nikki first explains how a comic works by defining what a panel is and offering an example. Then, there are pages dedicated to a planning activity that encourages the reader-writer to engage in the writing process—reflecting on the pieces she will be writing—before she actually begins to draw the comic. While the majority of the other prompts in the book feature traditional narrative, a number also feature opportunities for the audience to engage in other modes of writing, and, like *The Wimpy Kid Do-It-Yourself Book*, the book ends with ample blank, lined pages for the reader-writer to continue journaling.

One of the most interesting differences between *How to Dork Your Diary* and *The Wimpy Kid Do-It-Yourself Book* is the amount of space allotted for creation within the guided portion of the text. For instance, the *Wimpy Kid* narrative provides two or three lines for responding to a prompt. By contrast, the *Dork Diaries* book includes multiple blank pages with its prompts, encouraging longer responses. Perhaps this difference arises from the fact that the latter book seems to take its role of encouraging readers to become writers much more seriously, or perhaps this differential emerges because of the publisher's expectations that girls are more willing to write than boys. In both books, though, the audience is encouraged to interact with the characters by participating in the same processes that they characters do, especially when it comes to multimodal writing through comics, which both Greg and Nikki model more extensively than the other types of writing readers are asked to do. This modeling hints at an assumption that writers will be less familiar with comics and will need this type of writing to be broken down into incremental steps, a belief that is supported by recent outside research about what kids actually know about reading and creating multimodal texts (Risko, Walker-Dalhouse, Bridges, and Wilson 377–78). Because both of the do-it-yourself books expect active reader interaction with various modes of communication, including comics, the two books encourage readers to look at how those same modes are used within the two narrative series with a more careful eye.

🗨 ✱ 🗨

While I have focused exclusively on the do-it-yourself books, both series also have vibrant online communities that promote guided fan fiction (*Dork Diaries*) and digital literacies (*Wimpy Kid*). Additionally, beyond those types of participation directly encouraged and moderated by the authors and publishers, fans have taken to independent sites such as fanfiction.net to publish their own original creative works about each title. By encouraging participation through the paratexts provided by the print journals and online environments, the *Dork Diaries* and *Wimpy Kid* series allow spaces for increased user interaction, and, consequently, increased critical thinking. The reflection that is inherently necessitated by keeping a journal extends to the readers who are processing these journals and reflecting on not just their own participation in a wider community of readers but ultimately on their experiences as denizens of a global culture.

As the readers combine their voices with Nikki and Greg's through the do-it-yourself diary books, they develop multiple literacies that will help them to better navigate multimodal environments. Many assume that today's middle grade readers are multimodally competent because they have grown up surrounded by technology and transmedia writing; however, this assumption is only true in some instances. Children do not always innately "know" multimodal literacy skills, and providing them with opportunities to practice—especially in the context of a variety of literacies—is one of the key (and complex) benefits of these seemingly "light" books. Whether or not the readers engaging with these series are "reluctant" when it comes to reading and writing, the books' numerous opportunities to participate in both reading and writing through the paratexts ultimately enable both weak and strong readers to learn critical thinking skills in conjunction with the texts. Greg and Nikki may not be "ideal" middle schoolers, but their diaries and the paratexts surrounding them are fantastic models of the multimodal engagement essential for success in modern reading and composition.

## Notes

1. The second *Dork Diaries* supplemental book, *OMG! All About Me Diary!*, is a 365-day journal, which encourages readers to answer one prompt every day for two years. Each day has its own prompt for the reader to answer and space for a Year One and Year Two response. It contains much less narrative than *How to Dork Your Diary*, and will not be discussed at length, but it still encourages active and consistent writing. Notably, this journal does not provide prompts asking the reader to draw; all prompts are writing based.

## Works Cited

Albers, Peggy, and Jerome C. Harste. "The Arts, New Literacies, and Multimodality." *English Education* 40.1 (2007): 6–20. Print.

Balzalgette, Cary, and David Buckingham. "Literacy, Media, and Multimodality: A Critical Response." *Literacy* 47.2 (2013): 95–102. Web.

Bezemer, Jeff, and Gunther Kress. "Writing in Multimodal Texts: A Social Semiotic Account of Designs for Learning." *Written Communication* 25.2 (2008): 166–95. Print.

Bitz, Michael. "The Comic Book Project: Forging Alternative Pathways to Literacy." *Journal of Adolescent & Adult Literacy* 47.7 (2004): 574–86. Print.

Cavna, Michael. "'Dork Diaries': The Book Empire Built One Awkward Moment at a Time." *Washington Post.* 21 May 2015. Web.

Collins, Tom. *Notes from a Totally Lame Vampire.* New York: Aladdin, 2010. Print.

Common Core State Standards Initiative. *Common Core State Standards for English Language Arts & Literacy in History/Social Studies, Science, and Technical Subjects.* Common Core State Standards Initiative, 2015. PDF.

Curwood, Jen Scott. "*The Hunger Games*: Literature, Literacy, and Online Affinity Spaces." *Language Arts.* 90.6 (2013). 417–27. Web.

"'Dork Diaries' Reveals Secrets of 'Not-So-Fabulous' Teen Life." Backseat Book Club. NPR. 8 August 2013. Podcast.

Green, Beth H. "Dork Diaries #6: Tales from a Not-So-Happy Heartbreaker." *School Library Journal.* October 2013: 53. Academic OneFile. Web.

Hammond, Heidi. "Graphic Novels and Multimodal Literacy: A High School Study with *American Born Chinese.*" *Bookbird: A Journal of International Children's Literature* 50.4 (2012): 22–32. Print.

Hatfield, Charles, and Craig Svonkin. "Why Comics Are and Are Not Picture Books: Introduction." *Children's Literature Association Quarterly* 37.4 (2012): 429–35. Print.

Hunt, Sue. "Boys and Books-Again!" *The SLJ* 59.4 (2011): 205–6. Web. 2 October 2013.

"Jeff Kinney: Diary of a Wimpy Kid." *The Wheeler Centre: Books, Writing, Ideas.* The Wheeler Centre, 2012. Podcast.

Jenkins, Henry. *Convergence Culture.* New York: New York University Press, 2006. Print.

Juchniewicz, Melissa. "Different Paths: Books in the Differentiated Classroom." *New England Read Association* 44.2 (2009): 76–82. Web.

Katz, Farley. *Journal of a Schoolyard Bully.* New York: St. Martin's Griffin, 2011. Print.

Kinney, Jeff. *Diary of a Wimpy Kid*. New York: Amulet Books, 2007. Print.

———. *Diary of a Wimpy Kid: Dog Days*. New York: Amulet Books, 2009. Print.

———. *The Wimpy Kid Do-It-Yourself Book*. New York: Amulet Books, 2011. Print.

Lawler, Terry Ann. " Dork Diaries: Tales from a Not-So-Fabulous Life." *School Library Journal*. July 2009: 92. Academic OneFile. Web.

McCabe, Cynthia. "Is All Reading Good?" *National Education Association Today Magazine*. 2010. Web.

McCloud, Scott. *Understanding Comics*. New York: William Morrow, 1993. Print.

Mills, Kathy A. "Shrek Meets Vygotsky: Rethinking Adolescents' Multimodal Literacy Practices in Schools." *Journal of Adolescent and Adult Literacy* 54.1 (2010): 35–45. Print.

Risko, Victoria J., Doris Walker-Dalhouse, Erin S. Bridges, and Ali Wilson. "Drawing on Text Features for Reading Comprehension and Composing." *The Reading Teacher* 64.5 (2011): 376–78. Web.

Russell, Rachel Renée. *Dork Diaries: Tales from a Not-So-Fabulous Life*. New York: Aladdin, 2009. Print.

———. *Dork Diaries: How to Dork Your Diary*. New York: Aladdin, 2011. Print.

———. *OMG! All About Me Diary!* New York: Aladdin, 2013. Print.

Serafini, Frank. "Reading Multimodal Texts: Perceptual, Structural, and Ideological Perspectives." *Children's Literature in Education* 41 (2010): 85–104. Print.

"Scholastic Experts Issue List of 'Ten Trends in Children's Books from 2010.'" PR Newswire. UBM Pic, 8 December 2010. Web.

Shine, Brandi. "Dork Diaries: Tales from a Not-So-Fabulous Life." *Childhood Education* 86.5 (2010): 338. Web.

Shipka, Jody. "A Multimodal Task-Based Framework for Composing." *College Composition and Communication* 57.2 (2005): 277–306. Web.

Taber, Nancy, and Vera Woloshyn. "Dumb Dorky Girls and Wimpy Boys: Gendered Themes in Diary Cartoon Novels." *Children's Literature in Education* 42.3 (2011): 226–42. Print.

Young, Terrell A., and Barbara A. Ward. "Companion and Series Books: Invitations for Many Happy Returns." *Reading Horizons* 50.1 (2010): 67–79. Print.

# 6

## Parodic Potty Humor and Superheroic Potentiality in Dav Pilkey's *The Adventures of Captain Underpants*

*Joseph Michael Sommers*

Within the field of children's literature, author and illustrator Dav Pilkey stands out as an anomaly given the differing receptions afforded him by adults and children. The winner of the Randolph Caldecott Honor for 1997's *The Paperboy* garnered academic renown for a picture book that poeticized the humble efforts of the eponymous paperboy. Pilkey uses the construction of the paperboy as a metaphor of a valorized and an endorsed subject position for a child from an era of childhood romanticized by the parent: a paperboy being a fine choice for a child's first job, signaling the onset of maturity and responsibility, where a youth might make as much as twenty dollars a week doing honest work that taught a boy or girl "how to [properly] deal with people and money" ("Paperboy"). What parent would not encourage such noble aspirations and hope to press such a book into their child's hands?

However, such valorizations prized by academic organizations of children's literature that "assert value beyond the merely or crudely utilitarian" of good and honest children are not where Pilkey has gained his celebrity within youth culture (Kidd 178; 167). Actually, quite the contrary: Pilkey's favorable reputation with children comes by way of his more subversive, if not plainly grotesque, depictions of characters who specifically seek to defy the entrenched values of those parents, those adults atop the dominant hierarchy of childhood, searching for traditional boys and girls who might partake of "*good . . . acceptable* literature for children" (Lenters 121, 127; italics added). Or, as Pilkey's own graphically constructed autobiography states quite plainly, "Dav Pilkey was born on March 4, 1966, . . . and from the very start he was trying to make kids laugh . . . and getting into trouble!" (figure 6.1). Pilkey may be prized by librarians who select the Randolph Caldecott Medal and value him for the power of his "distinguished" artistry and message; however, to many children, Dav Pilkey is the author and illustrator of *The Adventures of Captain Underpants*, a

Fig. 6.1. Apropos of a cartoonist, Pilkey's biography in sequential art. In Dav Pilkey, "The Almost Completely True Adventures of Dav Pilkey." Dav Pilkey Bio. indd. Pilkey.com. Cover.

paragon of the "humor and juvenilia" of childhood (Lenters 118). That is, Pilkey crafts toilet whimsy for children, and he does that quite literally.

Captain Underpants, Pilkey's parodic reconstruction of superheroes, is the protagonist created from his own late-1960s Silver Age childhood doodlings and presented, from his adult perspective, to children in 1997 as being "faster than a speeding waistband . . . more powerful than boxer shorts . . . and able to leap tall bildings [sic] without getting a wedgie," all in the name of "fighting for truth, justise, [sic] and all that is pre-shrunk and cottony" (11). This notion is possibly not recognizable to those late twentieth-century children, but more to older generations as a playful, slightly mocking, parody of the catchphrase that began the George Reeves television serial of no coincidentally paralleled name, *The Adventures of Superman* (1952–58).[1] The juxtaposition of Captain Underpants's superheroic mission statement and the impossibly contrarian depiction of a bald, egg-shaped man of considerable juvenescence regaled in nothing more than a cape and a pair of tighty-whiteys illuminates that which makes him immediately successful to an audience of beginning readers. He is absolutely ridiculous. Take for example, the Captain's initial "success" as a crime fighter: confronting two masked thieves, conspicuously hiding their identities with black domino masks, and holding large sacks of purloined cash adorned with dollar signs, Captain Underpants stands directly in the way of the escaping bandits and declares, "Surrender . . . or I will have to resort to *Wedgie Power!*" (*The Adventures of Captain Underpants* 63). The Captain is successful in stopping the robbery; yet this feat is primarily due to the fact that the robbers are apprehended by the police after falling to the ground and laughing "in hysterics" at the hero (64). However, who and what Captain Underpants ridicules underpins his success with children and simultaneous revulsion by many parents: at a moment in time when superheroic valorization is potentially at its zenith, Captain Underpants is a superhero designed specifically to mock industrious adults: perhaps the greatest villains threatening a child's youth with their needs for respectability, maturation, and growing up.

This chapter examines the first volume in Pilkey's series, *The Adventures of Captain Underpants*, and argues that its success with contemporary children arises from a constellation of phenomena that connects comics, a child's perceived subjugation in their childhood, and the construction of a cross-generational heroism overlapping the late 1960s culture of Pilkey's childhood and the present historical moment's fascination with that era's superheroes. Viewing *The Adventures of Captain Underpants* through M. M. Bakhtin's theory of the carnivalesque, it can be seen that the book acts as a "prose allegorization" (Morson and Emerson 403), a visual, autobiographical narrative "whose eccentricities make the nature of all our inner lives more visible" (403), of childhood from a child's perspective. Through his parodic constructions of a superhero in Captain Underpants and a bifurcated reconstruction of himself through the protagonists George Beard and Harold Hutchins, Pilkey creates a moment for the reader to empathize with both the plight and shenanigans of his dual protagonists, children just like the reader. What makes Pilkey's superhero particularly effective as a site of carnival is his blatant construction as both a fool, Mr. Krupp, a metonymic mockery of adults and their authority over children, and his capacity to be manipulated into a child's hero, Captain Underpants, an embodiment of all that could be juvenile, delinquent, and unacceptable to *good, little children* and their parents alike. Remarkably, however, Captain Underpants is still able to be laughed at by children as both a paragon of a young child's romantic need of a hero and as the adult undermined and defeated by children who are doing things deemed subversive at best.

## Laughter: Sanctioned Shenanigans through Carnival

In the children's book *Absolutely Almost*, Lisa Graff writes about young Albie, a boy constructed as intellectually below average, and his mother, who is markedly concerned with his self-improvement and development in school. When she picks up his school reading log, a log noted by his teacher, Mrs. Rouse, as having accomplished "Great Reading," a disgusted look crosses his mother's face; she pointedly asks him, "What on earth are these books you've been reading, Albie?" (64). The books Albie has been reading are, of course, from the Captain Underpants series. His mother tells him that he is "way too old for these books" which are "for babies," and she tosses them away to be replaced by *Johnny Tremain*, a book she loved as a child (65–66). The idea Graff conveys here is one symptomatic of *The Adventures of Captain Underpants*'s general reception, which has landed it consistently atop the banned and challenged book lists since its arrival: anomalous as it is of what an adult recognizes or endorses as a positive or responsible text for their children, the book is determined to be disagreeable and rejected, here, quite literally, out of hand. Critics such as Roderick McGillis concur and have found it a "subversively" ridiculous series that undermines "adult and societal expectation of the child in the process of learning self-control" (69). As such, the book has been critically viewed as "unauthorized" reading material and determined to be a "waste of time," as opposed to more "authorized" fare such as normative and recognizable "chapter books" (Norton 144) like *Johnny Tremain*.

Another critic, Maria Nikolajeva, commenting not on *The Adventures of Captain Underpants* but on J. K. Rowling's Harry Potter series, explores the place in children's literature for texts deemed subversive, and the motivation for their construction in the first place. She writes:

> Children in our society are oppressed and powerless, having no economic resources of their own, no voice in political and social decisions, and subject to laws and rules that the adults expect them to obey without interrogation. Yet paradoxically enough, children are allowed, in fiction written for their enlightenment and enjoyment *by adults*, to become brave, right, powerful, independent—on certain conditions and for a limited time. Even though the fictional child is usually brought back to the security of home and parental supervision, the narratives have a subversive effect showing the rules imposed on the child by the adults are in fact arbitrary. (227)

What Nikolajeva describes here echoes M. M. Bakhtin's theory of carnival, an interpretation of literature whereupon the disenfranchised, for a limited time, are allowed "the superior position of the romantic hero" in a "temporary reversal on the established order when power structures change place" (226). It is an interpretive position that promotes analysis of "grotesque, scatological humor" specifically as a "liberating process, [an] interrogation of authorities" (226), which, in the case of *The Adventures of Captain Underpants*, when one considers that superheroes by their very nature operate for the good of the public *without* the endorsement of sanctioned authorities, fits a discussion of a parody of a superhero who liberates children from the enforced onset of maturity by the authoritative adult.

*The Adventures of Captain Underpants* thus is no stranger to Bakhtinian readings. Its carnivalesque tenor and design, its appropriation and parodization of the superhero motif, and its unabashed joy at poking the bear of adulthood from a position of juvenilia seen as "bad behavior [that] can infect their children with disrespect for authority" (Holley 82) virtually packages the work as threatening and requiring parental mediation. However, Jackie Stallcup looks past the juvenile humor and considers its purpose in the discussion of subversive literature (171–72). She notes that "Pilkey's *Captain Underpants* series, while seemingly simplistic and hopelessly overrun with potty humor, provides a deep well of material for exploring the implications of these parallels. Conflicting reactions of adults and children to the books suggest that they participate in a rich history of subversive literature that has long been feared by the dominant culture—literature that has been dismissed or suppressed by those who fear its effects" (174). As Stallcup observes, the series is entirely subversive in its parodic construction; for instance, from the cover of the first volume, Pilkey hides nothing from the reader in his intention to articulate the character of Captain Underpants as proudly ridiculous in all his splendor: he is depicted as a pear-shaped man with a head gleaming with baldness, displayed atop a building in white, spandex underwear pulled taut to his chest garnering a mischievous smile indicating nothing less than a propensity for shenanigans and nothing more than hilarity (figure 6.2). And on that same cover, George and Harold are shown comically imperiled behind the Captain hanging from a rooftop, mouths agape in some real terror with comic book emanata[2] shooting from their brows as they wonder why they are not being aided by the superhero standing before them; the answer, of course, is because the Captain is mugging for the cover to his book and cannot be bothered with superheroics as he strikes a dramatic pose demonstrating his status as a hero. Nothing about this construction gives weight to Captain Underpants's propensity for success as a superhero: though he possesses all the essential outward markers intrinsic to recognition as a superhero (cape, underwear outside his clothes, heroic pose), he neither understands the costuming of the superhero (the superhero does not wear *literal* underwear as costume) nor the responsibilities of his position (saving the children from certain doom) as he neither looks the part nor looks healthy enough to leap over a small cat let alone a tall building. One cannot dismiss the visual comics attributes presented in this depiction: the Captain is a parodic inversion of the over-muscled, super-attenuated superhero construct while the overtly expository "boom *fumetti*"[3] next to him promises action, thrills, and laughs as if the cover illustration does not make that explicitly and demonstrably clear. As Annette Wannamaker aptly notes, this parody "undermines the relationship" between superheroism and adulthood ("Battle" 85) as the Captain clearly has little ownership of the responsibilities of his position as superhero. Likewise, attention paid to the Captain's Rubenesque figure is not mockery in the sense of body-shaming; rather, it acts as the calculated inversion of the ridiculous if not entirely impossible hyper-masculinized bodies most often seen of male superheroes in comics. Both body types, as hyperbole, are grotesque, but the fleshy, zaftig construction of Captain Underpants is unexpected, "a special carnivaleque image,"

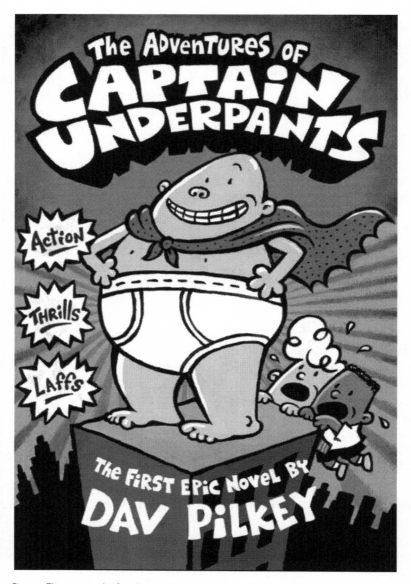

Fig. 6.2. The cover to the first Captain Underpants sports tropes reminiscent of comic's covers. In Dav Pilkey, *Captain Underpants*. New York, NY: Scholastic, 1997. Cover.

where "debasement" of it becomes "idealized" in the readership's capacity to laugh at the entirety of the juxtaposition (Morson and Emerson 444).

Both Stallcup and Wannamaker point out Pilkey's uses of the grotesque in an effort to allow children the opportunity to disenfranchise adult self-considerations of their own importance; Stallcup particularly draws attention to the binary construction of Mr. Krupp/Captain Underpants. From the boys' perspective, Krupp wields the terror of authoritarian might as the school principal in his starched white shirt and black tie, while Captain Underpants's "grotesque, joyful body . . . with his silly grin and triumphant cry of 'Tra-La-Laaaaa!" (190) completely eradicates any such capacity to fear him as an adult, since, as Bakhtin argues, "terror is conquered by laughter," and a grown adult standing in underwear and a cape made of his own office curtains would likely be hilarious to a child (*Rabelais*, 336). Wannamaker echoes these remarks, stating, "The carnivalesque aspects of the Captain Underpants books also come from their deliberate and self-referential position" ("Attack" 247).

In this self-referentiality, Pilkey constructs opportunities for humorous juxtaposition where the laughter created is "nothing more than the ridiculing of another's language and another's direct discourse (Bahktin, "From the Prehistory" 50), whether that differentiation of language be between a chapter book and a comic book, or the construction of the adult and the child, or even considerations of the orthodox and the taboo. The comparisons presented are offered up hyperbolically to articulate the ridiculous similarities of exaggerated differences via vulgar, low humor emphasized by Bahktin in "From the Prehistory of Novelistic Discourse" (50). Laughter here, in all directions and at all things, is key; nothing is sacrosanct and, thus, nothing is privileged. And while inextricably tied up in what Wannamaker and Stallcup register as the carnivalesque, this mockery is also distinctly associated with what Morson and Emerson call a "laughing truth, indebted to the parodic genres," meaning a distinct time and place where a "high value is placed on particularity and heterogeneity" where the disparate and dissimilar are celebrated as opposed to being feared (433). This opportunity occurs when the discourse conventions of a *different* time and place such as the 1960s are used in a time and place a contemporary setting where they can be found as not only acceptable but encouraged (while also being seen as gleefully anachronistic). Stallcup wonders if "perhaps it is time for analyses of *Captain Underpants* and other children's books to infuse academic discussions with the fresh air of such restorative laughter" (195), as Kathryn James openly notes that "humorous literature's potential for subversion and its tendency to address differing ways of being and acting should mark it as a site for special consideration" (368–69). Pilkey, and his audience of giddy child readers, agrees.

It is that absurdity found within the movement of something from the past into the present moment that lies at the heart of this parodic inversion. Captain Underpants should not be seen, by any conventional standards of superheroism, as anything less than laughable. In fact, that is partially his purpose: in being at least partially the villainous Krupp, the distillation of that pedantic authoritarian teacher who made Pilkey's younger self miserable through the enforcement of rules and order of the schoolroom,[4] the reader can laugh at how the boys undermine Krupp's authority in his transformation into the somewhat mindless automatonic reconstruction of everything the child loathes. Pilkey writes: "Mr. Krupp *hated* George and Harold. He hated their pranks and their wisecracks. He hated their silly attitudes and their constant giggling. And he especially hated those awful *Captain Underpants* comic books" (*Underpants* 19).[5] Yet in the duality of Krupp's construction, he is the living embodiment (and, given the similarities, likely the body model) of George and Harold's superhero and, in his secret identity, he, as villain, is the comic inversion of Captain Underpants. Pilkey constructs Krupp as the thing he actually despises, and, absurdly enough, Krupp doesn't actually know that he is Captain Underpants; when the boys use their 3-D Hypno Ring to mockingly turn Krupp into Captain Underpants, they *actually* turn him into Captain Underpants (49, 55).[6] This fact allows Krupp to operate both heroically as both a symbol of nobility while being parodied as a laughable foil simultaneously.

### Parodic Inversions, Silver Age Silliness, and Qualified Attempts at Bonding

While I have already noted the most obvious area of focused laughter, the construction of Captain Underpants, himself, what I have not yet discussed is the idea that Captain Underpants, before becoming actualized in a chapter book about comic books, is a localized construct of George and Harold within a comic book of their own making. He is a parody in so many ways of the iconography, and certainly the musculoma (Walker 58), of Jerry Siegel and Joe Shuster's seminal construction of Superman. That character, as Bradford Wright argues, was constructed by the duo, both of whom themselves were "shy and unpopular in school, unsuccessful with girls, and insecure about their bespeckled appearance and physical abilities," as a "modern adolescent fantasy" crafted after "body-building magazines" and "fantasies of power and success" (1). Upon closer inspection, the parallels of Siegel and Shuster to George and Harold are somewhat obvious, but the Captain's parodic parallels to Superman are likewise clear; Pilkey writes:

> Harold loved to draw, and George loved to make up stories. . . . But the all-time greatest superhero they ever made up *had* to be "The Amazing Captain Underpants."
> George came up with the idea.
> "Most superheroes *look* like they're flying around in their underwear," he said. "Well, this guy actually *is* flying around in his underwear." (*The Adventures of Captain Underpants* 6–7)

Not only did Pilkey seek to parodize Siegel and Schuster's creation, but, through the construction of the boys themselves, he crafts a parodization of the origins and the originators of the greatest superhero of all time, the one who "spawned an industry," Superman[7] (Wright 1). That Pilkey deftly slips himself into the parody (being the actual creator of *The Adventures of Captain Underpants*) only further cements his laughing truth about the initial cultural importance of his superhero and his creating it.

Yet while mining the characterization of Superman, the superhero that spawned the Golden Age of Comics, Pilkey goes to great lengths to fortify his position not within that time period; rather, he builds his superhero out of the same Silver Age of Comics he grew up within. Pilkey was born into the era, and he leaves markers throughout *The Adventures of Captain Underpants* that articulate his indebtedness to a particular moment from the era: the period of underground comix. Formed and fomented in the minds of R. Crumb and Denis Kitchen in the late 1960s, the underground comix movement arose as a countercultural response to the chilling effect caused by the adoption of the Comics Code Authority in 1954 ("Censorship," Munson 29–30). Preceded by EC Comics' own *MAD Magazine*, itself a more satirical publication that avoided CCA safeguards by switching to a magazine format as opposed to a comics one, the underground comix movement "dealt with issues important to [Crumb, Kitchen, and their associates], spiced with a liberal dose of *MAD*'s scathing humor . . . known then as underground comix (ending with an "x" to denote their uncensored nature). . . . These cartoonists both wrote and drew their own comics and cartoons, and retained ownership of the copyrights to their work" ("Mainstream," Munson 137). As Kim Munson notes, the issues central to underground comix often involved "political commentary, personal stories and characters, and exposés of corporate crime" (138), and while this subject matter may appear to be a stretch by way of comparison to George and Harold's work, parodic discourse analysis allows one to age-adjust for Pilkey's intended audience, the beginning reader. The indebtedness that Pilkey feels toward pioneers such as Crumb is reflected in George and Harold's imprimatur of "Treehouse Comix, Inc." on the back cover of the first publication of "The Really Cool Adventures of Captain Underpants" (figure 6.3). While this issue initially parodies the Silver Age intro to *The Adventures of Superman* (figure 6.4), upon turning the page, readers find Harold and George making political comment on "Stinky Taco Day" in the school's cafeteria and criticizing corporate malfeasance by the "principel [sic]," who is more concerned with the loss of "15 folding chairs" than a gym teacher who has been eaten by the "Inedible Hunk," a send-up of Marvel Comics Silver Age creation the Incredible Hulk (12–13). Given that the publication is crafted directly in George and Harold's treehouse and distributed by hand to children at recess, the parallels Pilkey

Fig. 6.3. Pilkey plants a sly allusion to the underground comix scene.
In Dav Pilkey, *Captain Underpants*. New York, NY: Scholastic, 1997. Cover.

draws between underground comix creators' subversion of the Comics Code Authority are readily apparent in Pilkey's mockery of the establishment of the Jerome Horowitz Elementary School.

One of the defining tenets of the Silver Age of Comics (1956–c. 1970) is a generally perceived ideological shift in perspective away from the overly

Fig. 6.4. Pilkey spoofs the George Reeves serial *The Adventures of Superman*.
In Dav Pilkey, *Captain Underpants*. New York, NY: Scholastic, 1997. Cover.

'super,' or perhaps better, superior, Golden Age characters to superheroes who were constructed as more "unlikely" heroes (Wright 209), "alienated and neurotic individuals" (203) who became more relatable to a younger market due to their own "self-absorbed obsessions with rejection, inadequacy, and loneliness" (210). While these characteristics are most often associated with

Marvel's Spider-Man, there are remarkable similarities between them and Siegel and Schuster's youthful insecurities. The difference, of course, is that while the latter duo sought to construct a superlative fantasy in reaction to that awkwardness, Stan Lee and Steve Ditko, Spider-Man's creators, embraced these shortcomings and "[reinvented] the superhero concept around younger characters, with whom readers could identify," creating one of the most clearly defined hallmarks of the Silver Age ("Trauma," Sommers 191). In other places and contexts, I have argued that this sort of Silver Age writing aims at creating a dialogism between reader and reading material where through "a steady mix of humor and pathos" ("Judy Blume" 263) where a sort of empathic bonding occurs that liberates both protagonist and readership by virtue of crafting "safe havens for adolescents to overcome what has been called the 'ignorance' of adolescence, and to do so from an adolescent's perspective of a 'safer way': that is, a way free from adults and through the networking of likeminded adolescents" ("Are You There" 260).[8]

In a single panel of his illustrated autobiography (figure 6.6), Pilkey synthesizes the adversity he faced as a child: hyperactivity, learning difficulties, etc., but the very next panel collapses the entirety of the time of his growth and shows him as an adult male adorned in traditional superhero regalia called "OK Guy." He's not *Super*man; he's just *OK* Guy—Pilkey diminishes and humbles himself before the audience by being willing to laugh at himself as both an adult and in his own youth, while articulating why being mediocre, as opposed to superior (as *super*heroes, by definition, seem to be), is not a bad thing at all. The final panel's message cements the bonds between not just young Pilkey and children but also older Pilkey, the chronicler of his own *roman à clef* of youthful exploits; it reads: "If a silly, smart-allecky goofball like Dav Pilkey can turn out all right . . . then there's hope for every kid." Not unlike Spider-Man, a superhero who started as a boy in high school "defined by his ability to crack wise, making oblique social comments" (Sommers 196), Pilkey demonstrates to his youthful readership that they too still can be children, and childish as well. And *when they do grow up*, they may still become successful in their own right (just as he did). In other words, Pilkey encourages his audience to hold on to their youth while they are still young. Having survived his own childhood, he encourages them to resist maturation right now; children can be successful in adulthood, even if that success leaves them less super and more okay.

This same concept can be found, adapted for beginning readers, in *The Adventures of Captain Underpants*. I have noted already that Pilkey constructs George and Harold to be a parodic construct of superhero creators; so why would it be a surprise that he crafts the two protagonists as a parody of a partitioned version of himself as well? In his comics autobiography, Pilkey states: "In elementary school, Dav was a responsible kid—Whenever anything bad

Fig. 6.5. Self-deprecating humor builds trust with Pilkey's audience. In Dav Pilkey, "The Almost Completely True Adventures of Dav Pilkey." Dav Pilkey Bio.indd. Pilkey.com. np.

happened, Dave was responsible" (figure 6.5). Not coincidentally, when a reader examines the initial handiwork of Harold and George, one finds remarkably similar language from Pilkey about them: "George and Harold were usually responsible kids. Whenever anything bad happened, George and Harold were responsible" (16).[9] This parallelism between the comic reconstruction of Pilkey as a boy and Pilkey's construction of George and Harold creates a remarkable set of bonds for the reader, akin to a tenuous analogy: George and Harold, with whom children can identify, were a lot like Dav Pilkey . . . who took cues from people like Siegel and Shuster who created Superman. Rhetorically speaking, analogy is one of the weaker forms of argument, but it does create a very attractive bond with Pilkey's intended audience.

The protagonists with whom the reader empathizes, these scampish boys who are both the construction and split personification of the book's author, are countercultural underdogs who subvert and undermine not only the primary authority figure of their elementary school but also the authorized discourses and practices of the school Krupp controls. Subverting those authorized discourses and practices here includes undermining anyone who participates in endorsed school activities as, essentially, collateral damage in the boys' shenanigans: In one instance, Harold and George sabotage a football game, with the football game constructed as a distillation of all that is endorsed as good, clean fun by their school, by doing nothing less than lacing

Fig. 6.6. Pilkey teaches his reader that they can always be children and still become successful adults. In Dav Pilkey, "The Almost Completely True Adventures of Dav Pilkey." Dav Pilkey Bio.indd. Pilkey.com. np.

the cheerleaders' pom-poms with black pepper, filling the band's brass instruments with bubble solution, overfilling the team's football with helium (causing it to rocket into space), and replacing the team's muscle rub with "Mr. Prankster's Extra-Scratchy Itching Cream" (21–26). Enacting these actions, mocking the endorsed and authorized practices of the school, effectually destroys their relationship with any of their youthful comrades who come that afternoon to partake in the football game; as Pilkey notes, their shenanigans left "the entire school [feeling] *miserable*" (27).

While naughty behavior as such likely would be amusing to a child reader as subversive tomfoolery, generally, it gains little traction in elevating Harold and George as underdog heroes to the reader *until* Krupp reveals the fact that he has been secretly videotaping the boy's shenanigans, which he threatens he will release to the public unless the boys become model students who "didn't tell jokes," "didn't pull pranks," and "didn't even smile" (40). These threats are designed to strip the boys of their power and capacity to construct mischief (which is what Pilkey hopes the reader will find attractive in the boys from his endorsement of them as narrator in the first place) and to reassert the power of the authoritarian base of the school's adults by diminishing the boys' hierarchal position through the enforced abeyance of their glorified childhood nonsense. Even children who might be angry with George and Harold might not want to see them kowtow before the adult authority figure and common enemy of the childish and immature.

Krupp's choice to blackmail George and Harold has the potential to concretize the audience's acceptance of Krupp the villain and provides the catalyst to move George and Harold's hijinks into the realm of an absurd superhero origin story. Laughter, here, provides elision over logic and even narrative gaps. For example, when George and Harold obtain a 3-D Hypno

Ring, itself both a *deus ex machina* and vestige of a bygone era of shoddy toy advertisements targeted at kids in the pages of publications like *Cracked* and *Mad* (44), they have found the exculpatory device to their woes. Originally, they plot only to use it to wipe Krupp's memories of their videotaped mischief (44); yet when they discover that they can *actually* transform him into Captain Underpants (figure 6.7), Pilkey unveils two game-changing truths to the audience: 1. While Krupp may have been hording the issues of *Captain Underpants* that he confiscated from children in his office, in order to take on the tenants and know both the hero's vocabulary and mannerisms, Krupp must have read the comics as well. 2. As George rightly notes, "[Krupp] kinda *looks* like Captain Underpants" (56). This identification, which initially strikes the boys as funny, underpins a truth about Krupp/ Underpants that they do not immediately realize: they modeled their hero after their greatest adult antagonist. Pilkey plants the seed of the idea that within all adults still exists the childlike hero who once made mischief and believed that humans could fly in ridiculous costumes flouting authority in name of justice or, at least, in what children might perceive justice to be.

In so many ways, Pilkey's narrative seems to demonstrate life's joke on us all that the older we get, the more childish we—hopefully—become. Bakhtin argues, "Life is shown in its two-fold contradictory process; it is the epitome of incompleteness" (quoted in Stallcup 190). Stallcup notes the remarkable similarities Pilkey instills into the Krupp/Captain Underpants construction—both somewhat adultlike and both somewhat infantile in their design, "vitalized childhood and grotesque adulthood" simultaneously (190). Pilkey laughs at himself while the reader can laugh at him as well as with him as he mocks the authority figures who said he would never amount to much being as childish and immature as he was as a young boy. Laughter and gentle mockery, as such, creates bonding through a construction of oppressed communities (school age children and the adult world paralleling comics creators) *a la* carnival. In other words, this laughter parodies not merely the state of oppression placed on children by adults, but also squarely takes aim at the condition of being a child, represented in this case by Pilkey's childhood, itself replete with opportunities for laughter at being young and foolish. Thus, *The Adventures of Captain Underpants* somehow becomes a site of critique, parody, and even satire not only lampooning the superhero genre of comics and the generation from which they came from but also mocking the adults in the process. Some have stated that it could be seen as "grounded in a playfulness which situates itself in positions of nonconformity. It expresses opposition to authoritarianism and

"Tra-La-Laaaaaaaa!" he sang.

Mr. Krupp stood before them looking quite triumphant, with his cape blowing in the breeze of the open window. George and Harold were dumbfounded.

"You know," said George, "he kinda *looks* like Captain Underpants."

"Yeah," Harold replied.

After a short silence, the two boys looked at each other and burst into laughter. George and Harold had never laughed so hard in all their lives. Tears ran down their faces as they rolled about the floor, shrieking in hysterics.

After a while, George pulled himself up from the floor for another look.

"Hey," George cried. "Where'd he go?"

60

Fig. 6.7. Sometimes villains make the best heroes as Krupp becomes Captain Underpants. In Dav Pilkey, *Captain Underpants*. New York, NY: Scholastic, 1997. 44.

seriousness, and is often manifested as parody of prevailing literary forms and genres" (Stevens 121). In other words, Pilkey appropriates the survival of his own traumatization of his youth and weaponizes it to children living today in an acceptable medium; by way of parody, he crafted a new type of chapter book that looks and acts like a comic book making it a difficult to classify thing that vexes parents and delights children simultaneously. Or, to put it another way, Pilkey subverts the form he has been valorized in by authorized agencies and gets the last laugh by creating something subversive that requires even further scrutiny and consideration by adults and children alike.

## Notes

1. The opening spiel from every episode of "The Adventures of Superman" mirrors Pilkey's phrasing:

> Faster than a speeding bullet! More powerful than a locomotive! Able to leap tall buildings in a single bound! ("Look! Up in the sky!" "It's a bird!" "It's a plane!" "It's Superman!") ... Yes, it's Superman ... strange visitor from another planet, who came to Earth with powers and abilities far beyond those of mortal men! Superman ... who can change the course of mighty rivers, bend steel in his bare hands, and who, disguised as Clark Kent, mild-mannered reporter for a great metropolitan newspaper, fights a never-ending battle for truth, justice, and the American way! And now, another exciting episode, in The Adventures of Superman! (Cronin)

However, the dating of the program places it interstitially between the Golden Age of Comics (c. 1938–c. 1950) and the Silver Age of Comics (c. 1956–c. 1970).

2. Another Walker term articulating tear-shaped drops emanating from the brown indicating a strong emotional response to an event (28).

3. *Fumetti* being Italian for "little puffs of smoke" and, by Mort Walker's construction, the "boom" aspect describing the balloon holding the words showing a star-like attributes much akin to an explosion. The notion here is that the word balloons being described are "yelling" the message to the reader, indicating their importance (38).

4. Pilkey's comic autobiography notes that his "sense of humor was getting him into so much trouble, that his teacher moved a desk out into the hallway just for *Him!*"; it is little surprise he labels such punishment as "cruel and unusual" (emphasis in original).

5. It is further noted by Pilkey that Krupp "hated children altogether" (18).

6. Or, at least, they craft a partition in Krupp's mind between himself and the hypnotized superhero who leaps into action whenever the boys snap their fingers.

7. This parody extends so that, not unlike when everyday citizens cannot tell that Superman is Clark Kent due only to the latter wearing glasses and the former not, Pilkey only differentiates Krupp from the Captain by virtue of Krupp donning a toupee as opposed to Captain Underpants more folicly disinclined state.

8. Admittedly, in the original context, I spoke of a sororal dialogism of oppressed young women through the work of Judy Blume. In adaptation of that earlier work, I suggest that such dialogism could be extended out to other marginalized communities based on identity and similar mitigating factors. In this remark, I do not seek to *directly* analogize the plight of young women to comics fans in 1960s; rather, I would only seek to argue that both were trodden on by superior hierarchies who would rather force them into silence and disregard.

9. It is also important to note that even with tongue firmly embedded in cheek, Pilkey reminds the reader that Harold and George are also "good, sweet, and loveable ... no matter what everybody else thought" (4). Regardless of their shenanigans and the trouble arising in light of it, Pilkey insists the good nature of the boys as "silly," an endearing trait that might describe any other five-year-old child.

# Works Cited

Bakhtin, M. M. "From the Prehistory of Novelistic Discourse." *The DialogicImagination: Four Essays*. Austin: University of Texas Press, 1981. 41–80. Print.

———. *Rabelais and His World*. Bloomington: Indiana UP, 1984. Print.

Cronin, Brian. "Comic Book Legends Revealed #276—Comics Should Be Good! @ Comic Book Resources." *Comics Should Be Good Comic Book Resources RSS*. 3 September 2010. Web. 16 August 2014.

Graff, Lisa. *Absolutely Almost*. Philomel Books: NYC, 2014. Print.

Holley, R. P. "Random ramblings—Does the focus on banned books subtly undermine intellectual freedom?" *Against the Grain* 24.6 (2012): 82. Print.

James, Kathryn. "Subversion or Socialization? Humor and Carnival in MorrisGleitzman's Texts." *Children's Literature in Education* 35.4 (2004): 367–79. Print.

Kidd, Kenneth. "Prizing Children's Literature: The Case of Newberry Gold." *Children's Literature* 35 (2007): 166–90. Print.

Lenters, Kimberly. "From Storybooks to Games, Comics, Bands, and Chapter Books: A Young Boy's Appropriation of Literacy Practices." *Canadian Journal of Education* 1 (2007): 113–36. Print.

McGillis, Roderick. "'Captain Underpants Is My Hero': Things Have Changed—or Have They?" *Children's Literature Association Quarterly* 27.2 (2002): 62–70. Print.

Morson, Gary Saul, and Caryl Emerson. *Mikhail Bakhtin: Creation of a Prosaics*. Stanford, CA: Stanford UP, 1990. Print.

Munson, Kim. "Hiding the Forbidden Fruit: Comics Censorship in the United States." *The American Comic Book*. Ed. Joseph Michael Sommers. Amenia, NY: Salem Press, 2014. 20–35. Print.

———. "From the Mainstream to the Margins: Independent Comics Find a Voice." *The American Comic Book*. Ed. Joseph Michael Sommers. Amenia, NY: Salem Press, 2014. 136–52. Print.

Nikolajeva, Maria. "Harry Potter and the Secrets of Children's Literature." *Critical Perspectives on Harry Potter*. Ed. Elizabeth Heilman. 2nd ed. Routledge: NY, 2009. 225–42. Print.

Norton, Bonny. "The motivating power of comic books: Insights from Archie comic readers." *The Reading Teacher* 2 (2003): 140–47. Print.

Pilkey, Dav. "The Almost Completely True Adventures of Dav Pilkey." Dav Pilkey Bio.indd. Pilkey.com. Web. 15 August 2014.

———. *Captain Underpants*. New York, NY: Scholastic, 1997. Print.

*The Randolph Caldecott Medal*. American Library Association, ala.org. n.d. Web. 1 May 2015.

Sommers, Joseph Michael. "*Are You There, Reader? It's Me, Margaret*: A Reconsideration of Judy Blume's Prose as Sororal Dialogism." *Children's Literature Association Quarterly* 33 (2008): 258–79. Print.

———. "Judy Blume." *Magill's Survey of American Literature*. Rev. ed. Ed. Stephen Kellman. Pasadena, CA: Salem, 2006. 263–69. Print.

———. "The Traumatic Revision of Marvel's *Spider-Man*: From 1960s Dime-Store Comic Book to Post-9/11 Moody Motion Picture Franchise." *Children's Literature Association Quarterly* 37.2 (2012): 188–209. Print.

Stallcup, Jackie E. "'The Feast of Misrule': Captain Underpants, Satire, and the Literary Establishment." *Genre* 41.1–2 (2008): 171–202. Print.

Stephens, John. *Language and Ideology in Children's Fiction*. London: Longman, 1992.

Walker, Mort. *The Lexicon of Comicana*. Lincoln, NE: IUniverse.com, 2000. Print.

Wannamaker, Annette. "'The Attack of the Inedible Hunk!': Food, Language, and Power in the Captain Underpants Series." *Critical Approaches to Food in Children's Literature*. Ed. Kara K. Keeling and Scott T. Pollard. New York: Routledge, 2009. 243–55. Print.

———. *Boys in Children's Literature and Popular Culture: Masculinity, Abjection, and the Fictional Child*. New York: Routledge, 2008. Print.

"While You Were Sleeping, the Paperboy Grew up." Msnbc.com. 25 April 2006. Web. 16 August 2014.

Wright, Bradford W. *Comic Book Nation: The Transformation of Youth Culture in America*. Baltimore, MD: Johns Hopkins UP, 2003. Print.

# 7

## Multimodality Is Magic: *My Little Pony* and Transmedia Strategies in Children's Comics

### *Aaron Kashtan*

One of my most vivid memories of the 2004 San Diego Comic-Con is Michael Chabon's keynote address at the Eisner Awards. Speaking to an audience largely composed of comics creators and publishers, Chabon urged his listeners to make not just more comics for kids, but ones of better quality. "Children did not abandon comics; comics, in their drive to attain respect and artistic accomplishment, abandoned children. . . . We have simply lost the habit of telling stories to children." Attending the same convention a decade later, I realized that the comics industry had finally started to take Chabon's critique to heart. In 2004, the Eisner Awards ballot included a single category for Best Title for a Younger Audience, and three of the six nominees were translations of foreign comics. By 2014, this category had been split into three categories (Best Publication for Early Readers, Best Publication for Kids, and Best Publication for Teens), reflecting the explosion of material targeted at children and teens. On Sunday, the traditional kids' day of Comic-Con, I attended panels featuring YA cartoonists like Kazu Kibuishi, Gene Luen Yang, and Raina Telgemeier, whose books regularly outsell the top Marvel and DC comics. My trip to Comic-Con gave me the distinct impression that children's comics, after having been nearly driven into extinction over the past four decades, were finally emerging again as a central segment of the industry.

Between 2004 and 2014, one particular category of children's comics exploded: children's comics based on licensed properties. Two specific companies—IDW Publishing, founded in 1999, and Boom! Studios, founded in 2005—have recently emerged as major players in the comics market thanks largely to their comics based on licensed properties, including many, such as IDW's *My Little Pony* and Boom's *Adventure Time*, that appeal primarily to children. As of March 2015, IDW and Boom were respectively the fourth and sixth largest American comics publishers, with market shares of 6.51 percent and 2.41 percent respectively, according to Diamond Comic Distributors sales figures (Elfring).

Of course, comics based on intellectual properties from other media are nothing new. Publishers have used these venues as a source for content at least since the 1899 debut of a comic strip adaptation of Palmer Cox's children's book series, *The Brownies*.[1] Dell Comics, which primarily published comics adaptations of movies and TV shows, was by far the most successful comics publisher of the 1950s, although historiographies of this period tend to focus on more notorious publishers like EC (Gabilliet 39–40). However, IDW and Boom!'s approach to licensed comics represents something substantially new. While earlier comics based on licensed properties have often been mere knockoffs of their source material, IDW and Boom! publish comics that expand the scope of their parent franchises, introducing new concepts and characters or expanding on obscure aspects of the source material. Moreover, IDW, in particular, has sought to use licensed-property comics to attract new readers to the medium, aggressively pursuing licenses for intellectual properties targeted at children and placing comics in venues that are more kid-friendly than the typical comic book store. IDW's Micro Comic Fun Packs, which include miniature comic books and stickers and are offered at stores like Wal-Mart, GameStop and Toys R Us, had sold half a million copies by July 2014. IDW's Skylanders comic, that will be published both in Micro Comic Fun Packs and as a traditional comic book, is projected to "have a "high six-figure" distribution for the first issue in all its forms, which will make it the best-selling comic release this fall" (ICv2). As IDW CEO Ted Adams has observed: "I think that growing our business we can't just do books that are of interest to the 30-and 40-year-old people. We've got to have content that spans demographics . . . If we can get kids into comics via our Fun Packs and grow them as not just comics readers, but readers in general. It's a really satisfying thing" (ICv2, ellipsis in original).

IDW and Boom! have helped to revitalize the moribund children's comics market through their successful use of the narrative and marketing strategy that Henry Jenkins calls transmedia storytelling. In transmedia storytelling, "integral elements of a fiction get dispersed systematically across multiple delivery channels for the purpose of creating a unified and coordinated entertainment experience" and "ideally, each medium makes [its] own unique contribution to the unfolding of the story" (Jenkins, "Transmedia Storytelling"). IDW and Boom! have proven that comics can be an effective component of transmedia marketing strategies, because reading comics promotes the type of reflexive awareness of media that transmedia narratives demand. Through the analysis of one particular test case, IDW's *My Little Pony* comics, this essay seeks to demonstrate that comics, when used as a component of larger transmedia narratives, can help young readers develop a critical awareness of media. In reading comics, children can learn media literacy skills that are applicable across all components of a transmedia franchise. In other words, comics make children better transmedia readers, and potentially better transmedia players and producers, as well.

In 2010, The Hub launched *My Little Pony: Friendship Is Magic* (hereafter *MLP: FIM* or just *MLP*), a TV series which reimagined a franchise originally created by Bonnie Zacherle in the early 1980s. *MLP: FIM*'s creator, Lauren Faust, saw it as an opportunity to dismantle traditional stereotypes about girls' entertainment and to prove that "cartoons for girls don't have to be a puddle of smooshy, cutesy-wootsy, goody-two-shoeness" (Faust).[2] The series takes place in the fictional land of Equestria, inhabited primarily by ponies, including unicorns and pegasi. Its stories typically revolve around six primary characters, known collectively as the Mane Six: scholar Twilight Sparkle, athlete Rainbow Dash, fashionista Rarity, animal lover Fluttershy, farmer Applejack, and comic relief Pinkie Pie. While these descriptions make the characters sound like stereotypes, each has received significant development over the course of the show's four seasons—and a fifth one underway at the time of writing. Collectively, they complement each other's personalities and show viewers that "there are lots of different ways to be a girl. You can be sweet and shy, or bold and physical. You can be silly and friendly, or reserved and studious. You can be strong and hard working, or artistic and beautiful" (Faust).

IDW's comic book adaptation of *MLP: FIM* was first published in November 2012, with an initial story arc by writer Katie Cook, already well known for her *Star Wars* fan artwork, and artist Andy Price.[3] The first issue sold over 100,000 copies, and by October 2013, the series as a whole had sold over a million copies. It has spawned two spin-off titles, *My Little Pony Micro-Series* (2013) and *My Little Pony: Friends Forever* (2014–present). These figures were shocking given that the comic was based on a franchise targeted at young girls, an audience that the American comics industry has mostly ignored (see Gabilliet 205–9). But from another perspective, the success of the *MLP* comic was perhaps inevitable given the *MLP* franchise's massive popularity among the adult males who make up the primary clientele of comic book stores. Thus, IDW's *MLP* comic is perhaps notable less for its success than for its quality. As Henry Jenkins points out, adaptations of licensed properties are traditionally low-quality knockoffs:

> The current licensing system typically generates works that are redundant (allowing no new character background or plot development), watered down (asking the new media to slavishly duplicate experiences better achieved through the old), or riddled with sloppy contradictions (failing to respect the core consistency audiences expect within a franchise). These failures account for

why sequels and franchises have a bad reputation. Nobody wants to consume a steady diet of second-rate novelizations! (Jenkins, "Transmedia Storytelling")

This description applies to many of the licensed-property comics that I read as a child, such as Marvel's *Pirates of Dark Water* (1991–1992) and *X-Men Adventures* (1992–1994). IDW could probably have published an equally substandard *MLP* comic book and gotten away with it. Instead, they produced an *MLP* comic book that expands on the source material in innovative ways and makes effective use of its medium. Therefore, the *MLP* comic book is an exemplary demonstration of how comics, when comics are used as part of a large transmedia narrative, can benefit young readers by encouraging critical awareness of media.

Instead of confining themselves to the scope of the TV series or following its narrative formulas, IDW's *My Little Pony* comics expand the scope of the franchise's narrative world by taking advantage of the unique affordances of comics. Cook and Price's stories introduce new characters, like Princess Luna's pet possum Tiberius or the hippie farmers Flax Seed and Wheat Grass, and new settings, like the Equestria versions of Seattle Hollywood and Mount Rushmore. They also expand on characters and settings that are not fully explored in the source material. For example, their story in *MLP* #17–20 prominently features Starswirl the Bearded, a character mentioned but never actually shown in the TV show. *My Little Pony: Fiendship Is Magic*, a five-issue spinoff miniseries published in April 2015, narrated the backstories of five prominent villains from the TV show, providing information not revealed in the episodes where these villains appeared. As Jenkins points out, in transmedia stories the "process of world-building encourages an encyclopedic impulse in both readers and writers. We are drawn to master what can be known about a world which always expands beyond our grasp" (Jenkins, "Transmedia Storytelling 101") and the *MLP* comics both partially satisfy and further encourage the reader's desire to know more about the world of Equestria.

However, the *MLP* comics are effective examples of transmedia storytelling not only because they expand on the narrative framework of the TV show, but also because they do so in ways that are specific to the comics medium. Some *MLP* comics take advantage of the serial nature of the comic book format in order to tell stories of greater length and scope than would be possible on the TV series. For example, Cook and Price's two longest stories, "The Return of Queen Chrysalis" (#1–4) and "Reflections" (#17–20), are four-issue epics in which the ponies fight against dastardly villains, with the fate of all Equestria at stake. The length and epic scope of these stories makes them unsuitable for the TV show because they would require massive animation budgets and would take many episodes to tell. Because the *MLP* comics are serialized rather than episodic, and because comics have an "unlimited special effects budget" (Wolk 68), Cook and Price are less constrained in the types of stories they can tell.

Other *MLP* comics tell stories which could not be told effectively in a moving image medium. For example, "Zen and the Art of Gazebo Repair," appearing in *MLP* #9–10, spotlights Applejack's brother Big McIntosh. This character hardly ever says anything other than "eeyup" and "nope," and this may explain why he tends to play a minor role in the TV show, which relies heavily on dialogue as a storytelling mechanism. In the comic book, Cook and Price are able to circumvent Big Mac's lack of spoken dialogue by using caption boxes to depict his internal monologue. Even more radically, *MLP: FIM* #23 focuses on the Mane Six's pets. The bulk of this issue features no written dialogue; instead, the pets' speech is represented with word balloons containing punctuation marks or images. This technique could not easily be replicated on the TV show because it depends on the comics medium's ability to use visual images to depict sound.

All these examples suggest that the *MLP* comic takes advantage of the property of transmedia storytelling that Jenkins calls multimodality: the simultaneous exploitation of the varying representational capabilities of different media. As Jenkins explains, "different media involve different kinds of representation—so what Green Lantern looks like differs from a comic book, a live action movie, a game, or an animated television series. Each medium has different kinds of affordances—the game facilitates different ways of interacting with the content than a book or a feature film. A story that plays out across different media adopts different modalities" ("Transmedia Storytelling 202"). Through multimodality, a transmedia narrative exploits the differing affordances of multiple media at the same time, using each medium to tell parts of its story that could not be told (at least not as effectively) in any of the others. This is why transmedia storytelling is potentially effective in building critical media literacy, especially among young readers. By following a transmedia narrative across multiple media, children can acquire sensitivity to both the differences between media and the ways in which multiple media work together. As Becky Herr-Stephenson and Erin Alper point out, "In order to take part in a transmedia play experience, children must learn to read both written and multimedia texts broadly (across multiple media) and deeply (digging into the details of the narrative)." They continue: "Transmedia play can support new approaches to reading across media, helping children develop broad literacy skills necessary to navigate a media-saturated society" (10). In this sense, transmedia narratives have the ability to teach young readers to use multiple media both simultaneously and sequentially, and to perceive the interrelations between one medium and another.

While the *MLP* franchise clearly encourages multimedia literacy by encouraging young readers to follow its story across multiple media, it also does more than this. In addition to helping readers develop functional literacy in multiple media. They can also encourage critical media literacy: the ability to make distinctions between media and to understand the ways in which media shape the creation and perception of content. One way in which a narrative (whether transmedia or not) can encourage critical awareness of media is by deploying what I will call reflexivity, the phenomenon in which a text directly acknowledges and calls attention to its own mediated nature. When a narrative employs reflexivity, it reminds the reader that s/he is having a mediated rather than a real experience, and that his or her reception of the narrative is shaped by the medium through which s/he encounters it. This effect is augmented when reflexivity appears in a transmedia narrative, where it encourages the reader to compare versions of the narrative and to understand how their mutual differences stem from their use of different media.

Jenkins emphasizes this point in his discussion of Jon Stone and Michael Smolin's Sesame Street book *The Monster at the End of This Book* (1971). As Grover reads the title page, he discovers that there is a monster at the end of the book. Horrified, he tries everything imaginable to stop the reader from reaching the end of the narrative, but of course he fails, and on the final page, the reader and Grover learn that the monster is Grover himself. This text is fascinating not just because of the joke but also because it draws attention to the book's physical structure and incorporates this physical structure into the narrative. As Jenkins writes, "Part of what makes *The Monster at the End of This Book* so compelling is that it is as reflexive about the nature of the printed book as a medium as *Sesame Street* was about our experiences of watching and learning from television" (quoted in Herr-Stephenson and Alper 5). This book could only work as a book and not as a TV show, and it encourages the child reader to notice this fact, and to reflect on the ways in which the *Sesame Street* TV show itself uses narrative strategies that are specific to this medium.

Similarly, the *MLP* franchise is particularly effective at building the sort of critical media literacy I have been describing, because reflexivity is a central strategy in both its TV and comic book versions. The *MLP* TV show makes extensive use of reflexivity because it is full of moments where the reader is reminded that s/he is watching a TV show. Rather than trying to create a seamless presentation of an immersive fictional narrative, *MLP: FIM* often violates the rules of its own fictional world, breaking the fourth wall or depicting occurrences which are clearly impossible even in a world where magic works. For example, at the end of the first season episode "Over a Barrel," a closing iris is used to signify that the episode is over, but Pinkie Pie climbs through the iris and holds it open so that she can complain about something.

This gag is repeated in the third season episode "Magic Duel" (This is a common fourth-wall-breaking trope in animation, going back at least as far as the 1928 Felix the Cat cartoon "Comicalamities"). In both instances, the reflexive gesture reminds the viewer that s/he is watching an animated cartoon and that both the "iris" and Pinkie Pie are drawn rather than real. In other episodes, Pinkie Pie looks directly at the viewer, extends her head into the frame from above, appears multiple times in the same frame, and so on. Notably, all these gags involve the same character, Pinkie Pie. When reflexivity is overused, it can prevent the reader or viewer from becoming immersed in the fictional world of a text. Perhaps in an effort to limit the damage that could be done in this way, the MLP creators decreed that Pinkie Pie would be the *only* character capable of breaking the fourth wall or violating the laws of physics. In an interview after the end of season one, Lauren Faust said she "encouraged people to keep the wacky gags exclusive to Pinkie" (Tekaramity). However, while fourth-wall jokes are typically associated with Pinkie Pie in particular, other characters are also capable of them. In the second season episode "Lesson Zero," Twilight Sparkle shouts, "If I don't send her [Princess Celestia] a letter by sundown, I'll be . . . *tardy!*" and on the word "tardy," a red sunburst background appears behind her. The viewer assumes that the background is intended as an abstract depiction of Twilight Sparkle's emotional state, but a moment later, Twilight Sparkle's dragon assistant, Spike, wheels it out of the frame to the left. Similar gags appear on two later occasions in this episode. Through such uses of metatextuality and reflexivity, *MLP: FIM* reminds the viewer of its own status as a constructed, medial artifact, thereby helping the reader develop critical awareness of mediacy and materiality.

In addition, the *MLP* TV show also uses reflexivity in a less literal way: it includes numerous references to other media, which help the young viewer understand that *MLP* functions within a larger media ecology. The Daring Do book series, featured in "Read It and Weep" from season two and "Daring Don't" from season four, is obviously a loose parody of Harry Potter. Rainbow Dash's obsession with Daring Do parallels many viewers' obsession with the Harry Potter books, and Daring Do's creator and alter ego, A. K. Yearling, is named after J. K. Rowling. Even more interesting in the context of comics is the fourth-season episode "Power Ponies," wherein the Mane Six are transported inside the fictional world of Spike's "enchanted comic book" and acquire superhuman powers. The humor in the episode depends partly on the viewer's recognition of how the episode parodies familiar superhero tropes. For example, inside the comic book, Fluttershy acquires the power to turn into a "huge, super-strong monster" when provoked. Although this superhero nod is funny on its own, it becomes funnier if the reader realizes the similarity between Fluttershy and the Hulk, both of whom are normally shy and mild-mannered but become furious if they are antagonized. Other prominent examples occur in the fifth-season episode "Tanks for the Memories," where Rainbow Dash tries to prevent winter from happening so that her pet tortoise Tank will not have to hibernate. When Rainbow Dash gets the idea for this scheme, she grins evilly, and her facial expression is identical to that of Dr. Seuss's Grinch. Later in the episode, when Rainbow Dash accidentally triggers a disastrous winter storm, Twilight Sparkle comments, "Prepare yourselves, everypony! Winter is coming!" This makes perfect sense in context, but will also be recognized by media-savvy viewers as a reference to House Stark's motto in the novel series and TV show *Game of Thrones*. In episodes like this, *MLP* acknowledges that television is only one of a wide variety of contemporary narrative media, and presupposes that the reader is aware of television shows other than *MLP* and of media other than television. References like these, of course, are examples of what Barbara Wall calls double address, in which a children's text is overtly aimed at children, but "will also address adults, either overtly, as the implied author's attention shifts away from the implied child reader to a different older audience, or covertly, as the narrator deliberately exploits the ignorance of the implied child reader and attempts to entertain an implied adult reader by making jokes which are funny primarily because children will not understand them" (35). *MLP*'s cross-media references sometimes seem like examples of Wall's second type of double address. For example, child viewers are clearly not supposed to understand the *Game of Thrones* reference because that franchise is blatantly inappropriate for children. Here, *MLP* is clearly addressing either the parents of its child viewers or its adult fans (like this writer). However, some of the other references listed above, like the Grinch reference, are closer to Wall's category of dual address, in which a text speaks to both child and adult audiences at once. Such references as these are intended to interpellate the child viewer, in particular, as a savvy consumer of multiple media. Thus, even in isolation, the *MLP* cartoon succeeds in alerting viewers to the way in which each medium has particular means of presentation that can be leveraged in particular ways. When *MLP* is adapted into other media, this lesson is reinforced because the reader is able to compare the media strategies used in one medium to those used in another.

This effect is especially strong when *MLP* is adapted into a comic book, because reflexivity is a particular strength of the comics medium. Due to their emphasis on surface over depth and their exploitation of their own material properties, comics are uniquely effective at calling attention to their own mediated nature and promoting critical reflection on mediacy. As Charles Hatfield notes, "Like traditional books, but perhaps more obviously, long-form comics can exploit both design and material qualities to communicate or underscore the meaning(s) available in the text. Indeed, many comics make it impossible to distinguish between text per se and secondary aspects such as design and the physical package, because they continually invoke said aspects to influence the reader's participation in meaning-making" (58–60). Reading comics effectively requires attention not just to the semiotic meaning of the text but also to its physical, material, and medial aspects, as I have argued elsewhere (see for example Kashtan 2013). This condition, I suggest, is why comics have the ability to make a unique contribution to the promotion of media literacy through transmedia storytelling: because comics have a unique ability to promote reflexive awareness of mediacy. To demonstrate this claim, I turn back to the *MLP* comic book: Katie Cook and Andy Price do a brilliant job of exploiting the inbuilt reflexivity of the comics medium, and because of this, their comics work in tandem with the *MLP* TV show to make readers more informed consumers of media.

The most obvious way in which Cook and Price encourage critical media literacy is through their use of the literal form of reflexivity, in which characters directly acknowledge their own fictional and mediated status. Again, as in the TV show, Pinkie Pie tends to do this more often than the other characters. In *MLP* #19, Twilight Sparkle tries to figure out the relationship between her reality and the alternate King Sombra's reality by making a giant wall chart. When Fluttershy comments that Twilight Sparkle may be overthinking things, Twilight Sparkle says, "But . . . but . . . *what if this world doesn't make 100% sense?* I need to record it all for posterity!" Pinkie Pie replies, "*Our world doesn't even make sense! Why should this one? Who needs continuity?*" (Cook and Price 2014c 3). To underscore Pinkie Pie's critique of fans who are excessively obsessed with continuity, one of the papers on the wall chart reads "If you're reading this, you may be overthinking this comic book" (3). In the following issue, the alternate Celestia fires a magic bolt at the alternate Luna and knocks her off a roof. In the panel below, Pinkie Pie points at Celestia up through the panel border and shouts "You can't do that! This is a kid's comic!" (Cook and Price 2014d 9). Here, as in the cartoon, Pinkie Pie is aware of the fact that she is in a comic book. Cook and Price also alert the reader to Pinkie Pie's inexplicable ability to generate objects from thin air. In *MLP: Fiendship Is Magic* #5, Rarity produces a couch out of nowhere, and when Spike wonders where Rarity got it, Fluttershy says "She's been around Pinkie a lot" (Cook and Price 2015 4). Thus, the comic alerts the reader to the fact that Pinkie Pie (along with Rarity) is capable of violating the logical consistency of the show's fictional universe.

A final way that Cook and Price encourage critical awareness of media is through their constant use of intertextual references, both to other components of the *MLP* franchise and to unrelated texts. In the first place, Cook and Price's pony comics extensively reference other parts of the pony universe. For instance, in *MLP* #18, on a visit to an alternate reality, the Mane Six pass by stained-glass windows depicting Flim and Flam, Trixie, Derpy Hooves/Ditzy Doo, and Queen Chrysalis, with captions reading FAIRNESS, HUMILITY, WISDOM and LOVE (Cook and Price 2014b 12–13). In order to get this joke, the reader has to realize that in the TV show's primary reality, these characters are notable for having exactly the opposite qualities; for example, Flim and Flam are notorious snake oil salesmen. At moments like this, the comic situates itself as only one part of a larger transmedia story, and rewards the reader for being familiar with other *MLP* texts in other media.

Similarly, Cook and Price's intertextual references to other media remind the reader that *MLP* is only one intellectual property among many. Each of their stories is packed with what can be called visual and textual "Easter eggs"—a concept taken from the world of video gaming and that refers to hidden gifts, surprises, or effects—that reference other works of popular culture. An "Easter egg" strictly refers to "a message, trick, or unusual behavior hidden inside a computer program by its creator" (Montfort and Bogost 59), but the meaning of the term has expanded to include hidden references in other non-interactive media. For example, in issue 2, when the Mane Six enter an abandoned mine, they pass by two statues of Diamond Dogs, creatures who first appeared in a first-season TV episode and were named after a David Bowie song. The two statues are labeled "Ziggy" and "Stardust," an obvious reference to another Bowie song (Cook and Price 2012b 3). Later in the issue the ponies pass by signs that read "RED LIKE JUNGLE BURNING BRIGHT" and "NEVER LOOK BACK / WALK TALL / ACT FINE" (19) which are quotations from the Bowie songs "Cat People" and "Golden Years." In addition, the series also includes numerous Easter eggs in visual form. For example, Price's crowd scenes often include background characters who are pony versions of the Blues Brothers, Doctor Who, the Marx Brothers, and so on. Half the fun of reading a Cook/Price *MLP* comic is trying to identify all the references, and the website Comics Alliance has even published a set of annotations to the early issues of the series. Again, many of these references are examples of double rather than dual address, in that they are likely to go over the heads of the comic's intended audience of child readers. Such references are apparently aimed either at parents reading the comic to their children, or, more likely, at adult fans, who are admittedly a significant part of the comic's audience. When Andy Price did a Twitter chat with my ENGL 1102 class in Feburary 2015, in response to my question "Why did IDW market the comic so aggressively, e.g. with multiple alt covers?" (Kashtan 2014), Price responded, "Also, it's a tried product-MLP already had an audience, so aggressive marketing to reach beyond just them" (Price 6:32 am). He continued, "Kids are always first-but fans do influence marketing" (Price 6:44 am), and presumably this factor also explains the presence in the comic of references specifically targeted at adult fans. Still, like the TV show, the comic includes numerous references and in-jokes that are likely to be noticed by children as well as adults. By deploying so many references to other media, Cook and Price interpellate even the child reader as a genre-and media-savvy consumer, a fan whose interests are not confined to *MLP* or to comics but who shares Cook and Price's fascination with a wide variety of texts dispersed across multiple different media.

Here, moreover, we begin to see how reflexivity functions differently in the *MLP* comics than it does in the TV show. Cook and Price are able to include so many Easter eggs because of their use of a medium composed of static moving images, where it's possible to include a large number of references and Easter eggs in the background of each page without drawing the reader's attention away from the story. The TV show does include some similar Easter eggs, but often they can only be seen by pausing the show, thereby interrupting the normal flow of the narrative. In comics, such background references can be integrated much more smoothly into the normal progress of the story.

Thus, Cook and Price's Easter eggs are an example of their use of reflexivity in a way which is specific to comics. Cook and Price's comics constantly draw attention to the graphic surface of the page, thereby reminding the reader of their own status as constructed, authored artifacts. Andy Price's pages are obsessively detailed, full of both visual and textual Easter eggs. An example is the splash page of *MLP* #1, which depicts the main street of Ponyville early in the morning (Cook and Price 2012a 3). Near the top of the page we see Derpy Hooves/Ditzy Doo flying erratically; just below her is Bulk Biceps, who has just dropped a 100-pound weight on another pony's head; to the left of that are two ponies dressed as the Blues Brothers; slightly below that are three ponies who are visually based on Andy Price, his wife Alice, and Katie Cook; and that's just the left half of the page. The only narrative function of this page is to establish that the story is set in Ponyville in the morning, so the reader could easily skip past this page quickly, but that would be missing the point. The reader is supposed to scan this page slowly and carefully, examining every character and every detail, as s/he might do with a *Where's Waldo* book. Through such sequences, Price calls attention to the graphic surface of the page. Another way he does so is through his page design. Rather than following a regular panel grid, Price uses a wide variety of creative and distinctive page layouts, which sometimes have narrative significance. For example, on the eleventh page of *MLP* #17, Twilight says that she always expected to become a magician like Starswirl the Bearded, rather than a princess, as she is now: "It's like looking at two paths, isn't it?" (Cook and Price 2014a 11). This page is formatted as a circle divided into four parts by a cross; each of the four panels is a quadrant of the circle, and the four panel borders are the two arms of the cross. At the center of the circle, where the four panel borders meet, is a depiction of Twilight Sparkle's cutie mark. This panel structure is a visual metaphor: the panel borders represent the "two paths" Twilight Sparkle mentions, and the appearance of her cutie mark at the intersection of the panel borders suggests the way in which she is poised between these paths. On a page like this, the panel structure is just as important as the actual content of the panels; in addition to serving its normal function of dividing the panels from each other, this panel structure actively creates meaning. A third way in which Cook and Price's *MLP* comics draw attention to the surface of the page is through expressive typography, in which words convey additional layers of meaning through their visual appearance. In issue 11, Twilight Sparkle's brother Shining Armor tries to talk to his love interest, Princess Cadence, but only manages to say "hello" in a squeaky voice (Cook and Price 2013 9). The five letters of the word "hello" are drawn in five different styles, indicating Shining Armor's paralyzing anxiety.

Through the use of all these graphic devices, Andy Price's pages make the reader aware of surface rather than depth. The reader is encouraged to scan across the surface of each panel, instead of seeing it as a transparent window into a three-dimensional world existing beyond it. In turn, this makes the reader aware that s/he is reading a comic book, just as the TV show makes the reader aware s/he is watching a TV show. These reflexive strategies are more powerful in comics than they would be in TV, because comics naturally tend to emphasize surface rather than depth. In comics, devices such as word balloons and panel borders constantly draw the reader's attention to the surface of the page, preventing the reader from becoming fully immersed in the narrative, and this is potentially beneficial because it encourages the reader to become aware of the comic as a mediated, constructed phenomenon. Furthermore, when comics function as part of a larger transmedia narrative, readers can take the lessons they learn about media literacy from reading comics and apply these lessons to other media that tend to encourage a less critical mode of reading. In other words, comics can make children better readers not only of comics but also of other media.

In all these ways, the *MLP* comic is an exemplary case of how comics, when used in the context of a larger transmedia narrative, can help young readers develop critical media literacy. As Herr-Stephenson and Alper have argued, transmedia narratives have the capacity to help young readers develop the ability to navigate an increasingly media-saturated world, and comics have an important role to play in this effort. Through integrating comics into transmedia narratives, publishers like IDW and Boom! have not only carved out a niche in the market, but have also helped to develop the comics medium's potential to educate young readers in the critical interpretation of media, and this is one reason why, ten years after Michael Chabon's keynote address, comics for children have reestablished themselves as a central component of the industry.

# Notes

1. I am grateful to Robert Beerbahm for this reference.

2. *MLP: FIM* might be most famous in the wider culture because of its gender politics and its highly surprising adult male fanbase, but for reasons of scope, this essay will not focus on these issues. However, see Carolyn Cocca's chapter in this book, which discusses representations of gender in the MLP comics.

3. I will focus on the *My Little Pony* comics by Katie Cook and Andy Price both for reasons of scope, and because I think their work on the series is the most successful in terms of using transmedia strategies to encourage media literacy among child readers. However, many other talented writers and artists have worked on the series.

# Works Cited

Chabon, Michael. Keynote Speech. Will Eisner Comics Industry Awards. Comic-Con International San Diego. 23 July 2004.

Cook, Katie (w), and Andy Price (a). "The Return of Queen Chrysalis." *My Little Pony: Friendship Is Magic* #1 (Nov. 2012), IDW Publishing.

———. "The Return of Queen Chrysalis Part II." *My Little Pony: Friendship Is Magic* #2 (Dec. 2012), IDW Publishing.

———. "Neigh Anything . . ." *My Little Pony: Friendship Is Magic* #11 (Sep. 2013), IDW Publishing.

———. "Reflections Part 1." *My Little Pony: Friendship Is Magic* #17 (March 2014), IDW Publishing.

———. "Reflections Part 2: Back to Where You've Never Been Before." *My Little Pony: Friendship Is Magic* #18 (Apr. 2014), IDW Publishing.

———. "Reflections Part 3: I'll Be Your Mirror." *My Little Pony: Friendship Is Magic* #19 (May 2014), IDW Publishing.

———. "Reflections, Conclusion." *My Little Pony: Friendship Is Magic* #20 (June 2014), IDW Publishing.

Elfring, Mat. "Top Selling Comics & Publisher Market Share: March 2015." *Comic Vine News.* Comic Vine. 24 April 2015. Web. 28 April 2015.

Faust, Lauren. "My Little NON-Homophobic, NON-Racist, NON-Smart-Shaming Pony: A Rebuttal." *Ms. Magazine Blog.* Ms. Magazine, 24 December 2010. Web. 1 September 2014.

Gabilliet, Jean-Paul. *Of Comics and Men: A Cultural History of American Comic Books.* Oxford, MS: University Press of Mississippi, 2010. Print.

Hatfield, Charles. *Alternative Comics: An Emerging Literature.* Jackson, MS: University Press of Mississippi, 2005.

Herr-Stephenson, Becky, and Meryl Alper with Erin Reilly. *T is for Transmedia: Learning Through Transmedia Play.* Los Angeles and New York: USC Innovation Lab and the Joan Ganz Cooney Center at Sesame Workshop. March 2013. Web. 1 September 2014.

Jenkins, Henry. "Transmedia Storytelling." MIT Technology Review, 15 January 2003. Web. 1 September 2003.

———. "Transmedia Storytelling 101." *Confessions of an Aca-Fan.* 22 March 2007. Web. 1 September 2014.

———. "Transmedia 202: Further Reflections." *Confessions of an Aca-Fan.* 1 August 2011. Web. 1 September 2014.

Kashtan, Aaron. "My Mother Was a Typewriter: *Fun Home* and the Importance of Materiality in Comics Studies." *Journal of Graphic Novels and Comics* 4:1 (2013): 92–116.

——. "#transmediaclass

New question for the class and @AndyPriceArt: Why did IDW market the comic so aggressively, e.g. with multiple alt covers?" 28 Febuary 2014, 6:30 a.m. Tweet.

Montfort, Nick, and Ian Bogost. *Racing the Beam: The Atari Video Computer System*. Cambridge, MA: MIT Press, 2009. Print.

Price, Andy. "@aaronkashtan #transmediaclass

Also, it's a tried product-MLP already had an audience, so aggressive marketing to reach beyond just them." 28 February 2014, 6:32 am. Tweet.

——. "@farkum @aaronkashtan #transmediaclass

Kids are always first-but fans do influence marketing. Equestria Girls is flawless example." 28 February 2014, 6:44 am. Tweet.

"'Skylanders' Comic Gets 'High Six Figures' Launch." ICv2, 10 August 2014. Web. 1 September 2014.

Tekaramity. "Exclusive Season 1 Retrospective Interview with Lauren Faust." *Equestria Daily*. 16 September 2011. Web. 28 April 2015.

Wall, Barbara. *The Narrator's Voice: The Dilemma of Children's Fiction*. New York: St. Martin's Press, 1991. Print.

# 8

# Framing Agency: Comics Adaptations of *Coraline* and *City of Ember*

*Meghann Meeusen*

As evidenced by the range of this collection, comics for children engage a variety of critical perspectives, including an examination of the power dynamics of an adult author in relation to the child reader, a concept that is a subject of continued critical debate.[1] I would like to put discussions of child agency in conversation with other recent critical conceptions, and specifically, the role of evolving media in an understanding of children's artifacts and culture. As Margaret Mackey points out, "Today's children are at home in a vast world of mutating and slippery literature. . . . We need more research that explores the tri-fold nature of literary materials, interpretive responses and institutional enablements and constraints, preferably as they all relate to each other" (505). Katharine Capshaw Smith similarly invites critics to consider "the particular dimensions and stakes of children's texts in relationship to source materials" (134), and Dirk Vanderbeke emphasizes comic adaptation as a much needed element of this approach, writing that "adaptation theory has not yet dealt satisfactorily with this topic, and comics and graphic novels are frequently neglected" (104). I would take up this critical call by asking how different kinds of textual transformations affect child agency, seeking the answer by analyzing two children's texts that have been adapted into both comic and film: Neil Gaiman's *Coraline* and Jeanne DuPrau's *City of Ember*.

I contend that in comparison to film adaptations, comic adaptations of text-only narratives offer children greater degrees of agency over their reading experience and frequently portray adult-child relationships with more emphasis on childhood independence and power. Still, both comic and film adaptations also reinforce adult-child power dynamics that place adults in power over children, a tradition in children's literature created in part by the unique situation of adults writing for children. This paradigm, however, also enculturates children into a system that often limits their agency. My study considers how the addition of visual imagery to retell a text only, or alphabetic, narrative affects child agency both over and within adaptations. Analyzing this pattern can help readers more fully understand not only the mediums of film and comics, but also the complexity of power in children's literature. Moreover, I suggest such examination provides an important first step in teasing out the inherent differences between wholly alphabetic texts and those with visual components, delving into the complexity of how different visual adaptations alter a story in unique ways.

## Reading Comic Adaptations: Power by Panel

In comparing comic and film adaptations in terms of child agency, there are two related elements worth considering: first, the agency afforded by the actual experience of reading/viewing these texts, and second, the way such elements are mirrored in portrayals of child/adult characters and their relative power and positionality. In analyzing the structure and form of comics in comparison to film, Scott McCloud describes alphabetic narratives as offering "perceived information," while visual narratives have a unique power because pictures are "received information" (49). Herein lies a crucial contrast in the ways readers understand visual media: while the addition of visuals brings a comic closer to the line between received and perceived information by combining both image and text, a film adaptation falls more squarely into received information. Each representation allows for a different kind of understanding, but I would suggest that comics offer more opportunities for reader engagement, and thus perhaps a greater agency in the reading experience.

McCloud explores this comics/film dynamic by noting that "the partnership between creator and reader in comics is far more intimate and active than cinema" (39), and Thierry Groensteen further writes that because comics' "narrative potential is not intrinsic, it can only arise, when it does arise, out of a certain internal relationship between the objects, motif, and characters represented" (21–22). Pascal Lefevre notes the reader's role in the interpretation of these relationships by explaining, "from the moment various pictures are grouped together in a series or sequence, the viewer or reader is prompted to look for relations among them" (26). What all three of these critics allude to is the active role a reader must take in reading comics, but I would take this further, suggesting that in contrast to film, comics ask more of the *child* reader, requiring mediation and active connection-making to a greater degree.

Of course, both comic and film adaptations utilize the specific techniques of their individual mediums, a notion especially emphasized by film adaptation scholars. Building from theories developed by Bakhtin and Genette to examine transtextuality, for example, Robert Stam concludes that because film adaptations, like novels, can be seen as situated utterances, a "source text forms a dense informational network, a series of verbal cues which the adapting film text can then selectively take up, amplify, ignore, subvert, or transform" (46). Creators of both adapted comics and film interpret such verbal cues to produce their respective texts, but the individual medium with which they work also shapes the product, as well as the reader/viewer's engagement with it.

In a comic, the reader controls the movement from image to image, and as a result of medium-specific features, as Henry John Pratt describes, "comics allow for types of control that cannot be achieved in film" (160). This is due, in great part, to what Vanderbeke discusses as the temporal gap between panels in adaptations, a concept McCloud also emphasizes in his discussion of the gutter and closure. McCloud calls comics a "medium where the audience is a willing and conscious collaborator" in ways different than film, in which the creator directs closure (65). Comics require, as Groensteen and Lefevre describe, readers to interpret relationships between images, which suggests an element of control over the text. A child reading a comic makes interpretive leaps, determines the speed of movement from panel to panel, and chooses the order to view images juxtaposed on the page, intuiting temporal and spatial contexts of the gutter and within frames themselves. While both comics and film adaptations present a series of images that make visual their source texts, comics require the reader to take a more active role in the adaptive experience.

This divergence can be noted in examining the comic and film adaptations of *City of Ember*, for example. The story of *City of Ember* revolves around two young people, Lina and Doon, who live in what they come to understand is an underground world, saved from apocalyptic destruction but unaware for most of the novel that their world's "builders" intended them to emerge above ground before their power and resources run out. Lina and Doon unravel the mystery of their home throughout the text, eventually escaping Ember with Lina's sister, Poppy.

Like the novel version, the comic includes images of note pieces Lina finds early in the story, which eventually prove to be instructions out of Ember. Because the child reader controls the reading pace, she can work to solve this mystery with the protagonists, deciphering the language of the note by piecing together letters and trying to surmise those that are missing. Chiefly due to the nature of film pacing, this element does not exist in the movie adaptation. While this aspect of the story is certainly facilitated by an adult author, thus reinforcing adult-child power structures, it also affords the reader greater agency by presenting her the opportunity to work out a mystery for herself, rather than passively watching the characters do so.

Although this medium-specific difference seems to suggest that comics allow readers greater agency than film adaptations, adult/authorial directing of the reader also bears some striking similarities in both film and comics.

In film, a variety of specific structural choices direct viewer's attention, with such elements as lighting and camera angles controlling the viewing experience in much the same way as comics' use of framing, position of thought bubbles, etc. For example, in the *Coraline* film, initial shots of Coraline exploring her new home are taken from behind trees and bushes, and the resulting appearance that someone is watching her reinforces notions of danger related to child observation, achieved by placing the viewer in the position of observer. This fits well with the story's overall tone and message, for at its heart, *Coraline* is the story of a young girl struggling to explore her own independence. In Gaiman's initial text and both adaptations, Coraline travels to a world seemingly like her own, but ruled by her "other mother," who attempts to force Coraline to stay forever. It thus makes sense, for example, that one of the dominant shots in the film is a canted angle, where the camera is literally titled so that the image appears skewed on a diagonal. This technique typically produces an "an overwhelming sense of the world's being unbalanced or out of kilter" (Mamer 9), and in *Coraline*, the effect makes the reader aware of the danger that the protagonist is about to encounter.

In the comic version, other visual techniques create a sense of a threat or foreboding relevant to adult power, as when the eye position of adult characters in the center of a large panel makes it appear they stare directly at the reader, especially when they have button eyes (see 4.3; 23; 31.1; 37.2; 51.2; 69.6; 70.2; 79.1; 89.3; 90.9; 102.4; 103.2; 104.7). This emphasis on the unwavering stare created by the button eyes highlights the malevolence of the characters and the other mother's attempts to assert power over Coraline, for as Christine Wilkie-Stibbs describes, the other mother's "unseeing, black-button eyes bore into Coraline in endless and ever-controlling surveillance" (45). Here, the power of adults in the text is demonstrated through visual technique, and the adult creator is controlling the reading experience in very purposeful ways.

I argue, therefore, that although the medium of comics appears to offer greater agency because readers have more control over their experience of the text than in film, a strong adult authorial presence is actually similar in film and comic adaptations. Maria Nikolajeva writes of this "child/adult power hierarchy," claiming that "nowhere else are power structures as visible as in children's literature, the refined instrument used for centuries to educate, socialize and oppress a particular social group" (8). This she terms aetonormativity, mirroring Perry Nodelman's description of the "basic opposition between adult and child implied by the very circumstance of adults writing for children" (*Hidden* 249).

Nikolajeva analyzes children's literature as "a unique art and communication form, deliberately created by those in power for the powerless," but still capable of "[subverting] its own oppressive function, as it can describe situations in which the established power structures are interrogated without necessarily being overthrown" (8–9). Still, Nikolajeva also explicates how children's texts almost always promote, establish, or eventually re-establish an aetonormative model (one in which adulthood is posited as the norm) that reinforces adults in positions of power over children. I suggest that adaptations reflect this model, often even more strongly than their source texts, and while comics seem to do so to a lesser degree than film, both reinforce traditional adult-child power dynamics. This phenomenon, I stress, is consistent across both kinds of visual representation, and thus is a quality worth tracing as a reoccurring element of visual adaptations of all sorts, and even a quality related to visual imagery itself.

## Autonomy and Rebellion: Agency in *Coraline* Adaptations

Of course, the reading experience is only one part of the question of agency in adaptations of children's texts, and just as comics seem to afford greater reader control in comparison to film only to actually reinforce traditional adult-child power structures, this concept is also reflected in adaptive choices related to plot, especially in alteration of adult-child relationships. While comics seem to present representations of child agency to a greater degree than film, both still fall under Nikolajeva's ideas of aetonormativity. For example, Gaiman's novel describes a conflict between eleven-year old Coraline and her parents, which critics have suggested reflects her internal conflict between autonomy and dependence. Coraline's struggle to navigate her burgeoning desires allows her to develop a self apart from her mother, for she is, as Karen Coats describes, "caught in that liminal moment when she finds herself cut off from her parent's desire, and not yet sure of her own" (87). This negotiation shifts in *Coraline* adaptations, especially in their differing depictions of Coraline's other mother.

Gaiman describes Coraline's first encounter with the other mother as follows: "She looked a little like Coraline's mother. Only . . . Only her skin was white as paper. Only she was taller and thinner. Only her fingers were too long, and they never stopped moving, and her dark red fingernails were curved and sharp" (27–28). Appearing several pages earlier, Dave McKean's illustration depicts the other mother's button eyes, but her posture hides her hands and sharp fingernails, and Coraline's subsequent encounter with her does not include any indication that she feels threatened or that the other mother seems particularly dangerous, a factor that comes to light only later.

In contrast, in the comic version, P. Craig Russell's first depiction of the other mother with back turned includes her curled and sharp fingernails clearly visible, and in the next panel (the large central focal point of the spread), the reader sees her clearly, including sharp diagonal points to her hair and thin angled eyebrows, elongated upper teeth, and a hatching used to denote facial lines (31.1). McCloud notes that "lines carry with them an expressive potential" (124), and Russell's use in this panel nearly matches McCloud's examples of lines that "seem savage and deadly—or weak and unstable" (125). Additionally, this image is especially frightening given its context, for the other mother is depicted in sharp contrast to Coraline's real mother, whose hair is wavy and flipped up, and whose face is drawn with curved eyebrows and infrequent facial lines.[2]

Moreover, Coraline's reaction to the other mother in the comics version is different than her reaction in the novel. In two panels adjacent to the first portrayal of the other mother's face, Coraline's is depicted leaning away from her starkly vertical other mother. Drawn on diagonal, which children's picture book author Molly Bang describes as reflecting "motion or tension" (46), Coraline leans away at a progressively greater angle as her other mother leans in, and Coraline's eyes appear as tiny dots indicating fear and distrust. In this adaptation, the other mother is immediately menacing, and Russell figures Coraline as readily apprehensive. While some subsequent panels do show her intrigue regarding the other world's wonders, Russell consistently depicts the other mother using visual clues to indicate malevolence, and Coraline consistently looks at her with suspicion and fear.

I draw distinct attention to the visual choices characterizing the relationship between Coraline and her other mother in the comic because I believe they indicate that Coraline does not, even initially, prefer the other world to her own, despite the other mother's attempt to manipulate her. Instead, Coraline's figural placement even before she meets the other mother reflects rebellion, making the resulting battle seem a conflict between a clearly evil adult villain and a teen or pre-teen protagonist asserting her power. While rebellion can certainly be part of a negotiation between autonomy and dependence, the comic portrays Coraline's attitude as not simply boredom, but anger, or even angst, especially in her interactions with adults.

Russell also utilizes visual cues to show Coraline as older than Gaiman's description of an eleven year old. Will Eisner writes, "the employment of body posture and facial expression . . . can carry the narrative without resorting to unnecessary props or scenery" (111). With a tall, lanky, pre-pubescent body, Coraline's posture seems like a teen character from a TV drama, reflecting an attitude perhaps best exemplified when her mother leaves for groceries and Coraline is depicted with crossed arms and leaning back in her chair, face tilted to the sky in desperate irritation (27).[3] Gaiman's Coraline is certainly bored, but Russell's frequent depiction of arms crossed, eyebrows arched, clothes ruffled, and posture slouched associate her with the frustrations of a teen. This, combined with the immediately menacing depiction of the other mother, creates a clear adult-child binary, and one where Coraline's conflict with the other mother reflects her strong assertion of power.[4]

Unlike the comic variant, the film adaptation of *Coraline* initially portrays the other mother as a near replica of Coraline's mother, with the exception of the button eyes. In the film, the other mother's visual depiction alters in small ways each time Coraline sees her, from minute changes in dress to an eventually distinctive spiderlike appearance, and a final transformation into a metallic creature that does not even seem human. As this occurs, Coraline also changes, able to interpret the other world with greater accuracy as she uncovers some of its darker elements. This interpretation is supported by some of the production choices of the film, such as the score. Adding suspense and excitement, the music first makes the world seem magical, but over time increases in both speed and intensity; these instrumental choices make clear that Coraline faces great peril, but they also position her as a frightened child.

In the film version, Coraline is wary throughout and is depicted as increasingly adversarial in response to the other mother's manipulation. However, this attitudinal change occurs slowly, and Coraline only takes action when the other mother clearly shows her malevolence. According to Lindsay Myers, who analyzes the film from an adaptation theory perspective, "in contrast to children's literature, which is predominantly author-driven, the family film is entirely market-led" and as a result, the film "does little to empower its child viewer, eliminating the child's perspective almost entirely, perpetuating victim stereotypes and fetishizing childhood innocence" (245; 254). While Myers's analysis engages somewhat problematically in the hierarchical structures that suggest changes to a source text necessarily diminish an adaptation, her commentary does highlight an element of the film that I believe is very different from the comic version, which portrays Coraline not a victim, and far more as a child who is empowered to act.

Additionally, the distinction between the real and other world is treated very differently in the film and comic. In the film, the real world appears drab, with filmmakers using special techniques like ranking or angling of the scene backdrops to create the appearance of flatness, while the scenes in the other world use 3D technology, appearing to extend beyond the screen.[5] Producers also use dull coloration when Coraline is at home, which acts in sharp contrast to the other world's brilliant coloring and similarly creates a more significant binary between what is real and other, whereby one seems to reflect an absence of the characteristics of the other.

In the comic, there are no changes in the other world or other mother over time, resulting in a very different kind of adult-child interaction and a divergence in the power negotiations portrayed. Russell offers haunting images of the rats and other Mr. Bobinski, and uses posture and facial expression to show

Coraline consistently enacting rebellion and power, which continues as she more actively battles the other mother. In the film, Coraline is initially swept up in the other world's wonderment, only later seeing the malevolence and deciding to fight. Both versions show Coraline exerting power, but the comic depicts this agency visually from the very beginning, while in the movie, Coraline first loses power and then gains it back.

Overall, Russell's Coraline consistently attempts to wield power and agency, but the film's more manipulative other mother changes this adult-child dynamic. As Myers writes, "Selick's decision to put the Other Mother 'in the driving seat' so to speak, severely limits Coraline's agency" (248). Conversely, Coraline is far more rebellious in the comic, never fooled by the other mother and shown asserting her power as an adolescent even at the level of facial expression and posture. Still, while Coraline seems to assert more agency in the comic than film, both adaptations still return to norma-tive adult-child power structures. For example, the comic shows Coraline cel-ebrating her triumph by showing appreciation for the adults in her life. First, in a panel greatly resembling the first other mother's appearance, readers see Coraline's real mother with curled hair, rounded eyebrows, closed mouth, and only horizontal facial lines (reflecting greater stability). While in the earlier panel, Coraline leaned away from her other mother, she now embraces her real mother, and on subsequent pages, Russell depicts no characteristic arms crossed, scowls, or postures similar to the beginning (expect in one school-related instance). Instead, Coraline smilingly kisses her father and connects with the neighbors. She has asserted her power by defeating the other mother, but returns from her ordeal appreciating the adults in her life more, thus maintaining the power structures from the story's beginning; it is Coraline, not society, that has changed.

Selick's film, however, far more strongly emphasizes this return to adult-child hierarchies, especially in eliminating the tea-party scene that is a crucial part of the ending of the novel and comic. Analyzing Gaiman's novel, Richard Gooding points to Coraline's defeat of the other mother using "protective col-oration . . . that is, the acquisition of a false identity designed to protect the self against hostile forces" (398). This defense is mimicked in the comic, wherein Coraline similarly stages an uncharacteristically child-like tea-party in order to lure the other mother into a trap. By presenting herself as the child the other mother has desired, Coraline turns the tables of manipulation by perform-ing (rather than simply embracing) her role as a child. Selick's film eliminates these purposeful and performative signs of her maturation, again creating a divergence between depictions of agency in the film and comic. While in the comic, Coraline performs as a child to assert agency over the other mother, the film's end lacks such purposeful wielding of agency.

Similarly, the film's use of a gardening motif also presents a re-established adult-child power dynamic. The film's other mother creates an awe-inspiring garden for Coraline, filled with majestic wonders, but also symbolizing an activity defined by control, a taming of the natural world to fit exacting parameters. At the story's end, Coraline re-appropriates this control by throwing a garden party, but she also appears changed, deciding to use the garden to entertain the adults rather than asking them to entertain her. She facilitates the activity, but her seeming nonchalance over her mother's hesitation to participate reflects a relationship that balances autonomy and dependence. Yet she also works within established structures to show herself more adult than child, revealing that while she has grown, her agency has not disrupted adult-child paradigms.

In all of these elements I have described, it is the choices of the adaptor in utilizing the visual medium that creates a unique experience for the reader, and one that shifts the portrayals of child agency from its representation in the alphabetic source text. While further study might be required to fully trace increased aetonormativity as an element inherent to visual representations, it seems worthy to take the time to speculate whether visual texts always more strongly reinforce this power dynamic of children's literature. To consider this further, I look to a second example, questioning the consistency of this concept within children's texts.

## Powering the World: Adult-Child Relationships in Ember

In the comic and film versions of DuPrau's *City of Ember*, the visual elements of these adaptations primarily change depictions of child agency by shifting the representation of adult presence, resulting in a seemingly greater degree of child agency portrayed in the comic variant when compared to the film. Nonetheless, just as in *Coraline* adaptations, closer analysis of this element reveals that this power is undercut to reinforce aetornormativity. In the comic version, the key change that the visual representation creates is a removal or downplaying of adult characters. For example, in the novel and film, Doon's father and Clary offer encouragement to the protagonists, but this support is largely absent from the comic (in which Clary is eliminated and Doon's father is only briefly mentioned, but never pictured). As a result, the comic adaptation includes only two primary adults: the mayor, a malevolent force, and Lina's grandmother, whose suffers from memory loss and ailing health, and is thus presented as having little power or influence. With adults either absent, negative influences, or having little power, child characters are placed in a position of greater responsibility in the comic variant, and are thus given increased power within this text.

The only other named adult given at least one line of dialogue in the comic is Mrs. Murdo, who briefly helps watch Granny and then returns when Granny dies to care for Lina and Poppy. In this case, as in *Coraline*, the visual elements reinforce child agency, for Mrs. Murdo's depiction is striking in its use of distancing. Drawn with glasses, the reduction of her eyes to small lines or dots limits her expression in comparison to that of other characters. More importantly, she never makes eye contact with Lina. In several panels, Mrs. Murdo is looking over Lina's shoulder or only visible in part, but even in panels where visible eye contact would be possible given the stance of the characters, the direction of her gaze does not appear fixed on Lina. This creates a sense of distance in their relationship, and one that results in a representation of Lina holding even more power in the story.

While the film also changes portrayals of adults, visual choices do not eliminate, but exaggerate these characters to caricatures, creating a different power dynamic. Billy Murray's film depiction of the rotund, villainous mayor is even more striking than in the comic, offering comedy in hyperbole and critiquing adult politicians through his ridiculousness. This and other exaggerated portrayals make clear that adults cause the problems of Ember, thus giving them a warped sense of power, while establishing the young protagonists as possessing the necessary ingenuity, foresight, and willingness to seek solutions.

As with the increased manipulation of Coraline's other mother, this element polarizes the adult-child binary in ways different from the comic. While the adaptation in comic form eliminates supporting adult characters, the film either presents them as villains like the mayor or, like Clary or Doon's father, supportive and kind, but also exceptionally unhelpful. For example, Doon's father and Clary both protect the children when they run from the guards in the film, but throughout, their advice is hesitant; they err on the side of safety instead of taking necessary action. Doon's father even discourages his son's investigation, saying it will "give him a headache" or that he is being "dramatic," thus limiting Doon's power in the story. Doon's father only encourages him at the very end, saying, "if you have proof you have to pursue it." Even this, however, is distanced through visual representation, as he yells it through a grate when hiding Doon. Doon's father may finally support his son, but also holds a position of power over him, even though he fails to exert his own power to enact positive change. Instead, this responsibility is placed with the children, but only within adult-child paradigms that seem stronger than the comic variant.

In both adaptations, the responsibility of saving Ember rests on the child protagonists who have little adult aid, and this combined with greater adult-child binaries puts the children in position of seeming power—they are the heroes able to facilitate action in opposition to or despite the limits of adults. However, just as in the *Coraline* adaptations, wherein a child character seems to have more power and agency only within an established adult-child paradigm, this is also the case in the *Ember* adaptations, and in particular, power hierarchies favoring adults are especially reinforced in the film version, even more than the comic.

In the comic, portrayals of power held by the young protagonists are subtle, created through an absence of characters from the source text. The child protagonists simply seem wise and strong, able to independently assert agency to save their city. In the film version, however, adults are not absent, and while they are chiefly unhelpful, they still occasionally take the role of "wise" intercessors. For example, while Doon's father and Clary refuse to take action to save Ember, deferring power to Lina and Doon, another adult presence exists at the periphery of the movie: the legacy of Lina's father. Although he has died before the film begins, details not found in the novel or comic highlight the connection Lina and Doon share in carrying out the work her father began and his father is too disillusioned to continue.

Thus, although Lina and Doon seem to have the power to save Ember in the film, it is only as a continuation of adult work, a concept reinforced by the idea of the builders, who are the ultimate architects of Ember's salvation. The film begins with Tim Robbins narrating the story of the builders, establishing him as an authorial presence immediately, even if he proves to be a less powerful agent of change. Furthermore, his ending narration is particularly telling, and as viewers watch the rock containing Lina and Doon's message of salvation tumble eventually into his hands, his voiceover suggests that despite the danger of it being lost, "fate ran another course and the message found its way." By focalizing this narration through the adult character and including this final image of Tim Robbins, complete with his characteristically knowing smirk, the adult authority of the text seems to resonate despite the agency demonstrated by its youthful protagonists. What is more, this element of adult presence within the film seems to limit the children's agency in more obvious ways than in the comic adaptation.

At first glance, it seems that both adaptations' emphasis on the power of the child to work against social structure and rebel against authority represents the kind of recasting Nikolajeva calls for, one which places the "child in power as norm and the powerless child as deviation" (8). Yet Nikolajeva also notes that "the absence of parental authority allows the space that the fictive child needs for development and maturity, in order to test (and taste) his independence and to discover the world without adult protection" (16). In the case of both the *City of Ember* film and comic, child characters do assert independent agency to varying degrees, but as they eventually move toward an independence that places them in a position of greater power, they are also maturing and becoming far more adult themselves.

Thus, in both the comic and film adaptations of these two children's texts, aetonormativity is seemingly dismantled, but eventually reinforced. Again, it seems intriguing to consider whether this aspect of the adaptations is related to the visual medium itself. For example, DuPrau's written novel also depicts child agency, but it seems somewhat tempered by lessons the children learn about the vices of arrogance and greed; in this way, the alphabetic text seems more directly didactic, affording less agency to the child protagonists. Still, while the written narrative presents a perhaps more consistent adult-child power hierarchy, the visual texts depict children in more powerful positions only within the overall context that Nikolajeva describes.

Is it possible, then, that visual portrayals offer children as heroes in intrinsically different ways than wholly alphabetic texts, enabling them to seemingly take on power, only to require a clear reinforcement of traditional adult-child power structures? While discerning this element as part of the very essence of visual representation lies beyond the scope of what I seek to assert in this study, it is certainly worth considering what role the very nature of visual imagery plays in these shifting power dynamics.

In a field for which the question of child agency is continually a major concern, critics must continue to examine how various mediums remediate this element when comics creators and filmmakers adapt a children's text. As critics analyze the specific affordances and portrayals that comics and films provide, it seems also important to consider how the depictions of independent, rebellious, and powerful children in visual texts still exist within established power structures. Whether read panel by panel or watched up on the big screen, the ways texts frame agency is a topic worthy of continued examination.

## Notes

1. For example, while Richard Flynn suggests children are capable "of creatively misappropriating the cultural artifacts they inherit from adults and transforming them into their own texts" (66), Perry Nodelman writes that the "idea that children inherently and always possess the agency to do more than just improvise within the framework the adults in charge provides represents a kind of wish-fulfillment fantasy" ("Discovery" 51).

2. See pages 10–11, 18, and 25–26.

3. Similar depictions show a building to this epitome of her frustration. See page 4.5, 9.1, 10.418.1–4, 29.2–4, 25.8, and 26.6.

4. I draw primarily from Jacques Derrida's definition of a binary as "a violent hierarchy" wherein "one of the two terms governs the other" (41), a concept critics like Perry Nodelman suggest is a key part children's literature.

5. Because the film uses stop-action animation, which utilized sets and figures built in miniature and then filmed, the producers control scenes in a way similar to live action cinema.

# Works Cited

Bang, Molly. *Picture This: How Pictures Work*. New York: SeaStar Books, 2000. Print.

Coats, Karen. "Between Horror, Humour, and Hope: Neil Gaiman and the Psychic World of the Gothic." *The Gothic in Children's Literature: Haunting the Borders*. London: Routledge, 2008. 77–92. Print.

Derrida, Jacques. *Positions*. Trans. Alan Bass. Chicago: University of Chicago Press, 1981. Print.

DuPrau, Jeanne. *The City of Ember*. New York: Random, 2003. Print.

——, writer. *The City of Ember: The Comic*. Adapted by Dallas Middaugh. Illustrated by Niklas Asker. New York: Random House, 2012. Print.

Eisner, Will. *Comics & Sequential Art*. Tamarac: Poorhouse Press, 2006. Print.

Flynn, Richard. "Culture." *Keywords for Children's Literature*. Philip Nel and Lissa Paul, eds. New York: New York UP, 2011. Print.

Gaiman, Neil. *Coraline*. New York: HarperCollins, 2002. Print.

——, writer. *Coraline*. Illustrated by P. Craig Russell. New York: Harper Trophy, 2008. Print.

Gooding, Richard. "'Something Very Old and Very Slow': *Coraline*, Uncanniness, and Narrative Form." *Children's Literature Association Quarterly* 33.4 (2008): 390–407. Print.

Groensteen, Thierry. *Comics and Narration*. Jackson: University Press of Mississippi, 2013. Print.

Kena, Gil, dir. *City of Ember*. 20th Century Fox, 2009. Film.

Lefèvre, Pascal. "Some Medium-Specific Qualities of Graphic Sequences." *SubStance* 40.1 (2011): 14–33. Print.

Mackey, Margaret. "Spinning Off: Toys, Television, Tie-Ins, and Technology." *Handbook of Research on Children's and Young Adult Literature*. Eds. Shelby Wolf, Karen Coats, Patricia Enciso, and Christine Jenkins. New York: Routledge, 2011. Print.

Mamer, Bruce. *Film Production Technique: Creating the Accomplished Image*. Belmont, CA: Wadsworth Centgage Learning, 2009. Print.

Myers, Lindsay. "Whose Fear Is It Anyway? Moral Panics and 'Stranger Danger' in Henry Selick's Coraline." *The Lion and the Unicorn* 36.3 (2012): 245–57. Print.

Nikolajeva, Maria. *Power, Voice and Subjectivity in Literature for Young Readers*. New York: Routledge, 2010. Print.

Nodelman, Perry. *The Hidden Adult: Defining Children's Literature*. Baltimore: Johns Hopkins UP, 2008. Print.

——. "Discovery: My Name Is Elizabeth." (*Re*)*imagining the World: Children's Literature's Response to Changing Times*. Eds. Yan Wu, Kerry Mallan, and Roderick McGillis. Berlin: Springer, 2013. Print.

Pratt, Henry James. "Making Comics into Film." *The Art of Comics: A Philosophical Approach*. Eds. Aaron Meskin and Roy T. Cook. Malden, MA: Wiley-Blackwell, 2012. Print.

Selick, Henry, dir. *Coraline*. Focus Features, 2009. Film.

Smith, Katharine Capshaw. "Middle Age." *Children's Literature Association Quarterly* 38.2 (2013): 133–36. Print.

Stam, Robert, and Alessandra Raengo, eds. *Literature and Film: A Guide to the Theory and Practice of Film Adaptation*. Malden, MA: Blackwell, 2005. Print.

Vanderbeke, Dirk. "It Was the Best of Two Worlds, It Was the Worst of Two Worlds: The Adaptation of Novels in Comics and Comics." *The Rise and Reason of Comics and Graphic Literature*. Eds. Joyce Goggin and Dan Hassler-Forest. Jefferson, NC: McFarland & Co., 2010. Print.

Wilkie-Stibbs, Christine. "Imaging Fear: Inside the Worlds of Neil Gaiman (An Anti-Oedipal Reading)." *The Lion and the Unicorn* 37.1 (2013): 37–53. Print.

PART THREE

The PEDAGOGY of the PANEL

COMICS STORYTELLING in the CLASSROOM

# 9

## From Who-ville to Hereville:
## Integrating Graphic Novels into
## an Undergraduate Children's Literature Course

*Gwen Athene Tarbox*

Ben Hatke, the comics creator behind such bestselling children's graphic novels as *Zita the Spacegirl* (2011) and *Little Robot* (2015), notes that while "comics are a great tool for the developing reader, there can be a temptation to think of them as gateways to 'real' reading. ('Real' reading being any kind of reading that doesn't involve a lot of artwork)" ("Zap!"). Rather than accepting this view, Hatke joins a growing chorus of authors, artists, educators, and scholars who emphasize the value of the comics medium as a vehicle for storytelling that encourages young readers to appreciate the often complex relationship between image and text. Shelley Hong Xu, an associate professor of teacher education at California State University, Long Beach, extends Hatke's argument, highlighting the ability of the comics medium to "teach about making inferences," especially since "readers must rely on pictures and just a small amount of text" ("Using Comics"). Xu includes comics in her literacy methods courses, asking students to reflect on the reading strategies they employ. Moreover, given the contemporary emphasis on visual literacy put forward by state and national accreditation bodies, the need for preservice teachers to develop an awareness of visual literacy skills has only intensified. Speaking in 2014 about the increasing clout of children's comics, Jesse Karp, a New York City public school librarian, points out that comics appeal to K-12 curriculum developers because "they reinforce left-to-right sequence," and the images aid "in word/sentence comprehension" and provide "a deeper interpretation of the words and story" (Alverson). These benefits, combined with evidence that young people build confidence as readers by interacting with comics, have encouraged instructors of children's literacy and children's literature to integrate the use of graphic novels into undergraduate courses.

In most university-level children's literature classes, visual literacy in the form of picture book instruction has long been emphasized, and instructors have access to a plethora of resources on picture book interpretation, including monographs by Denise I. Matulka, Perry Nodelman, and Maria Nikolajeva. Additionally, there are dozens of scholarly articles and chapters in every major children's literature text book that focus on the subject. However, for those instructors who wish to expand their curricula beyond familiar picture books such as Seuss's *Horton Hears a Who!* to include comics and graphic novels such as Barry Deutsch's Hereville series, the process may seem daunting. Children's literature survey courses are notoriously content rich already, as students are expected to gain familiarity with a variety of forms, including picture books, fairytales, fantasy, poetry, nonfiction, realistic fiction, and film.

Adding to the perceived barriers of using graphic novels in children's literature courses is the fact that no children's literature textbook to date includes a dedicated chapter on the comics medium, and critical studies such as Scott McCloud's *Understanding Comics: The Invisible Art* (1993) or Barbara Postema's *Narrative Structure in Comics: Making Sense of Fragments* (2013) are too lengthy to introduce in the one or two class periods that an instructor might be able to devote to teaching a graphic novel in an undergraduate course. As a result, many educators find themselves treating comics in much the same way they would text only narratives, focusing primarily on the tools of literary analysis that place an emphasis on words over images.

By 2007, with the publication of award winning texts such as Brian Selznick's hybrid graphic novel *The Invention of Hugo Cabret* and Gene Luen Yang's *American Born Chinese*, as well as the soaring popularity of Jeff Kinney's *Diary of a Wimpy Kid* series and Shaun Tan's *The Arrival*, I decided that my students, most of whom planned to teach in elementary or secondary educational settings, needed to develop a set of interpretative skills that would enable them to share comics with their own students. I realized that I had to find a way to convey the basic principles of comics interpretation without taking too much class time away from the existing curriculum, and I decided to work on developing a unit on children's comics that could be integrated into a 15-week undergraduate course in children's literature and could be taught competently by an instructor who was interested in comics studies, but was not an expert.

This essay sets out a model for comics studies instruction that I have developed for use in ENGL 3830, Literature for the Intermediate Reader, a children's literature survey course offered at Western Michigan University to students majoring in education or the humanities. I want to acknowledge from the outset that the approach I describe is only one of many possible ways to introduce students to comics form and interpretation, and I appreciate the work that has already been done by scholars such as Charles Hatfield, Philip Nel, Joe Sutliff Sanders, and many others who advocate for the use of comics in children's literature courses and who share their syllabi and teaching ideas so generously with their colleagues in the field.

Before I cover primary and secondary materials, teaching methods, and discussion prompts for a unit on children's comics, I want to emphasize the usefulness of introducing comics studies as part of a longer process that focuses on the acquisition of visual interpretation skills. The units that I offer during the second half of the semester begin with illustrated chapter books and transition to film adaptations of these chapter books, to picture books, to hybrid text/comic narratives, and finally, to graphic novels. I place the comics-centered units at the end of this sequence so that students have the chance to immerse themselves in visual theory and to practice what they learn across a variety of genres. Of course, in addition to focusing on visual interpretation, I continue to emphasize the foundations of literary interpretation, including an attention to thematic elements, language, genre, and various socio-cultural critical approaches. However, with each successive unit, students apprehend the presence of visual imagery as the driver of narrative progression, one of the key course learning objectives.

In the unit on illustrated texts that begins the visual sequence, I might teach a classic such as Michael Bond's *A Bear Called Paddington* (1958) and ask students to apply Denise I. Matulka's scholarship on the various relation-ships (symmetrical, complementary, and contradictory) that occur between words and pictures on a page. I then introduce the issues involved in film adaptation, relying on excerpts from Robert Stam's introduction to *Literature and Film* and Margaret Mackey's "Spinning Off: Toys, Television, Tie-Ins, and Technology." Students watch the 2014 film adaptation *Paddington* and con-sider what remains, both visually and thematically, from the origin text and what has been removed. This exercise encourages students to appreciate how the medium affects the use of visuals. For example, Peggy Fortnum's line style for the black and white illustrations in *A Bear Called Paddington*, with their impressionistic depictions of a small, slightly unkempt bear going about his workaday adventures, complement the slow paced narration and the focus on Paddington's attempts to understand a new and perplexing culture in environ-ments such as the home, the neighborhood, and the market that are already familiar to young readers. Although each chapter presents a minor mishap from which Paddington must extricate himself, the illustrations underscore that most misunderstandings can be easily sorted out with gentle humor and good will by Paddington and his adoptive family, the Browns. Moreover, Paddington's placement at the center of almost every image, often in the embrace of the Browns, underscores how well he fits in to his new home.

Prior to showing the film adaptation, I assign Molly Bang's *Picture This: How Pictures Work* (2000), a text that proves useful throughout the rest of the semester. Bang's emphasis on the shape, size, color, and placement of objects in an image aids in students' apprehension of the aesthetic differences between the chapter book and its adaptation, especially as the live action, Technicolor, fast-paced, plot-driven film relies heavily on depictions of domination over Paddington by a fame-hungry zoologist, Millicent Clyde, who hopes to display the Peruvian bear as a taxidermy trophy in the British Museum of Natural History. The repetition of camera angles in which Millicent, played to chilling perfection by Nicole Kidman, lurks in the shadows, towers over Paddington, and menaces him with sharp instruments not only serves to captivate an audience of young cinemagoers, it reinforces Bang's claim that viewers' emotions can be manipulated via the purposeful use of visual techniques. In many of the scenes in which they appear together, it is Millicent who fills the screen, pushing Paddington to the edges, thus demonstrating his vulnerability and underscoring the centrality of the capture-and-kill plot to the adaptation.

In the next unit on picture books, students read about the postmodern turn in children's literature via excerpts from Lawrence Sipe and Sylvia Pantaleo's *Postmodern Picturebooks: Play, Parody, and Self-Referentiality* (2008), combined with a close reading of a text such as David Wiesner's *The Three Pigs* (2001), a picture book in which readers are invited to enjoy the various textual and visual deviations that Wiesner embeds in his rendition of "The Three Little Pigs" fairytale. Next, I introduce students to Shaun Tan's *The Arrival*, a wordless comic that provides both an overarching narrative of one immigrant family's experience, along with embedded flashbacks of other migration stories told by secondary characters. As they work through the wordless text, students learn to pick up on visual cues in order to discern how motif, point of view, and temporality can be conveyed by elements such as color, shading, line style, character placement, and page layout, thus reinforcing Molly Bang's principles articulated in *Picture This* and underscoring the narrative potential of visual imagery. For a fine example of how instructors can integrate *The Arrival* into their classrooms, I would recommend an essay in this volume, "Looking beyond the Scenes: Spatial Storytelling and Masking in Shaun Tan's *The Arrival*," by Cathy Ryan and Christiane Buuck.

The pairing of Wiesner's *The Three Pigs*, a picture book, with *The Arrival*, a text that author Shaun Tan terms a picture book, but that most children's literature scholars, comics scholars, and book reviewers have termed a "comic" or a "graphic novel," introduces students to the fluid boundaries that exist among children's texts that are visually centered.[1] The fact that there is no definitive categorization for *The Arrival* encourages students to view themselves as participants in a field that is continuously changing in terms of its definitions and its subject matter.

For the next unit, I assign a hybrid text/comic novel such as Kate DiCamillo's *Flora and Ulysses: The Illuminated Adventures* (2013) that combines narration and illustrations, while also including comic strip sequences, all drawn by illustrator K. G. Campbell. *Flora and Ulysses* tells the story of the relationship between a young comics fan, Flora Buckman, and a squirrel who develops the ability to fly and to write poetry, after being sucked up by a magical vacuum cleaner. Working with a hybrid text that is invested in familiar fantasy and superhero tropes paves the way for students to practice their interpretative skills regarding word/text relationships and page layout, while also incorporating the comics terminology and ideas on closure that are featured in texts such as McCloud's *Understanding Comics* and Postema's *Narrative Structure in Comics*. If I were teaching an upper division comics studies course, I would assign both of these critical texts in their entirety, but given the time constraints, I set up exercises that increase students' ability to recognize how comics grammar begins with the individual panel and expands out to include the relationship among contiguous panels on a page and then across the entire comic in a process known as braiding.

To get started, I introduce my students to basic comics terminology, noting that the "medium of comics" refers to sequential art, though many scholars, myself included, would consider individual panels such as those created by Bil and Jeff Keane for their long running comic strip *Family Circus* to be part of the comics medium as well. Will Eisner, a prolific US comics artist, is credited with coining the term "graphic novel" in the 1970s to refer to a long-form comic that features a compelling narrative, such as his classic 1978 text *A Contract With God*.[2] Many comics artists and academics have gravitated towards this term, in part to try to distinguish high art comics from the comic books that are so often associated with children and with popular culture. The phrase "graphic narrative" serves a similar function. Most contemporary comics scholars use the term graphic novel or the term "long-form comic" to refer to a text such as Shaun Tan's *The Arrival*.

I go on to explain that the basic unit of a comic is the panel, and as Scott McCloud has pointed out in *Understanding Comics: The Invisible Art* (1993), the relationship of panels that are set out in a sequence forms the basics of comics grammar. The term "gutter" refers to the space between contiguous panels, and we make reference to Scott McCloud's chapter "Blood in the Gutter," as students learn to become highly conscious of the process of filling in the gaps between panels, an action that they have been doing since the first time that they read a comic strip or a comic book, but might not have ever acknowledged. This process of filling in the gaps, which comics scholars term "closure," requires readers to attend to changes in detail between two contiguous panels and to recognize that these changes indicate the rate at which the narration unfolds (McCloud 69).

If text is present in the comic, it usually comes in two forms: narration, often set apart in captions within or just outside the panel, and dialogue, represented via speech or thought bubbles. At this point, I remind students of previous interpretative work that we have done using Denise I. Matulka's three interactions that typically occur between words and an image on a page: symmetrical, complementary, and contradictory. In comics, most creators avoid symmetrical relationships in which the words and the image are absolutely identical. This relationship is found most often in board books for children, where the text "A is for Apple" might appear next to an image of an apple. Instead, most comics creators will allow the text and the image to combine to create a complementary relationship, or they will use contradictory images and words in order to underscore disjunction (118).

Of course, the burden of comics narration is often carried without the use of words, and I explain to students that they will need to also pay attention to page layout, panel size, borders, line style, color choice, and emanata. These elements combine to convey meaning, regardless of whether text is present. The definitions listed below are taken from a handout that I use on the first day that we work with *Flora and Ulysses*:

**Page layout**: Most comics are arranged using what is known as a "waffle pattern," with three or four panels per row, and three to four rows per page. When a comics creator alters this pattern, typically it is in order to emphasize something in the story. A comics page with only one panel draws our attention to the subject in more dramatic fashion than if the panel had been set out as one of many on a page.

**Panel size**: In a typical waffle pattern layout, panels are of the same size, but comics creators will vary the size to establish a variety of effects. As Barbara Postema explains, "frames in a movie come in one standard size; in comics, panel sizes can vary very easily, and hence they can be used to create or emphasize meaning" (112). Panels are set out on the page in a variety of ways, and the choices that a comics creator makes about how the panels should be set up is called the breakdown. The term "spread" refers to two facing comics pages.

**Borders**: Most panels have borders, but occasionally, a comics creator will eliminate a border as a way of indicating a concept such as freedom or escape, or, the comics creator will obscure a border with a speech bubble or with an embedded object. As an example, in *Flora and Ulysses*, DiCamillo and Campbell use a jagged border in order to highlight the impact of Ulysses's superpowers (202).

**Line style:** The thickness of lines and the use of shading can help to set the mood and direct readers as to where they should be placing their attention. When the lines of a comic are uniform in size and contain little shading, the mood may seem lighter than if the lines of the comic varied in thickness and were jagged. That said, comics creators sometimes upend readers' expectations by employing a line style associated with one sort of emotion to convey a narrative that is out of keeping with the mood.

**Color choice:** When the comics industry was in its infancy, publishers asked comics creators to stick to basic primary colors because they were less expensive to replicate. As such, brightly colored layouts became associated with children's comics and lighthearted subjects (Baetens 112). In the later half of the twentieth century, as many comics creators hoped to differentiate their work from that of the traditional comic book, they turned to limited color palettes. For instance, Art Spiegelman's *Maus* helped influence subsequent generations of comics creators to depict serious and traumatic events in black and white.

**Emanata:** The use of lines to reflect a character's anger, fear, or joy enables comics creators to express these emotions without the use of words. Cartoonist Mort Walker, best known for his long-running comic strip *Beetle Bailey*, wrote a satire of comics emanata called *The Lexicon of Comicana* (1980), but many of the terms that he gave to the line devices used to show emotion have taken hold and are used by scholars today. I typically show one or two pages from *The Lexicon of Comicana* so that students can get a sense for these small, but useful devices.

**Lettering:** While most comics lettering is uniform in size and style, variations can help to convey emotion and mood. The insertion of italicized or bold font, or a shift in letter size for important words, provides readers with a sense for how a speaker may be feeling.

Once students are familiar with the basic terminology, I remind them that when they read a comic, they move forward by taking notice of the changes that occur from panel to panel; this process of filling in the gaps is central to comics grammar, and Scott McCloud devotes an entire section of *Understanding Comics* to identifying and labeling the potential relationships that occur between panels in a sequence. At this point, I take students through pages 70–73 of *Understanding Comics*, pointing out that McCloud categorizes transitions between panels based on how much work the reader must do in order to fill in the gaps.

In order to give students practice identifying and thinking through the relationship between juxtaposed panels, I project the first three pages of *Flora and Ulysses* on the classroom screen and ask students to volunteer a summary of the action that occurs on page 2. The students agree that the passage demonstrates what happens when a spouse gives a gift that ignores the recipient's interests. I then show students the various ways that text can be introduced in a comic through captions and speech bubbles, and I follow up by asking if their summaries of the action were included anywhere in the text itself. When students answer in the negative, they recognize that the narrative is being formed by more than just the words.

As the students study page 2 further, they realize that panels 2 and 3, which show tiny close ups of Mr. and Mrs. Tickham's expressions, are designed to emphasize their contrasting responses to the birthday gift, while also inviting readers to return to panel 1 and scrutinize it carefully. At this point, I introduce students to the idea that reading a comic is not an entirely linear exercise. Unlike film, where the sequence of frames is joined together to create a trajectory that the viewer perceives as a seamless product, comics layout encourages a more flexible visual experience. As Postema observes, "readers participate in making meaning by creating theoretical scenarios based on the information at hand and adapting as new information becomes available. In comics, this process often involves flipping backward and forward through the text to reexamine certain panels" (113). For many students, especially those who are new to reading comics, receiving guidance on how to read outside the linear mode improves their comprehension. It also encourages students to pay closer attention to the visual elements of a comics page and to contemplate what is conveyed by words versus what is conveyed by the rhetorical layout of the visuals.

For example, during their discussion of page 2 of *Flora and Ulysses*, students recognize that Mrs. Tickham's initially unenthusiastic response to her husband's utilitarian birthday gift, the "Ulysses Super-Suction, Multi-Terrain 2000X," is central to the narrative but is not primarily articulated via language. Instead, Mrs. Tickham's body posture in the first panel and her retreat back into her poetry anthology, symbolized by the narrow focus of panel 5 on her eyes and the book, unfold one after the other to highlight the tension that escalates between the couple. By paying careful attention to the contents of each panel (students note, for instance, that the Ulysses 2000X is shaped like a maid, underscoring the conflict that can occur when marital partners follow traditions in which household chores are gendered), the nonverbal elements such as figural placement, panel size, and panel layout, and the relationship between contiguous panels, students acknowledge the ability of visual elements to drive the narrative, a concept that they first encountered in the picture book unit and find that they can apply again.

By the time we begin the graphic novel unit, the practice of introducing students gradually to the principles of visual interpretation allows me to focus on braiding, a concept that adds significantly to a reader's ability to understand the interplay between form and meaning in the comics medium. In *The System of Comics* (1999), Thierry Groensteen argues that while it is important to look at the relationship between two panels situated next to each other in sequence, it is also important to identify the relationships that panels have with each other throughout the entire comic. Comics creators will often return to a specific panel or panel shape or page layout repeatedly in the text, and braiding refers to a reader's ability to recognize these repetitions and to accord meaning to them. Thus, an individual panel in a comic exists both in relation to the panels next to it on the page, but also in relation to any other panel in the entire comic.

The text I will be using to illustrate how braiding works, Barry Deutsch's *Hereville: How Mirka Got Her Sword* (2010), is representative of the aesthetically sophisticated and culturally diverse graphic novels that are increasingly being produced for elementary and middle grade readers, and it is a good candidate for structural analysis because of its clean lines, consistent color palette, and easy-to-follow page layouts.[3] Deutsch's *Hereville* series, begun in 2010, takes up the question of how a young woman can develop her individuality while remaining observant of religious and cultural practices valued in her community. The tagline for the first volume, *Hereville: How Mirka Got Her Sword*, points ironically to the uniqueness of his subject matter: "Yet Another Troll-Fighting 11 Year-Old Orthodox Jewish Girl." In the series to date, Mirka learns valuable lessons from her stepmother Fruma and from stories about her great, great grandmother, who emigrated from Europe to the United States to build a new life. Barry Deutsch's interest in creating *Hereville* was piqued by the fact that stories of female heroism have been largely missing from North American comics, as have stories about underrepresented groups—in this case, Orthodox Jewish communities. Deutsch explains that: "I am concerned with identity politics—I'd like to see more girl-centered pop fiction, and I'd like to see more Jewish characters in popular fictions. And if other readers, especially female readers and Jewish readers, have been feeling that same hunger and so get a bit of extra pleasure out of reading *Hereville*, then that's great" ("Author Interview"). Deutsch was raised in a reform Jewish family and found that writing Hereville gave him the chance to learn more about Orthodox Jewish communities and their practices. The series has been reviewed positively in both mainstream literary publications such as *The School Library Journal* and *The Horn Book*, and in periodicals with a predominantly Jewish readership, including *The Jewish Daily Forward* and *The Jewish Journal*.

In the *Hereville* series, Deutsch uses structural elements to indicate the bond between Mirka and her stepmother, thus minimizing those cloying instances that can occur in a text when a young protagonist states directly that she has benefited from adult mentoring. For example, early in story, Mirka, in the tradition of the tomboy figure, wants to trade in her knitting needles for a sword, and her homework and chores for a life of adventure as a dragon slayer (4). During an argument with her stepmother Fruma, Mirka is questioned regarding her rationale for wanting to slay dragons. Mirka has argued that dragons are evil and "*eat* people and stuff" (4.1), and Fruma's rebuttal takes a variety of tacks: she asks how Mirka's own enjoyment of fish and beef and chicken can go unpunished, but a dragon's eating of humans is considered to be evil. She notes that God created dragons to kill and eat people, and asks how this behavior could be considered evil. However, the minute that Mirka concedes, Fruma flips the argument: "Mirka!" she cries. "You mean you'd let a dragon devour me and the whole town? How could you?" (4.5). As Fruma progresses through what is obviously a lesson in argumentation, her figural placement changes with each claim, and speech bubbles surround her and dominate the page, indicating both the force of her words and her loquacious nature (4.2).

As the story progresses, Mirka makes a bargain with a troll: they will engage in a knitting contest, and if Mirka wins, the troll promises to give her a what she desires—in this case, a sword; however, if the troll wins, Mirka must agree, in time-honored fairytale fashion, to sacrifice herself and become his lunch (131). At the end of the allotted knitting time, the troll presents a traditional sweater, perfectly stitched, while Mirka presents what appears to be a garbled, hole-ridden monstrosity. With her life on the line, Mirka replicates Fruma's ability to get out of a difficult situation through the skilled use of language and argumentation. She tells the troll that hers is the better sweater: "I notice that all of your sleeves have openings," she begins. "Do you WANT people wearing your sweater to have their hands freeze and fall off? No worthwhile idea of 'better' penalizes originality! If your clichéd sweater wins, that's rejection the whole idea of innovation," and so on (131.2). Beyond the information that the text conveys, the page layout, the figural placement of Mirka and the troll, and the arrangement of speech bubbles create visual echoes, or what comics theorist Thierry Groensteen terms "braids": Mirka's body language and her expression mirror Fruma's, and her speech bubbles, like Fruma's, crowd out almost everything else in the panel. In terms of figural placement, the first, third, fourth, and fifth panels all parallel the panels on page 4, but now it is the troll who is bested by Mirka, rather than Mirka being bested by Fruma.

In *Comics and Narration*, Groensteen demonstrates that "the braiding effect that operates between spatially distant images can . . . assume as much importance as the friction between adjacent images" on a page (35). Similarly, Pascal Lefèvre has observed that "the reader is not just a passive agent: he or she looks at images with prior knowledge, and uses that context to make sense of visual" patterns (16). Thus, without any textual direction, readers *witness* the link between Fruma and Mirka; they can intuit that though she initially seemed resistant, Mirka did benefit from listening to the counsel of her stepmother. From this observation, students learn that comics creators often return to a specific image or panel shape or page layout repeatedly as they devise the rhetorical layout of the entire comic, and the braiding process encourages readers to recognize repetitions and to accord meaning to them. Moreover, an emphasis on braiding helps readers to view the graphic novel as a unified whole that is bound together by a series of braids, rather than as a simple sequence of linked panels.

## Exploring Further Resources

As the readership for children's comics continues to grow, a number of resources are available to educators who wish to enhance their understanding of the comics medium. In addition to the foundational work of McCloud, Groensteen, and Postema, I would recommend Jan Baetens and Hugo Frey's *The Graphic Novel: An Introduction* (2015), which includes sections on the historical context, form, and themes related to the graphic novel. I would also suggest Randy Duncan, Matthew J. Smith, and Paul Levitz's *The Power of Comics: History, Form, and Culture* (2014), which focuses on teaching comics, and includes in-class exercises and writing prompts. Charles Hatfield's *Alternative Comics: An Emerging Literature* (2005) provides an excellent overview of comics history and contemporary scholarship, and the most recent comics scholarship can be found in journals such as *ImageTexT: Interdisciplinary Comics Studies*, *Image and Narrative*, and the *International Journal of Comic Art*. A number of podcasts that focus on comics, including ones sponsored by the Comics Alternative and by comics creator Jessica Abel, also provide helpful background resources for educators.

In terms of resources to share directly with students, I often use a pamphlet released by the Comic Book Legal Defense Fund, *Raising a Reader! How Comics & Graphic Novels Can Help Your Kids Love To Read*, written by Dr. Meryl Jaffe, with an introduction by children's literature author Jennifer Holm, and illustrated by her brother, Matthew Holm, the artist behind their joint effort, the *Babymouse* comics series. Although the pamphlet is geared towards parents and educators, it includes an excellent primer on comics terminology and interpretation, and it is available as a PDF on the CBLDF website.

In his essay on the resurgence of children's comics, Ben Hatke suggests that today's young readers are living in a new "golden age" where in addition to traditional comic books, "kids have access to longer stories in multiple genres featuring a diverse cast of heroes" ("Zap!"). Over the last decade, graphic novels and graphic hybrid texts have won the Newbery Medal, the Caldecott Medal, the Printz Award, and the National Book Award; many series, such as *Diary of a Wimpy Kid* have sold tens of millions of copies, and comics creators such as Raina Telgemeier and comics script writers such as Neil Gaiman are encouraging more and more young people to become comics readers. Against this backdrop, developing a basic competency in comics interpretation and sharing graphic novels with students has never been more timely. The fact that scholars are actively debating the boundaries between, say, picture books and graphic novels, or that web comics are giving child readers the opportunity to interact with authors and to influence the composition process, enable educators to underscore the constructedness of literary culture and to invite students to view comics interpretation as an exercise in which they can become influential participants.

## Notes

1. For a discussion of the generic properties of Shaun Tan's *The Arrival*, see Gene Luen Yang's "Stranger in a Strange Land." *The New York Times*, 11 November 2007: np. Web. 15 February 2016.

2. The earliest known use of the term "graphic novel" was made by Richard Kyle, in his comics magazine *Wonderworld* 1.2 (1964): 4. Print. I want to thank Joe Sutliff Sanders for providing me with a copy of the magazine.

3. Students who are beginning their work with literary interpretation will often be intimidated by the comics medium, as it foregrounds what will be, for most of them, an unfamiliar set of practices and terms. For this reason, I select children's graphic novels that provide very clear instances of braiding so that students can readily identify patterns and feel the satisfaction of adding to their skill set. At the end of the graphic novel unit, I will preview more advanced scholarly techniques and employ them with a few sample comics, just to give those students who are deeply interested in comics interpretation a chance to see what lies ahead, but that supplemental work is not required by any means.

## Works Cited

Alverson, Brigid. "Teaching with Graphic Novels." *School Library Journal*. 8 September 2014: np. Web. 1 September 2015.

"Author Interview: Barry Deutsch and *Hereville*." *People of the Books Blog*. Association of Jewish Libraries. 31 October 2010: np. Web. 15 September 2015.

Baetens, Jan. "From Black & White to Color and Back: What Does It Mean (Not) to Use Color?" *College Literature* 38.3 (2011): 111–28. Web. 25 September 2015.

Baetens, Jan, and Hugo Frey. *The Graphic Novel: An Introduction*. Cambridge, UK: Cambridge University Press, 2015. Print.

Bang, Molly. *Picture This: How Pictures Work*. San Francisco: Chronicle Books, 2000. Print.

Bond, Michael. *A Bear Called Paddington*. 1958. New York: HarperCollins, 2014. Print.

Deutsch, Barry. *Hereville: How Mirka Got Her Sword*. New York: Amulet Books, 2010. Print.

DiCamillo, Kate, and K. G. Campbell. *Flora and Ulysses: The Illuminated Adventures*. Somerville, MA: Candlewick Press, 2013. Print.

Duncan, Randy, Matthew J. Smith, and Paul Levitz. *The Power of Comics: History, Form, and Culture*. London: Bloomsbury, 2009. Print.

Groensteen, Thierry. *Comics and Narration*. Trans. Ann Miller. Jackson, MS: University Press of Mississippi, 2011. Print.

———. *The System of Comics*. Trans. Bart Beaty and Nick Nguyen. Reprint, 1999. Jackson, MS: University Press of Mississippi, 2007. Print.

Hatfield, Charles. *Alternative Comics: An Emerging Literature*. Jackson, MS: University Press of Mississippi, 2005. Print.

Hatke, Ben. "Zap! Pow! Comics Are for Kids Again." *BoingBoing*. 2 May 2015: np. Web. 10 October 2015.

Jaffe, Meryl. *Raising a Reader! How Comics & Graphic Novels Can Help Your Kids Love To Read!* New York: Comic Book Legal Defense Fund, 2014. Web. 10 October 2015.

Lefèvre, Pascal. "Some Medium-Specific Qualities of Graphic Sequences." *SubStance* 40.1 (2011): 14–33. Web. 1 September 2015.

Mackey, Margaret. "Spinning Off: Toys, Television, Tie-Ins, and Technology." *Handbook of Research on Children's and Young Adult Literature*. Eds. Shelby Wolf, Karen Coats, Patricia Enciso, and Christine Jenkins. New York: Routledge, 2011. Print.

Matulka, Denise I. *A Picture Book Primer: Understanding and Using Picture Books*. Westport, CT: Libraries Unlimited, 2008. Print.

McCloud, Scott. *Understanding Comics: The Invisible Art*. New York: William Morrow, 1993. Print.

*Paddington*. Dir. Paul King. Perf. Nicole Kidman, Sally Hawkins, Hugh Bonneville, and Julie Walters. StudioCanal. 2015. Film.

Postema, Barbara. *Narrative Structure in Comics: Making Sense of Fragments*. Rochester, NY: Rochester Institute of Technology Press, 2013. Print.

Sipe, Lawrence, and Sylvia Pantaleo. *Post-modern Picturebooks: Play, Parody, and Self-Referentiality*. New York: Routledge, 2008. Print.

Stam, Robert, and Alessandra Raengo, eds. *Literature and Film: A Guide to the Theory and Practice of Film Adaptation*. Malden, MA: Blackwell, 2005. Print.

Tan, Shaun. *The Arrival*. 2006. New York: Arthur A. Levine Books, 2007. Print.

"Using Comics and Graphic Novels in the Classroom." *The Council Chronicle*. 1 September 2005: np. Web. 10 October 2015.

Walker, Mort. *The Lexicon of Comicana*. New York: Comicana Books, 1980. Print.

Wiesner, David. *The Three Pigs*. New York: Clarion, 2001. Print.

# 10

## Looking beyond the Scenes: Spatial Storytelling and Masking in Shaun Tan's *The Arrival*

### Christiane Buuck and Cathy Ryan

From the moment readers pick up Shaun Tan's *The Arrival*, they are invited to step into an immersive and subversive visual narrative. The cover has the appearance of a worn leather scrapbook onto which a black and white photograph is affixed. This photograph depicts a man carrying a suitcase, stooping to inspect a white, four-legged creature with a long tail. The man resembles someone captured in an early twentieth-century photograph, complete with suit and hat and suitcase secured by a strap. The white creature, however, with its unshelled-pistachio-shaped body and cartoonish appearance, seems out of place when set within the book cover's otherwise photorealistic art. This juxtaposition is the first hint that the reader is entering a visual world in which the familiar and the surprising coexist.

The sense of dislocation in *The Arrival* continues when the reader opens the book and is greeted with an inside cover and flyleaf decorated with sixty square black and white portraits. The subject of each image looks directly at the viewer and, collectively, their ethnicities are so diverse that the portraits seem to have been inspired by historic anthropological photographs or the pages of *National Geographic*.[1] Given the title of the book, these portraits may even be passport photographs. The reader turns the page and gathers more visual clues.

For the purposes of this study, we identify the next two right-hand pages as the title pages.[2] The first title page features several immigration-related documents on the top left and bottom margins, a centered starburst symbol, and fantastical writing above and below this starburst. The writing beneath the starburst appears to be the author's name in highly stylized font. The second title page includes a decorative floral border that frames the title of the book, the name of the author and publisher, and, at the very center, a familiar visual cue: a portrait of a man from the shoulders up. The shape of this photograph echoes the sixty portraits of the inside cover, only this time the subject is not looking at the viewer. He is turned three-quarters away, as if to look at something behind him. The reader might wonder what has attracted his attention—Something menacing? Something inviting? This visual cue, coupled with those that have come before, makes a nuanced suggestion to readers that there is something worthwhile to be seen just beyond the initial field of vision. Indeed, throughout the book, the reader's eye is invited to look beyond the characters that populate the story in order to explore the subtle, yet significant, peripheries and settings in which these characters are placed. Tan's settings offer readers of all ages some of the most compelling sites of interpretation in the visual narrative.

## Masking and Spatial Storytelling Devices in *The Arrival*

In addition to the story's content, *The Arrival*'s composition is important. Panels in the text come in a multitude of sizes and contain an equally diverse range of subject matter. Many of the smaller panels feature extreme close-ups of hands and faces (see pages 28–29) or specific repeated images (such as the clouds on pages 16–17). Meanwhile, many of the larger panels comprise intricate compositions with vanishing points and a clear sense of foreground, middle ground and background, and they showcase cityscapes, seascapes, countrysides, and vast interiors. There are certain patterns of detail, especially within the larger panels (such as the vacuum-wielding giants on pages 66–67) that are not clearly understood and, in our experience, invite the most attention.

Our study of backgrounds and spatial storytelling devices in *The Arrival* began in English 2367, a second-level honors composition course at The Ohio State University, piqued our scholarly curiosity. The course theme was immigration and newcomer identity. Early in the semester, we read Scott McCloud's *Understanding Comics* as context to study of Tan's *The Arrival*. During class discussions, we noticed how students were frequently drawn to investigate the settings in the graphic narrative. One section that particularly drew students' interest depicts a man and a woman fleeing from a city that is in flames and being attacked by what look like vacuum-wielding giants. The escapees pay a man with a piece of jewelry to show them an escape route through a sewer. They emerge from the underground into a landscape that is planar and vast, all sharp corners and tall walls.

Students were so intrigued by this section that we spent a majority of class time analyzing it. They offered many interpretations of these images, but the most frequent analysis was that this mini-narrative depicted the Holocaust. One student suggested that the giants represented the Nazis. Another student considered the almost cubist escape route the couple follows to be a reference to the art of the 1930s and 1940s. Still other students suggested science-fiction-inspired readings in which aliens arrive and destroy the planet save for a few lucky survivors. The debate swirled and each student was able to point to textual details that underpinned a grounded argument of "what this story is *really* about." Most revealing was the level of detail students were willing to parse to build their readings. Toward the end of our discussion, one student, Hayley Kick, synthesized what had just happened. She suggested, rightly, that it was important that we were not as concerned with the *people* in the story as we were in the *backgrounds*.

In this study we propose a new application of the comics term "masked" to backgrounds rather than to characters. The traditional usage of the concept of masking is explained by Scott McCloud in *Understanding Comics*. He suggests that one method by which readers intellectually, emotionally, and psychologically connect with a graphic narrative is by being able to imagine themselves within the world on the page. McCloud explains that graphic narratives are welcoming spaces in part because characters, especially in cartoons, are often masked, or rendered abstractly enough to avoid easy classification. These characters can then serve as "an empty shell that we inhabit that enables us to travel to another realm" (36). McCloud describes a style of masking in which simplistically drawn characters are placed against "unusually realistic backgrounds." He argues that "this combination allows readers to mask themselves in a character and safely enter a sensually stimulating world" (43).

Something different is happening in Tan's mode of graphic storytelling.[3] Whereas one could argue that creatures in *The Arrival* might be considered masked (such as the animal on the cover, which seems not unlike a character from Jeff Smith's *Bone* series), Tan's people are rendered in photorealistic detail. These human characters are so clearly unique that the reader is not encouraged to easily mask him-or herself in them. Instead, the characters' highly realistic appearance helps readers gain purchase and a sense of the familiar in a world that is often strange, intriguing, and unfamiliar. This is a new application of the principle of comics masking, wherein Tan's graphic narrative invites "arrivees" to explore the way hyper-realistic characters are incorporated within attention-grabbing, masked spatial contexts.

If, according to McCloud, the characters in comics can become vessels through which multiple readers might imagine themselves in a clearly delineated world, we propose that *The Arrival's* clearly delineated characters act more like guides to the book's unfamiliar, often fantastical settings. Caitlin McGurk, Associate Curator, Billy Ireland Cartoon Library and Museum, explains one precedent for how comics artists direct the reader's gaze. In a talk about the museum's collections, she uses an example of Ernie Bushmiller's *Nancy* (a comic strip originating in the 1930s) to show how the placement of spot-blacks and angle of a character's gaze and gestures pull a reader's eyes from panel to panel. Tan's characters likewise direct through their gaze and expressions, as well as through body language. In so doing, these characters encourage readers to travel with them through settings that are just familiar enough to be accessible, but just fantastical enough to seem foreign—settings that become sites of the most complex interpretation in the narrative.

John Berger, in *Ways of Seeing*, suggests, "When we 'see' a landscape, we situate ourselves in it" (11). This act of situating the self with respect to the visual landscape of the story is especially important in *The Arrival*. Berger suggests that when we perceive art, "we never look at just one thing; we are always looking at the relations between things and ourselves. Our vision is continually active, continually moving, continually holding things in a circle around itself, constituting what is present to us as we are" (9). This dynamic interplay between details in the visual narrative and the reader's perception of them is central to our theory.

For the purposes of this study, we use the term "setting" to denote several contexts into which Tan's characters are placed. The first of these contexts includes the detailed worlds in the book's larger panels (such as the one that features vacuum-wielding giants). The second context is the visual space on the page that surrounds (or frames) each panel—these spaces sometimes have the appearance of crumpled paper and at different points in the narrative the page colors alternate from white to gray or black. We also consider the narrative context that surrounds the character in the larger story.

Tan's use of photorealism for his illustration style in *The Arrival* merits some commentary. His visual narratives sometimes include collage (*Distant Rain*), occasionally incorporate found objects (*The Lost Thing, Eric*), and most often feature text embedded within illustrations (*The Red Tree*). In *The Arrival*, however, the use of collage is minimal. Readers find, for example, a variety of small tickets, official stamps, and inspection cards in the title pages.[4] Another example of collage-esque illustration appears in the back of the book where the "Artist's Note" appears to be printed directly on crumpled paper that features a child's drawing of a house. Even when used minimally, these collages highlight Tan's formula of mixing the familiar (birth certificate) and strange (title lettering) to surprise and unsettle the reader in his graphic narratives. The majority of such visual cues in *The Arrival*, however, are more subtle, and appear at the margins of the panels themselves.

In his foreword to Evelyn Arizpe, Teresa Colomer, and Carmen Martinez-Roldán's *Visual Journeys through Wordless Narratives*, Shaun Tan speaks of a process he describes as "open reading." He explains that "any good act of creativity is fundamentally an act of sharing and co-creation" and, in terms of scene, writes, "As a creator, you provide a little architecture, build some imaginary walls, add a few furnishings, then wait for an anonymous visitor to arrive." The titular "arrival," then, offers an invitation to the reader, whom Tan likens to the "conversationalist" who arrives via his or her engagement in co-producing what Tan calls "free-roaming interpretations." One of *The Arrival*'s chief pleasures for readers of any age is this continual navigation between the identity of the individual who is encountering the text and the world that is being presented on the page.

Further, the act of situating the self within the world of *The Arrival* is a topic that Evelyn Arizpe and colleagues explore. Their cross-cultural study (*Visual Journeys through Wordless Narratives*) examines the ways children from ethnic minority and immigrant backgrounds interact with Tan's graphic narrative. The authors focus on the movement into adolescence (what the authors call being "in flux"; see Introduction) and investigate reader responses to the story. Alan Pulverness reviews the book for *CLELE Journal*, and synthesizes the experience of student readers, as well as that of teachers, using Tan's narrative in classroom settings:

> *The Arrival*, in common with many postmodern visual narratives, is an open text, full of ambiguity and indeterminacy, which invites its readers to co-construct the story, bringing to it their own experiences of reading and their own life experiences. With its story of arrival in a strange, new country, and its dream-like visual language, populating its world with almost photo-realist depictions of human beings and creatures of the imagination, it 'defamiliarises' the reader in much the same way as the immigrant-protagonist is himself defamiliarised. The book thus provides a space in which readers can recognise themselves, speculate not only on what they can see, but also on the experience behind the images, and in quite a literal sense become co-authors of the book. (Pulverness 78)

Pulverness moves beyond Kick's observation about masking—past "ambiguity" and "indeterminacy" (what Tan characterizes as "open text")—to map how the visual narrative invites readers to "co-construct the story." The visual language Tan incorporates into his settings works to unsettle readers in such a way as to prompt them to "speculate not only on what they can see" but also "on the experience behind the images" (78).

In *Sketches from a Nameless Land* (2012), Tan provides insights into his own sense of the narrative.[5] For example, in a section entitled "Belonging," he introduces a "stylized, dream-like interpretation of figures in a 'foreign' landscape" and, in a section titled "The Companion Animal," suggests that the companion creature "can only be described in terms of a vague likeness." We propose that the experience of becoming immersed in the world of the narrative and working to construct relationships among the book's visual details becomes all the richer when readers interrogate *The Arrival*'s masked backgrounds and settings.

## Visual Literacy and Reading Visual Cues in *The Arrival*

The literature on visual literacy conveys how multiple encounters with Tan's visual narrative may teach students to become critical readers.[6] David Perkins suggests that "by cultivating awareness of our own thinking, asking ourselves good questions, guiding ourselves with strategies, we steer our experiential intelligence in fruitful directions" (11). Raney extends this observation by defining visual literacy as "the history of thinking about what images and objects mean, how they are put together, how we respond to or interpret them, how they might function as modes of thought, and how they are seated within the societies that gave rise to them" (38). Notably, Kenneth Clark classifies the interpretive process—what happens when we look at pictures—and postulates that patience and persistence factor into the impact art has on a viewer. He explains that when critical faculties "come into operation," the viewer (or reader) moves through active participation into re-examining more deeply, a process wherein previously overlooked details come into focus and new connections emerge (69). In his foreword to *Visual Journeys through Wordless Narratives*, Tan describes what he calls visual intelligence, or "making connections between things without the convenience of written or spoken language." An early University of Cambridge field study by Evelyn Arizpe and Morag Styles (2003) described this process as occurring when "looking [develops] into *seeing*, through memory, imagination, and thought" (43).

Comics theorist Will Eisner characterizes comics (and, perhaps, we may add the graphic novel tradition since his 1978 publication of *A Contract with God*) as being principally "composed of images" (xi). He explains that "while words are a vital component [in comics], the major dependence for description and narration is on universally understood *images*, crafted with the intention of imitating or exaggerating reality" (xi; emphasis added). *The Arrival* contains almost no recognizable text beyond the second title page and one later page where the author's name is secretly embedded (39.2 shows the protagonist holding a book. The first line of text on the left page of the book appears to spell "Shaun Tan."). While there is an invented language on the walls and documents in the story, there are no familiar words or thought balloons to tell the reader what the characters are saying or thinking, and there is no explanatory text to help readers interpret the visual landscape. Berger reminds us that "seeing comes before words. The child looks and recognizes before it can speak" (7). This observation, however, ought not to imply that the absence of words automatically limits the book to an audience of young

readers. Because *The Arrival* is a wordless text, it is accessible to readers of all
levels and ages. Tan allows his audience to inhabit his pages and be confronted
with a world crafted entirely of images.

## Case Study: Students Discuss *The Arrival*

Because we are especially interested in the ways college-aged readers interact
with *The Arrival*, we asked our former student, Hayley Kick, to write about
her sense of how Tan uses masking. Her in-class observation influenced our
own ideas about masked backgrounds and spatial storytelling devices in *The
Arrival*, and we wanted to invite her to more fully articulate her ideas here.
Reflecting on her experience with the text, Ms. Kick observed that

> throughout my first reading of Shaun Tan's *The Arrival*, I made notes on nearly
> every page. Each note contained a few words or phrases that described my emo-
> tions in response to the characters' circumstances. The words "fear," "uncertainty,"
> and "camaraderie" appeared most often, and I entered our class discussion with
> the intent to ask my classmates how those emotions shaped the theme of Tan's
> work. However, my peers seemed more perplexed by our collective inability to
> pinpoint how the setting contributed meaning to the plot than [on] the emo-
> tions of Tan's characters. Although I appreciated the critical thoughts that were
> shared in our discussion, I felt like our conversation discounted the significance
> of the characters' emotions to the meaning of the work.
>
> I returned to my copy of *The Arrival* to find a reason for the discrepancy
> between my thoughts and those of my peers. A new pattern emerged among my
> notes: There were no markings on the pages dominated by illustrations of the
> background rather than the characters. In my first reading I was so intrigued by the
> main character's experiences that I paid little attention to the backgrounds against
> which they occurred. This observation brought me to the conclusion that Tan
> masks his backgrounds with surreal places and creatures to draw readers closer to
> the characters in the story. Tan's ambiguous settings invite readers to project famil-
> iar places behind his characters in order to make sense of the protagonist's progres-
> sion of emotions. Since each reader in my writing class related the immigrant's
> reactions with a different experience, we could not agree on one obvious back-
> ground at any point in the story. Our collective discussion did not end in concrete
> conclusions about the setting of *The Arrival*, but our individual readings ended in
> a deeper relationship with the immigrant who brought those settings to life.[7]

As Ms. Kick suggests, readers do not mask themselves into the characters
of *The Arrival*. Instead, the space in Tan's text that most compels is the "sensually stimulating world" itself (McCloud 43). Her thoughtful reading highlights

some of the ways we suggest Tan simultaneously draws ambiguous settings and helps orient the reader of *The Arrival*. She notes how places help readers make sense of the immigrant's experience (e.g., backgrounds function as projections of a character's emotions), how individual readings end in "deeper relationship" with the protagonist, and how Tan's "ambiguous" settings offer space for readers to superimpose their own lived experiences. Ms. Kick observes that the backgrounds and creatures in the narrative are so unfamiliar that their very oddness helps the reader to connect with the people in the story, who are familiar and recognizable in comparison. While we agree with Ms. Kick about Tan's use of masking in backgrounds, we extend the comics principle of masking to encompass *settings*, and especially how, "behind the characters," spatial storytelling devices invite the reader to coauthor the narrative.

In our experience, students readily engage with the book's settings and want to make sense of *The Arrival* both through their own experiences and by adopting historical lenses.[8] These tendencies also reveal something of the power of visual metaphor when it is used as masked context: it opens space for readers to explore the ways in which the graphic narrative about a fantastical world can enlighten our own cultural and historical perspectives. An example of masked settings in large panels occurs early in the book, specifically on pages 5, 6–7, and 10, which all feature a detail our students have termed "dragon tails." On page 5 of the narrative, a shadow of what appears to be a dragon-like tail is cast on the wall of a building as the protagonist and his family walk below. Pages 6–7 offer a wide-angle perspective of the family traversing a grim neighborhood of high buildings around which the sinister tails curl. On page 10, the tails snake through the sky rather ominously as the mother and daughter return home again after sending the father off on a train. When students in English 2367 discussed *The Arrival*, these dragon tails were an early and frequent focus of their attention. Did these tails and their shadows represent real dragons? Were they metaphors representing menace and danger, or something else? What if these tails were just a feature of the land the protagonist leaves, not the reason for his leaving? And so on.

Students were so captivated by this visual detail that they found additional examples of the tails recurring in playful variation later in the narrative. On pages 64–65 (four panels), a boy beckons the protagonist to a small boat that holds an earthen pot. A tail begins to emerge from the pot, and by the fourth panel the tail resembles a small version of the dragon tails that haunt the beginning of the story. The protagonist recoils only to be reassured that this particular tail belongs to a domesticated creature. Because the protagonist does not have a shared spoken language to explain his fright, he draws a picture to show the boy's father. Panels 6 and 7 on page 65 depict his line drawing of a dragon tail over house tops—images that very closely echo the beginning of the book.[9] Students noted that the tails and their shadows are smaller with each representation. In the first iteration they are so large they seem to overtake a city; in the second, they can be held by a small boy; in the last, they are reduced to a line drawing in a notebook within a panel.

Students working to make meaning of Tan's graphic text took on a coauthoring role. Often, they compared the dragon tails to visual tropes in their experiences of pop culture—animal disaster films, fables or stories about dragons, dinosaurs, or mythological creatures. These themes easily translate across cultures. Each student provided a slightly different interpretation of the tails, and these interpretations were firmly rooted in each student's lived experience. As readers "assimilate" visual cues (Pulverness 78), the protagonist's world opens to wide interpretation. (It is interesting to note that despite the wide variety of readings students offered of the dragon tails, no one argued that they conveyed a happy message.) By sharing their unique interpretations, our students modeled how readers provide depth of meaning and "give voice" to the world Tan's silent protagonist inhabits.

Another masked scene occurs in the latter part of *The Arrival* and features a land of rolling hills outside the cities of the protagonist's "new world." This setting features an object that students describe as a sun, a star, or a wheel. Many of the "suns" appear to rise out of the hills and plains on pages 98–99, and again on page 101. It is impossible for readers to know exactly what these sun/star/wheels really are, but because Tan has so carefully constructed the narrative's visual landscape, our students intuit that these objects are a foil for the earlier, more ominous dragon tails. The serrated shapes of the sun/star/wheels mimic the curling, serrated tails of the "dragons," but while the dragon tails are depicted as terrestrial and menacing, the sun/star/wheels are bright and buoyant. This contrast illuminates the emotional realities of the protagonist's journey. Indeed, it is *because* of objects that populate the settings around the characters that the reader comes to understand the emotional resonance of the protagonist's—and the reader's own—arrival to a light-filled space full of possibility. The illustrations of the protagonist can provide clues through physical gesture and facial expression, but it is the masked context that surrounds the protagonist that invites the reader to interpret the full canvas of nuanced, psychological character development.

When we studied *The Arrival* in English 2367, students were initially drawn to the most obvious details within the panels (e.g., dragon tails), but upon further analysis the text offered many subtler background and setting details to parse. For example, throughout the book, Tan employs visual cues at edges of his panels and on panel pages to highlight moments when the narrative passes from the protagonist into the hands of another character. These special pages frame moments of exchange that seem to manifest a commentary *at the margins* of the panels. Among these transitional exchanges in character's point of view, we have already begun to discuss the sixty-fifth page of Tan's text where the protagonist is befriended by a man and his son. In this visual sequence, the protagonist draws a picture of his homeland, which is exemplified by simple houses overshadowed by a sinister dragon tail. The man in the white shirt and suspenders seems to understand something fundamental from this drawing, and in images 65.8–11 each panel focuses more tightly on his face until in 65.11 the reader sees only the man's eye and the reflection of fire against the iris. Then on pages 66 through 72, the text gives this man's backstory.

This secondary character's narrative is so artfully drawn that readers may focus only on the action-packed story without noticing what is happening in the visual space that surrounds the main plot. It was only upon closer inspection that one student asked, "Did anyone notice how the pages change colors here?" Some students had noticed; some had not. But once the fact was voiced students quickly recognized a visual pattern wherein different color frames mark transitions into a secondary character's story. We use the term "frame" to identify the border that frames story background (housing secondary character sequences or backstory). Such frames may also be considered "boundary spaces." Frames in the escape narrative section stand out because each story panel is housed within a black boundary space. In addition, several of the framed panels in this section (example 69.1) have the *trompe l'oeil* appearance of wrinkled and worn photographs.

As soon as this framing cue was noted, the students began to question the significance of frames and panel colors, working to classify their experience of the wordless narrative. What we discovered, upon closer investigation, was that the backstory of the young girl working in the factory (55–57) appears to be framed on light gray pages. The backstory featuring the vacuum-wielding giants appears framed on the aforementioned black pages. The final secondary character narrative context, that of the soldier returning from war (89–95), appears as dark panels framed by rumpled white boundaries, approximating the look of a scrapbook. Further, students noticed how the white panels look like aged paper; these panels have the appearance of scrap papers affixed within gray and sepia-toned frames. The twice-bordered story panels themselves are like pencil etchings with a rough, cross-hatch pattern that evokes diminished memory or the haze of war and settings within the panel grow progressively darker. This multi-layered framing acts as a spatial storytelling device that provides resonance for story panels—frames contextualize and carry meaning such as sentimentality (e.g., Ellis Island-themed immigrant pictures), in so doing deepening the text's emotional impact (e.g., the degraded, irregular borders of the young girl's "furnace" sequence), forming a type of commentary without words, and conveying atmospheric aspects of story within the larger graphic narrative.

Our discussions focused exhaustively on these spatial storytelling devices. Students wanted to know both the purpose of and the meaning behind different frames. Why, they asked, were all secondary stories not pictured within the same colored frame? What sense could be made of differences in panel coloration? They agreed that all three of the secondary characters' stories featured images of oppression, from forced labor to engagements in times of war, and they wondered aloud if it were possible to rank the different kinds of oppression depicted in each. Based on feedback from students, we assert simply that questions about spatial storytelling devices are significant and that they play a large, if subtle, role in the ways readers analyze *The Arrival*.

While the questions the students raised offer no concrete answers, it is significant that spatial storytelling devices outlined in our study do generate keen interpretive curiosity. Comics scholar Christophe Dony asserts that the fragmented layout of Tan's narrative corresponds to a "multiplicity of voices" and that inherent in this form is a suggestion that the "whole" (the page) can only be thought of "in terms of its various parts or fragments" (panels, localities). This reading of Tan's narrative corresponds to how our students worked to situate themselves within the narrative and how they labored to parse meaning and significance from all the visual cues before them. As suggested earlier, the contexts surrounding the panels offered ample opportunity for interpretation. For instance, after noticing the significance of coloration on bordering spaces, students began to notice other visual cues: including tears and stains that made the panels resemble worn photographs, panels that appeared to be crumpled pages, and even soft, mottled borders (such as on the last page of the story where the young girl directs a newcomer with a map toward an unknown direction beyond the book's boundary). Indeed, the students continued to see greater visual complexity in Tan's illustrations, and it is a testament to Tan's artistry that even small patterns of visual detail are able to offer significant opportunity for interpretation. *The Arrival* rewards the reader who lingers and looks longer.

## Spatial Storytelling, Masking, and the Classroom: Looking Back and Looking Ahead

Tan designs visual spaces that endlessly challenge the "inquiring mind" that Ernest H. Gombrich describes in *Art and Illusion* as "[knowing] how to probe the ambiguities of vision" (264). Our students report that reviewing and rereading *The Arrival* produces "ever-new insights" and "connections" that lead them to modify former interpretations: this negotiation process, arguably, approximates Jean Piaget's process of assimilation and accommodation (Wood 106). Alan Pulverness, in his review of Arizpe, Colomer, and Martinez-Roldán's *Visual Journeys through Wordless Narratives*, asserts that the data demonstrate, again and again, "the way in which the textual indeterminacy of a wordless narrative offers children a peculiarly rich and suggestive ground, both for articulating their own experience and for empathetic understanding of the experience of others" (79). W. J. T. Mitchell further asserts that more clearly than any other use of the eyes, "wrestling with a work of visual art reveals how active a task of shape-building is involved in what goes by the simple names of 'seeing' or 'looking'" (36). Readers of visual narratives will want to test their skills in articulation and literary interpretation. Upon revisiting Tan's *The Arrival*, they will be delighted to find that new readings yield fresh insights.

In today's test-hungry educational milieu we suggest, first, that graphic narratives may foster the development of "vision" (itself a function of intelligence) and "perception" (a cognitive event) and that, as Will Eisner suggests, "interpretation and meaning are an indivisible aspect of seeing" (foreword to Arnheim's *Visual Thinking*; quoted in Arizpe and Styles 35). Second, we propose that use of Tan's visual narrative in teaching adolescents fulfills the National Council of Teachers of English Executive Board's call, issued in 2005, for students to learn "different modes of expression." NCTE's William Kist declared that young students should be able to read critically and write functionally "no matter what the medium." We cite Kist's dictum now because his words apply to readers across the age spectrum, and because the NCTE publication seems as fresh today as a decade ago. He writes (in words that strike at the heart of what Tan does in *The Arrival*): "Has there ever been a time when we have not been awash in a remarkable torrent of symbols and opportunities for reading and writing them?" Our research indicates that study of visual works may function as an essential component of knowing. Beyond helping students acquire much needed skills in visual literacy, lively discussion of wordless narratives further empowers students to learn and practice skills, especially how to build cogent literary interpretations.

There is not space in this chapter to fully develop all the ways in which *The Arrival*'s settings are masked. We suggest that historical and cultural lenses seem apropos for study of Tan's work, and have only begun to explore these lenses here. At the time he authored *The Arrival*, Shaun Tan was reading broadly and reviewing historical photographs (see, for example, the "Artist's Note" at the end of the book). Jerry Griswold asserts in his review that "for teens keen on manga," Shaun Tan's novel resides "at the top of the top." Comics scholar and historian Jared Gardner adds his idea that a precedent for our theory of masked backgrounds may be investigated in Japanese manga. In conversation, he told us that these ideas of masking brought to mind the art

| Table 1. Spatial Storytelling and Masking: Directions for Future Study |
| --- |
| 1. Shedding light on persistent stereotypes. |
| 2. Lending voice to the marginalized. |
| 3. Encouraging readers to question their own perceptions. |
| 4. Examining socio-political and economic disparities/realities. |
| 5. Seeing difficulties in assimilation or navigating across cultures (symbols, language, and customs). |
| 6. Highlighting the horrors of war and displacement. |
| 7. Enacting societal traditions—including family, friendship and camaraderie, etc. |

of Fumi Yoshinaga. Gardner followed up in an email, explaining that "many manga leave backgrounds largely underdeveloped or even blank for extended sections." He asserts, "This is by no means universally so (some is invested in very photorealistic backgrounds, often photo referenced), but it is frequent enough to have come to mind when we were first talking [about masking and backgrounds]." An investigation of the ways masking works in blank or under-developed backgrounds would be fascinating, especially because the spare manga backgrounds Gardner mentions are as much a means to invite the reader into a text as are the unsettling, highly detailed backgrounds in Tan's work. Researchers and comics historians may want to test our hypotheses and more fully explore and develop a theory of masked backgrounds. We encourage scholarship that bridges into related studies.

Studying graphic narratives for evidence of masked backgrounds and settings surely will produce rich and viable research efforts. Marjorie Allison's treatment of Marjane Satrapi's *Persepolis*, "(Not) Lost in the Margins: Gender and Identity in Graphic Texts" (*Mosaic*, 2014), for example, poses useful questions about framing and pictures in graphic narratives, such as "Who takes pictures?" "In what contexts?" and "In what role?" (81). In keeping with our discussion of frames and spatial storytelling devices, Allison identifies a selective type of framing that Satrapi uses (e.g., the father's Polaroid images strewn on a table) where readers must "step outside the normal boundaries of passively viewing" (81) to assess and engage more actively in the graphic narrative. In the short term, we look forward to seeing more comics scholarship in this vein.

Beyond questions of history, culture, gender and identity, future researchers may want to explore our spatial storytelling and masking arguments to assess how Tan's visual narratives apply, more broadly speaking, to international readers, to readers of different ages, to marginalized groups, and other populations. Among questions teachers may want to explore with their students or theorists may want to investigate in future publications, we propose a handful of possible directions in table 1. New studies may also want to explore the relationship of masked settings to the way in which Tan juxtaposes the familiar and the fantastical. *The Arrival* works so effectively because the reader is grounded in background images that are just recognizable enough to be familiar.[10] We contend that this juxtaposition is strategic.[11] Tan's narrative takes place in a world that shares many similarities with our own, especially in terms of human interactions, but the places that these humans inhabit are ones that the reader, too, must decode.

Looking ahead, we anticipate further study into the creative processes of graphic storytellers and visual artists. Researchers may want to investigate how the use of metaphor in *The Arrival* extends beyond the realm of what Lynd Ward (*Storyteller Without Words*) has termed the "purely visual" (77). We see potential for teachers to develop new exercises and collaborative activities, especially based on masking theory, that explore and help readers understand Tan's backgrounds while improving literacy and critical thinking skills. Above all, we affirm that sometimes the most profound insights about graphic narratives come from readers themselves.

## Notes

1. Tan explains in his companion text and sequel to *The Arrival, Sketches from a Nameless Land* (2010), that the portrait galleries on the cover flaps of The Arrival are directly inspired from actual photographs of migrants from the Ellis Island archives. In addition to archival photographs, Tan says he also includes a reworking of his father's passport picture on the cover-flaps. In this context, Christophe Dony discusses how "[Tan] affirms the importance of the personal and the familial into the collective. He brings different histories into relief, proposes different kinds of narratives, mixes the personal with the historical, and intersperses his (post) memory with that of other people."

2. Because *The Arrival* does not contain page numbers, we propose a numbering system that begins on the first page of the primary visual story. Page 1, as we are counting, is the right-hand page following the numeral "I," featuring nine small square images arranged in a grid. (The first row pictures an origami bird, a clock and a hat hanging from a peg.)

3. Award-winning graphic novelist, David Small, was so taken with Tan's work as a graphic artist in *The Arrival* that he incongruously proclaimed it "a major new literary genre" (see www.thearrival.com.au).

4. One is an inspection card for 23 March 1912, for the ship Caledonia, and passenger Bedane Breilman, whose last residence is listed as "Nikoleff," and landing in an unnamed American port. The traveler is instructed to attach the card to clothing to assist inspection. Another scrap of ID at the bottom of the page says, "ANMERKUNG UWAGA," and post locale "Urodzenia." One is of the translations from the German for "Anmerkungen" is "a place for notes." From the Polish, "Urodzenia" translates to "short/abridged copy of birth certificate."

5. See <http://shauntan.net/books/Sketches.html >. Tan published this book as a companion volume to *The Arrival*. It comprises fifty pages of Tan's preliminary sketches, research materials and commentary on the evolution of the project. It is currently part of a special boxed edition of *The Arrival* produced by Hachette Australia, from September 2010. In the deluxe collector's

edition, both books are innovatively housed within a suitcase (vintage worn and stained interior) with travel luggage tag and strap. For further information about the special editions, or to see more about Tan's artwork and ideas related to *The Arrival*, visit http://www.thearrival.com.au/.

6. Hayley Kick, Personal Communication. Email. August 2014.

7. Readers looking for a more comprehensive literature review should consult pages 17–52 of Evelyn Arizpe and Morag Styles's definitive publication on how children interpret visual texts (*Children Reading Pictures*, 2003). We also recommend the last two chapters of Evelyn Arizpe, Maureen Farrell, and Julie McAdam's essay collection *Picture Books: Beyond the Borders of Art, Narrative and Culture* (2013).

8. A helpful treatment of this type of student reading and associated exercises has been published by Maureen Bakis in *The Graphic Novel Classroom* (2012). See pages 14–31, where she introduces teachable concepts and skills based on Scott McCloud's *Understanding Comics* (see p. 16) and follows with her lesson based on "Interpreting Images" by juxtaposing study of Tan's *The Arrival* with Rachel Masilimani's *Two Kinds of People* and Gene Luen Yang's *American Born Chinese* (chapter 2, pp. 31–49). Chapter 2 focuses on student responses, as well as introduces how to question texts and defend interpretations in what Bakis calls "The Spectrum of Interpretation" (38).

9. We suggest that teachers may use Katie Monnin's comics vocabulary to help students engage in more focused class discussion of Tan's graphic narrative. Her *Teaching Early Readers Comics and Graphic Novels* (2013) introduces a vocabulary for story panels such as these. For example, the panels in which the dragon tails occur could be interpreted as "symbols panels," which, in Monnin's definition, contain "images and/or words that represent something larger than themselves."

10. Scholars have yet to fully explore and interpret the fantastical and familiar elements of Tan's visual narrative. Tan writes in his Artist's Note at the end of *The Arrival*, for example, that he sometimes draws inspiration from iconic historical images and period photos such as those of Ellis Island. Tan's characters in the old world and in the new engage in familiar behaviors (in the "new world" people still eat, even if the food looks different). This grounding in the familiar allows the reader to feel confident in making meaning out of the protagonist's journey even as the backgrounds contain tee pee-like structures and flying ships (51); in the Cinque Terre-esque seaside village ordinary laundry hangs from windows but the entire scene is overlooked by giant owl-like sentinels that are many times larger than the buildings themselves (74). Meantime, students have offered fascinating interpretations using the historical lens, such as one student's theory about the song "Waltzing Matilda" and the Battle of Gallipoli and their application to Tan's narrative (see p. 8, Kurkjian and Kara-Soteriou).

11. Because of this carefully constructed juxtaposition, the reader is able to engage in a journey not unlike the protagonist's, encountering unreadable words, unrecognizable foods, and inscrutable forms of public transportation. The fantastical elements of the masked backgrounds allow space for more creative engagement with the text than do graphic novels with completely realistic backgrounds.

# Works Cited

Allison, Marjorie. "(Not) Lost in the Margins: Gender and Identity in Graphic Texts." *Mosaic* 47.4 (2014): 73–97. Print.

Arizpe, Evelyn, Maureen Farrell, and Julie McAdam, eds. *Picture Books: Beyond the Borders of Art, Narrative and Culture*. London: Routledge, 2013. Print.

Arizpe, Evelyn, and Morag Styles. *Children Reading Pictures: Interpreting Visual Texts.* London and New York: RoutledgeFalmer, 2003. Print.

Arizpe, Evelyn, Teresa Colomer, and Carmen Martinez-Roldán. *Visual Journeys through Wordless Narratives: An International Enquiry with Immigrant Children and 'The Arrival.'* London: Bloomsbury, 2014. Print.

Arnheim, Rudolf. *Visual Thinking.* Will Eisner, Foreword. London: Faber, 1970. Print.

Bakis, Maureen. *The Graphic Novel Classroom.* New York: Skyhorse Publishing, 2014. Print.

Berger, John. *Ways of Seeing.* London: Penguin, 1977. Print.

Clark, Kenneth. *Looking at Pictures.* London: John McMurray, 1960. Print.

Dony, Christophe. "Moving Between Worlds: *The Arrival.*" *Comics Forum.* 23 January 2012. Web. 6 May 2015.

Eisner, Will. *Graphic Storytelling and Visual Narrative.* Rev. ed. 2008. New York: W. W. Norton, 2005. Print.

Gardner, Jared. Personal Interview. 26 April 2015.

——. Personal Interview. 2 June 2015.

Gombrich, Ernest H. *Art and Illusion.* London: Phaidon Press, 1962. Print.

Griswold, Jerry. "Shaun Tan and the Graphic Novel." *Parents' Choice.* 22 June 2015. Web.

Kick, Hayley. "Response to Reading Shaun Tan's *The Arrival.*" Personal Communication. 18 August 2014.

Kurkjian, Catherine, and Julia Kara-Soteriou. "Insights into Negotiating Shaun Tan's *The Arrival* Using a Literature Cyberlesson." *SANE Journal: Sequential Art Narrative in Education* 1.3 (2013): np. Web. 8 August 2014.

McCloud, Scott. *Understanding Comics: The Invisible Art.* New York: Harper Perennial, 1994. Print.

McGurk, Caitlin. Personal Interview. 10 April 2015.

Mitchell, W. J. T. *Iconology: Image, Text and Ideology.* Chicago: University of Chicago Press, 1986. Print.

Monnin, Katie. *Teaching Early Reader Comics and Graphic Novels.* Gainesville, FL: Maupin House, 2013. Print.

National Council of Teachers of English. *Position Statement on Mulimodal Literacies.* NCTE Executive Committee. 2005. Web. 30 August 2014.

Perkins, David. *The Intelligent Eye: Learning to Think by Looking at Art.* Cambridge, MA: Harvard Graduate School of Education, 1994. Print.

Pulverness, Alan. Rev. of *Visual Journeys through Wordless Narratives: An International Enquiry with Immigrant Children and "The Arrival."* Eds. Evelyn Arizpe, Teresa Colomer, and Carmen Martinez-Roldán. *Children's Literature in English Language Education.* 2.2 (2014): 78–82. Web. 4 May 2015.

Raney, Karen. *Visual Literacy: Issues and Debates.* London: Middlesex University, School of Education, 1997. Print.

Tan, Shaun. Foreword. *Visual Journeys through Wordless Narratives: An International Enquiry with Immigrant Children and "The Arrival."* Eds. Evelyn Arizpe, Teresa Colomer, and Carmen Martinez-Roldán. London: Bloomsbury, 2014. Print.

——. *The Arrival.* New York: Arthur A Levine Books, 2007. Print.

——. *Lost and Found: Three by Shaun Tan.* New York: Arthur A Levine Books, 2011. Print.

——. *Sketches from a Nameless Land.* 2012. Melbourne: Lothian Children's Books. Print.

——. *Tales from Outer Suburbia.* New York: Arthur A Levine Books, 2007. Print.

Ward, Lynd. *Storyteller Without Words.* New York: Harry N. Abrams: 1974. Print.

Wood, David. *How Children Think and Learn.* London: Blackwell, 1998. Print.

# Suggested Resources for Teachers

Arizpe, Evelyn, Maureen Farrell, and Julie McAdam, eds. *Picture Books: Beyond the Borders of Art, Narrative and Culture*. London: Routledge, 2013. Print.

Arizpe, Evelyn, and Morag Styles. *Children Reading Pictures: Interpreting Visual Texts*. London and New York: RoutledgeFalmer, 2003. Print.

Arizpe, Evelyn, Teresa Colomer, and Carmen Martinez-Roldán. *Visual Journeys through Wordless Narratives: An International Enquiry with Immigrant Children and "The Arrival."* London: Bloomsbury, 2014. Print.

Cohn, Neil. "Un-Defining 'Comics': Separating the Cultural from the Structural in Comics." *International Journal of Comic Art* 7.2 (2005): 236–48. Print.

Eisner, Will. *Comics and Sequential Art*. Rev. ed. 2008. New York: WW Norton, 1985. Print.

———. *Graphic Storytelling and Visual Narrative*. Rev. ed. 2008. New York: W. W. Norton, 2007. Print.

Kurkjian, Catherine, and Julia Kara-Soteriou. "Insights into Negotiating Shaun Tan's *The Arrival* Using a Literature Cyberlesson." *SANE Journal: Sequential Art Narrative in Education* 1.3 (2013): np. Web. 8 August 2014.

Madden, Matt. *99 Ways to Tell a Story*. New York: Chamberlain Bros., 2005. Print.

McCloud, Scott. *Understanding Comics: The Invisible Art*. New York: Harper Perennial, 1993. Print.

Monnin, Katie. *Teaching Early Reader Comics and Graphic Novels*. Gainesville, FL: Maupin House, 2013. Print.

———. *Teaching Graphic Novels: Practical Strategies for the Secondary ELA Classroom*. Gainesville, FL: Maupin House, 2013. Print.

———. *Using Content-Area Graphic Texts for Learning: A Guide for Middle-Level Educators*. Gainesville, FL: Maupin House, 2013. Print.

Monnin, Katie, and Rachel Bowman. *Teaching Reading Comprehension with Graphic Texts: An Illustrated Adventure*. Gainesville, FL: Maupin House, 2013. Print.

Stein, Daniel, and Jan-Noël Thon, eds. "Introduction." *From Comic Strips to Graphic Novels: Contributions to the Theory and History of Graphic Narrative*. Berlin/Boston: Walter de Gruyter, 2013. 1–23. Print.

Walker, George A., ed. *Graphic Witness: Four Wordless Graphic Novels by Frans Masereel, Lynd Ward, Giacomo Patri, and Laurence Hyde*. Buffalo, NY: Firefly Books, 2007. Print.

# 11

# When Young Writers Draw Their Voices: Creating Hybrid Comic Memoirs with *The Absolutely True Diary of a Part-Time Indian*

*Michael L. Kersulov, Mary Beth Hines, and Rebecca Rupert*

> I draw because words are too unpredictable.
> I draw because words are too limited.
> If you speak and write in English, or Spanish, or Chinese, or any other language, then only a certain percentage of human beings will get your meaning.
> But when you draw a picture, everybody can understand it.
> —**Sherman Alexie**, *The Absolutely True Diary of a Part-Time Indian*

Graphic novels are the fastest growing category of young adult literature today, only relatively recently gaining acclaim as part of our literary tradition and literacy curricula (Brozo, Morman, and Meyer 6). In the twentieth century, comics texts were relegated to the margins or dismissed by critics who claimed that comics used simplistic plots, limited written text, and flat characters, thus requiring minimal literacy skills (Bitz 2). Naysayers argued that these texts valorized sex and violence and thus were inappropriate for schools. In addition, reading these texts did not prepare students for the rigors that awaited them either in higher education or in the workplace (Bitz 2; Pagliaro 32). Hence, comics merited a place in literary annals and in schools only because they served struggling readers, providing a stepping stone to the more complex texts of the canon and/or traditional curricula (Bitz 4; Hammond 25).

These longstanding views are currently being challenged by a variety of teachers, librarians, and literary critics who argue the value of comics for students of all ability levels, content areas, and purposes (Jaffe; Brozo, Moorman, and Meyer 22; Gavigan and Tomasevich 7; Jenkins and Detamore 16). Furthermore, focusing on comics in the classroom encourages visual literacy skills and provides development of verbal skills, self-expression, motivation, comfort with self-image, and confidence in literacy (Jaffe; Simon 519–21; Whitlock and Poletti, xix).

Although enthusiasm about using comics in the classroom is a relatively recent phenomenon, teachers can find excellent educational resources, including course descriptions, pedagogical strategies, curricula guides, instructional resources, Common Core standard alignments, assessments, and testimonials about student learning (Brozo, Moorman, and Meyer 9–10, 131–35; Gavigan and Tomasevich 47–158; Jenkins and Dentamore 23–127; Monnin 15–132; Novak 23–150). To further our understanding of the impact of comics on student learning, the field also needs empirical research that renders fine-grained portraitures of teaching and learning with comics. This chapter attempts to fill the gap in research by showcasing the dynamics of one English classroom studying comics.

In our former roles as secondary English teachers and our current roles as researchers, we have witnessed the affordances of using comics in the classroom. In this chapter, we aim to illuminate the value of comics by focusing on one ninth-grade student's response to Sherman Alexie's hybrid text, *The Absolutely True Diary of a Part-Time Indian*. The narrative combines Alexie's conventional prose writing with comics illustrations by Ellen Forney, so that the book is neither completely verbal nor wholly visual, but an integration of the two. Although *True Diary* has garnered multiple awards-including the 2007 National Book Award for Young People's Literature-it also has been the subject of controversy (Dicker). In April of 2014, one school district in Idaho, for example, removed it from the curriculum when community members labeled images and references to masturbation as pornographic and depictions of poverty-stricken Native Americans as racist (Roberts). After an outcry from parents and teachers, the school district returned the book to English classrooms with several restrictions: that parents would have to provide consent for children to read the book; that the book would only be used in small groups, and that it would not be read aloud to the whole class. These policies were designed to prevent children without permission from hearing the book. Furthermore, this event was not an isolated incident of censorship. In fact, the book appeared on the American Library Association's list of 2014 banned books after ranking in the top five from 2011–2013 (Missing). *True Diary* offers powerful verbal and visual depictions of the protagonist's struggles with identity, poverty, race, bullying, and peer acceptance. As such, it provides access to issues that are salient not only to young adult readers, but also to the wider community.

It was the potential appeal of the text to young adults that had prompted coauthor and high school English teacher Rebecca Rupert, or Becky, as her students called her, to select Alexie's text for use in her classroom. Becky was a National Board Certified teacher with fifteen years of teaching experience, and she recognized that *True Diary* embodied an exemplary hybrid text that would be of interest to students. After reading *True Diary*, she invited students to write coming-of-age memoirs consisting of three prose vignettes accompanied by three comics that elaborated on them. Becky chose the genre not only so that students could tell their stories, but also so that they could articulate what they had learned from their experiences.

In examining how students used Alexie's semi-autobiographical work as a springboard for creating comics, we argue that while using *True Diary* and the hybrid comics medium in the classroom, Becky's students were able to gain voice, signify vulnerability, and convey nuanced understandings of distressing and emotionally charged topics in their lives-elements that were not conveyed in other course work or even in the prose vignette memoirs. In order to make this case, this chapter focuses on the work of one student in the class, Harper. Before turning to Harper's work, we present a brief look at the text and an overview of the larger study.

## Connecting Themes of *True Diary* to the Classroom

In an interview with National Public Radio, Sherman Alexie describes *True Diary* as "an immigrant story . . . an indigenous kid who's an immigrant in the United States . . . [searching] for identity" (Montagne). This coming-of-age YA novel, which combines diary entries with a variety of drawings, delves into the life of Junior, a teenage Spokane Indian, and his struggles with identity, poverty, and discrimination. While Junior is a fictional character, he shares commonalities with Alexie, who, like Junior, was diagnosed as a child with hydrocephalus (born with too much fluid in the head), experienced poverty, and attended an inadequately funded school on the Spokane Reservation (Montagne). Junior's struggle with self-esteem is apparent from the beginning when he writes in his diary, "I am a zero on the rez. And if you subtract zero from zero, you still have zero" (Alexie 16). Furthermore, his family's fight with alcoholism and generational poverty fuel his lack of self-confidence. As Junior puts it, "My parents came from poor people who came from poor people who came from poor people, all the way back to the very first poor people" (11). As a result of this generational struggle, Junior's parents are depressed, lack education, and have difficulty putting food on the table. At school, Junior is bullied because of his appearance, his lisp, and his occasional seizures. Moreover, his struggles at school are compounded by a lack of diversity on the school's faculty. After being told by a teacher on the reservation that "we were supposed to make you give up being Indian. . . . We weren't trying kill Indian people. We were trying to kill Indian culture" (35), Junior decides to leave the reservation school and attend a predominantly white school in a neighboring town. While hoping the school transfer would improve his quality of life, Junior finds out that his difficulties with identity, poverty, and racism resurface in new ways, limiting his prospects of ever escaping the social inequalities he endures. Throughout the semi-autobiographical novel, Alexie depicts what may seem like an extraordinary tale. However, the strength in the work lies within the real world obstacles that resonate with Alexie's young readers who see themselves in the text-the same young readers in Becky's class who, like Junior, find their lives to be complicated by low self-esteem, school transfers, and discrimination.

## The Larger Study

This chapter has been culled from a qualitative case study that explored the ways in which students produced texts and identities in Becky's classroom at Last Chance High (pseudonym), a school that could be described as an alternative to expulsion for many of the students who transferred in from other schools. The data set collected and analyzed in preparation for writing this chapter consisted of the entire class set of memoirs and comics created by the English 9–10 class, handouts, interviews with six students about the unit, Becky's teaching notebook, observations, and the other two researchers' twice weekly observations and field notes. We began by analyzing data to establish preliminary categories and then added data to test and refine the early categories. This process, what researchers refer to as the constant comparative method, involved a recurring process of analyzing additional data, tweaking provisional categories, and attempting to discern relationships across the patterns (Creswell 86). One researcher completed a content analysis of the memoirs to identify recurring patterns across the class set. We then recursively examined the data in light of those patterns, attempting to explain the themes generated by the content analysis. We also re-examined the focal student's work in light of the content analysis. Using axial coding to discern relationships among codes and categories, we developed provisional hypotheses as we attempted to reconcile tensions across the data set (Charmaz 60–63). In the next section, we situate our study within and against related literacy research.

## Multiliteracies, Multiple Identities, and Transmediation:
## *True Diary* in Becky's Classroom

Working within a sociocultural framework, we regard texts and identities as social and discursive constructs, produced within particular social contexts that are animated by the interplay of social, economic, and political systems at work in the larger society (Lewis, Enciso, and Moje xi). Advocates for using comics in the classroom articulate the ways in which the production and interpretation of verbal and visual media require forms of literacy that go beyond the deciphering of print-based texts. These multimodal texts involve flows of information across several mediums (i.e., music, print, and graphics). Learners producing and responding to multimodal texts harness literacy practices that extend beyond print—sharpening visual, audio, and kinesthetic skills that contribute to the development of students' multiple literacies, or multi-literacies (New London Group 61). The notion of multiliteracies is frequently referenced in discussions regarding the twenty-first-century digital media skills that students need to be successful in the near future (Hull and Nelson 225).

Well before the emergence of digital media, experts argued that teachers should enrich student comprehension and encourage creativity by inviting students to express meaning in ways other than standard written responses. They argued for transmediation, the process of converting messages or texts in one sign system to another. The pedagogical strategies built on transmediation are still valuable today as they enrich student understanding of text and showcase students' abilities in art, dance, drama, and music (Leland and Harste 384). Marjorie Siegel argues that transmediation became an important aspect of digital practices. "What was important about . . . transmediation was the idea that moving across sign systems was a generative process that could produce new meanings" (70). In other words, the use of multiple sign systems requires audience members to reconcile meanings that can never be exactly the same because there is no absolute one-to-one correspondence between a sound and a picture and a word. Thus, "when a learner moves from one sign system to another, semiosis becomes even more complex . . . and the two different sign systems create an anomaly that sets generative thinking in motion" (70).

Comics serve as the catalyst for generative thinking because they require readers to interpret visual and linguistic cues that typically work interdependently to create meaning. With comics, readers view interdependent narratives expressed in verbal and visual modes, and the reader must negotiate the intertextuality of the two in order for the text as a whole to make sense (Jacobs 7). The total effect of the two modes generates what Lawrence Sipe calls "text-picture synergy" (27). In order to produce meanings, readers need to draw on print and visual interpretative strategies, reinforcing the importance of multiliteracies in contemporary classrooms. While some scholars have argued that comics can help struggling readers,[1] we argue that the affordances of multimodality make comics beneficial for all students as they learn to construct meanings from simultaneous informational flows with digital media (Bakis 4–5; Jaffe).

By combining his prose text with Forney's illustrations, Alexie weaves evidence of transmediation throughout *True Diary*. Additionally, as Junior's diary, the prose and images are not only mediums to tell the story, but they are to be products of Junior's own hand and creativity. As such, Junior enhances his narrative by intertwining multiple flows of communication, juxtaposing written text with images for multiple purposes. At times, Junior's comics depict events as they actually happen, while many of Junior's drawings invoke his fantasies and situational irony. For example, Junior's drawing of his best friend from the reservation, Rowdy, depicts him with two competing faces: a contemplative Rowdy calmly reading comics, superimposed with an overly embellished caricature erratically yelling at Junior, "What're you drawing??" (Alexie 23). The image demonstrates how Junior sees through Rowdy's tough exterior, perceiving a softer personality that others do not recognize. Junior writes on the same page of the image, "[Rowdy] loves my cartoons. . . . So I draw cartoons to make him happy, to give him other worlds to live inside" (23). Here, Junior produces and comprehends multiple streams of information simultaneously, creating a highly rich message about his friend's identity.

## Background and Context

Last Chance High was an alternative middle and high school that served students who had not been successful in the three mainstream schools in town. Some administrators from those schools had previously given their unsuccessful students the option to attend Last Chance High or face expulsion, so many students entered the school with behavior problems, anger management issues, and disdain for traditional school settings. Others chose to attend because they preferred smaller classes and wanted more support from teachers. At the beginning of the 2013–14 school year, 90 percent of Becky's English (9–10) students entered the class reading at below grade level (as determined by NWEA measures).

In the next section, we introduce our focal student, Harper. From there we describe her three memoir vignettes and the accompanying comics before presenting our data analysis.

## Harper

Harper was a 9th grader at Last Chance High, enrolled in a 9–10 level language arts course. As a Caucasian young adult with free/reduced lunch status, Harper was at a sixth grade reading level and was also enrolled in a reading support class. While bright, she frequently attempted to hide it in front of her peers. With a father in prison and a mother in and out of jail during the past year, she lived with an aunt in a household of ten other family members. She was sent to Last Chance High as a middle school student because she had a history of conflict with teachers and administrators. We selected her as a case study participant because she was loud, unruly, and angry; we wanted to understand her practices of engagement and disengagement in Becky's class.

At the beginning of the year, Harper actively and very vocally resisted academic tasks and authority. She was removed from the classroom on several occasions and suspended twice. She slowly began to apply herself to her schoolwork after her best friend was expelled from school for similar behavior. As a learner, Harper expected (and received) a great deal of individual attention and feedback from her teachers. In class she asked many questions and consulted her teacher while she worked to ensure that what she was doing was "right."

## Becky's Rationale for the Assignment

Becky chose *True Diary* because she thought many of her students would be able to relate to the struggles of the protagonist. Like Junior, Becky's students had struggled with bullying, low economic households, parents' substance abuse, racism, and systemic marginalization in their previous schools. Becky hoped that students would be drawn to these salient experiences and would be open to discuss the novel's themes of identity, poverty, and discrimination. Likewise, she hoped that Alexie's novel, with its humorous take on real world coming-of-age struggles and its semi-autobiographical nature, would serve as a model for students when writing about their own experiences. After completing the book, all the students were required to create a memoir, an assignment labeled, "Who I Am as a Learner." Becky wanted to incorporate comics and illustrations in students' reading and writing because many of her students, though not avid readers of traditional prose-only texts, had excelled at expressing themselves in visual mediums. Becky's intent was for students to connect with Junior through shared values and experiences. She then wanted students to replicate Junior's multimodal writing practices as a way to communicate and investigate their real world obstacles. As a multimodal practice, reading and creating hybrid comics would "allow for the expression of a much fuller range of human emotion and experience ... [that] acknowledge the limits of language, [and] admit the integrity of silence" (Stein 95). It would engage students in transmediation and would require students to demonstrate multiple literacies in the process. To complete their memoirs as a hybrid comic, students would have to utilize the stages and standards of the writing process (brainstorming, drafting, editing, etc.) while invoking parallel design skills in drawing and illustration.

## Harper's Prose Vignettes

One of the goals of the assignment was for students to develop an understanding of the literacy skills that they already possessed. Additionally, Becky wanted students to learn how comics could not only stand alone in storytelling, but also enhance the prose version of the accompanying vignette. The prose vignette and the comic were to work together to render a narrative that would be incomplete if one of the two modes were absent. Additionally, students replicated *True Diary*'s visual presentation of characters (avatars), such as when Junior draws his parents (Alexie 12), his grandmother (69), and himself (57). Students created avatars of themselves to introduce their hybrid comics, what Becky referred to as a visual "user's manual." They depicted themselves in the center of a page surrounded by words, phrases, and images that generated a full representation of who they were both inside and out. Drawing the self-portraits served as a brainstorming activity. Students formalized elements of their identity on the page that would fuel the next steps in writing their memoirs. Moreover, creating their avatars gave students time to become comfortable with the visual aspects of the project.

The prose text of Harper's hybrid comic follows the assignment's instructions by including an introduction, three vignettes, and a conclusion. Within the text itself she incorporates metaphors, similes, a logical structure, and other rhetorical devices to narrate her story. Following each prose section, Harper continues the narrative of the vignette with a comic, adding details and action to the plot.

When Harper was originally prompted to begin drawing, she, along with other students, proclaimed that she could not draw well. Becky anticipated that students would resist, but she did not want to delve into a complex discussion of drawing aesthetics that would intimidate her students even more; thus, she suggested they simply draw stick figures. As students progressed, many of the drawings, including Harper's, started with stick figures and matured into fuller, more detailed depictions. As her finished work indicates, Harper employs images that range from iconic to abstract, and she displays in her work perspective to depict distance, images as metaphors, and synesthetic lines. Additionally, while she mostly uses a standard waffle-grid panel structure, she includes bleeding and panel-within-panel manipulation. In general, Harper has a good grasp of the grammar of comics.

## Harper's Memoir

Harper introduces her memoir by addressing the plot and goals of each of her three short vignettes. The memoir, appropriately titled, "Then and Now," guides the reader through her experiences of change, from attending "Normalton" (pseudonym), the mainstream middle school she had attended before Last Chance High, to moving in with her aunt, changing schools, and becoming more mature and academically minded. Below her introduction on the same page, Harper depicts an avatar of herself smiling and wearing her typical school attire of a t-shirt, blue jeans, and flip flops. Over a hundred words

Fig. 11.1. Harper's "user manual": a self-portrait with accompanying phrases and images that Harper attributes to her identity.

surround her avatar, some linked to her body with an attaching line. The style of the picture is similar to the visual depiction of Junior's sister in *True Diary* (Alexie 27); both Harper's and Junior's drawings emphasize their subject's clothes, shoes, and neck tattoos. Harper's words describe her physical appearance: "glasses and mascara, nose pierced, tattoo, nails always painted, long curly hair." She also includes a variety of self-disclosed characteristics: "I'm good on catching on to something (emotions)," "patient, determined, hardheaded," and "I've been told I'm fun and easy to talk to." The medley of words, lines, and images circle around her avatar as she stands on the phrase, "I love my friends & family." On her chest, a line connects a heart to the phrase "being success-ful." Through the combination of images and text, Harper uses the avatar to introduce herself to the reader, leaving the prose portion of the introduction to outline the events of the memoir. Just as Becky intended, Junior's drawings of himself and family acted as effective scaffolding for Harper.

Like Junior, Harper illustrates her struggles at her former school, Normalton Junior High, with her first comic and prose vignette titled, "5 Reasons [Normalton] Saved My Education" (figure 11.2). The comic mim-ics the language and structure of the first prose vignette, referencing the five reasons that her first school experience was so alienating. Using *True Diary* as a mentor text, Harper structures the panels of first comic similarly to Alexie's "Are You Poor?" (128), with six panels, titling and numbering each sequentially. Harper's first panel displays the title of her comic, and the sec-ond, "Dropping Out," depicts Harper lying in bed, declaring, "I'm so bored I'm gonna go crazy!" A line connects the bed and computer to the narrative box. "This was my life when I didn't go to school," she explains from her bed. The second panel features Normalton as the Normalton Junior High Prison with students who are trapped behind barred windows. Here, Harper's character says, "Teachers and students were [too] high class for me." The third panel transitions to inside the school, showing a hallway crowded with students. A word balloon emanates from the bottom of the panel, signaling her inability to move: "Can't get to my classes." Harper does not depict herself in the hall-way, but out of the frame. The crowd of students in the corridor almost seems to crush Harper, piling on top of her, pushing her out of the panel. After a fourth panel, showing an empty cafeteria with a note about how the food smells like pickles and dirt, the final panel depicts Harper and her classmates, divided by a harsh, bold line. Her classmates are smiling and moving around within the top portion. A caption reads, "The whole school." Meanwhile, Harper stands alone in a vacant space frowning. To ensure that her readers recognize this figure as Harper, the word "Me" is above her. Harper's comic not only communicates her distress while at Normalton, but also her need to find a school where she feels welcomed, one that will improve her quality of life just as Junior does.

In four panels, the second comic highlights the benefits of moving in with her aunt (figure 11.3). The comic opens with Harper standing at a road that leads to her aunt's house, luminous rays extruding from the building. The next panel takes us inside the house as Harper and her cousin, Terrin, wake for

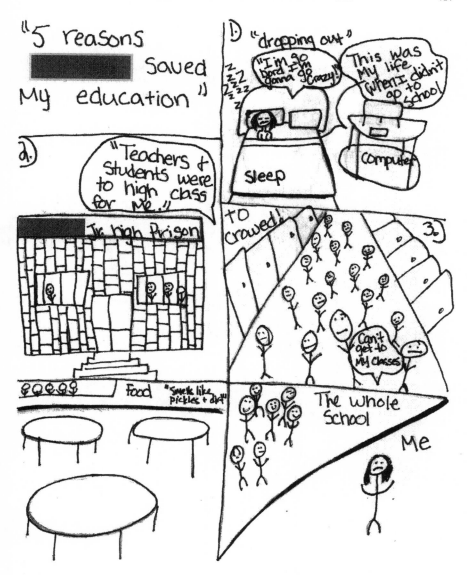

Fig. 11.2. Harper's first comic. "5 Reasons—Saved My Education."

school in the morning. The third panel shifts to a bull's head, representing her zodiac sign Taurus (a personal characteristic with which she strongly identifies). It hovers over a bulleted list, "determined, hardheaded, blunt, outgoing," that feeds into the image of a diploma with similar illuminating lines as the aunt's house. The last panel highlights Harper's goals: a diploma, college, and a graduation hat all float above her with lines attached to an image of her head.

Fig. 11.3. Harper's second comic

The third and final comic uses the same four-panel structure to address shifts in behavior and attitude regarding school (figure 11.4). However, she divides the first three panels into two smaller frames to establish a "then and now" transition. This divide reveals Harper's thoughts on her progression toward education. The bull's head returns with the caption, "I used to be this heated bull," contrasting with Harper's head below it, with the narration, "Now I'm cool, calm, collective [sic]." The following panel moves into the

Fig. 11.4. Harper's third comic.

classroom where Harper depicts herself resisting lessons and distracting her classmates. Harper contrasts this image with herself sitting alone at the same table, focusing on her assignment, saying, "Quiet." Harper demonstrates her dedication to attendance in the third panel, showing a group of students who "skip school and go smoke pot" next to a smiling Harper who is "over here getting my education on." The comic concludes with a panel showing an image of Harper's brain filled with text, "Don't be a dropout. Don't be like the rest of your [family]," as an illuminated high school diploma shines underneath it.

## Findings from the Study: Harper, the Brassy yet Vulnerable Student

Harper's memoir—the three hybrid comics with accompanying vignettes—renders versions of this student that were not apparent in class or in her other course work. In the classroom, Harper worked to present herself as tough, matter of fact, and willing to speak her mind. She routinely yelled out to Becky and at her friends as she stormed the classroom, burping loudly, slamming her books onto her desk, and announcing that she did not want to work. In the midst of quiet reading or writing time, she would impulsively blurt out her feelings, whether confused, mad, frustrated, or unable to proceed, until Becky could assist her. When she was tired and cranky, she threatened anyone who crossed her path. Early in the school year, Harper publicly derided a mixed race classmate who had shifted from her regular speech pattern to formal English usage when talking to a teacher by saying, "Look at you—trying to talk all white." During class and in the hallways, Harper seemed to present a durable exterior that protected her from what she referred to as "drama in the classroom." Defining this in an interview, she explained that she did not want conflicts or issues with peers: "I'm not the kind [of person] to take a lot of shit from people." And she did not.

The version of herself that Harper presents on the page, however, is not the brassy young woman that we saw in class. Her memoir and hybrid comics reveal a more vulnerable individual. In her vignette, "The Silver Lining," she attributes dropping out of middle school to excruciating experiences at Normalton Junior High: "This school made me so uncomfortable that I didn't even want to get up in the morning." Responding to the teachers and students, she describes herself as simultaneously isolated and exposed, a condition that she likens to being "naked in the middle of Times Square." These emotions telescope even more dramatically in the accompanying hybrid comic. As described earlier, Harper signals in her comic her emotional distress and social seclusion while at Normalton. The stark contrast between Harper and her peers brings the emotional pain she had endured during her days at Normalton into sharp relief. In interviews Harper corroborated our interpretation of her persona in the vignette comic series, explaining that, "It was really rough to adapt" to Normalton. Consequently, she skipped school, had behavior problems, and failed classes.

While we had witnessed Harper's social as well as academic struggles in the classroom on a daily basis, we had no inkling of the myriad emotions, negative prior experiences, and even personal trauma prompting it. She had been carrying with her the anxiety, anger, alienation, and emotional pain from her days at Normalton. In representing herself as a vulnerable individual who was not only capable of being hurt, but who had been hurt many times before,

Harper reveals experiences that shaped her sensibilities about school, aspects that none of us were aware of before.

During this unit, Becky noticed that Harper began to change. Harper turned in more of her class work. In addition, her behavior improved; she became less unruly. Becky attributed much of this transition to Harper's best friend being expelled from Last Chance High. Perhaps as a reaction to her friend leaving, Harper chose to reflect on her own experiences of dropping out and returning to school. In her vignette, "The Silver Lining," she reveals the reasons she left Normalton. Harper also emphasizes the consequences of dropping out, including a depressing image of herself, alone with no contact with others, literally bedridden with grief. This image contrasts sharply with the socially rambunctious student that we witnessed who freely announced to the class she had "done weed and pills."

The Harper of the hybrid comic recognizes the need to stay in school, writing in one of her vignettes, "I never thought I would actually be as good in school as I am now. I never thought I would actually go to school, let alone get good grades. I thought I'd be working at Burger King by now." In her comics Harper outlines additional motives to change. She represents her thoughts with a picture of a brain with text inside of it: "Don't be a drop-out. Don't be like the rest of your [family]." It is difficult for us to read her work and not see connections between her experiences and Junior's, especially those tied to identity construction, troubles at home, and discrimination. Resonating with Junior's experiences, the nuances of Harper's situation become increasingly complicated as she unveils the multiple layers of conflict she carries with her: the threat of turning out like her rest of her family, of being expelled and lacking future opportunities, and of ultimately leading an unfulfilling life. With the memoir assignment as an opportunity and *True Diary* as a model text, Harper tells stories about events in her life. Furthermore, within her comics she finds a space to reflect on her actions, assess what type of future she wants, and determine the attitude toward education that she needs to accomplish her goals.

## Gaining Voice with Authenticity

Becky noted that even though she taught other YA classics such as *To Kill a Mockingbird* (Lee) and *Lord of the Flies* (Golding) to Harper and her classmates, it was during the *True Diary* unit that Harper really shined. Becky indicated Harper's hybrid comic was unlike anything that she had turned in before, and was in fact of much higher quality than her previous work. In an interview, Becky reflected on why she felt the assignment had affected Harper so strongly, noting,

I think her voice in [the hybrid comic] was very authentically and safely hers. I think she took some risks, and stretched herself a bit, doing so successfully, trying on a different, wittier, wiser voice in the comics. In a couple of instances, her comics included and also seemed to "talk back" to the substance of her writing. I think she implemented in her comic-making the strategies we looked at in the mentor text to make this move.

Becky offered a testimonial to Harper's burgeoning skills as a writer and to her sophistication as a reflective young adult. Furthermore, she remarked that the young woman's growth as a person was tied to her growth as a writer. Perhaps Harper became comfortable with the hybrid medium over time. Or she may have felt connected with Junior's struggles with school and family. Nevertheless, Harper demonstrated a sophisticated approach to her past and present outlooks on education that breathed life into both the vignettes and comic texts. As Becky put it, "Harper knew [her hybrid comic] was better than her previous writing when she turned it in, and [she] was proud of it."

At the end of the unit, when Harper turned in the final version of her hybrid memoir comic, she returned to her seat, rolled up the previous drafts she had been working on into the shape of a tube, put them to her mouth as if a bullhorn, and exclaimed exuberantly, "What! What!" This moment of celebration, no doubt, marked the end of a long and tiring assignment for her, but it also revealed her investment in the completed work. As Becky noted, unlike Harper's previous writing assignments, she was proud of her memoir, and her commitment to the assignment shows as she took risks, displayed vulnerability, and expressed an authentic voice through the combination of prose and comics that she had been unable or unwilling to reach beforehand.

It was during *True Diary* and this multimodal production that Harper chose for the first time in Becky's class to address distressing and emotionally charged topics, such as failing at school, dropping out, and being a social outsider-themes that were no doubt culled from reading Junior's narrative. In addressing these topics, reflecting on painful aspects of her past, Harper made herself vulnerable to her teacher and to her peers. The drafting of prose and comics provided Harper with the opportunity to revisit difficult experiences with a reflective and critical eye. Thus, the memoir assignment became the catalyst for generative thinking about her life, present and past. Moreover, through the process of constructing the prose vignettes and visual comics, she demonstrated how she channeled her oppositional behavior into more productive activities. In a poignant example of this phenomenon, Harper writes in one vignette: "The events are not all positive, but the outcomes are. It's funny how life works; it makes me think that things can't get any worse, and then I rethink it all and realize maybe everything I have gone through was for the best." The act of reflection resulted in Harper producing a nuanced representation of the past, exposing a transformation of behavior and perspective. Harper came to see that her struggles not only with education, but with life itself, had allowed her to envision a more hopeful future for herself.

*True Diary* helped Harper see memoir as a way to investigate the struggles within her life. More specifically, the hybrid comic assignment pushed Harper towards greater complexity in her writing by employing a multiliteracy approach, namely by having her integrate writing skills with visual elements. Becky's assignment invoked the benefits of transmediation, mimicking Junior's celebration of multimodal writing when he comments, "I draw because words are too limited . . . But when you draw a picture, everybody can understand it" (5).We saw his words embodied as Harper's drawings gave emotional depth to her writing-a depth we had not seen before this unit. Becky's use of *True Diary* and Harper's case demonstrate the possibilities that hybrid comics possess to engage students and to provide them with tools to create thoughtful, innovative, and even inspirational work in the language arts classroom.

## Notes

1. Researchers, teachers, and librarians have urged the use of comics in classrooms to boost the confidence and literacy skills of reluctant readers. Some have argued that the visual nature of the comics medium provides readers with context clues and an overall ease of readability that increase vocabulary and encourage struggling readers to participate more in class and explore a diversity of genres (Hughes et al. 603; Snowball 43–44).

## Works Cited

Alexie, Sherman. *The Absolutely True Diary of a Part-Time Indian*. New York: Little, Brown, 2007. Print.

Bakis, Maureen. *The Graphic Novel Classroom: Powerful Teaching and Learning with Images*. New York: Corwin, 2011. Print.

Bitz, Michael. *When Comics Meet Kryptonite: Classroom Lessons from the Comic Book Project*. New York: Teachers College Press, 2010. Print.

Brozo, William, Gary Moorman, and Carla Meyer. *Teaching with Graphic Novels across the Curriculum*. New York: Teachers College Press, 2014. Print.

Charmaz, Kathy. *Constructing Grounded Theory: A Practical Guide through Qualitative Analysis*. Thousand Oaks, CA: Sage, 2006. Print.

Creswell, John. *Qualitative Research & Research Design: Choosing among Five Approaches*. 3rd ed. Thousand Oaks, CA: Sage, 2013. Print.

Dicker, Ron. "Sherman Alexie's *True Diary of a Part-Time Indian* Pulled from School Reading List Over Masturbation Mention." *Huff Post Parents*. 2 August 2013. Web. 17 April 2015.

Gavigan, K, and M. Tomasevich. *Connecting Comics to Curriculum: Strategies for Grades 6–12*. Santa Barbara, CA: Libraries Unlimited, 2011. Print.

Golding, William. *Lord of the Flies*. London: Faber & Faber. 1954. Print.

Hammond, Heidi. "Graphic Novels and Multimodal Literacy: A High School Study with American Born Chinese." *Bookbird: A Journal of International Children's Literature* 50. 4 (2012): 22–32. Print.

Hughes, Jannette Michelle, et al. "Adolescents and 'Autographics': Reading and Writing Coming-of-Age Graphic Novels." *Journal of Adolescent & Adult Literacy* 54.8 (2011): 601–12. Print.

Hull, Glynda, and Mark Nelson. "Locating the Semiotic Power of Multimodality." *Written Communication* 22.2 (April 2005): 224–61. Print.

Jacobs, Dale. *Graphic Encounters: Comics and the Sponsorship of Multimodal Literacy.* New York: Bloomsbury. 2013. Print.

Jaffe, Meryl. *Raising a Reader! How Comics and Graphic Novels Can Help Your Kids Love to Read!* New York: Comic Book Legal Defense Fund. 2013. Print.

Jenkins, Richard, and Debra Detamore. *Comics in Your Curriculum: Teacher-Friendly Activities for Making and Integrating Comics with Reading, Math, Science, and Other Subjects in Your Classroom.* Marion, IL: Pieces of Learning. 2008. Print.

Lee, Harper. *To Kill a Mockingbird.* New York: Hachette. 1960. Print.

Leland, Chris, and Jerome Harste. "Multiple Ways of Knowing: Curriculum in a New Key." *Language Arts* 71.5 (September, 1994): 337–45. Print.

Lewis, Cynthia, Pat Enciso, and Elizabeth Moje, eds. *Reframing Sociocultural Research on Literacy: Identity, Agency, and Power.* Mahwaw, NJ: Lawrence Erlbaum Associates. 2007. Print.

Missing: Find a Banned Book. Web. ALA.org. 30 April 2015.

Monnin, Katie. *Teaching Graphic Novels: Practical Strategies for the Secondary ELA Classroom.* New York: Maupin House Publishing, Inc., 2010. Print.

Montagne, Renee. "Author Sherman Alexie Targets Young Readers." NPR. 21 September 2007. Web. 28 April 2015.

National Book Foundation. http://www.nationalbook.org/nba2007_ypl_alexie.html

New London Group. "A Pedagogy of Multiliteracies: Designing Social Futures." *Harvard Educational Review* 66.1 (1996): 60–92. Print.

Novak, Michael. *Teaching Graphic Novels in the Classroom: Building Literacy and Comprehension.* Waco, TX: Prufrock Press. 2014. Print.

Pagliaro, Michael. "Is a Picture Worth a Thousand Words? Determining the Criteria for Graphic Novels with Merit." *English Journal* 103. 4 (2014): 31–45. Print.

Roberts, Bill. "Meridian School Board Votes to Remove Controversial Book from Curriculum." *Idaho Statesman* (2014): Web. 20 April 2014.

Siegel, Marjorie. "Rereading the Signs: Multimodal Transformations in the Field of Literacy Education." *Language Arts* 84. 1 (2006): 65–77. Print.

Simon, Rob. "'Without Comic Books, There Would Be No Me': Teachers as Connoisseurs of Adolescents' Literate Lives." *Journal of Adolescent & Adult Literacy* 55.6 (2012): 516–26. Print.

Sipe, Larry. *Storytime: Young Children's Literacy Understanding in the Classroom.* New York: Teachers College Press, 2008. Print.

Snowball, Clare. "Teenage Reluctant Readers and Graphic Novels." *Young Adult Library Services* 3.4 (2005): 43–45. Print.

Stein, Pippa. *Multimodal Pedagogies in Diverse Classrooms: Representation, Rights and Resources.* Routledge, 2007. Print.

Whitlock, Gillian, and Anna Poletti. "Self-Regarding Art." *Biography* 31.1 (2008): v–xxiii. Print.

PART FOUR

REPRESENTING GENDER and SEXUALITY

in the COMICS MEDIUM

# 12

## Unbalanced on the Brink: Adolescent Girls and the Discovery of the Self in *Skim* and *This One Summer* by Mariko Tamaki and Jillian Tamaki

*Marni Stanley*

In *Skim* (2008) and *This One Summer* (2014), Mariko and Jillian Tamaki present adolescent protagonists hovering at crucial points of development. Kimberly Keiko Cameron, the heroine of *Skim*, is a sixteen-year-old, half-Japanese, half-Caucasian student at an all-girls school. The plot focuses on her first feelings of love, which are both painfully unrequited and not heteronormative. These experiences are made more difficult by Kim's struggle with identity in a school community where she feels acutely different from her peers and where she lacks supportive friends. The Tamakis' most recent book, *This One Summer*, has as its protagonist Rose Wallace, a girl of twelve, who spends her annual summer vacation at the lake in Ontario's cottage country with her mother, Alice, and her father, Evan. Rose and her summer friend Windy swim, play, scare themselves silly with horror movies, and get drawn into the dramas of the older local teens who hang out and work at the local convenience store that serves the transient summer community. Rose also experiences the confusing feelings of her attraction to an older boy, as well as the pain caused by the now troubled relationship between her parents. Unbeknownst to Rose, her mother had miscarried the previous summer at the lake. This event caused her mother's depression, which has been exacerbated by the family's return to this locale. Throughout both *Skim* and *This One Summer*, the Tamakis detail the emotional and intellectual lives of these characters, as well as the complexity of the girls' perceptions and their struggle to understand adult motivations. In so doing, they provide readers with rich portrayals of girlhood that foreground the intense vulnerability of young hearts in a world of grownup rules. Moreover, in each narrative, the portrayal of the domestic and intimate worlds of the characters reveals the vulnerability of these young girls, both while they struggle to understand their lives without all of the information that full understanding requires, and as they struggle with the adults who seek to protect them from this precise knowledge. As the girls try to understand the older teens and adults around them through observation and eavesdropping, they learn that not everything is knowable—that knowledge of others is limited by what they choose to share and that other people's actions cannot be predicted, controlled, or even accurately interpreted. Through the Tamakis careful attention to the minutiae in these girls' lives—Kim's doodles and the objects that she has collected for her altar, Rose's Manga and her pile of beach treasure pebbles—the reader is drawn into their struggle to understand complex issues such as race, class hierarchies, sexuality, and the power and limitations of adults, both parents and teachers.

Stylistically, both works, while complexly plotted, move at a relatively calm visual pace. If, as Hillary L. Chute and Marianne DeKoven claim, "Graphic narrative, through its most basic composition in frames and gutters . . . calls a reader's attention visually and spatially to the act, process, and duration of interpretation" (767), then both these works deliberately slow us down, especially *This One Summer*. Both graphic novels are punctuated by full splash pages or spreads which frequently show quiet scenes of characters walking in the middle distance, surrounded by pleasant landscapes or, in *Skim*, residential neighborhoods. In *This One Summer* there are ten spreads which are also silent, ensuring that no text disrupts the reader's focus on the image. Chute and DeKoven argue that "the form's fundamental syntactical operation is the representation of time as space on the page" (769). In some of these spreads in *Summer*, a character is represented in multiple exposures, swimming or dancing or cycling across the pages. This stop-action image capture effect, combined with the nostalgic indigo wash of the book, create dreamy, contemplative moments that interrupt the momentum of the story and return the focus from action to emotion.

Appropriately, since it tells of a summer vacation, *This One Summer* is also full of individual panels, scattered through the text, that look like photos in a holiday album. These many wordless panels encourage the reader to slow down and consider the image. In *Skim*, splash pages are rarely wordless, but the text on them is usually rendered as narration from Kim's diary, not as speech balloons. These diary entries sometimes relate directly to the illustration, but other times they provide a counterpoint, inviting the reader to work out the interaction of text and image. For example, one such page shows the upper part of a street light with a street sign, a Neighborhood Watch sign, and a no parking sign attached. The very top of Kim's head appears at the bottom of the page, which is diagonally bifurcated into lit and unlit sides. Part of the diary entry reads: "This is strange. This is the strangest ever. I feel like I have wings but my bones are bricks. Because . . . Because . . . Because . . ." (58.1). At first glance the text seems unrelated but as the reader contemplates the page the high contrast use of black and white becomes an image of the highs and lows of Kim's feelings in relation to Ms. Archer. The street sign, "Deneuve," is Ms. Archer's street, but it is also the name of a French actress famous for her alluring and glamorous beauty. The Neighborhood Watch sign has three little houses with large eyes gazing out of them reminding Kim of the panoptican, of all the people who are keeping an eye on her. Thus the page, at first a puzzle, is revealed to perfectly illustrate Kim's heightened state of emotion where she has wings to fly, but is weighted to the earth by her bricks for bones. The watching eyes and the diagonal cut across the page also draw attention to the impossibility of a relationship between these two characters even though Kim, in the throes of first feelings, is compelled to pursue the focus of her desire even when she can see the futility of it.

Together with emotional issues, both *Skim* and *This One Summer* engage with a number of social issues, namely race, while demonstrating the ways in which race intersects with other ideas of difference, such as sexuality. Race is more prominent in *Skim* where the protagonist, Kim, is half-Japanese and half-Caucasian and attends a school with little racial diversity. Kim is regarded as not simply different by her classmates but at times even "other." A teenage boy who was dating a girl at her school recently committed suicide and this event has sent the school, along with many of the students, into a heightened state of vigilance. Kim is isolated within this environment—she has only one friend, Lisa, who is not very nice to her. For example, when Kim admits that she is making a card for the bereaved girl in their class, as they have all been invited to do, Lisa mocks her participation and claims, "I'm more independent than you are" (33.2). The next panel, the largest on the page, shows the back of Kim's head in close-up on a dark ground. This is followed by a small panel showing Kim in the shadows gazing through a door frame with two brightly lit girls, with whom she is not engaging, in the background. Later on the same page, when Kim questions something Lisa has said, the latter swears at her and makes fun of her studying. At one point in this sequence, Kim is merely a reflection in the mirror. Kim's black sweater and hair against the other girls' white shirts and light hair, and the way she is framed as occupying a liminal position to the other girls, combine to emphasize her alienation in the school.

Indeed, Kim's limited social network, combined with her melancholic state, has placed the young girl on the radar screen of both the guidance counselor and the clique of popular girls. Images throughout *Skim* present Kim being stared at by both her peers and by the adults at the school. These illustrations are emphasized in the text by occasional panels of life in the school which are rendered from an acute overhead angle as if from surveillance. In addition, the eye imagery on the Neighborhood Watch signs on the street and her friend Lisa's verbal reports of other girls' close scrutiny of Kim also reinforce the idea of Kim under observation. When the school invites a special facilitator to conduct a "self-love" exercise and invites the students to share what makes them happy as well as sad, Kim opts not to participate. As a consequence, the guidance counselor follows her out and asks to see her list of happy and sad items anyway, violating the agreement that the facilitator made with the students that the exercise would be both confidential and purely voluntary. As Kim notes in response, "so much for feeling comfortable" (61.7).

Afterwards, she receives an equally uncomfortable hug from the guidance counselor as well as by the leader of the powerful clique of popular girls in the school, Julie Peters. This gesture of understanding, care, and even empathy aside, readers soon learn that Julie Peters had been the instigator of one of the worst racist experiences in Kim's life. Three years earlier, at Julie's thirteenth birthday party, Julie attacked Kim and another girl, Hien, who is Vietnamese. Kim was invited to the party at the last minute, a gesture which she understood to mean that Julie's mother must have made her invite Kim. It is a costume party, but all the girls except Kim and Hien are dressed as either ballet dancers or figure skaters. Kim is dressed as the cowardly lion and Hein as a soldier. As soon as Julie's mother leaves the room, Julie and her friends throw Kim and Hien out into the dark. The two girls at first think this is some kind of game and wait patiently to be let back in. Eventually Hien leaves. Kim notes in her diary "Hien's parents adopted her from Vietnam two years earlier and she never got invited to parties. Maybe she thought that's how people left parties in Canada, Asians first" (86.10).

What follows is a beautiful panelless page in which Kim, in her cowardly lion costume, rises from the bench, plucks a small branch from a tree, and walks off into the dark alone. Although she says that she is scared of the dark, she also does not want to return to the horrible party. There are a number of places in the text where the Tamakis place Kim's words under erasure (the words are clearly visible but crossed out). These episodes offer insight into the young girl's thought processes as well as inner emotional life. On the occasion of the unpleasant costume party, for example she notes: "At first I was scared to walk home on my own . . . But in the end . . . it was ~~scarier~~ stupider to sit outside, waiting for Julie Peters and the ballerinas to let me in" (87). Kim rescripts her reaction to the other girls' cruelty. By changing her thoughts she instructs herself not to be scared, but to simply leave. In her terms, it would be stupid to stay and give them the satisfaction of having scared her. Kim understands, as the school administration does not, that the differences they perceive in her—sadness and an interest in the gothic—are not as important as the difference that everyone pretends they do not see. In this very homogenous school, it is Kim's minority status which is the real cause of her isolation.

Alterity in *This One Summer* is created by race, class, and geography, but also by age. The novel reflects the trope of a community invaded by vacationing outsiders who bring their big city views and judgments into a semi-rural space. The subject of race is embodied by the character Jenny, one of the local teens whom Rose watches, who may or may not be a member of the First Nations[1] and who works at the Historic Heritage Huron Village performing as a native interpreter. Rose tells Windy that "No one here is Huron. I think they are all, like, white" (207.1). Jenny could be a member of the indigenous peoples of Canada since Rose is just speculating that no one at the Heritage Village is Huron. The reader is never given enough information to definitively resolve the question. Whether Jenny is aboriginal or not, she is subject to a verbal assault by a pair of local boys which is both racist and sexist. Jenny is pregnant and the local kids have been gossiping about it. As Rose and Windy watch, two local boys start harassing Jenny in front of a group of park attendees, including young children. They interrupt her work at the Heritage Village to ask what kind of birth control the Huron used. When she doesn't answer, one of the boys calls out, "Like, fuckin' condoms made from squirrel skin or something" (213.4). An unseen adult in the crowd intervenes, but Jenny is completely humiliated by this point and she runs off crying. Jenny's perceived social, cultural, and especially ethnic difference makes her a target for harassment and ridicule. Moreover, the fact that she is verbally insulted while performing a First Nation's identity—whether she is actually Huron or not—reflects Canada's long and ongoing history of disregard, oppression, and racism in relation to the First Nations peoples.

In *This One Summer*, economic class as a marker of social difference and as the basis for cultural hierarchy plays a larger role than race. Nonetheless, it also intersects with race in the presentation of Jenny. The Tamakis make clear that Rose and Windy are learning the importance of reinforcing class hierarchy from some of the adults around them. The cabins are located at Awago Beach, Ontario—a fictional place in the actual Muskoka region. As they drive by a turkey farm, Rose's father performs his fake uneducated farmer voice (which is not unlike Foghorn Leghorn) to tease Rose about her origins: "Hyuk hyuk! Lookee Lee. I say, it's tha TURKEY HATCHERY! Official birthplace of one Rose Abigail Wallace" (9.3). Throughout the novel, the family has a running joke mocking the "world famous turkey jerky" produced at the farm. Later her father instructs Rose to "wave to the youth of Awago" (13.2) in what is clearly a mocking tone since Rose's mother admonishes him for it. Indeed, Alice never participates in her husband's mockery of the locals. Later, at a family dinner, while eating corn on the cob, Rose's father tells her that the cobs are "AWAGO TOILET PAPER" (95.1) and pretends to save his for later use. Alice twice intervenes in her husband's joking around, but to no effect. Far from mirroring her father's prejudices, Rose has a crush on one of the locals, an older teenage boy named Dunc, who works at the convenience store.

*[margin annotation: socio-economics]*

When Windy and Rose play a fortune telling game called MASH, Windy tells Rose to add Dunc to the list of potential husbands as "the Dud. It's the one you don't want. Like, 'garbage man'" (75.5). Windy reinforces his status by referring to him as "the Dud" numerous later occasions as well (114, 148), whereas Rose imagines a future with him where he goes to medical school and she has "One Perfect Baby" (80.1). On the one hand, Rose's optimistic vision of Dunc's future with her demonstrates that she does not share her father's contempt for the locals. On the other hand it is also evidence of her naïve belief that educational opportunity exists equally for Dunc as it does for her. Rose and Windy walk through the locals' impoverished housing area as tourists, and Windy comments loudly that it's "weird" and "everything's, like, crappy" (148.4). When they accidently encounter the local teenagers' litter-strewn hangout spot in the woods, Rose sifts through the detritus for clues to their lives. When Rose picks up a flip-flop, Windy warns her that she will "get HERPES" (153.3) from touching their possessions. Wendy then refers to the hangout as "BUM headquarters" (154.3). As evidence of her differing response to the space, Rose takes a Niagara Falls button she finds and some bottle caps as souvenirs of their adventure and adds them to her beachcombing collection of pebbles and driftwood. Rose romanticizes Dunc by imagining a future where she can take him away from all this while at the same time sharing in her father's view that this is a foreign culture to be examined with an anthropologist's investigative, analytical, and collecting eye. Rose's "summer cottage friend" (19.1) Windy is not someone who lives locally but is an urban child with educated, professional parents just like Rose. While *This One Summer* foregrounds class by contrasting the poor locals with the wealthier summer visitors, *Skim* does so by contrasting socio-economic differences within the school population: namely, through the portrayal of Kim versus the powerful clique of popular and wealthy girls.

When it comes to the subject of developing desire and sexuality, the Tamakis again deploy characteristic complexity and thought-provoking ambiguity. In *Skim*, Kim falls in love for the first time. The object of her attraction is Ms. Archer, her English and drama teacher. Ms. Archer is not like the other teachers in the book who have tidy hairdos and business-like clothes. Ms. Archer appears for the first time as a body without a face—in class, drawn from the neck down, seated on her desk, legs crossed, with a teacup by one hand and a partially eaten apple in the other, wearing an ankle-length elaborately patterned swirling skirt, a fringed shawl wrapped around her slim waist, with long tendrils of hair falling out of an up-do and jewellery to spare. Later on the same page, she appears to be dancing among the students' desks as she reads aloud from a book. In the next panel, Kim gazes up at her enraptured. Kim sees both Ms. Archer and herself as "freaks" (13.1; 13.4). Ms. Archer is very animated, colourful (even in a comic that uses only black and white), and dramatic. Her pronouncements make Kim feel noticed.

When Kim sneaks off to the wooded ravine behind the school to smoke, she encounters Ms. Archer, a fellow smoker, and they begin a kind of friendship. Kim has a cast on her arm from a fall, and Ms. Archer draws a rebel heart on it and encourages Kim to speak up in class. She also asks Kim how her nickname, Skim, originated. Kim replies that the girls call her Skim "because I'm not" (27.5)—a reference to her weight. Ms. Archer reflects that she must prefer her name, Kim, a gentle acknowledgement that Kim is bullied in the school by this subtle name calling. Eventually, at one of these meetings in the ravine Kim and Ms. Archer share a kiss. The kiss is drawn as a splash spread, in a single image, without sequence (40–41). Preceding the kiss is a scene about Halloween and following it is the title page for Part II. In the Halloween scene the narration records Kim's enigmatic remark in her diary "technically nothing has happened" (38). Because the kiss occurs without any sequence of events either before or after, the reader cannot know who initiated or ended the kiss, nor do they have any sense of the duration, intensity, or even the level of intimacy. As Ariel Kahn argues, "the image of the kiss subverts the authority of the textual claim on the previous page that "nothing happened. . . . Skim attempts to both re-present and deny her forbidden desire for her teacher, and its consummation" (341). Jillian Tamaki's wonderful art shows a single frozen moment of lips touching, no hands. By choosing to create just the one image, the Tamakis leave the reader wondering did Ms. Archer kiss Kim or did Kim kiss Ms. Archer? Did the teacher pull back first? Or did Kim?

The ambiguities of the kiss are borne out by further ambiguities in Part Two of *Skim*. Kim visits Ms. Archer's home a number of times, always uninvited, as Ms. Archer points out to her. On one occasion Kim arrives unannounced. Ms. Archer invites her in and then disappears for so long on a phone call that Kim eventually leaves. Is this a deliberate strategy on Ms. Archer's part? Is she trying to let Kim down gently? No other physical contact between Kim and Ms. Archer takes place, nor is there any evidence that Kim sees herself as a lesbian, or that her desire for Ms. Archer, in spite of the kiss, is particularly sexual. But her feelings are passionate and intense. Kim feels transformed, inspired, and even ignited. Accordingly, she starts to take seriously the idea that some kind of force is at work in the universe. Her heart sounds different to her and she cannot understand why others cannot hear it. On one page, her heartbeat appears as a rhythm of black bars walking across the panels of a page about school (44). Elsewhere in both books, sounds are usually represented by words. This page, made up mostly of snapshots of moments Kim is seeing through the day, is the exception. The page begins with a line of narration, "it feels like there's a broken washing machine inside my chest" (44.1) and ends with Kim lying in the dark holding her cat on her chest, and listening to her own heart, which we see as rapidly increasing black vertical bars.

The subject of homosexuality also appears, equally ambiguously, in the sub-plot about the boy who killed himself, John Reddear. Because he was dating Katie Matthews, a girl from their school, many of the students are gossiping about him. A rumour has been circulating that he was gay and, as a conse-quence, someone writes the word "fag" (89.2) on his photo, which is posted on a bulletin board in the school hallway. Just as readers never definitively learn whether Jenny is actually First Nations in *This One Summer*, they like-wise never ascertain from the information available in *Skim* whether John was actually gay. Ultimately, however, the question of John's potential homo-sexuality does not matter, because Kim sees how her peers treat the issue. Nonheteronormative identity constitutes another form of personal difference, akin to racial otherness, which, in this school, is regarded as negative by the majority of her peers. Because her feelings are unrequited, she also does not get to follow up on them and learn the extent to which her feelings are actually sexual. Ms. Archer's decision to quit the school removes her from Kim's world. As a consequence, Kim cannot be sure what her feelings mean in terms of her developing sexuality and nor can the reader. It is arguably the Tamakis' point that the lives of their protagonists are works in progress and many things, most importantly their futures, are unresolved and unforeseeable. Both Rose and Kim seek to know their futures since both are shown engaging in fortune-telling activities. The Tamakis' creative use of ambiguity indicates the varying futures that could branch from the present for their protagonist.

Rose in *This One Summer* is younger than Kim by some years, and she is not yet beginning to act on her nascent sexual feelings. Rose develops her ideas around sex through observation, not experimentation, so the book focuses on her watchfulness and study of the older teens and adults around her. Anna Fitzpatrick describes her as "a practiced spectator, impatient to become the main character in her own story, positive that she won't make the same mis-takes that the grown-ups around her did" (11). Rose experiences the first stir-rings of heterosexual desire through her crush on Dunc. The reader also learns that she has already had a crush on Mitch, her swimming instructor back home. Sexuality is primarily represented in the text through Rose's voyeuristic attention to the older teens and their interpersonal and sometimes romantic relationships.

The two boys who work at the convenience store each have a girlfriend. Dunc and his girlfriend Jenny are the main focus of Rose's gaze. The first time that Rose sees them together, they are flirting in the store. The close-up panel of Dunc teasing Jenny and leaning towards her while she puts her hand up to still his progress is followed by an angle shot looking down on Rose and

Windy at the counter. While Windy is glaring angrily at Dunc who is failing to serve her, Rose is gazing up through her bangs at Dunc and Jenny with a wistful expression on her face. As she and Windy sit behind the store eating their gummy candies, Dunc and Jenny come out of the back door and kiss. While Windy makes a face and says, "Barf!" (29.1), Rose picks up a gummy and squints through this semi-translucent improvised lens at the kissing couple, filtering their actions so that they appear blurred. Jillian Tamaki draws the kissing couple distorted through Rose's jellied lens in contrast to her clear and fluid drawing of them on the facing page when they were subject to Windy's disgusted gaze.

*distortion of sex*

Later, Rose watches Jenny sunbathe through the slats of a fence in a sequence of three panels (37.1–3). In the first one, Rose is looking through the fence; in the second one, Jenny's face and bikini-clad breasts are visible through the gap Rose peers through; finally, in the third panel, Jenny is holding a book and her hands and groin area are visible between the planks. This sequence of fragmented images highlights Rose's fragmented understanding of what is happening: she is not seeing the whole picture of Jenny's life. On another occasion, Rose and Windy see Sarah and Jenny flirting with their boyfriends and on yet another, they overhear the girls talking about sexual subjects. Sarah's boyfriend refers to Sarah and Jenny as sluts, a derogatory term to which Jenny strenuously objects. Her protest, however, is ignored, just as Alice's attempts to hush her husband's classist remarks were also ignored, a pattern that provides the girls with a subtle primer on gendered relationships within their society. The Tamakis underscore the power and impact of such repetitions by showing the younger girls picking up the term "slut" and using it to refer to the older girls whom they also refer to as drunk, without any evidence for either insult. Only much later, on a single occasion, will Jenny be shown to be drunk. When their mothers overhear Rose and Windy using derogatory terms for Sarah and Jenny, they are each admonished and instructed not to use such language. The sequence ends with Rose following her mother home—the panel shows only their feet and legs in the landscape, but the word slut is repeated across the spread as if it were the sound made by Rose's flip flops (44–45). Later, Windy asks Rose why she was so harsh in her criticism of Jenny, calling Jenny "stupid" and saying she "deserves" being pregnant (240.4), and that "all the girls here are sluts" (241.3). Windy, who has clearly had a chat with her mother, calls Rose "sexist" and walks away from her (242.1).

*impact of repetition/ slut shaming*

As the Jenny plot develops, it is clear that Rose lacks empathy for this young woman. However, it is less clear whether this condition arises from Rose's age, her crush on Dunc, or her possible race and class prejudice. When she watches Jenny sobbing in the car shortly after learning that she's pregnant and again after being humiliated at the Huron Heritage site, Rose is curious but not sympathetic. When a young co-worker of Jenny's comforts her and offers to drive her home, Rose misinterprets the gesture and decides that Jenny is cheating on Dunc. She locates Dunc's home, trespasses into his yard, and begins writing "she is cheating" on the dusty screen of an old arcade game. She gets as far as the "t" in cheating and then goes back and puts "I think" above it (252.3).

Like the words that Kim puts under erasure in her diary in *Skim*, this act shows Rose's thought process as she realizes partway through that this is not a fact but merely her own speculation impelled by her jealousy. Dunc comes out of the house and confronts Rose, and she tries to tell him but gets scared by his mood and runs off instead. Later, Jenny either intentionally tries to drown herself or nearly drowns herself by accident after a humiliating public fight with Dunc in which he is unsupportive of her pregnancy and acts out his own fears in a hostile manner. Echoing the uncertainty, doubt and equivocality that have run throughout *This One Summer*, Jenny's actions are ambiguous. Jenny is rescued by Rose's mother whom Rose has called for help. A few days later, a girl about Rose's age, who strongly resembles Jenny (perhaps her little sister?) asks Rose to tell her mom that "Jenny says 'thank you'" and that "Jenny is cool now' (309.1). As the young girl walks back to her cabin, Rose ponders the meaning of being "cool now"—does it signal that Jenny intends to keep the baby? If so, does it also mean that Dunc will be emotionally, logistically, and financially supportive? Rose concludes, "I hope she's cool. I hope it's true" (310.3–4). That last sentence appears in a panel that has an overhead point of view. As Rose walks along the tall fence, readers can see the debris strewn across the yard. Rose understands, with her repetition of "hope" that Jenny may be in trouble. Through watching Jenny over the summer, Rose has progressed from harsh judgment to sympathy. As April Spisak argues; "empathy is one of the milestones that helps Rose find a way to channel her loneliness into independence and self-fulfillment" (493). She may not understand systemic oppression, but she is beginning to understand that plans for the future can be swiftly changed by events and, furthermore, not everyone has the same range of choices. Even if Jenny is not Huron she is local—native to the area. Unlike Rose and her family she has nowhere else to go and few opportunities to pursue. Rose sees Jenny as older, more sophisticated, doing adult things; at the novel's end Rose is just beginning to see the limitations of Jenny's world.

The other couple that Rose has been observing, also with limited and often incorrect data, is her own parents. Her mother Alice is filled with grief from the miscarriage the summer before. Moreover, all this misery has been refreshed by the return to the location where the miscarriage took place. Meanwhile, her father Evan is frustrated by what he is beginning to regard as her lack of effort to stop mourning. Happy memories of being on the beach or learning to swim with her mother are juxtaposed with images of her mother

*[handwritten marginal note: Rose maturing *]*

this summer—withdrawn, refusing to swim (the miscarriage occurred when she was swimming), working on an academic article while her family plays, hunched and sad-looking in every panel. The most telling juxtaposition of panels contrasts Rose picking up little pebbles on the beach against a close-up image of her mother's hands, one hand pouring pills into the other (51. 4; 51.5). One evening after dinner, she watches her father flirt with her mother. When Alice pulls away, Evan accuses her of not trying to be close with him and Rose—or, even worse, of not wanting to be. The argument accelerates until Rose runs into her room and pulls the duvet over her head. Her father takes her out to the beach and tells her not to worry because "It's all just adult junk that doesn't mean anything" (105.2), but his words offer little comfort because they offer little explanation about what is happening. Rose overhears snippets of a conversation between her mother and her mother's sister Danielle, but only enough to learn that her mother is sad, angry and feeling so unlike herself that she wishes she could "just disappear" (129.1). Alice and Danielle stop talking when they realize Rose is outside the open window, but she has overheard enough to be confused and upset.

That same night, her parents sit in the car parked out in the driveway in order to talk privately—and they quickly end up screaming at each other. Eventually, Rose's father decides to return to the city and leaves her and her mother alone. Alice tries to deal with Rose's anger at her Dad's absence, but her daughter ends up attacking her, saying that she is the one who should have gone since she is the one who is not swimming or enjoying the lake. Rose accuses her mother of being dissatisfied with her and wanting another child because Rose isn't good enough. Tellingly, when Rose had imagined her own future with Dunc, "one perfect baby" was all she wanted. Echoing her father's allegation, Rose accuses her mother of not trying to be happy. She then walks out, leaving her mother crying. After rescuing Jenny, Alice has a long talk with Windy's mother about the miscarriage and about her anger and sorrow. Windy's mother urges Alice to tell Rose but the reader can see that Rose has been eavesdropping on this conversation from its beginning (297.1). Unlike her earlier attempt at listening in, this time she overhears the explanation of her mother's deep sorrow. Perhaps this knowledge of her mother's situation—her yearning for a child that she will never have—helps Rose to develop empathy for Jenny, pregnant with a child for whom she is not ready.

In *Skim*, Kim also observes the adults around her for clues about love, with equally mixed results. Her parents are divorced. Her mother has no interest in a relationship and seems to prefer work to love. By contrast, her father is actively looking, but has had no long-term success thus far. In one wonderfully awkward sequence, her father takes Kim out for dinner with his current girlfriend who presents Kim a "teen drama queen" (65.5) mug she has made for her. The mug licenses her father to dismiss the seriousness of her feelings by asking her "any teen drama I should know about?" (65.6). A subsequent close-up of her father saying "you know you can talk to me about anything right?" (66.1) is followed by a panel with an even tighter close-up of his current girlfriend staring askance at Kim. Both her belittling gift and her focused stare seem designed to silence Kim. Even so, Kim desperately wants to answer her father. The words "I think I'm in love" (66.3), in fact, appear across a large close-up of her partially eaten meal in the next panel, but they are clearly a thought, not an utterance. Does her father ask her to speak in front of a virtual stranger because he doesn't actually want to do so? Or is he so caught up in his own emotional life that he doesn't think that his daughter will not want to have a heart-to-heart in these circumstances? Would Kim speak if her father took her out alone? The scene is only two pages long. Additionally, there is no later episode with Kim and her father where they revisit this conversation, so these questions are never resolved.

Similarly, readers can also never resolve the question of Ms. Archer's role in Kim's crush. On the one hand, she tells Kim more than once that her eyes are fascinating, which could be seen as flirtation but also as an attempt to build up the young girl's confidence, especially given the way in which her racial identity makes her a target for bullying and relegates her to a highly marginalized status among her peers. Talking to Kim about class assignments or the nickname that other girls use for her does not seem unprofessional in these instances. While the counselor regards Kim as a high-risk student and gives her unwanted hugs, Ms. Archer actually notices that Kim has been ostracized and so offers something that the young girl desperately needs: a friend to talk to and, especially, a friend who will listen. As noted above, the reader can not tell the extent to which Ms. Archer is engaged in the one kiss that occurs. After Kim repeatedly visits Ms. Archer's home without her permission, the teacher accepts another professional position and leaves the school. Is Ms. Archer the innocent target of a schoolgirl crush or did she actually have feelings for Kim? These questions reinforce the struggle that Kim has been experiencing to understand the actions of the adult around her. Why is her mother so anti-romantic and her father so romantic? Did Ms. Archer like her in the way that she had hoped that she would? Is that why she left? Kim does not get a chance to speak to Ms. Archer before she leaves, so once again all of these questions are left unresolved in the text.

The level of ambiguity in these works is appropriate for the adolescent characters that they feature. In spite of their interest in fortune telling, Kim and Rose do not know what the future holds for them. They are both still in the midst of adolescent discovery. The rich and thought-provoking ambiguity of Mariko Tamaki's written text for the two books is reinforced by the richness of Jillian

Tamaki's art. Occasionally they appear to deliberately play with the reader's desire to know. There is a scene, for example, in *This One Summer* where Windy and Rose are eavesdropping on the two boys working in the convenience store. One boy says something to the other, but the speech bubble is cropped by the panel in such a way that the reader gets only a few scattered words—a wonderful visual reminder of the importance of having enough information before one draws conclusions, which is an issue for Rose (39.1). Likewise, by the end of *Skim*, Kim has come to the conclusion that "everything you do and everything people do to you leaves a mark, or at least it affects who you are" (125). She, too, is beginning to understand the unpredictability of life. Kim makes a new friend, Katie, who is nice and fun but also sad and wounded. Katie doesn't criticize and mock her as Lisa, her previous friend, sometimes did.

The final sequence of the novel begins with Kim and Lisa talking. Lisa hurries off to see her new boyfriend in what is presented as a casual goodbye but which actually seems more final. Then Kim walks back towards the wooded ravine in two panels inset onto the final splash page. As Ariel Kahn observes, "Skim's . . . leaving behind her previous disappointments and the constrictions of 'home,' represented by the linear corner of her house, as she literally "turns a corner" and moves purposefully into an open ended future, which she actively seeks out" (342). The final splash page also shows the top of Katie's head as she disappears into the ravine, followed, presumably, by Kim. Everything points to Katie being a happier friendship for Kim, one that will help her think ahead, set new goals, and be a better student. Facing that final sequence of the story is a small drawing, low on the endpaper, of one of those folded paper fortune tellers that children make. Presented on an otherwise blank page, it is a final reminder that Kim's future is yet to be written.

The conclusion of *This One Summer* shares the modest hopefulness of *Skim*. Rose and Windy sit on the hood of the car breathing deeply, trying to inhale all the smells of summer. Windy reminds Rose that they used to think that they could save that smell in their lungs. Windy says goodbye, and Rose goes into the cabin for a final check. We see her parents looking comfortable together, her father's arm around her mother as they walk to the car. The rooms of the cabin appear in a sequence of panels as time ticks on. The sense that the time of summer is running out is emphasized by the word "tick" which travels across each image until we reach the final panel of Rose's bed with her collection of summer pebbles, bits of driftwood and other little objects dumped into the middle, a tiny cache of memories (317–18). She and Windy had talked and laughed on a number of occasions over the summer about the imminent onset of puberty and their attendant development of breasts. Accordingly, in her farewell, Windy tells Rose: "you have to come back next summer. So I can see your massive boobs" (312.5). On the endpaper, facing the final drawing, there is no image, just

*ambiguity for the reader & Rose*

the words "tick" and "boobs would be cool" (319). This closing sequence encap-
sulates the tension in Rose's young self between wanting her family to stay the
same and for every summer to be the same and wanting, as her voyeuristic
fascination for the teenagers demonstrates, to grow up and have the drama and
excitement of romance. The reader is reminded by the "tick, tick, tick" across
the final pages that time does indeed move on, and that stasis is not a legitimate
option even if sometimes it may seem desirable. Rose's little cache of objects
holds the memories of this summer; the next one will have its own souvenirs.

Both of these books attend to the everyday and the ordinary. In so doing,
they convey that the drama of commonplace experiences is an essential part of
the adventure of growing up. The cover of *This One Summer* shows Rose and
Windy leaping into the lake—captured in a moment of anticipation and joy. The
cover of *Skim* has Kim shading her eyes as she looks up and into the distance—
a gesture that can be read as a sign of anticipation, of seeing into the distance
and striving to discover what is up ahead. The lack of resolution for many plot
points, along with the visual techniques that show key characters changing their
minds and struggling to understand, serve to remind readers of the intensity of
change and the uncertainty of perception in adolescent life. During this stage of
life, there is much to learn, including the serious task of learning about sexuality and race. In the world of youthful crushes, everything is intense, dramatic,
and fascinating. As a result, everything is ripe for discovery, inquiry, and debate.
Ultimately both *Skim* and *This One Summer* celebrate the challenge, the possibility, the risks, and the adventure of coming-of-age in the lives of ordinary girls.

## Notes

1. In Canada, First Nations is the preferred term of the Indigenous or Aboriginal Peoples.
Though the Government still uses the word "Indian," as in the infamous "Indian Act" legislation,
the term is generally perceived as inaccurate and racist.

## Works Cited

Chute, Hillary, and Marianne DeKoven. "Introduction: Graphic Narrative." *Modern Fiction Studies* 52.4 (Winter 2006): 767–82. Print.

Fitzpatrick, Anna. "The Shores of Childhood; Lethargic Cottage Days Stretch a Young Girl's Understanding in Mariko and Jillian Tamaki's *This One Summer*." *National Post*. 24 May 2014. Toronto ed.: WP 11. Print.

Kahn, Ariel. "On Being Unique: Gender Subversion in Two Graphic Novels for Young Adults." *Journal of Graphic Novels and Comics* 5.3 (2014): 336–43. Print.

Spisak, April. "*This One Summer*; Review." *Bulletin of the Center for Children's Books* 67.10 (June 2014): 493–94. Print.

Tamaki, Mariko and Jillian Tamaki. *Skim*. Toronto: Groundwood Books, 2008. Print.

———. *This One Summer*. Toronto: Groundwood Books, 2014. Print.

# 13

## The Drama of Coming Out:
## Censorship and *Drama* by Raina Telgemeier

### *Eti Berland*

*Drama* by Raina Telgemieier, a graphic novel that focuses on a whirlwind theatrical production in a middle school, as well as the emotional complications and romantic mishaps of its company, has seen its own share of acclaim and behind-the-scenes drama. Since its release in 2012, the graphic novel has received the Stonewall Honor from the American Library Association's Gay, Lesbian, Bisexual, and Transgender Round Table; a nomination for a Harvey Award for excellence in comics; and appearances on prestigious booklists like the Young Adult Library Services Association's Great Graphic Novels for Teens Top Ten, the Association for Library Service to Children's 2013 Notable Children's Books list, School Library Journal's Top 10 Graphic Novels of 2012, and Publishers Weekly's Best Books of 2012. In spite of these critical accolades, public conversations about *Drama* routinely focus on the reasons *not* to share this award-winning book with young readers because of Telgemeier's choice to feature queer characters. During National Library Week in 2015, in fact, the American Library Association released their list of the most frequently challenged books for the previous year. According to the Office for Intellectual Freedom, they "received 311 reports regarding attempts to remove or restrict materials from school curricula and library bookshelves" (American Library Association). *Drama* was ranked as #10 on the list for being "sexually explicit" (American Library Association), but "it has no sex at all, unless you consider a kiss to be 'sexually explicit'" (Alverson). According to Teen Librarian Robin Brenner, "it's not the romance they are objecting to, but the homosexuality" (Alverson).

In their findings, the Office for Intellectual Freedom demonstrated that "authors of color and books with diverse content are disproportionately challenged and banned," which includes books with "LGBT main and/or secondary characters" or "LGBT issues" (American Library Association). While the Office for Intellectual Freedom collects reports of formal complaints, "for each challenge reported there are as many as four or five that go unreported" (Office for Intellectual Freedom), which can include self-censorship and quiet bans. Information is scarce about the formal challenges,[1] but the Internet is rife with commentary censuring *Drama*. One-star Amazon reviews provide extensive feedback to encourage future readers to reject this title. Reviewers argue that it has inappropriate and mature content that they encountered due to misleading book descriptions that did not make clear that there are gay characters in the book. According to Amazon user Sunshinewest, "This is not a book about a young girl having a crush and dealing with it. This is an introduction to homosexuality and bisexual behavior in children" (Sunshinewest). XCPilot criticizes the medium of the story, arguing, "The entire book is a 'comic book' . . . and considering the simplicity of that dialog, it's absolutely targeted at a very young audience . . . (Anyone older would be reading books written in prose instead of pictures—books with an actual literary structure.)" (XCPilot). Incorrectly citing Lexile and Accelerated Reader classifications[2], they assert that *Drama* has been marketed for young children in primary school (according to Scholastic's online Store, *Drama* is listed as a title for children grades 5–8), which shows these reviewers' lack of understanding of *Drama* as a verbal-visual text about tweens in middle school.

*Drama*'s distinction as a visual text has been noted by visual literacy scholar Meryl Jaffe of Johns Hopkins University Center for Talented Youth, who argues that "it depicts school-girl crushes and travails with humor and sensitivity, relayed through [Telgemeier's] engaging text, wonderfully expressive characters, and her colorful and engaging visual montages. . . . The art conveys a sense of place, touch, and feel" (Jaffe). However, since many critics who write reviews for Amazon do not understand, or at least appreciate, the visual format, they vilify individual panels outside the context of the rest of the story. Because the images are immediate and accessible, those who challenge *Drama* can point out pages without having to invest the time in reading the entire work or recognizing how the scenes fit within the larger narrative. Instead, they narrowly focus on the "sexually explicit" content.

While the public reaction to *Drama* has been marked by tumult and controversy, the LGBTQ identity of the characters in the text itself is markedly different. Coming out in *Drama* is challenging, but affirming, a moment when these characters find community. In her landmark article, "Mirrors, Windows, and Sliding Glass Doors," Rudine Sims Bishop's emphasizes the importance of narratives that reflect the experiences of flesh-and-blood readers, stating that "literature transforms human experience and reflects it back to us, and in that reflection we can see our own lives and experiences as part of the larger human experience. Reading, then, becomes a means of self-affirmation, and readers often seek their mirrors in books" (Bishop ix–xi). Diverse books like

*Drama* can serve both as a window and as a mirror for teens. The graphic novel can help adolescent readers develop compassion and empathy for others, while simultaneously enabling them to see their own experiences represented. In so doing, *Drama* has expanded the canon of children's literature by presenting the coming out narrative as part of the everyday fabric of young people's lives. Examining the realities of modern teen identity formation within the framework of Queer Studies illuminates an added facet to the literary merit and social value of *Drama* while it also underscores the necessity of protecting young people's right to read it. While much of the previous public conversation about Raina Telgemeier's graphic novel focuses on the LGBTQ content as a reason to keep the book out of the hands of young people, I argue that these elements are precisely why young people ought to have access to it.

*Drama* was inspired by Raina Telgemeier's middle and high school experiences in theater and choir (Author's Note), with characters drawn from actual people like her friendship with a pair of twin gay brothers (Author's Note; "Frequently Asked Questions"). In *Drama*, students at Eucalyptus Middle School are tasked with producing the (imagined) classic musical about star-crossed lovers, *Moon Over Mississippi*. The action is focused on Callie, who has ambitious plans in her role as set designer while dealing with friendships and various unreciprocated crushes. The cover image of Callie walking on stage between twin brothers, Jesse and Justin, with a red heart above her head establishes the interdependence of the theatrical drama and romantic drama in the text. At the beginning of their romantic lives, these middle school pupils deal with first crushes, unrequited love, and "confused, chaste love affairs," as they determine what they want in their interpersonal relationships in the midst of putting on the musical (Brenner). Jaffe emphasizes the excellence of "Telgemeier's portrayal of diverse characters from the stage crew—from geeks to the cool kids and jocks. There are kids of different ethnicities and cultural heritages, and all of them, regardless of color, background, size, or shape, are wrestling with who they are." *Drama* reflects the realities of teen identity formation in that awareness of their burgeoning sexuality, including sexual orientation, is a significant part of early adolescent development. According to the American Psychological Association, "the core attractions that form the basis for adult sexual identity typically emerge between middle childhood and early adolescence. These patterns of emotional, romantic, and sexual attraction may arise without any prior sexual experience." As Benoit Denizet-Lewis notes in a *New York Times* article, "sex researchers and counselors say that middle-school students are increasingly coming out to friends or family or to an adult in school" (Denizet-Lewis MM36). Adolescence is a time of tremendous change when social and cultural structures shape teens' identities. Gender, in particular, is "a process that changes as the subject comes into contact with people and the omnipresent hierarchies in which individuals are sorted" (Malaby and Esh 52). Michael Messner describes gender identity as "not a "thing" that people "have," but rather as a *process of construction* that develops, comes into crisis, and changes as a person interacts with the social world" (Messner 416).

In *Drama*, Telgemeier shows how young males develop their masculine identities particularly through the characters of Matt and Jesse, who struggle with hegemonic masculinity, coming "under increased external pressure due to encounters with institutional and social structures, such as work, sports, and dating, that sort males into hierarchies" (Malaby and Esh 39). R. W. Connell coined the term "hegemonic masculinity" to refer to normative forms of masculine behavior within a society. Historically, hegemonic masculinity "embodied the currently most honored way of being a man, it required all other men to position themselves in relation to it, and it ideologically legitimated the global subordination of women to men" (Connell and Messerschmidt 832). In Telgemeier's graphic novel, Matt expresses his desire to determine Callie's choices based on his preferences and self-styled wisdom. He judges Callie's pincushion purchase at Yoshi's J-Mart, saying, "Their stuff's way too cutesy for me," with an image of his hand pointing to his chest in authority (62.3). This comment asserts his superiority over Callie with a subtle dig at femininity. After Matt meets Justin, he tells Callie, "I wouldn't get too attached to the performers. . . . It'll only distract you from what's most important. Our job is to stay focused on what's *behind* the stage" (emphasis in original; 68.3–68.4). Again Matt shows his craving for dominance by telling Callie to isolate herself from Justin and the other performers—with the clandestine intention of becoming the object of her affections. At the end of a series of negative interactions, Matt apologizes and admits to Callie, "I treated you weirdly all year . . . because I liked you," [and after Greg kissed you], "I was so mad at him that I took it out on you. Which wasn't really fair of me" (225.4–225.6).

According to Mark Malaby and Melissa Esh, while "adolescent boys experience gendered social and institutionalized pressures and respond to them," they are not "always aware of the structures of the larger forces that create these pressures" (39–40). Matt finally recognizes some of the ways he has tried to dominate Callie, expresses his remorse for these errors, and starts pushing back against hegemonic masculinity. As a sign of his growth, he asks Jesse to invite Justin to the stage crew meeting, saying, "You two have earned your wings. It's cool if he wants to come" (227.5).

While Matt is able to begin challenging himself, the stakes are much higher for Jesse to resist masculine norms. Hegemonic masculinity can be characterized by promoting heteronormative identities, which comes into conflict with Jesse's eventual coming out. Jesse struggles with his hidden desire to perform, which could reveal too much of himself to the wider world and allow for others to judge him (78.3–78.4). Jesse also encounters attitudes about masculinity from his father, who asks both his sons if Callie is their girlfriend, resulting in grave embarrassment for all and reinforcing the patriarchal approach to male-female relationships (125–26). When Jesse challenges hegemonic masculinity and takes on the role of Miss Maybelle to save the play, he resists gender norms and eventually comes out. Telgemeier's depiction of Jesse underscores the way that many tweens undergo a time of self-discovery as they determine who they are and where they belong, which makes labels and identifiers particularly significant to them.

A static understanding of sexuality and gender is at odds with the field of Queer Studies that thrives on the fluid nature and ongoing evolution of identity; thus, Queer Studies provides a productive space for critical examinations of texts like *Drama*. While many scholars use the acronym "LGBT," the addition of the category "queer" to this moniker is "an empowering statement about the emancipatory strength of a word that was once used as hate speech and as a collective noun to capture the multiplicity of sexualities and gender expressions that are usually captured as lesbian, gay, bisexual, transgendered, questioning/queer" (Logan, Lasswell, Hood, and Watson, 31). As David L. Eng, J. Jack Halberstam, and José Esteban Muñoz point out in the special issue of *Social Text*, "What's Queer about Queer Studies Now": "Around 1990 *queer* emerged into public consciousness. It was a term that challenged the normalizing mechanisms of state power to name its sexual subjects: male or female, married or single, heterosexual or homosexual, natural or perverse" (Eng, Halberstam, and Muñoz 1). Queer Studies seeks to overcome "the danger of a single story," as Chimamanda Ngozi Adichie has called it, by providing a variety of frameworks for understanding the complexity of identity.

Of course, Queer Studies is an ever-evolving field, as each successive generation employs it in new, unexpected, and unpredictable ways. For this reason, in fact, Judith Butler pointed out that "it is necessary to affirm the contingency of the term . . . to let it be vanquished by those who are excluded by the term but who justifiably expect representation by it, to let it take on meanings that cannot now be anticipated by a younger generation whose political vocabulary may well carry a very different set of investments" (Butler 21). In this sense, "queer" is by nature fluid, malleable, and subject to change. This diverse mindset allows for multiple perspectives and an equally diverse range of frameworks for understanding human experiences. Queer Studies resists entropy and apathy since "the reinvention of the term is contingent on its potential obsolescence, one necessarily at odds with any fortification of its critical reach in advance or any static notion of its presumed audience and participants" (Eng et al. 3). This openness allows individuals to see beyond prescribed and even entrenched understandings about non-heteronormative people and helps them to better understand how actual queer figures construct their identity.

This phenomenon is especially true when it comes to considerations of queer youth. Queer Studies challenges assumptions that how young people conceptualized their sexuality in the past is an accurate predictor of what is occurring in the present, let alone in the future. The lives of actual queer youth are much more complex than they way these lives are often depicted in typical coming out narratives. In *The New Gay Teenager*, Ritch C. Savin-Williams discusses how claiming one's sexual identity often involves a process of "[recognizing] that they are different; then . . . [realizing] that this difference might be linked to their sexuality. At this point they give a name to it, publicize their sexual status to others, and integrate their same-sex sexuality into their sense of self" (70–71). Sexual identity theorists have developed variations on this process to devise their own "universal" models of identity formation. Within these configurations, the final stage is often static, a label that one chooses as their definitive stamp of identity.

Modern queer youth transcend "master narratives" that seek to fit them into often ethnocentric models of development (Savin-Williams 80). Savin-Williams challenges sexual identity models that do not reflect the richness of real life experiences, but create limiting end points since "people's lives are far more chaotic, fluid, and complex than any simple model might suggest" (Savin-Williams 74). Rather, "sexuality . . . is an ongoing process formed by the interaction of our psyche, body, and environment" (Bronski et al. 60). Adolescents are in the process of discovering and forming all the parts of themselves. If coming out is the process of synthesizing one's identity, many young people do this by defying labels and boxes, checking several, none at all, or coining their own identifiers. Self-identification allows teens to resist the flawed binary of sexual identity and instead recognize that they embrace its vicissitudes.

Queer identities are given equal billing with the heteronormative identities in Telgemeier's *Drama*. Just like Callie's crushes on various boys are part of her identity, so too the various crushes that the queer characters experience are presented in an open, matter-of-fact, and fully formed way. Good Comics for Kids blog editor Brigid Alverson asserts that Telgemeier "treats being gay as a normal part of life, not something exceptional, and it's a part of the story but by no means the most important part" (Alverson). In her review of *Drama*, School Librarian Esther Keller points out that "today's issues aren't ignored, though they're not actually issues in the book, such as characters coming to terms with their sexual identity" (Keller). In *Drama*, three characters come out in the course of the novel, expanding the literary genre of the coming out narrative through the bravura way Telgemeier depicts these scenes.

For instance, Telgemeier shows that coming out is a facet of middle school life in Justin's revelation to Callie. Before Justin's confession, Telgemeier grounds the scene in a panoramic panel that shows Callie and Justin on a hill outside by the baseball field (Telgemeier 64.3). She then focuses the next series of panels (64.4–65.5) solely on Justin and Callie, with the majority of the frame focusing on them, revealing the intimacy of the experience of Justin's coming out. When Justin opens the conversation by sharing that he thinks Greg is cute, the subsequent panel (64.5) shows surprise on Callie's face and eagerness on Justin's face as they both make clear eye contact. Showing Justin's process of coming out to Callie reveals added dimensions of his character, expecting to be accepted by his friend in the way he positions himself during the conversation. When he reveals, "Like, I like boys, yeah," Justin's huge smile and relaxed body language demonstrates his comfort with sharing his sexual identity with Callie (65.1). After Callie tells Justin that "It's cool" that he has told her, the next panel shows Justin even more at ease, almost lying down on the hill (65.5). Justin's demeanor and body language shifts only when Callie asks if Jesse is gay since Justin is uncomfortable revealing his brother's secret. This message is conveyed through subtle changes in Justin's facial expressions and figural placement (66). Telgemeier shows Justin's formerly happy face frown in panel 66.3 when Callie questions him about Jesse's sexuality, then looks downcast when responding "No . . ." and finally turns his entire body away from her and looks away, expressing Justin's desire to shut down the topic (66.4). Even the background of the scene changes, with the open blue sky replaced with the baseball field fence, a visual metaphor for the boundaries of their conversation. These graphic elements demonstrate Telgemeier's superior ability to show the various layers of the story within a single scene.

Throughout the graphic novel, body language plays a significant role in revealing the characters' thoughts and feelings. During the conversation, Callie remains in close physical proximity to Justin. She mostly stays in the same position until she sweeps Justin into an affirming hug and tells him, "Your secret's safe with me" (67.1). Callie's natural reaction is to accept her friend for who he is and, accordingly, offer unconditional love and support. Supporting Justin means respecting his wishes to keep his secret. Later, when Callie and Justin discuss going to the eighth grade formal, Justin responds to Callie's question if he would take another boy as a date, "Well, my dad would probably flip out, and I'm not sure if he's ready for that," adding in another speech bubble, "I'm not sure if *I'm* ready" (131.2; emphasis in original). Justin's family plays a pivotal role in when, where, how, and to whom he will reveal his sexual identity. The young man tells the protagonist, "I'm sure [my father] suspects. But we don't discuss it" (131.3). From Justin's facial expression, with his eyes drooped and half of his face not shown in panel 131.3—a graphic representation of a substantial part of himself that is hidden—it is clear that he is dissatisfied with this situation. However, Justin is not tortured by his circumstances or treated differently by his peers, as is the case in many of the previous LGBTQ narratives in the canon of young people's literature. Justin's story is approached with age-appropriate sensitivity and thoughtful characterization that transcends defining him solely by his sexuality. *Drama* introduces young readers to the idea that LGBTQ people exist without making them caricatures. Aptly, Callie demonstrates this condition when she says, "I guess I was never really sure if anyone I knew was actually . . . um . . . ," which prompts Justin's response: "Gay? You can say it! I don't mind" (65.5). Caring about marginalized individuals is what makes people allies. Having an ally like Callie, with whom he can be honest, makes the experience of being a gay boy in middle school that much better for Justin.

Jesse eventually finds an ally in Callie as well, but his process of coming out in middle school is more complicated. Jesse resists performing in the play despite his obvious talent, since "all this audition stuff is just too much for me. I don't like being judged. . . . I mean to stack myself up against all of these guys" (78.3–78.4). As Mark Malaby and Melissa Esh point out, "Boys of this age often struggle to navigate the structural and social hierarchies that surround them" (39). The strictures of masculinity prevent him from embracing his true self, so Jesse is much more guarded about his identity. While Justin talks to Callie about the issues with coming out to his family, Jesse's body language shows he is extremely uncomfortable, with subtle clues like a small frown on his face, his hands in his pockets, and positioning his body away from Callie and Justin, essentially cutting himself out of the excruciating conversation (Telgemeier 131.1–131.6). Throughout Callie and Justin's conversation, Jesse does not speak. His discomfort boils over after Callie asks him, "Er, So . . . What about you, Jesse?" His reaction is expressed in bold, oversized letters, "WHAT ABOUT ME?!!" with alarm written all over his face (132.1). While the text does not reveal his thoughts in this moment, the visuals in the scene and the revelations later in the narrative support the conclusion that Jesse is triggered by Callie's question, worried that he has been outed (132.1). Jesse keeps his feelings close to his chest, literally smacking his mouth shut after declaring that "he's perfect" after school heartthrob West auditions for the play (79.6). Telgemeier provides subtle clues like this that show Jesse is attracted to West, from his disgusted reaction after spotting West and Bonnie kissing (110.1) to his attentive medical care when West slips on stage (170.5; 171.3; 172.1).

Jesse's coming out process is gradual and intertwined to facing his fear of being judged. When Bonnie leaves the play abruptly, Jesse unexpectedly steps in to save the day. In an apropos demonstration of Shakespearian gender nonconformity, the young man assumes the role of Miss Maybelle, opposite his crush, the male romantic lead, West. The subtext of the scene is embedded in the musical itself. West as Bailey Johnson tells Jesse as Miss Maybelle, "I won't run, please don't hide. You'll be safe by my side" (186.4–186.5). During this scene, Jesse starts to find his voice as well as a venue in which to express his true self, especially with West's acceptance. As they sing, their faces grow flush, their eyes stare deeply at each other, and even the word balloons' tails intertwine, demonstrating both that they are singing in harmony and that they are experiencing a profound moment of connection (188.1). Another lyric from the musical, "such a secretive kiss only happen beneath the magnolia tree" (77.1), foreshadows the cinematic kiss that Jesse and West exchange at the end of their big musical number. After the kiss, there are some snickers from the audience, but the show does not stop and Jesse receives thunderous applause and cheers for his performance.

During the cast party, Matt casts aspersions on Jesse's character in general and his sexual identity in particular by saying, with his arms crossed in smug satisfaction, "What *guy* sits around studying a woman's role in a musical?" (194.4). When Callie defends Jesse, Matt remarks, "Hasn't tonight made anything especially *obvious* to you? . . . Maybe it's time you started chasing after *real* men" (195.2–195.3; emphasis in original). Oblivious to the homophobia embedded in his comments, Matt reinforces hegemonic ideology about masculinity as he tries to manipulate Callie into considering him as a love interest by criticizing Jesse. However, Matt is clearly depicting a minority viewpoint within the Eucalyptus Middle School community, who see Jesse as a hero who saved the play by defying gender roles.

Performing in the play is a turning point in Jesse's process of identity formation. This liberating experience leads Jesse to be more honest about who he is through a series of dramatic events. Unbeknownst to him, he becomes entangled in Callie's romantic machinations when she develops a crush on him during the time they spend together working on the stage crew. After she receives a text from Jesse wishing her sweet dreams, her affection begins to grow, as shown by the pink hearts floating around her head (103.6). As a result, some predictable middle-school chaos, or perhaps more accurately, drama ensues. At the cast party, Jesse invites Callie to the eighth grade formal, only to abandon her (after showing visible discomfort during an intimate slow dance, sweat dripping from his brow) to spend time with West (201.3–201.4). The signs that Callie has been oblivious to for so long finally come together when Callie finds Jesse and West together talking. Keeping with the awkwardness that is so common among romantic attachments in middle school whether gay or straight, Jesse has no idea what to do about Callie's overwhelmingly strong feelings for him and Callie herself is challenged to accept that her crush on Jesse is not going to be reciprocated. Callie has channeled the passion of her crush on Jesse into desperation for him to invite her to the formal, which makes this rejection at the formal all the more painful.

Telgemeier uses sophisticated literary and artistic techniques to reveal Callie's slow acceptance process that manifests itself through deliberate body language. When Callie confronts Jesse at the formal, she feels betrayed and rejected, so her arms are folded and her gaze is averted from Jesse (211.5). When she and Jesse finally meet to discuss what happened, the scene is set with panoramic images of the auditorium, showing the great distance between them as Callie heads towards Jesse without him looking at her. Their conversation begins with Callie's arms folded and her eyes looking down and away from Jesse (221.1). After they both apologize, Jesse finally comes out to Callie, saying, "It was *you* who told me to go after what makes me happy" (222.1; emphasis in original). As Callie and Jesse mend the rift between them, the perspective of the panels shifts. In panel 222.4, there is a significant amount of space between them, with their backs facing the reader. Then, panel 222.5 adjusts the perspective so Jesse and Callie are facing the reader with their bodies side by side. Their physical proximity reveals their emotional connection. Callie resumes her role as a supportive friend, engaging Jesse in a discussion about his relationship with West with a wide smile on her face, showing her entire lack of judgment (222.6).

Homophobia is never part of Callie's reaction or her moral makeup. She unconditionally accepts Jesse for who he is. As determined from the mirrored positions of their bodies in panels 223.2 and 223.3, it is clear during their hug that they are now synchronized in their understanding of their relationship. Callie's true affection for her friend helps her overcome any hurt feelings. When Jesse tells her, "And if I was going to like any girl . . . it would've been you," Callie reacts in good humor, shoving him playfully and saying, "Fat load of good that does me now" (223.3–223.5), causing Jesse to laugh in kind. In joking with Jesse, the drama concluding, Callie shows she has come to terms with the end of her crush and they can move forward together. This scene paints a picture a modern queer teen who is "breaking . . . out of [his] shell" by sharing an essential facet of his identity with a friend who accepts him wholeheartedly (223.2). Telgemeier creates a refreshing and innovative coming out narrative where prejudice does not exist.

West's coming out is still a work in progress. He defies the stereotype of the closeted gay guy and instead exhibits the nuances of questioning tweens who recognize the fluidity of identity. As Savin-Williams points out, for the new queer teenager, "sexual diversity is becoming normalized, and gay-straight divide is becoming blurred" (219). Queer youth "[repudiates] the appropriateness and artificiality in dichotomous definitions of sexual identity as they challenge cultural identifications of gay lives" (Savin-Williams 209). At the beginning of *Drama*, West and Bonnie kiss in the basement prop room. Their relationship ends when West learns that Bonnie asked Jesse to help her cheat on a test. West and Jesse's performance together reveals the growing chemistry between them, especially in the magnified image of their flushed faces before their stage kiss (Telgemeier 188.1). This enjoyable experience prompts Jesse and West to spend most of the formal together outside. West runs back inside when Callie discovers him and Jesse, a private moment between the two boys that West does not know how to handle and thus causes him to panic. Jesse reveals to Callie that "West still doesn't know if he's really gay, or, I dunno, bi, or whatever" (222.4). As a modern queer teen, West continues to ponder his sexuality without selecting a specific label, determining for himself how he wants to self-identify.

*Drama*'s presentation of queer identity offers a more realistic view of young adolescent lives that echoes the groundbreaking work of Savin-Williams in this area. Queer tweens' existence in middle school is presented matter-of-factly in Telgemeier's story, reflecting the current developments in early adolescent identity formation. Telgemeier recognized that "finding your identity, whether gay or straight, is a huge part of middle school" ("Interview with Raina Telgemeier"). *Drama* offers several coming out stories that all have acceptance at their core. By showing, not just telling the story, in text and pictures, Telgemeier offers an innovative and different approach to the coming out narrative. The artist's deliberate creative choices show young adolescents contemplating their queer identities unscathed by the distant specter of prejudice or homophobia. Coming out in *Drama* provides opportunities to find a community of supportive allies and personal self-actualization. In *Drama*, it is possible to be queer and happy, adjusting the negative coming out narrative with "an acknowledgement that many teens with same-sex desire are healthy, life-affirming individuals capable of effectively coping with the stresses of life, including those related to their sexuality" (Savin-Williams 183).

Those who seek to remove *Drama* from collections and restrict access to this graphic novel fail to recognize the realities of millennial teenagers who are questioning their sexuality and seeking ways to self-identity. In response to the controversy surrounding *Drama*, Telgemeier asserted that "I knew it was a story that needed to be told" (Cavna). According to Children's Services Specialist Scott Robins, "There is very little out there for the middle grade audience that deal with LGBT issues and I'm hoping this book starts a trend that issues of sexuality can be explored in younger works provided they're done with sensitivity and appropriateness. *Drama* is the perfect model for further works" (quoted in Brenner para. 13). Young adults are examining their sexuality in new ways, defying labels and challenging entrenched patterns of identity formation. This necessitates that the literature for them be "more than coming out stories. It needs to include more stories about young people whose homosexuality is simply a given and who are dealing with other issues and challenges—emotional, intellectual, physical, social, developmental, etc. that are part of teens' lives" (Cart and Jenkins 166). Integrating queer literature into libraries and classrooms communicates to children that queer youth exist and their stories have value. Reading and discussing books like *Drama* by Raina Telgemeier provide important opportunities for teens to affirm and expand their identities as both mirrors and windows. It shows how beautiful the ordinary lives of present-day tweens can be without the drama of the past.

## Notes

1. The Texas ACLU indicated in its Annual Banned Books Report in 2014 that *Drama* had been banned from Chapel Hill Elementary (Williams).
2. The Lexile score is 400GN, but Lexile states that "the impact of the pictures on reading comprehension is not captured in the Lexile measure of a graphic novel" (Lexile). The Accelerated Reader Level is 2.3, but for middle grades plus.

## Works Cited

Alverson, Brigid. "Roundtable: Why all the Drama about 'Drama'?" *School Library Journal: Good Comics for Kids*. 20 April 2015. Web. 21 April 2015.

American Library Association. *The State of American Libraries Report*. ALA. 12 April 2015. Web. 15 April 2015.

American Psychological Association. *Sexual Orientation and Homosexuality: Answers to Your Questions for a Better Understanding*. APA. 2008. Web. 15 April 2015.

Bishop, Rudine Sims. "Mirrors, Windows, and Sliding Glass Doors." *Perspectives: Choosing and Using Books for the Classroom* 6.3 (1990): ix–xi. Web.

Brenner, Robin. "YALSA Hub Challenge: Drama by Raina Telgemeier." *School Library Journal: Good Comics for Kids*. 12 February 2013. Web. 17 April 2015.

Bronski, Michael, Ann Pellegrini, and Michael Amico. *"You Can Tell Just by Looking": And 20 Other Myths about LGBT Life and People*. Boston: Beacon Press, 2013. Print.

Butler, Judith. "Critically Queer." *GLQ: A Journal of Lesbian and Gay Studies* 1.1 (1993): 17–32. Web.

Cart, Michael, and Christine Jenkins. *The Heart Has Its Reasons: Young Adult Literature with Gay/lesbian/queer Content, 1969–2004*. Lanham, Md: Scarecrow Press, 2006. Print.

Cavna, Michael. "'Persepolis,' 'Saga,' and 'Drama' among 'Most Challenged' books in U.S. libraries." *Washington Post*. 13 April 2015. Web. 13 April 2015.

Connell, R. W., and James W. Messerschmidt. "Hegemonic Masculinity: Rethinking the Concept." *Gender & Society* 19.6 (2005): 829–59. Web.

Denizet-Lewis, Benoit. "Coming out in Middle School." *New York Times*. 23 September 2009: MM36. Web.

Eng, David L., Judith Halberstam, and José Esteban Muñoz. *What's Queer about Queer Studies Now?* Durham, NC: Duke University Press, 2005. Print.

"Interview with Raina Telgemeier." *Teenreads*. n.d. Web. 24 April 2015.

Jaffe, Meryl. "Using Graphic Novels in Education: Drama." Comic Book Legal Defense Fund, cbldf.org. 24 April 2015. Web. 24 April 2015.

JAM12. "Not appropriate material for elementary age children!" Amazon.com. 5 February 2015. Web. 16 April 2015.

Keller, Esther. "Review: Drama." *School Library Journal: Good Comics for Kids.* 17 September 2012. Web. 23 May 2015.

Lexile. "Drama." *MetaMetrics.* 2015. Web. 16 April 2015.

Malaby, Mark, and Melissa Esh. "'Nice Cape, Super Faggot!' Male Adolescent Identity Crises in Young Adult Graphic Novels." *Journal of Graphic Novels & Comics* 3.1 (2012): 39–53. Print.

Messner, Michael. "Boyhood, Organized Sports, and the Construction of Masculinities." *Journal of Contemporary Ethnography* 18.4 (1990): 416–44. Print.

Office for Intellectual Freedom. "Frequently Challenged Books." ALA. April 2015. Web. 16 April 2015.

Savin-Williams, Ritch C. *The New Gay Teenager.* Cambridge, Mass: Harvard University Press, 2005. Print.

Sunshinewest. "Parents beware! This book is not in line with the previous two books." Amazon.com. 17 November 2014. Web. 16 April 2015.

Telgemeier, Raina. *Drama.* New York: Graphix/Scholastic, 2012. Print.

———. "Frequently Asked Questions." GoRaina.com. 2015. Web. 17 April 2015.

Williams, Meren. "What Do We Know about Frequently Challenged Comics of 2014?" Comic Book Legal Defense Fund, cbldf.org. 17 April 2015. Web. 17 April 2015.

XCPilot. "Inappropriate from Several Perspectives." Amazon.com. 11 February 2015. Web. 16 April 2015.

# 14

## "What the Junk?" Defeating the Velociraptor in the Outhouse with the *Lumberjanes*

*Rachel Dean-Ruzicka*

Upon its debut in 2014, *Lumberjanes* was lauded by readers and critics alike as an accessible, all-ages comic. The series is not only created by a group of women, but it also features strong female protagonists in a genre that remains dominated by men. Much has been written about the problems with representations of women and girls in comics, graphic novels, and anime. There are excellent recent academic resources, such as Suzanne Scott's "Fangirls in Refrigerators: The Politics of (in)visibility in Comic Book Culture" and Sallye Sheppeard's "Entering the Green: Imaginal Space in *Black Orchid*," as well as web-based articles including Laura Hudson's "The Big Sexy Problem with Superheroines and Their 'Liberated Sexuality,'" focused on problematic representation. Scott, Sheppeard, and Hudson critically evaluate the violence and sexualization performed on women's bodies, with a particular focus on superhero comics. As the analysis by these figures indicates, comics texts have historically contained and remain riddled in the present day with sexist elements. The ongoing sexism is, of course, never separate from race, gender presentation, and sexuality. It would be a serious misstep to imply that female characters exist within a vacuum where there is no need to also consider their other identity characteristics. These narratives lack complex female characters, but they often also lack multifaceted development of non-white or nonheteronormative characters. This article presents an analysis of *Lumberjanes* that takes into account the intersectional concerns of recent feminist theory, contrasting the comic against third-wave "Girl Power" and the *Powerpuff Girls*.

All too often in mainstream media, "comic book" is synonymous with "superhero story." Given the heavily sexualized representation of female bodies in narratives of this nature, the assumption is that women in comics exist as adolescent male fantasies. However, many contemporary texts challenge this longstanding practice. In fact, current comics readership, including many titles that are best sellers, exemplify this shift. *Lumberjanes* is one of many comics created by women and prominently featuring young girls as protagonists to be found on recent *New York Times* lists.[1]

Accordingly, this chapter breaks from recent trends in comics scholarship. Instead of examining problematic representations of female characters, this essay traces the development of *girls* and *power* in a post-Girl Power moment. In this manner, I provide insight on how feminist movements are transforming and on how popular culture can contribute to a feminism that embraces a wide variety of ways to present oneself in the world. *Lumberjanes* marks a new kind of collectivist *and* intersectional feminism. Primarily, *Lumberjanes* presents new forms of feminist identity by working outside of the neoliberal frameworks that often, as well as unfortunately, characterized third-wave feminist discourse, especially in the "Girl Power" movement. One of the most important aspects of *Lumberjanes* is how it employs collectivism. Growing out of the comic's primary motto "Friendship to the Max," I define collectivism as a prioritization of group success over individual attainment. It requires cooperation, a flexible leadership model, and trust in the abilities of others. Power, in this model, is inseparable from the group working together to accomplish often radical goals. We see this in how Roanoke Cabin campers, their counselor Jen, and the camp headmistress all collaborate at various points the comic also has an all-ages appeal that creates a connection between adult and child readers without sacrificing complexity of plot or character due to perceptions of what child readers need. *Lumberjanes*, particularly the first eight issues that I examine here, is a text that "does not condescend to the idea that kids are dumb or weak," according to author Shannon Watters (Kahn). Modeling agency and strength to middle-school girls as well as young adult and grown-up readers helps to craft a sense of collective empowerment that stretches across race, class, and sexuality. For readers, the comic offers exiting possibilities for how feminism may grow and change after the third wave.[2]

◗ ✸ ◖

The series, written and illustrated by Grace Ellis, Noelle Stevenson, Shannon Watters and Brooke Allen,[3] was created to challenge the token girl character often found in mainstream comics, one who was automatically assumed to be a role model because she was the only girl (Kahn). Stevenson comments on how she often had a hard time identifying with these characters because "girl" is not really a personality, but merely a placeholder. *Lumberjanes* was always designed to have multiple points of identification for readers, which is how it creates an all-ages appeal. There are many girls, a young adult counselor, and a headmistress. All have unique personalities, moving past the trend in the 1990s–2000s of "[having] the team and [having] the *girl*" (Kahn). When commenting on creating books for a broad audience, Watters notes "the most important thing you could do when making all-ages entertainment is to remember when you were a kid you had this incredibly rich life and you were an incredibly rich being already" (Kahn). That acknowledgement of the rich life that children lead is the guiding force behind the comic, where Roanoke Cabin campers Ripley, Jo, April, Mal, Molly, and their counselor Jen are regularly faced with defeating the supernatural elements that live in the woods surrounding Miss Qiunzella Thiskwin Penniquiqul Thistle Crumpet's Camp for Hardcore Lady Types.

Each character in Roanoke Cabin is clearly endowed with her own personality and talents. Additionally, as in the liminal space of adolescence itself, the campers are at different developmental stages. Instead of assuming the category "girl" means the same point in each character's life, we see Ripley as the tiniest and the most obsessed with rainbows and kittens, while Molly and Mal have moved into the more teenage concerns of relationships and leadership challenges. However, *Lumberjanes* gives us a world where the protagonists, regardless of maturity level, are able to use their own skills to explore the nearby forest and rise to the challenges presented to them. They do this largely without adults and decidedly without patriarchal control, unlike the representatives of Girl Power and children's culture I examine here, the *Powerpuff Girls*. The campers rely on proficiencies they have gained through education, such as the "Everything Under the Sum" and "Robyn Hood" badges, in order to deconstruct traditional nature/culture binaries. In fact, the book itself opens up new spaces for gender performances, breaking down the assumption that we can simply talk about women versus men, separate from a multitude of other identity categories. One category to consider in light of *Lumberjanes* is the binary of children versus adult, particularly in how comics readership and consumption has been characterized.

## Sex Doesn't Sell; or, The Current Appeal of Middle-Grade Comics

*Lumberjanes'* engagement with children's entertainment is one good example of a recent series that moves away from the trend in the mid-1980s to 2000s of serious and dark superhero comics.[4] Comics like Alan Moore's *Watchmen*, Frank Miller's *Batman: The Dark Knight Returns*, and Warren Ellis's *Transmetropolitan* inspired the cliché that Charles Hatfield refers to here:

Unfortunately, the recent reevaluation of comics in the United States has, to some extent, been based on a denial of childhood and childishness. Popular journalism, review criticism, and academic study have all partaken of the idea that "comics aren't just for kids anymore"—a cliché that has circulated with teeth-grinding regularity since the late 1980s. That has led, belatedly, to an anguished realization that most comic books are not for children *at all*, and a concerted effort among comics professionals to reclaim child readers. (377)

*Lumberjanes* is one of a number of texts that have recently emerged that are both "serious" and written for children or young adults. Comics publishing has moved beyond the *Archie* and *Richie Rich* books I read as a child as readers today can find a wide variety of books that may be serious or dark, yet are written to appeal to children and young adults. The *Lumberjanes* crew finds a balance that appeals to ages five and up by Watters's insistence that "a good all-ages book is one that tells a truly good story and does not condescend to the idea that kids are dumb or weak. Kids are smart and powerful beings, and I think that the best way that you can make good all-ages entertainment is to make good entertainment for you that does not condescend 'what kids want'" (Kahn). Reclaiming comics for children's culture is one goal of the contemporary comics publishing industry. However, more radical than reclamation alone is the idea that children's culture has something to offer adults as well, and adults and children are not such separate beings as popular culture often makes out.

Looking at J. Jack Halberstam's "Gaga Feminism" highlights how contemporary theory also focuses on the new collective and intersectional feminism I am arguing exists in *Lumberjanes*. Halberstam ties the future of feminism directly to children's culture. (S)he writes, "It is this generation of kids—kids growing up in the age of divorce, queer parenting, and economic collapse— who will probably recognize, name, and embrace new modes of gender and sexuality within a social environment that has changed their meaning forever" (xxi). *Gaga Feminism* reads *SpongeBob SquarePants*, *Finding Nemo*, and *Fantastic Mr. Fox* as important sites for the reconsidering gender in contemporary society. Halberstam's view of how diversity can be deployed and how collective action is both necessary and possible is reflected in *Lumberjanes* Vol. 1. It is perhaps not so surprising then that this new picture of powerful girls is not uniformly white, as we have Black, Asian, and possibly Latina or Southeast Asian characters. The girls also do not serve a traditional patriarchal power structure, or even have to identify as "girls" at all. *Lumberjanes* is one of several current comics drawing young female readers to the genre, and it highlights the playful growth of feminism beyond the Girl Power movements of the preceding decades.

Of course, finding YA texts with crossover appeal is no problem these days. And despite the tutting that may come from some critics,[5] it is largely accepted that adults will seek out and read YA texts. However, this is rarer in children's or middle-grade books. Indeed, outside a sense of nostalgia, I doubt many adults are picking up *Kristy's Great Idea* for themselves. *Lumberjanes'* true all-ages appeal is a step forward from 2006 when Charles Hatfield noted the attempts to reclaim child readers "informs the various 'all-ages' series recently distributed to comic shops, many of which unfortunately suffer from rank sentimentality" (377–78). Sentimentality has clear overlap with the condescension that Stevenson and Watters state they are trying to avoid. Sentimentality is marked by shallow or uncomplicated emotions, and it is easy to see why Hatfield rejects this as a marker of quality all-ages entertainment. As an example of what a strange category "all ages" can be, Milwaukee comic book store Lost World of Wonders' 2005 list of all-ages suggestions for librarians includes Will Eisner's adaptation of *Moby Dick*, Chris Duffy's *Scooby Doo: Ruh-Roh*, Grant Morrison's *JLA: New World Order* and A. Denson's *Powerpuff Girls: Titans of Townsville*. This seems a strange combination of attempts to get children interested in classic literature, Cartoon Network crossovers, and a superhero comic featuring a version Wonder Woman who would certainly be criticized by the Hawkeye Initiative.[6] *Lumberjanes* appeals across generational boundaries because it refuses shallowness when building complex characters.

### Saving the World *After* Bedtime; or, Earning An "Up All Night" Badge

So how do these complex characters differ from children's culture in third wave "Girl Power" movements? One point of analysis is to compare some "all-ages" representatives of 90s Girl Power with the cast from *Lumberjanes*. Looking back to the Lost World of Wonders list, one suggestion for an all-ages comic is *Powerpuff Girls: Titans of Townsville*. The Powerpuff Girls are a useful point of comparison as they have some similarities to the Lumberjanes. The former are a close-knit group, work together to defeat dangerous challenges, and embodied a particular moment in American gender politics. The comic is an adaptation of the television show *Powerpuff Girls* (1998–2005), which was one of Cartoon Network's most successful shows in its first ten years as a stand-alone cable network. *Powerpuff Girls*, like *Lumberjanes*, had an all-ages appeal that some other popular texts may not, including the *Babysitters Club* sitting on the Best Seller list in 2015 and *Scooby Doo: Ruh-Roh* in 2005.[7]

The comparative analysis between third wave girl power politics and contemporary feminist collective texts that I explore here would be remiss to not acknowledge the history of collectivism in feminist politics. First wave feminist activism was rooted in several important aspects of women's relationships. First, there was the intense and loving female friendships that characterized the era, as detailed in Carol Smith-Rosenberg's *Disorderly Conduct* and Ken Burns's *Not for Ourselves Alone*. Women had long-standing correspondence with other women, often using the language of romantic love.[8] Indeed, "both

men and women praised women's lifelong friendships, their passionate decla-
rations of love for other women" without any assumption of sexual impropri-
ety associated with this passionate friendship (Smith-Rosenberg 39). Second,
there is the power of women's clubs in this era. Groups such as the Women's
Christian Temperance Movement and the General Federation of Women's
Clubs were essential in promoting feminist causes of the era, including claiming property rights and women's suffrage. Members of these clubs "learned
that only through strength in numbers could they gain access to traditionally-
male pursuits and activities" (Tarbox 2). Women found power in these societies where they could invite activist speakers such as Susan B. Anthony, as well
as make claims for civic responsibilities outside of the home. Of course, club
relationships were complicated on the grounds of class and race. While the
slogan of General Federation of Women's Clubs was "Unity in Diversity," that
diversity did not extend to African American women as delegates, particularly
when the club was presided over by Georgian Rebecca Douglas Lowe (Smith
479). The theme of feminism's vexed relationship to the concept of diversity
extends through second wave and into contemporary discourse.

The often-seen slogan of second wave feminism "Sisterhood is Powerful"
is an acknowledgement of the need to come together in order to accomplish
political goals. Yet second wave feminism has a troubled relationship with a
variety of identity categories. Betty Friedan famously referred to lesbians as
the "lavender menace" in 1969 while president of the National Organization
of Women. While she retracted this phrasing in 1977, the implications for radical politics in the 1970s was clear: Women's Rights was a straight women's
movement (Fetters para. 33–34). It's no surprise then that lesbian-separatist
collectives sprung up throughout the United States, as women "dissociated
themselves from the feminist movement" and created all-lesbian communities
where sexual politics, rather than concerns about abortion or battered wives,
were the activist focus (Faderman 238).

The complications with the idea of sisterhood and second wave inclusivity
were recently highlighted in a keynote conversation between Erica Jong (*Fear
of Flying*, 1973) and Roxanne Gay (*Bad Feminist*, 2014) at the 2015 Decatur
Book Festival in Decatur, Georgia. The event was an uncomfortable reminder
that generational divides between feminists do clearly exist, and they often
fall along the lines of what inclusive politics look like. Jong, herself a member
of Friedan's "lavender menace," was defensive about second wave feminism's
racial politics. Her claim that white feminists reclaiming the history of black
women for the (largely) white audience of *Ms.* magazine seems like an excellent first step, but one that demands we move beyond just historical knowledge
(Schachner). Certainly, bringing awareness of the historical contributions of
women of color is essential, but the collective impulse of first and second wave

feminism can do more than just that, and critics like Roxanne Gay and texts like *Lumberjanes* are examples of how we can mobilize a history of "sisterhood" that also takes intersectionality as a core value.

For Girl Power movements of the third wave, the focus was on one as *a* girl and how that single identity was powerful. We can contrast that against the collective power that we find in *Lumberjanes* through a continued examination of the differences between *Powerpuff Girls* and *Lumberjanes*. As Dick Hebdige points out in his work *Subculture: the Meaning of Style*, the revolutionary possibilities seen in Third Wave Riot Grrrl feminism gets coopted and commodified into the Spice Girls and Avril Lavigne, in music, and made adorably powerful in the *Powerpuff Girls*. Lisa Hager notes the similarities between the two, commenting "Powerpuff Girls occupy a space more closely related to the 'contested terrain' of Riot Grrrl third wave feminism because they reclaim and reinvent girlhood by insisting on simultaneity of femininity and power" (64). While this is true, the Powerpuff Girls' power is often safely maintained by patriarchal structures, different from the experience of the girls in *Lumberjanes*.

Unlike the Powerpuff Girls' Townsville, "Crumpet's Camp for Hardcore Lady Types" demands readers think more directly about how race and sexuality are inseparable from gender. *Lumberjanes* differs from the Girl Power that viewers saw in *Powerpuff Girls* as it acknowledges that the richness of children's lives cannot be boiled down to one girl's experience. Certainly, Blossom, Bubbles, and Buttercup are not one girl, but their experience as super-enhanced triplets means they look and act in a very similar fashion. In *Lumberjanes* versus *Powerpuff Girls*, there are very different power structures at play. In *Powerpuff Girls*, there are clear male authority figures and villains who drive the story. Professor Utonium, or Dad, creates the girls with the help of the mysterious Chemical X. The ineffectual mayor calls for their help "before bedtime," locating them within the service of the State, as Hager points out. The *Powerpuff Girls* end up supporting the culture (versus nature) side of a complex set of binary relationships (other value relationships in this system: white/black, male/female, strong/weak) where culture is generally aligned with progress and patriarchy. Hager is aware of the problematic side of the *Girls* as well, saying, "the necessity of such a powerful element as Chemical X for the girls to be superheroes suggests the strength of the American construction of girl in that their very natures as girls must be altered for them to claim super-heroism" (Hager 68).

In *Lumberjanes*, we have no such thing as Chemical X or emergency calls from the State. While there is a supernatural amulet that Jo finds and carries in her bag, it causes more problems than powers for the girls. Instead of getting superpowers, it brings the threat of velociraptors. The *Lumberjanes* villains, for the most part, are unnatural-nature (and the occasional zombie boy from the camp next door) and hyper-culture from the West's founding "civilization." The culture of city/civilization is not the preferred side of this debate, but rather a chance to illustrate how the power of civilization can be just as destructive and frightening as the power of nature.

## The "Moo Moo Express"; or, Nature and Culture Made Absurd

Feminist theory has long sought to deconstruct value-laden binaries. Girl Power framed this deconstruction in the melding of feminine and strong, claiming a space where both ideals could exist simultaneously. Yet there is a considerable potential for this to be merely a very market-driven movement: where girls were able to consume feminism in the form of clothing, albums and concerts by female musicians, and *Powerpuff Girls* handbags. Girl Power, however, did not require that girls have an investment in social change (Zaslow 6). Many did, but many also coopted the subculture into a style, rather than a political ethos. In *Lumberjanes*, the girls cooperatively use their *learned* skills and abilities, rather than their Chemical X driven superpowers, to work together to conquer the menaces that they face. Collectivism is an ethos on its own, and working together to deconstruct problematic binaries is where we find the political import of what the *Lumberjanes* do together.

Camp is far from a well-ordered place. Chaotic versions of what should be average natural creatures pop up throughout the first eight issues as the girls fight three-eyed foxes, river monsters, and those velociraptors. Nature is untrustworthy because it has been meddled with from seemingly all sides, as camp leaders and campers alike come under suspicion, not to mention those zombie boys across the lake. Yet the Roanoke Cabin girls also defeat cultural constructs put in place by the Gods themselves (thank goodness for that "Myth-tery" badge!) Both sides of the culture/nature binary are represented, and both must be overcome in order to solve the camp's mysteries. In this way, we see how the story of a feminist summer camp becomes a refusal to side with traditional binary structures of male/female, culture/nature, white/black, and queer/straight. Rather than incorporating both sides of the culture/nature binary into a fusion of girl and power, the *Lumberjanes* make both sides seem absurd, and easy to defeat when using their most important motto: "Friendship to the Max!" In fact, we could also read this as a deconstruction of Girl Power itself: girl is replaced by "lady type" and power becomes a quality of the collective, not the individual. The importance of the phrase "lady-type" is underscored by the revelation in *Lumberjanes* #17 that the character Jo is transgender (Finn).

The girls have to function effectively as a group in order to succeed. They need to synthesize knowledge, to draw on individual skills, and to think flexibly about solving problems together, examples of my earlier definition of collectivism. Cabin counselor Jen is often portrayed as a bit of a wet blanket, yet her lessons prove invaluable to the girls' success at different points. Due to her concerns about the dangers lurking in the woods, she refuses to let the girls attend the Raccoon Rodeo. Instead, she teaches everyone (including readers) to make friendship bracelets. While initially seen as a disappointing and fearful response to the strange goings on at camp, the velociraptors could not be tamed without those recently learned bracelet making skills. Ripley uses her newfound ability to make a bit and bridle for one monster, effectively vanquishing her dinosaur.

The Lumberjanes' adventures are similar to Halberstam's *Gaga Feminism*, as "Wisdom lies in the unexpected and unanticipated—to recognize new forms of politics, social structures, and personhood, we really have to take some big leaps into the unknown. Going gaga means letting go of many of your most basic assumptions about people, bodies, and desires" (27). Here I am interpreting that "leap into the unknown" very literally, as the girls find a cave and dive in (figure 14.1). This cave is the primary example of how civilization needs to be defeated, just as they have previously managed to subdue the river monster and three-eyed foxes. April, with Jo's encouragement, defeats a giant statue in an arm-wrestling contest, despite being the "girliest." Mal and Molly's romantic relationship begins to show more clearly, which asks readers to let go of any assumptions about universal heterosexual desire among the campers. Tiny Ripley becomes a fastball thrown by Mal, in a cooperative defeat of another fearsome statue. The varying challenges in the underground maze might hearken back to *Harry Potter and the Sorcerer's Stone*, but the resolution is very different. Harry's story is that of the chosen *one*, and therefore Hermione and Ron are there to help him reach *his* goals, as he moves on alone to defeat Voldemort for the first time. Later, in the eighth issue of *Lumberjanes*, the girls must again go into the cave, this time with another camper who we now know to be an incarnation of Artemis, put at the girls' camp while Apollo is at the boys', each to compete for the ultimate power offered by Zeus when he retires. Artemis is deeply surprised to find the girls have already defeated Zeus's obstacles and the once fearsome statues have become friends. She assumed the tasks at hand would require supernatural powers, when really, all that was needed was some good knowledge of physics (leverage), mathematics (Fibonacci), and language (anagrams).

When the architect of the strange events is revealed in Issue 8, he appears in a laughable form—king of all the Gods, a bull who just wants to be seen as the cool Dad as he offers ice cream for dinner. Zeus is represented with horns and

Fig 14.1. Leap into the unknown. *Lumberjanes*, Vol. 1 by Noelle Stevenson, et al.
Los Angeles: Boom! Box, 2015. 11.

a nose ring, indicating his masculinity and bull nature. However, he also wears an ugly tie and has a cell phone clipped to his belt—the epitome of uncool. He turns to Artemis and Apollo and says, "Your Mom has the car this weekend, so it looks like you're riding the moo moo express," a silly explanation of how Zeus conceptualizes a ride on a flying bull. Readers cannot take Zeus seriously here. He is neither a God (although he does fly) nor a fearsome bull. Instead, he's a huge dork, embarrassing his teenage kids. Here, a reminder that "Gaga feminism is a form of political expression masquerading as naïve nonsense but that actually participates in big and meaningful forms of critique" (Halberstam xxv). Is this cow merely naïve nonsense? Or does it point to a larger critique of the underlying structures that American gender roles are still so often based on? The promise of a "moo moo express" is funny to grades five and up . . . but also a meaningful choice in challenging the patriarchal status-quo. Nature and culture are conflated by melding the God Zeus and his natural incarnation as a talking bull. Through this both are made absurd, an effective critique of western binary relationships.

### Not That Type of Girl; or, Becoming a Hardcore Lady Type

Here, I want to return to the idea of intersectionality and feminism I mentioned in the introduction. Like the nature/culture binary being made absurd through the girls' defeat of Zeus, intersectional feminist analysis makes female/male binaries seem illogical. There is no such thing as a platonic ideal of "woman" or "man." Instead, we must acknowledge the importance of race, sexuality, and gender presentation as complicating forces at work. The sign in figure 14.2 asks us to move beyond "girls," which opens up a post-girl power space for these characters. The word "girls" has been replaced by "hardcore lady types" a queering of gender indicating new ways of being. Readers also see the camp's most important motto with the small sign reading "Friendship to the Max!" another reminder of the importance of collective action for the Lumberjanes. With each individual adding their abilities to the mix, it matters less that there is one leader to follow. Mal has to throw Ripley to make the attack on a giant statue work. Jo's confidence that April can win an arm wrestling contest helps the other girls believe in their friend. Ripley has to point to the correct anagram that Molly then solves to get them out of the cave on their first trip there. Looking again at Harry Potter, unlike *Sorcerer's Stone*, the girls' skills are intertwined and it is not only one of them that will win the day.

Figures 14.1 and 14.2 show the very different bodies and styles of the Roanoke Cabin girls. April is "girly," with the red hair and ribbon that might reference Blossom herself. Molly wears a raccoon hat (which is, yes, a real raccoon). Mal has a punk aesthetic, Jo has hit her growth spurt and is taller

Fig. 14.2. "Hardcore Lady Types." *Lumberjanes*, Vol. 1 by Noelle Stevenson, et al.
Los Angeles: Boom! Box, 2015. 46.

than the rest, and Ripley is all scraped knees and childish bravery. Mal, Jo, and Ripley are also not white, and Mal and Molly are not straight. While we have one nod to the *Powerpuff Girls* in April, the rest show readers a much more dynamic version of what a contemporary feminist coalition looks like. This transformation is necessary because "power emerges from the choice-making of individuals rather than from structural supports or systemic change and the emphasis on personal responsibility leads to increasing attempts at self-improvement and self-monitoring" (Zaslow 8). When feminism becomes about self-monitoring, rather than coalition building, we see a movement that actually limits girls' radical potential, rather than expands it. One moment of the radical potential of girlhood comes in a scene from Issue 8 featuring Molly and Mal's first kiss, a peck on the cheek that happens during a very tense moment. Their kiss gives Molly confidence and focus. As Mal and Molly begin to define themselves outside heteronormative values, they seem to access a significant source of personal, and perhaps in 2015, cultural power. This moment gives Molly the confidence she needs to focus on the anagrams and defeat the horde of Apollo-controlled zombie boys that have taken over the cave. Neither girl seems troubled by their desires, but instead empowered by them, perhaps a new manner of looking at young adult sexuality. Here we also see a challenge to the sentimentality that Hatfield identified in earlier all-ages comics. The moment is significant, particularly for Mal and Molly. Yet it is not a chance for emotion to overwhelm reason, instead it gives Molly even more brain power and focus.

### Refusing Neoliberal Uniqueness; or, Friendship to the Max

*Lumberjanes* clearly is not the only comic for middle-grade readers popular in 2015. In fact, it would be a fruitful project to evaluate other works from the current best seller list to see if they promote similar values and reject Girl Power's neoliberal tendencies. It may also be worth considering whether or not books like Telgemeier's are, in fact, as limited in age appeal as the publishers might imply. Finally, a useful site of research would be to contrast these new collective feminist values I identify here with the rhetoric of the "mean girl," another common construct from 1990s and 2000s popular culture. We see this character in films like *Mean Girls*, of course, but we also find her in *Buffy the Vampire Slayer*, *Gossip Girl*, and *Heathers*. However, a most applicable point of comparison to *Lumberjanes* is Hope Larson's 2008 summer camp-based graphic novel *Chiggers*. Looking at intersectionality and collective action in popular culture helps us go gaga, rather than self-improve or self-monitor as though we have a crowd of mean girls constantly on following and judging individual behaviors. I want to conclude with another quote from Halberstam:

> To go gaga is to be loud in a world of silent collaborators, to be crazy in a room full of nice and normal people, to be unpredictable in a world of highly structured systems of meaning. But being gaga is not a mindless commitment to some neoliberal concept of difference and uniqueness. It is not another version of the sad, worn-out notion of human diversity. It does not sacrifice the whole for the part, the group for the individual, the multitude for the singular. (141)

The Lumberjanes series embodies this unpredictability in what could have been a trite narrative space, the traditional summer camp narrative. Yet what I am highlighting is not merely that each individual is more "diverse" than, say, the Powerpuff Girls. Without the whole group, including wet-blanket counselor Jen, individual contributions would fail. The future of feminism, in the Lumberjanes, is one that requires historical knowledge, skill building, cooperation, and an acknowledgement that to be a woman also means one has a race, a class, and a sexuality. We do not mindlessly celebrate the individual at the expense of the group. Or to put it another way, Friendship to the Max!

## Notes

1. Comics and Graphic Novels created by women dominated the *New York Times* Best Sellers list in the summer of 2015. Raina Telgemeier dominated the July lists with three titles: *Drama*, *Smile*, and the graphic novel reboot of *Babysitters Club*. Other books that repeatedly made the lists were *Lumberjanes*, *Fun Home*, *El Deafo*, and *Roller Girl*. Notably, with the exception of *Fun Home*, these books are also all written to appeal to children and young adults.

2. I am hesitant to say this is an indicator of "Fourth Wave" feminism, because the wave metaphor often implies a false separation between generations of feminists. *Lumberjanes* is neither Third Wave nor post-Feminist in its presentation of collective power.

3. *Lumberjanes* was released on April 9, 2014 and has a monthly release schedule. The most recent issue is #16, released on July 15, 2015. Two more issues are currently scheduled for release, in August and September. On June 22, 2015 Stevenson announced that *Lumberjanes* #17 would be her last issue as head writer "for a while" (Lachenal).

4. I am defining the difference between "comic" and "graphic novel" as follows: comics are initially distributed in individual issues and often collected into trade paperbacks, as *Lumberjanes* Vol. 1 is. Graphic novels are initially published as one self-contained story. This is not a perfect definition, as we see graphic novels like *My Friend Dahmer* distributed in early drafts as a comic, then later revised into a graphic novel. Categorization of the genre of graphic storytelling is very complex and even the industry itself has a hard time fitting sometimes square pegs into round holes. In 14.2, the girls find a cave and dive in (figure 14.1). This cave is the primary example of s a large role in whether or not childr

5. See Ruth Graham's 2014 *Slate* magazine piece, "Against YA: Yes, Adults Should Be Embarrassed to Read Young Adult Literature."

6. Hawkeye is a male superhero and a member of the Avengers whose recent stand-alone titles feature storylines characterized by male-female relationships that are not required to be sexual in nature. His current iteration, written by Matt Fraction, is also tied to the Hawkeye Initiative, which seeks to use "Hawkeye and other male comic characters to illustrate how deformed, hyper-sexualized, and impossibly contorted women are commonly illustrated in comics, books, and video games" ("About THI and FAQ").

7. The popularity of *Powerpuff Girls*, which spawned a comic, a film, and products galore that were not merely limited to child consumers. A quick google search reveals six adult-sized t-shirts, a set of pint glasses, and business card holders on the Cartoon Network website, as well as newly released designer heels and handbags.

8. In children's literature we see this sort of relationship between Anne and Diana in the *Anne of Green Gables* series, although it wanes as the series goes on.

## Works Cited

"About THI and FAQ." *The Hawkeye Initiative*. Web. 8 July 2015.

"Best Sellers—Paperback Graphic Books." *Best Sellers—The New York Times*. 5 July 2015. Web. 8 July 2015.

Faderman, Lillian. *Odd Girls and Twilight Lovers: A History of Lesbian Life in Twentieth-century America*. New York: Columbia UP, 1991. Print.

Fetters, Ashley. "4 Big Problems with 'The Feminine Mystique'" *The Atlantic*. 12 February 2013. Web. 11 September 2015.

Finn, Charlotte. "Earning the Hindsight Badge: On Jo from 'Lumberjanes' #17." Comics Alliance. 28 August 2015. Web. 11 September 2015.

Graham, Ruth. "Against YA: Yes, Adults Should Be Embarrassed to Read Young Adult Books." *Slate Magazine*. 5 June 2014. Web. 9 July 2015.

Hager, Lisa. "'Saving the World Before Bedtime': The Powerpuff Girls, Citizenship, and the Little Girl Superhero." *Children's Literature Association Quarterly* 33.1 (2008): 62–78. Web.

Halberstam, J. Jack. *Gaga Feminism: Sex, Gender, and the End of Normal*. Boston: Beacon, 2012. Print.

Hatfield, Charles. "Comic Art, Children's Literature, and the New Comic Studies." *The Lion and the Unicorn* 30.3 (2006): 360–82. Web.

Hebdige, Dick. *Subculture: the Meaning of Style*. London, Methuen, 1979. Print.

Hudson, Laura. "The Big Sexy Problem with Superheroines and Their 'Liberated Sexuality.'" Comics Alliance. 22 September 2011. Web. 14 July 2015.

Kahn, Juliet. "'Girl' Is Not a Personality Type: An Interview with the Creators of 'Lumberjanes.'" Comics Alliance. 3 September 2014. Web. 8 July 2015.

Lachenal, Jessica. "BUT WHY: Noelle Stevenson Leaving Lumberjanes." *The Mary Sue*. 23 June 2015. Web. 8 July 2015.

Larson, Hope. *Chiggers*. New York, London, Toronto, Sydney: Aladdin MIX, 2008. Print.

"Recommended American Titles Sorted by Age." *Lost World of Wonders*, 14 April 2005. Web. 14 July 2015.

Rowling, J. K. *Harry Potter and the Sorcerer's Stone*. New York: Scholastic, 1999. Print.

Schachner, Anna. "Roxane Gay and Erica Jong Discuss Feminism and It Instantly Gets Awkward." *The Guardian*. 7 September 2015. Web. 11 September 2015.

Scott, Suzanne. "Fangirls in Refrigerators: The Politics of (in)visibility in Comic Book Culture." *Transformative Works and Cultures* 13 (2013): Web. 14 July 2015.

Sheppeard, Sallye. "Entering the Green: Imaginal Space in Black Orchid." *The Contemporary Comic Book Superhero*. Ed. Angela Ndalianis. New York: Routledge, 2009. 205–15. Print.

Smith, Mary Jane. "The Fight to Protect Race and Regional Identity within the General Federation of Women's Clubs, 1895–1902." *Georgia Historical Quarterly* 94.4 (2010): 479–513.

Smith-Rosenberg, Carroll. *Disorderly Conduct: Visions of Gender in Victorian America*. New York: Oxford UP, 1985. Print.

Stevenson, Noelle, Grace Ellis, Brooke Allen, and Shannon Watters. *Lumberjanes*, Vol 1. Los Angeles: BOOM! Box, 2015. Print.

Tarbox, Gwen Athene. *The Clubwomen's Daughters: Collectivist Impulses in Progressive-Era Girl's Fiction*. New York: Routledge, 2000. Print.

Zaslow, Emilie. *Feminism, Inc: Coming of Age in Girl Power Media Culture*. New York: Palgrave Macmillan, 2009. Print.

# 15

## Engendering Friendship: Exploring Jewish and Vampiric Boyhood in Joann Sfar's *Little Vampire*

### Rebecca A. Brown

Joann Sfar is a prolific French-Jewish filmmaker, musician, and comics artist. His graphic novels feature fantastical realms, haunted by human, animalistic, and monstrous characters. Most English-language criticism concentrates on representations of Jewish beliefs, rituals, and/or socio-historical struggles in three of his publications: *The Rabbi's Cat 1* and *2* (2005, 2008) and *Klezmer Book 1: Tales of the Wild East* (2006).[1] In contrast, *Little Vampire* (2008)[2], which chronicles the escapades of a diminutive monster and his preteen Jewish friend Michael, is typically given only causal mention in Jewish comics studies. This is likely because Jewish tropes and socio-cultural issues do not explicitly structure its storylines. My essay contributes to English-language criticism of Sfar's works by demonstrating that *Little Vampire* brings vampires, Judaism, and masculinity into an illuminating convergence.[3] The result is a text that implicitly provides a recuperative contribution to vampire studies by empowering two fictionally and culturally demonized figures through a friendship that challenges the constraints of normative western masculinity. Although most children between the ages of nine and eleven, the recommended American reading age for *Little Vampire*, will not understand how Sfar rewrites a metaphor with anti-Semitic overtones by making a Jewish boy and a vampire friends, they will readily appreciate the protagonists' highly comedic adventures and the child-friendly themes that emerge from the text.

### The Vampire as "Jew" within and beyond Comics

Many Jewish graphic novels focus on depictions of and responses to anti-Semitism. Some familiar examples include Art Spiegelman's allegorical use of cats as Nazis in *Maus I: A Survivor's Tale* (1993) and James Strum's angry mob of gentiles in *The Golem's Mighty Swing* (2003). Although these works may incorporate marvelous elements, such as golems, they do not usually address a

gothicized anti-Semitic image: the vampire as a metaphor for the Jew. Two reasons for this omission may concern setting and temporality. While texts such
as *Megillat Esther* (2006) rewrite biblical stories, others evoke a contemporary, urban, or specifically European World War II milieu for their narratives.
*Little Vampire* implicitly invites this metaphoric association due its two protagonists—a vampire and a Jewish boy—and its visual and narrative emphasis on Gothicism. The graphic novel's three stories take place roughly thirty
years after the War, but Sfar's use of familiar Gothic figures, settings, tropes,
and symbols draw on imagery from late eighteenth- and nineteenth-century
fiction as well as horror films. This complex stylization creates a disconnection
from the contemporary world, fashioning an atemporal milieu which allows
Sfar to rewrite this metaphor.

In European literature and culture, Jews have been negatively associated
with vampires due to their status as racially, religiously and socially marginalized figures (Robinson 63–68). Focusing on medieval European culture, Sara
Libby Robinson explores the significance of the blood-libel, which positioned
Jews as voracious creatures who "[wanted] to murder Christian children" (21).
Furthermore, Historian Howard L. Malchow discusses the literary trajectory of the Jew as socio-cultural outcast. Drawing on the first wave of Gothic
fiction in the late eighteenth century as well as the mid-nineteenth-century
French novel *The Wandering Jew* (1844) by Eugene Sue, Malchow contends,
"The most obvious connection [between Jew and vampire] is that of death-
lessness—like the vampire, the wandering Jew suffers the curse of immor-
tality" (161). Whether depicted as demons seeking warm Christian blood or
positioned as the eternally wandering living dead, literature and culture rei-
fied connections between the Jewish male body and these monsters. Although
nineteenth-century fiction produced several renowned female vampires, such
as J. S. Le Fanu's *Carmilla* (1872), they are rarely coded as Jewish. This is likely
due to the "persistent European representation of the Jewish man as a sort of
woman" (Boyarin 3), amongst other factors.

Bram Stoker's *Dracula* (1897) offers the quintessential metaphoric representation of the vampire as male Jew. In her analysis of this text, J. Jack
Halberstam scrutinizes Dracula's physical features, including his "aquiline
nose with 'peculiarly arched nostrils,' massive eyebrows and 'bushy hair,' a cruel
mouth and 'peculiarly sharp white teeth'" (18). He claims, "Visually, the connection between Dracula and other fictional Jews [such as George DuMaurier's
Svengali and Charles Dickens' Fagin] is quite strong" (92). Outside of fiction,
these corporeal attributes would have been linked to the "Jewish body as an
essentially criminalized and pathologized body" (Halberstam 95) as a result
of discourses propounded by Caesar Lombroso and other criminologists.
Stoker's creation has come to signify a form of Gothic monstrosity that not

only coalesces fears about gendered and sexual deviancy but also derogatory racist imagery of the late-Victorian imaginary provoked by localized cultural stereotypes and imperialist ventures.

Nonetheless, Dracula and other vampires' associations with a specifically Jewish racial-ethnic otherness are often severed or whitewashed in twentieth- and twenty-first-century popular culture.[4] In cinema, Dracula has been portrayed in a variety of ways, including as a hypermasculine sexual threat (*The Horror of Dracula* [1958] and other Hammer films) and as a mesmerizing Euro-African Judas (*Dracula 2000* [2000]). The Bronze Age American horror comic *The Tomb of Dracula* (1972–79) reinforces connections amongst masculinity, monstrosity, and violence, while rewriting the monster's racial difference as explicitly African American. American children's graphic novels circulate more domesticated images of the monster to emphasize child-friendly themes such as eating, socializing, family, and the subversion of horror stereotypes. These works may generalize representations of race and ethnicity—the caricatured Eastern European vampire in *Dear Dracula* (2008) or the elderly white man in *Sam and Friends Mystery: Dracula Madness* (2009)—or simply occlude this issue, as in *Upside Down: A Vampire Tale* (2012).

How then does Sfar's character, Little Vampire, engage with and help rewrite an anti-Semitic trope? Little Vampire is a diminutive purple-grey skinned cartoon version of F. W. Murnau's titular silent film monster *Nosferatu* (1922). While Julia Round discusses this monster's "animalistic" visage and actions (173), Brenda Gardenour investigates his visual associations with Stoker's Dracula, contending "Murnau sculpts a sinister creature whose anatomical traits and physiological drives are grounded in the imaginary body not just of the vampire but of the monstrous, blood-thirsty, rapacious Jew" (53). She additionally explores "Aristotelian categorical inversion," to explain Count Orlock's behavior and physical features: "Like the medieval Jew, Orlock is an inversion of the warm Christian male and as such is predominantly cold in humor" (56) and is an "un-manly" figure (57). Little Vampire's body and appearance, including his bald head, bulbous white eyes, pointed ears and nose, frequently hidden hands, and invisible feet, mark him as inhuman. Furthermore, his name, Little Vampire, and even his visage—a tiny, shapeless body hidden beneath a cloak—resists gender categorization. The monster is also endowed with several familiar vampiric features that magnify his otherness, such as the ability to fly (Sfar 4).

Sfar not only layers a range of cinematic, cultural, and literary associations onto Little Vampire but also draws from his own corpus. The character Little Vampire appears as an adult incarnation of himself in Sfar's *The Little World of the Golem* (Brod 169). He is also Ferdinand the Vampire, the cerebral, lovelorn adult protagonist of *Vampire Loves* (2006). In a short comic strip nestled within *Vampire Loves* the child monster tells Michael that vampires "can grow little." Ferdinand's "grandmother" elaborates the back-story by explaining, "One day, you'll be so sad to be leading an adult's life that you'll ask to go back to childhood" (94). Little Vampire represents Ferdinand's disavowal of adult life, a retreat from his romantic liaisons and problematic friendships. Unlike his adult doppelganger who persistently pursues females, the child monster's only female affinity is his mother, and he evinces few normative masculine qualities.[5] Instead, Little Vampire frequently espouses an ethics of nonviolence and ultimately promotes social activism. These are features that Paul Breines, Elliott N. Dorff, and Elise Martel have identified with stereotypic depictions of Jews and in some cases have directly linked to Jewish masculinity.

In sum, Sfar's heavily intertextual and extratextual graphic novel draws on multiple sources to fashion a novel child vampire. Due to his visual/corporeal resonances with vampires of the past, Little Vampire implies the vampire/Jew metaphor and ruptures conventional representations of masculinity. But he also behaviorally deviates from his predecessors. Similar to other contemporary vampires, such as the Cullens in *The Twilight Saga* or Nick Knight in the Canadian television series *Forever Knight*, Little Vampire is often coded as a monster with a "conscience" (76) who frequently "obeys human laws, respects Western society's norms, and shares its values" (Tenga and Zimmerman 77). These humanized aspects often overlap with normative Jewish ethics, further distancing him from earlier conflations between Jews and bloodsucking monsters. As I demonstrate below, Little Vampire functions as a cipher who implicitly enables his human friend Michael to activate his ethnoreligious heritage and helps the boy fashion a gendered identity that challenges normative gender paradigms.

## Night School

Michael and Little Vampire establish their friendship in the graphic novel's first storyline. Little Vampire informs his family that he would like to go to school. Although his father, the Captain of the Dead (the Flying Dutchman), reminds the monster that his paranormal abilities preclude him from a typical education, Little Vampire replies, "I'm bored here. There aren't any other children around" (5). Little Vampire's statement separates him from his family, underscoring his human-like impulses, such as his desire for a peer group. Sfar's drawings reinforce this disconnection: the child monster is initially pictured at the top of the stairs articulating his decision. The subsequent panel comedically breaks the fourth wall by showing the household's inhabitants, a motley group of colorful monsters, staring at the reader in disbelief. Since Little Vampire finds no children on his first school visit, the following night, the

Captain plays teacher, inviting several ghosts to fill the empty classroom. These efforts mark the specter as a father-figure and a kindly pedagogue, rather than a Gothic patriarch. Perhaps because of the Captain's kindness, Little Vampire flouts his rule—the living must not know about the dead—when he writes in Michael's notebook.

This transgression leads to a series of events wherein stereotypes of Jewish masculinity are given a comedic gloss. The next day at school, Michael discovers Little Vampire's existence by reading his notebook and decides not to do his homework for several nights, hoping that his unknown "benefactor" (Sfar 13) will do it for him. While few boys may be said to love school, Michael's behavior becomes significant in relation to his ethnoreligious heritage, even though he is not explicitly identified as Jewish until later in this storyline. Harry Brod emphasizes Judaism "as a culture that values education . . . and specifically an education that values independence of mind (as seen in the Talmudic tradition of debate and openness to divergent interpretations)" (28). Elise Martel, though, underscores the gendered stereotypes of this scholasticness: "Jewish men were understood by white Anglo-Saxon Protestant society to come from a religious culture that stressed morality and literacy" (351).[6] Reading the narrative retrospectively, since Michael waits for mysterious forces to do his homework, he demonstrates no affinity for education and places no value on independent thought, thereby rupturing these stereotypes. Furthermore, he and Little Vampire cast themselves as unethical in a subsequent series of panels where the latter writes, "If you want to be my friend then I'll keep doing your homework" (14).

The notebook incident leads to a meeting between monster and child that catalyzes their friendship. In this respect, Sfar, like other late twentieth- and early twenty-first-century writers, such as Anne Rice and Stephenie Meyer, refashions a pre-*Dracula* theme: "intimacy or friendship" between mortals and vampires (Auerbach 60). Little Vampire flies into Michael's bedroom window and awakens the initially frightened boy. But their dialogue instantly establishes intimacy based on the dead rather than conventional "boyish" subjects such as cars and sports. Michael reveals that his parents are dead while Little Vampire discloses that his parents are "the living dead" (18). The private site of meeting, the subject matter, and Michael's interest in Little Vampire's red bulldog, Phantomato, bind the two non-normative boys together in an intimacy that is homosocial rather than romantic. The youths' eyes reinforce this idea by serving as metaphors for the acquisition of social knowledge. Although the bedroom sequence begins with Little Vampire's objectification of Michael's sleeping body, once he awakens, the panels depict the two boys looking and talking curiously with each other. Consequently, the monster's bulbous, penetrating orbs subvert the "vampire's mesmerizing and animalistic qualities" that Julia Round identifies in vampire comics (168), while Michael's tiny, black pin-like pupils undermine nineteenth-century stereotypes of Jews possessing threatening "ocular power" (Stoddart 119, 122–24). Cheating served as the impetus for their friendship, but the knowledge the boys amass about each other through their social interactions here and subsequently at Little Vampire's house constitutes their relationship, rather than more normative masculine conventions of physical prowess or verbal aggression.

"Little Vampire Goes to School" concludes by restructuring Michael's relationship with his ethnoreligious heritage. At Little Vampire's house the boy takes an oath before the Captain of the Dead: "I swear to devote my life to protecting the dead and keeping their memory. And if I break my word, may a thousand curses befall me" (24). While the latter part of the speech hyperbolically links him to the Captain's pirate legacy and his own boyish desire to swear on a skull, these resonances are tempered by the first sentence, which pays homage to Jewish rites of mourning and memory. Ivan Marcus explains, "Although mourning [for Jews] ends after a stipulated period, remembering continues in different ways throughout the lifetime of a surviving relative" (221). He further adds that another "powerful motivation to create and to follow rites of memorialization of the dead is the ancient belief, still held by some Jews today, that an active relationship exists between the living and the dead, such that the two could affect one another in significant ways" (222). The bright yellow glow that suffuses these panels' backgrounds reinforces the boy's vow to honor the dead because it suggests a lit Yahrzeit candle, an object integral to commemorating the anniversary of one's parents' death. The Captain, already a father to Little Vampire and the monsters in his house, functions here and later in the narratives as a paternal figure for the orphaned Michael.[7] Michael tells the Captain afterwards that he cannot seal the oath with the sign of the cross because he's Jewish, but the boy also adds, "I don't believe much in God" (24). The boy's uncertainty about God's existence due to his parents' demise might be read as a stereotypic Jewish response to the almighty after loss, particularly following on from the Holocaust. These panels, in short, explicitly expose the boy's nascent Jewish identity and provide a compelling context for his adventures at school.

Because Michael relies on Little Vampire to complete his homework and the two play all night, the next day at school Michael receives a failing grade and endures an embarrassing punishment: he stands in the corner, facing the wall, wearing donkey ears. Visually, the boy is entrapped by the green chalkboard and teacher's desk to his left and the closed door to his right; behind him, two pupils' heads stare at his back. Michael's disgrace figures as an ironic instance of emasculation: instead of enduring emasculation because he is a studious Jewish boy (Martel 351), he is emasculated by his teacher and objectified by his classmates for not studying. This punishment leads to a change in his scholastic habits: "From then on, Michael vowed he would always do his own homework . . . which would leave him more time to play with Little Vampire" (32). The storyline's final panel shows Michael sitting outside, writing in a book beneath a light green tree; several darker green and brownish ones appear in the background, suggesting symbols of growth and knowledge. Little Vampire's friendship thus becomes the impetus for Michael's first explicit associations with his ethnoreligious heritage, literacy and ethics, albeit in ways that subvert expectations. This conclusion dovetails with the next narrative which downplays cerebral learning to explore Michael's physical emasculation.

## Kung Fu Makes the Man?

"Little Vampire Does Kung Fu!" opens with Michael's poignant conversation with his grandfather. The boy explains that Jeffrey, the schoolyard bully, called him a "loser" and an orphan. Michael chronicles his disempowerment, which is conveyed in flashback through a series of panels. He states that he "wasn't strong enough to defend" himself when his peers pummeled him, and he additionally explains that the situation was compounded when "They hit . . . [him] in front of Sabrina . . . and they even took . . . [his] pants off in front of her!" (33). This humiliating schoolyard incident reinforces the problematic nature of heteronormative masculinity and its social and cultural institutionalization. Michael Reichert and Sharon Ravitch draw on several gender critics to discuss the "ideals" of hegemonic masculinity, contending that they "are enforced by violence, bullying, and constant threat" (107). Sfar's drawings imply that Michael "falls short of masculine expectations" (Reichert and Ravitch 106) and as a result, must endure social repercussions. The boy never explicitly addresses his rotund, un-athletic build, but the panels highlight these physical differences between himself, Jeffrey, and the other boys. As the panels further demonstrate, the bully gives Michael a "shove" (33), and then Jeffrey menaces the boy, while a group of his male peers surround him. Taking these details into consideration, one may say that gendered norms (masculinity) and familial norms (his orphan status) entrap the boy at the beginning of this narrative in ways more constricting than closed doors, teacher's desks, and donkey ears in the previous story.

Michael's ethnoreligious heritage additionally contributes to his situation. Although the boys at school never mention his Jewish identity, his interpretation of masculine Jewish identity is attenuated to it. Michael misreads his grandfather as a "tough Jew," because he "killed a Nazi" in World War II and seeks to identify with him: "I wanted to be just like you in the war and take a shotgun and kill every last one of them!" (33). Elise Martel uses Paul Breines's formulations of (American) Jewish masculinity to contend, "There comes a time for many Jews when no longer can they stand back and bear the brunt of deeds perpetuated against them" (352). This sense of injustice serves as the basis for the "tough Jew" archetype (352), which draws on the biblical and social history. Michael, who is too young and emotionally distraught to comprehend his grandfather's command, "I never want you to fight," views retaliation against his aggressors in physical terms. His desire to "kill every last one of them!" offers his own interpretation of the tough Jew archetype, and mirrors his being bullied. Violence, in this case, turns into a proverbial cycle of violence.

Little Vampire, who is outraged by Michael's aggression and his monster friends' offer to beat up Jeffrey, takes the boy to see Rabbi Solomon, "a kung fu master" (35). The rabbi is a Catbalist, a clever pun on the Jewish spiritual advisor, the Kabbalist. This rotund, green-bodied, violin-playing cat resides in a painting; the Catbalist thus visually pays homage to Marc Chagall's painting "The Fiddler" (1912), considered by some as the artistic inspiration for *Fiddler on the Roof* (1964). Michael instantly typecasts the rabbi based on these clues, remarking to Little Vampire, "He's a rabbi. And rabbis don't know the first thing about Kung Fu" (37). This implied emasculating labeling proves errone-ous, though. Reinforcing his status as a Catbalist/Kabbalist, the rabbi initially offers to create Michael the quintessential, violent, indestructible Jewish super-hero: "a golem" (Andrae and Gordon 38–41). However, the boy rejects this solution on the basis of school's rules: "We're not allowed to bring giant dudes to school" (37). Implicitly, the refusal of the Golem can be read as a rejection of ethnoreligious heritage as well as a desire for self-sufficiency. Instead, when the rabbi offers a solution that appeals to Michael's restrictively masculine norms of a (self-) defense system, the "Wushu kung fu, the boxing style of the Shaolin Temple monks," he accepts the Catbalist's help (38).

When Michael enters the lush, green garden in search of the kung fu book that will teach him Wushu, an "embedded story" (Round 158) begins. Sfar crafts a hybrid defense system for Michael that visually pays homage to DC, Marvel, and Charlton Comics' martial arts and body-building ads as well as kung fu movies and video game imagery. The boy beats up several monkeys, climbs a temple's steep steps, and is defeated by "the Siamese [boxing] Dragon" Lumpini (42). Determined to possess the tome, Michael challenges the monster to a re-match. Here, the boy appears as quintessentially hypermasculine in his bare feet, wearing only his pajama bottoms, and brandishing nunchaku. Towards the end of the match, a panel depicts Michael with his teeth bared, floating just above the fallen dragon, with six arms waving to show his speed and phys-ical prowess. This image contrasts one at the beginning of the story where Michael's waving arms signified disempowerment in the schoolyard. While

Lumpini's pain is confined to a jagged speech bubble reading "Ow! Ouch! Ow!" the words "Wham! Wham! Wham! Wham! Wham!" hover above Michael, unbounded, attesting to his power (44). If, as R. W. Connell writes, "The body . . . is inescapable in constructions of masculinity; but what is inescapable is not fixed," then the embedded story reveals this lack of fixity through the boy's movements in this panel and in the previous ones where he leaps in the air and rolls on the ground (56). Victorious, Michael returns to the Catbalist and Little Vampire only to discover that the book claims, "If you have managed to steal this book from the dragon, you are very skilled at kung fu. This book will teach you nothing more" (45). The entire incident thus provides Michael with an empowering male fantasy that contradictorily downplays intellectualism by positioning and then discarding a book as the source of knowledge.

The next day at school, Michael tries to defeat his adversary with his new-found martial arts skills. Unfortunately, the bully knocks him out in a series of well-aimed punches. Jeffrey still embodies masculine physical superior-ity, while Michael's attempt to perform the skills he mastered the previous night cast him an emasculated (Jewish) boy. Michael's kung fu training is thus revealed as a fantasy that can never be transferred to his schoolyard reality; in this sense the embedded story resonates with, but does not change, the other levels of narration. Significantly, Little Vampire, by taking the boy to the rabbi, shows his friend that he can neither escape his ethnoreligious heritage nor solve his problems in one evening. However, Sabrina, Michael's romantic interest, provides him with a temporary solution when she smacks Jeffery over the head with a book bag. In a storyline that seemingly emphasizes the sig-nificance of physical and empirical learning, the girl's violent gesture not only reminds the reader that books are powerful weapons, but implicitly returns Michael to the values he embraced at the end of the previous story.

### Canine Heroism

In the text's final narrative, "Little Vampire and the Canine Defender's Club," Little Vampire and Michael rescue three dogs from a mad scientist. This tale, although shorter than the other two, offers at least three significant contribu-tions to the Little Vampire stories. First, through Michael's interactions with canines, it recuperates negative associations between Jews and dogs. Phillip Ackerman-Lieberman and Rakefet Zalashik explain, "Jews have had long to reckon with the fact they were looked at the very same way as the dog," because they were religious, racial, and/or ethnic outcasts within societies (4). However, the graphic novel implicitly addresses a different facet to this rela-tionship: that Jews have had negative or ambivalent attitudes towards dogs, for reasons that extend beyond biblical literature (Ackerman-Lieberman 3–10), such as the use of German Shepherds "as guard dogs and tools of terror in the ghettos, forced labor camps, concentration camps, and extermination camps" (Zalashik 184). Second, Sfar's use of dogs establishes a significant connection to children's literature. As Zalashik explains, "Western culture widely uses animals in children's literature, with dogs playing a particularly prominent role. . . . In some tales, dogs display unusual devotion or shrewdness, making them seem like the most intelligent animal, the most capable of education, and even the only animal who can identify its owner and friends of the family" (181). Phantomato, Little Vampire's canine familiar, provides his owner and Michael with intelligence and side-kick humor in the other two stories; by the third narrative, he becomes an important protagonist. Finally, as a synthesis of these other two points, the story casts the boy, his monstrous friend, and Phantomato as superheroes. This is especially important in Michael's case due to the established Jewish identities of comics superheroes and their nemeses (i.e., Superman, Magneto, etc.).[8]

"Little Vampire and the Canine Defenders Club" begins with three exhausted canines seeking refuge from their pursuers, a scientist and his two sidekicks, in Little Vampire's house. The evil male scientist is a stock Gothic figure, given a cartoon-esque makeover. He is a tall, slender man dressed in white lab clothes, with a balding head, glasses, and perhaps significantly, given his later actions, such as capturing and torturing the dogs, a Hitler-esque mustache. In a series of panels, the scientist and his cronies blast their way into Little Vampire's house to hunt down and steal away the dogs. His phallic weapon (a shot-gun), verbal violence (towards Michael), and physical brutality (dragging Michael around by his ear) conspires to create an irrational masculine foe who must be defeated.

After this domestic invasion, the story positions the Captain's ethics of non-violence against Phantomato's desire for action/retaliation. The paternal character explains his decision to hide from the invaders by claiming, "I swore never to kill more humans. I could not intervene" (70). This statement establishes a doppelganger connection between the Captain and Michael's grandfather; both elderly wisemen value human life since they have killed. However, Phantomato counters, "Fact is, once you saw it was just a bunch of dogs, you didn't care." He elaborates, "If it'd been three children, or even three little pigs, you would've saved 'em, but who cares about dogs, right?" (70). Phantomato's statement alludes to the Captain's rescue of Jeffrey in the previous story, and the monsters' later attempts to save the boys within this story (which becomes retrospectively evident to readers). Human life is clearly the most highly valued making the dog's sarcastic reference to canine devaluation, he is not "man's best friend, all the more poignant. When Phantomato departs to save the animals, Michael and Little Vampire follow him, thereby reinforcing the identification between children and animals in children's literature (Zalashik 182).

At the aptly named "Secret Laboratory," an action-oriented dog rescue mission begins, marking the dynamic trio as miniature superheroes. One of the dog's statements attests to their courageous feats: "They're [the scientist and his minions] going to make us eat lipstick and toothpaste until we keel over" (74). The allusion to Proctor and Gamble's horrifying experiments suggest that Little Vampire and Michael and Phantomato will not simply save the animals from Gothic human forces, but from abusive corporate forces, a more pervasive source of evil within the late twentieth- and early twenty-first-century literature and culture. To enact this rescue, Phantomato crashes through the window to free the canines. When the scientist's sidekicks capture the dog, Little Vampire swoops in to save his familiar while Michael throws a cage at one of the scientist's sidekicks (77). In these panels, each character capitalizes on his physical strengths revealed in earlier stories, such as flying, musculature, and heavy lifting. Phantomato emerges as the heroic figure from this battle: he saves Little Vampire, who is hit with an anesthetized dart, and the canine also orchestrates the animals' liberation by commanding Michael to "free the dogs" (80). In this sense, the action sequence affirms Eric Tribunella's observation that within children's literature, "The relationship between boy and dog is sometimes hierarchical, sometimes egalitarian. Sometimes the boy is more competent than his dog; sometimes the dog is more competent than the boy" (153).

Competent rescue missions and defeating forces of evil are just two of several attributes associated with superhero comics. Richard Reynolds enumerates seven features of the genre that this Little Vampire tale exemplifies. For instance, Michael's status as an orphan "[marks him] out from society," and Little Vampire's and Phantomato infuse the story with "a sense of wonder" (106–7). Furthermore, the coexistence of "magic powers" with "science" pervades the narrative. When the boys arrive with Phantomato at the laboratory, they demonstrate their allegiance to and undermining of the notion that "devotion to justice overrides even . . . [their] devotion to the law" (106–7). The law is not literal or national but rather the law of the father, the Captain of the Dead, who has forbidden himself and his monsters from taking violent actions against the perpetrators. Their superheroism also reveals a vital connection to normative Jewish ethics. Dorff explicates the reasons why many Jewish Americans feel that a "strong commitment to social equality" structures their identities (1). He investigates the Torah and pre-Enlightenment Jewish culture to reveal that "Jewish law and theology protect the rights of individuals and minorities" (23). These discourses are focused on human beings, rather than animals. However, within Sfar's story, the canines may be considered minorities that the boys and Phantomato seek to protect.

The narrative's conclusion synthesizes several themes within this tale and the other two Little Vampire stories. Eric Tribunella claims, "Boy-and-his-dog stories are, as is much children's literature, about coming of age, and a central component of coming of age—except perhaps in some transgender kids—is coming of age *as* either a man or a woman" (153). At the story's conclusion, Michael comes of age when he presides over the "Canine Defenders Club Annual Picnic" in the woods. Here, the boy is a well-spoken leader and protector: he confidently addresses to a group of his peers having orchestrated adopted homes for the animals. He has finally harnessed a masculine identity that pays homage to his ethnoreligious heritage: Michael is a practitioner of "social equality" who "places strong emphasis on the worth of the individual" (Dorff 1, 5), in this case by rescuing and seeking care for an animal that has complex symbolic valence within Judaism and Jewish culture. In short, he has become a mensch, "an ethical or decent human being of either gender" (Martel 351).[9] In contrast to the boy who wished to assume a "tough Jew" identity in the previous story, the only violence he resorted to—against the scientist and his minions—was sanctioned by their own nefariousness. At the same time, Michael's physical prowess at the laboratory, including his brief performance as part of a superhero term, link him to more conventional constructions of masculinity. Ultimately, the identity he fashions pays homage to positive features identified with masculinity and to the social ethics of a religion that is still regarded by many as non-normative in western culture.

Given the vampire's media-saturation in the twenty-first century, with many western children's familiarity beginning with *Sesame Street*'s Count, children and parents will likely enjoy the way that Little Vampire himself follows recent humanized trends by befriending a preteen boy and avoiding blood-sucking. In terms of its depictions of masculinity, Reichert and Ravitch, in their study of urban American Jewish boys demonstrate "that active participation in Jewish identity strengthened boys' ability to adopt alternative masculinities" (123). They explain that many men, not just American, have already begun to fashion non-normative masculine identities (125). Nonetheless, Reichert and Ravitch recognize that much work needs to be done before hegemonic masculinity is thoroughly destabilized in western nations. Until that time, fictional works, such as Sfar's, serve as a potent reminder of ethnic and racial tolerance, as well as the work of social ethics, so important to Judaism, which can ultimately empower preteen children and diminutive vampires.

# Notes

1. *The Rabbi's Cat*, set in Algeria and France in the 1930s, chronicles the adventures of a talk-ing feline living a Sephardic Jewish household. *Klezmer*, set in Russia in the 1890s, concerns a traveling Klezmer musician, two outcast rabbinical scholars, and a Jewish woman's epic trek to St. Petersburg. The publication dates I list are for the North American translations.

2. All three *Little Vampire* stories were originally published in France in 1999, 2000, and 2001, respectively. In 2003, Simon and Schuster published translations of the first two stories. The publication date of 2008 reflects First Second's translated graphic novel, featuring all three stories.

3. Explicit references to religion, Jewish history, and/or Judaic values are generally absent from *The Horn Book* and *School Library Journal* reviews of the *Little Vampire* stories. Stephen E. Tabachnick's *The Quest for Jewish Belief and Identity in the Graphic Novel* (2014) mentions the book in passing (88). Harry Brod briefly comments on Sfar's integration of Judaism within the graphic novel (167–68), and Susan Honeyman provides a short discussion of Sfar's golem (170) in her study *Consuming Agency in Fairy Tales, Childlore, and Folkliterature* (2010).

4. I use the word "often" here carefully. As Clare Reed discusses, even the vampires in *Buffy: The Vampire Slayer* and *The Twilight Saga* "are [not] entirely denuded of the symbols of Judaism" (129). Per Gardenour's discussion, Roman Polanski's *The Fearless Vampire Killers* (1967) and Werner Herzog's *Nosferatu* (1979) both represent the vampire as Jew. In addition, Simon Bacon discusses this association in the film *The Breed* (2001) in his essay "The Vampiric Diaspora: The Complications of Victimhood and Post-Memory as Configured in the Jewish Migrant Vampire" in *The Modern Vampire and Human Identity*.

5. Michael Duffin in *Little Vampire* is likely the grown-up Michael Duffin in *Vampire Loves*. I do not examine this intertextual feature due to space limitations. Sfar has also said in interviews that the child character Michael is loosely based on himself.

6. It is important to note that Brienes, Dorff, Martel, and Reichert and Ravitch focus on the identity of American or Diaspora Jews rather specifically French Jews. However, as I hope I demonstrate, much of the information I draw on from their works concerns biblical sources and European social history and is thus highly applicable to what Sfar stages in his graphic novel.

7. Brod briefly discusses Jewish traditions of honoring the dead in the context of *The Rabbi's Cat*. He notes that "Sfar's concern with the dead plays an important role in his work, as his stories abound with all sorts of denizens of the worlds after death: vampires, mummies, ghosts, and others" (166). He quotes the full conversation between the Captain and Michael but does not analyze it.

8. The superhero as Jew, as well as Jews' roles within the comic book publishing industry, have been extensively explored in Harry Brod's study, Andrae and Gordon's study, Tabachnick's study, and Danny Fingeroth's *Disguised as Clark Kent: Jews, Comics, and the Creation of the Superhero* (2007).

9. As Martel explains, "the need of Jews to be ethical" is "historically formed" (not just by the Holocaust) (353).

# Works Cited

Ackerman-Lieberman, Phillip, and Rakefet Zalashik. Introduction. *A Jew's Best Friend? The Image of the Dog Throughout Jewish History*. Eds. Phillip Ackerman-Lieberman and Rakefet Zalashik. Brighton: Sussex Academic Press, 2011. 1–11. Print.

Andrae, Thomas, and Mel Gordon. *Funnyman: The First Jewish Superhero*. Port Townsend: Feral House, 2010. Print.

Auerbach, Nina. *Our Vampires, Ourselves*. Chicago: University of Chicago Press, 1995. Print.

Boyarin, Daniel. *Unheroic Conduct: The Rise of Heterosexuality and the Invention of the Jewish Man*. Berkeley: University of California Press, 1997. Print.

Brod, Harry. *Superman Is Jewish? How Comic Book Superheroes Came to Serve Truth, Justice, and the Jewish-American Way*. New York: Free Press, 2012. Print.

Connell, R. W. *Masculinities*. 2nd ed. Berkeley: University of California Press, 2005. Print.

Dorff, Elliot N. *To Do the Right and the Good: A Jewish Approach to Modern Social Ethics*. Philadelphia: The Jewish Publication Society, 2002. Print.

Gardenour, Brenda. "The Biology of Blood-Lust: Medieval Medicine, Theology, and the Vampire Jew. *Film and History* 41.2 (Fall 2011): 51–63. Web. 8 August 2014.

Halberstam, Judith. *Skin Shows: Gothic Horror and the Technology of Monsters*. Durham: Duke UP, 1995. Print.

Malchow, H. L. *Gothic Images of Race in Nineteenth-Century Britain*. Stanford: Stanford UP, 1996. Print.

Marcus, Ivan G. *The Jewish Life Cycle*. Seattle: University of Washington Press, 2013. Web. 15 April 2015.

Martel, Elise. "From Mensch to Macho? The Social Construction of a Jewish Masculinity." *Men and Masculinities* 3.4 (April 2001): 347–69. Web. 14 July 2014.

Reed, Clare. "Vampires and Gentiles: Jews, Mormons and Embracing the Other." *The Modern Vampire and Human Identity*. Ed. Deborah Mutch. Basingstoke: Palgrave Macmillan, 2012. 128–45. Print.

Reichert, Michael C., and Sharon M. Ravitch. "Defying Normative Male Identities: The Transgressive Possibilities of Jewish Boyhood." *Youth and Society* 42.1 (2010): 104–31. Web. 16 July 2014.

Reynolds, Richard. "Masked Heroes." *The Superhero Reader*. Eds. Charles Hatfield, Jeet Heer, and Kent Worcester. Jackson: University Press of Mississippi, 2013. 99–115. Print.

Robinson, Sara Libby. *Blood Will Tell: Vampires as Political Metaphors Before World War I*. Boston: Academic Studies Press, 2011. Print.

Round, Julia. *Gothic in Comics and Graphic Novels: A Critical Approach*. Jefferson: McFarland Press, 2014. Print.

Sfar, Joann. *Little Vampire*. Trans. Alexis Siegel and Edward Gauvin. New York: First Second, 2008. Print.

———. *Vampire Loves*. Trans. Alexis Siegel. New York: First Second, 2006. Print.

Stoddart, Helen. "Horror, Circus, Orientalism." *Empire and the Gothic: The Politics of Genre*. Eds. Andrew Smith and William Hughes. Basingstoke: Palgarve Macmillan, 2003. 118–35. Print.

Tenga, Angela, and Elizabeth Zimmerman. *Vampire Gentlemen and Zombie Beasts: A Rendering of True Monstrosity*. Gothic Studies 15.1 (May 2013): 76–87. Web. 10 April 2015.

Tribunella, Eric L. "A Boy and His Dog: Canine Companions and the Proto-Erotics of Youth." *Children's Literature Association Quarterly* 29.3 (Fall 2004): 152–71. Web. 4 August 2014.

Zalashik, Rakefet. "An Israeli Heroine? 'Azit the Canine Paratrooper.'" *A Jew's Best Friend? The Image of the Dog Throughout Jewish History*. Eds. Phillip Ackerman-Lieberman and Rakefet Zalashik. Brighton: Sussex Academic Press, 2011. 179–206. Print.

# 16

# Gothic Excess and the Body in Vera Brosgol's *Anya's Ghost*

*Krystal Howard*

In Vera Brosgol's graphic novel *Anya's Ghost*, the titular adolescent heroine struggles with the issues of body image, unrequited love, and the tensions between her Russian cultural heritage and her desire to assimilate into US culture. In an early scene, Anya is depicted falling into a well where she encounters the skeletal remains and ghost of a young girl. In a moment suggesting both terror and ecstasy, Anya's body appears sprawled across the bottom of the page while five smaller floating panels above her show her face and body just before she falls. Anya is depicted as overwhelmed by her thoughts, surprised as she realizes too late that she has lost control, and terrified as she steps directly into the mouth of the well.

This cluster of images demonstrates Brosgol's indebtedness to the Gothic tradition. From a visual perspective, reviewers of *Anya's Ghost* note the "moodily atmospheric spectrum of grays" ("Anya's Ghost"), "shades of indigo" (Bircher 143), and the "crisp, sophisticated purple, gray, black, and white palette" (Spisak 459) used in the comic; this color palette contributes considerably to the Gothic "feel" of the text, or as the reviewers put it, the comic is "creepy," "chilling," and full of "supernatural elements" ("Anya's Ghost"). Many of the distinguishing features of the Gothic tradition have remained of interest to contemporary theorists; most notably these include: its narrative structure and style that engender both desire and fear in the reader, its carnivalesque approach to representing the fragmented self, and its subversive approach to addressing social issues (Halberstam 2; Miles 4; Round 57). Brosgol's *Anya's Ghost* features each of these elements, producing both a fear of and desire for corporeal as well as unseen bodies, while examining the fractured sense of self experienced by the female protagonist and addressing the social trauma of body shame through Anya's encounter with a ghost.

Julia Round explains that "gothic narratives often rely upon notions of excess, whether stylistically . . . structurally . . . or thematically. . . . These tropes can be linked to the dichotomy of the seen/unseen, which can be conjured conceptually or linguistically in Gothic" (76). In *Anya's Ghost*, excess abounds through depictions of the female body in various manifestations. In this essay, I explore the seen and unseen bodies in Brosgol's *Anya's Ghost* as Gothic excess. Utilizing Thierry Groensteen's concept of braiding to trace the representation of and relationship between the human and specter body, arguing that Anya's perceived bodily excess and the terror of the excess represented by the ghost body are intimately connected.

In *The System of Comics*, Groensteen explains the phenomenon of what he calls "*tressage*," or braiding, within comics. This concept denotes "the way panels (more specifically, the images in the panels) can be linked in series (continuous or discontinuous) through non-narrative correspondences, be it iconic or other means" (ix). Additionally, Groensteen notes that comics is an "art of fragments, of scattering," as well as an "art of conjunction, of repetition, of linking together" (22). Barbara Postema elaborates on Groensteen's theory of braiding in her *Narrative Structure in Comics: Making Sense of Fragments*, noting that braiding is a function of discourse and "panels, which occur as fragments throughout the text, share a focus . . . and establish a series of images in the text that, through braiding, create thematic unity" (113). Postema argues that "what pulls together the fragments and needs to be inserted into the gap that is left in comics is, ultimately, the reader" (xx). Likewise, Charles Hatfield states that "comics solicit the reader's participation in a unique way" (xiii). Hatfield notes that comics urge "readers to take up the constitutive act of interpretation" by drawing attention to their "incompleteness or indeterminacy" (xiii). As Hatfield explains further, "The fractured surface of the comics page, with its patchwork of different images, shapes, and symbols, presents the reader with a surfeit of interpretive options, creating an experience that is always decentered, unstable, and unfixable" (xiii). The repetition of the corporeal body and the apparitional body as excess in Brosgol's narrative is significant because it focuses the reader's attention on Anya's shame surrounding the way her body appears and calls on the reader to trace Anya's eventual self-acceptance as the comic progresses. The visual expression of these concepts in the comics medium adds another dimension to what is offered by text-only narratives targeted at a readership of young women. Visual expression foregrounds the disconnect between the way Anya's body appears to the reader and the way Anya imagines that her body appears. By juxtaposing Anya's "real" and "imagined" bodies, Brosgol calls the reader's attention to the social and internal pressures about body image faced by young women. Moreover, the simultaneous visual presentation of multiple selves calls young readers to actively engage with the comic narrative and to call into question the various ideologies about women's bodies with which the text engages.

## Falling for You

In Brosgol's text, Anya experiences a crisis of identity that is specifically related to her body, and this condition is made manifest within the beginning pages of the narrative. The first 5 panels of the text feature food—her mother cracks eggs into a bowl and Russian cheese patties sizzle in a pan. The text begins by immediately immersing the reader into Anya's home life, which includes a major focus on the culinary traditions specific to a national culture. Anya's mother rejects North American ideas about body image, telling her daughter that in their home country, an ample figure is the sign of prosperity. Anya counters in a way that emphasizes her newfound understanding of US cultural mores, "I don't think American boys really go for girls that look like rich men" (4). These introductory images set the stage for a series of sequences in which Anya has a private thought or a dream about her dissatisfaction with her body, and her body is then shown in a sexualized way. Later in the narrative, these panels are followed by an encounter with a ghost. While taking a shortcut through the park, Anya becomes so distracted that she falls into a well where she is greeted by the ghost of a girl named Emily (11–14). Eventually, Anya is rescued from the well, and Emily hitches a ride (by traveling with her little finger bone in Anya's backpack) out of the well (35–38). At first, Anya enjoys having a ghost to help her cheat on tests and find out the secrets of the boy on whom she has a crush; in a section entitled "Ghosts Are Awesome," Anya exclaims to Emily, "Oh, man, having you around is the best! You're so useful!!!" (81). However, after researching Emily's death, Anya discovers that her apparitional friend died after committing arson and murder, all in the name of true love (152–56). Anya must then protect her family from the wrath of the ghost and banish her back to the bottom of the well.

Throughout Brosgol's text, narration boxes do not appear; instead, the story is told through image, dialogue bubbles, and thought bubbles. This approach emphasizes what the characters in the narrative do and say, in addition to how they appear in images, as opposed to what the narrator presents via explication. On page 12, in the first of a series of panels that run across the narrative, creating a narrative link or what Groensteen terms "a braid," Anya appears with a scowl on her face and the landscape of the park behind her (figure 16.1). A thought bubble with the face of her friend arguing with her appears above her on the left in panel one as she stares straight ahead. In panel two, Anya's face is depicted in great detail; her eyes appear averted toward the ground, and a thought bubble with the smiling face of her mother holding a plate of cheese patties appears above her head next to the first. The reader is aware that Anya is experiencing intense emotions of anger and frustration. This feeling is intensified as the reader's eye moves from panel to panel. In panel three, the same image of Anya appears, but her facial expressions have shifted slightly; her mouth tightens, her eyes become wide, and jagged lines on her cheeks represent her anger. In this panel, another thought bubble appears of the boy she likes, Sean, kissing his girlfriend. It is also clear that Anya is thinking about other things that the reader cannot see, as the edges of thought bubbles appear to rise up from beneath her face and the background of the park disappears from view. In panel four, a close-up of Anya's face fills the frame, her eyes narrow, and a thought bubble of her thighs appears in the upper right hand corner of the panel. In panel five, the intensity of Anya's thoughts explode on the page. Anya's face is almost obscured by the excess of thought bubbles that swirl around her: friend, mother, thighs, cheese patties, brother, cigarettes, and Sean kissing his girlfriend converge around her. Anya's face appears strained; her eyes close tightly and her mouth opens as if she is sighing. The final panel on this page moves to Anya's feet, alerting the reader that she has been walking this whole time, and thought bubbles creep down even near her knees.

On page 13, a full-page image of Anya falling down a well appears with five floating panels layered over each other near the top of the page (figure 16.2). As Mike Chinn notes, this effect asks the reader to look at the details in the larger image and creates a sense of intimacy (22). The large image offers a close-up of Anya's body from beneath as she falls. Her body appears sprawled across three-fourths of the page. Her arms reach both up as if grasping and down to brace her fall. Her legs and hair appear suspended in air, depicting her movement. Her face is almost fully shadowed, and her expression of fear is evidenced by her widened eyes gazing below her and her half opened mouth. This terror is confirmed in the 5 floating panels that recreate panels five and six from the previous page, along with an image of the well and the surprise and fear in Anya's eyes before she falls. In the floating panels, the panel borders become rough, thick, and sketched in, as opposed to the clean, uniform lines featured in previous panels. Although her face reads as terror in the large image, her body is contorted in an erotic pose: her back is arched, her breasts and thighs are prominently at the center of the image, her legs are open, and the reader is almost able to see up her skirt. As J. Jack Halberstam notes, the body within the Gothic tradition "inspires fear and desire at the same time— fear of and desire for the other" within the reader (13). The teenage body, like the monstrous body, is a potential sight of both sexuality and strangeness.

Laura Mulvey, in her oft-referenced essay "Visual Pleasure and Narrative Cinema," notes how the gaze of the reader on the female form is a loaded gaze; women in visual narratives are "simultaneously looked at and displayed" (2186). A female character's appearance is "coded for strong visual and erotic impact," and although her presence is a vital part of spectacle in the visual narrative, her "visual presence tends to work against the development of a story line, to freeze the flow of action in moments of erotic contemplation" (Mulvey 2186). Round, building on discussions of the gaze by Mulvey as well as Michel Foucault, explains, "the gaze is not just a way of looking at others' behaviors but also at our own as socialization influences us to make ourselves the subject of our own gaze. In comics, stylized art and mobile perspectives do not allow the reader the freedom of the panoptic gaze but instead assign them a series of different perspectives" (76). While the reader of a comic certainly has more freedom than a viewer of a film to move forward or linger longer on an image, that reader is influenced by the layout, size, and stylistic choices made by the comics artist, who may wish to encourage readers to adopt specific perspectives and to spend more or less time on certain images. During this sequence in Brosgol's narrative, much as in narrative film, the presence of Anya's body in the frame slows down the action of the narrative. The reader watches Anya's movements unfold in slow motion, and the use of the full page panel invites the eye to linger on the page and on Anya's body. As Scott McCloud notes, "Motion in comics is produced *between* panels by the mental process called *closure*" (107), and "when the *content* of a silent panel [a panel that lacks dialogue or narration] offers no clues as to its *duration*, it can also produce a sense of *timelessness* . . . because of its *unresolved nature*, such a panel may *linger* in the reader's mind" (102). While the six panels on page 12 require the reader to move quickly across the page as Anya's thoughts appear and take over the panels, the reader is asked to spend time in "erotic contemplation" as Anya falls in the image on the facing page. In *Anya's Ghost*, this particular gaze is assigned to the reader so that Anya's character must be viewed in a sexualized fashion.

It is clear in this spread, and the pages that follow it, that thoughts—and specifically thoughts directly related to the body (how it looks, what it consumes, how it might be sexual)—become so excessive for the protagonist that they overwhelm her. In the first instance of such braiding, Anya's overwhelming thoughts cause her to lose her bearings and become distracted from her sense of place. Anya can pay attention to nothing else, and thus falls into a well—a well symbolic for both the retreat into the unconscious and the dangers of excessive focus on the body. Once Anya is overcome with thoughts of her body, she encounters *her* ghost. The entrance and presence of this ghost becomes the visual manifestation of her internal thoughts and anxieties. Jeffrey Weinstock notes that in many contexts, the ghost, "neither living nor dead, present or absent . . . functions as the paradigmatic deconstructive gesture" and "suggests the complex relationship between the constitution of individual subjectivity and the larger social collective" (4). Weinstock explains further that ghosts "reflect the ethos and anxieties of the eras of their production" and do cultural work specific to the needs of the living subjects (6, 7).

Anya's ghost, Emily, performs the cultural work of representing conflicting historical and contemporary ideas about femininity and ideal womanhood that still haunt young women today. Emily has large, hollow eyes; her hair is styled in a short bob; and she wears a childish jumper (19). As the narrative progresses, Emily undergoes several physical changes as her true motives emerge, but in these initial panels of the comic, she appears harmless and is the picture of innocence. As the comic progresses, Emily adopts prevalent ideas regarding body image; she is very thin to begin with and eventually grows long flowing hair (130). She convinces Anya to dress in revealing clothes and use her sexuality in order to attract the attention of boys, explaining when she suggests a revealing outfit that she's "been doing [her] research. This is exactly the kind of thing men like nowadays" (112) and "do you want Sean to notice you or not?" (114).

## Smokin' in the Girls Room

Significantly, the appearance of Anya's ghost, and the reference of the comic's title to the ghost as "Anya's," plays on the fact that the ghost first appears out of the cigarette smoke that Anya exhales into the air of the well (18). Anya has taken up smoking in order to fit in with the popular girls at her school, including her friend Siobhan, the first person with whom she shares the news of Emily. As both girls lose themselves in a cloud of smoke in the school's bathroom, Siobhan finds Anya's encounter in the well "totally hardcore and awesome" (46), while Anya assures her that it is not. When Anya divulges the fact that she saw the skeleton of a dead girl when she fell down the well, Siobhan suggests that the well is haunted and wants Anya to get the skeleton to put in her room. Anya is mortified by these suggestions and tells Siobhan that this would be "the scariest thing ever" (47). In the second instance of the narrative link or braid, on page 48, after Siobhan leaves the bathroom, Anya continues to smoke her cigarette and examines her body in the mirror. In panel two, her body is turned toward the mirror and she leans in. The scene that follows contains many links to the Lacanian mirror stage (the idea that through the doubled self figured in an external mirror the fragmented body is made whole) and Sigmund Freud's discussions of the uncanny (the idea that surprising or frightening impulses can be strangely familiar), both of which are significant features of Gothic works.

The panel shows Anya's face just inches from her own reflected self with a cloud of smoke in between. Only the reflected image of Anya's face is visible to the reader. In the center panel, which takes up the width of the page, the perspective moves back into the bathroom stall, placing the reader into the position of a voyeur, observing Anya from behind, as she poses with her hands on her hips and stares at herself on the left hand side of the panel. Again, the reader is asked to view Anya's body as erotic while she poses in the private space of the bathroom, but at the same time is given insight into the protagonist's thoughts. A large thought bubble emerges from the head of Anya's reflected body, displaying her mother's body with Anya's face as almost the same size as Anya on the right hand side of the panel. Both Anya and her imagined mother-self frown and touch their hips. The size and central placement of this panel is significant, as the reader is asked to spend more time here, surveying the scene and comparing the *real* Anya, her reflected self, and her imagined self. In the fourth panel, the reader views Anya, as if from her reflection in the mirror. The shoulder of her reflection is visible on the left side of the panel, and Anya stares tightlipped and furrowed brow at the reader and her reflection. In the upper right hand corner of the panel, the ghost of Emily peers over the top of a stall. Again, Anya's ghost appears after Anya's private thoughts about her body materialize on the page. In the fifth panel, Anya sees the ghost, she starts, her pupils become smaller, and her mouth opens in surprise. As Karen Coats explains in her discussion of Neil Gaiman's Gothic literature for young readers, many Gothic motifs including doppelgangers (doubles) "operate rather obviously as metaphors for unconscious depths" (77–78). Freud describes the phenomenon of the double as "marked by the fact that the subject identifies himself with someone else so that he is in doubt as to which his self is, or substitutes the extraneous self for his own. In other words, there is a doubling, dividing and interchanging of the self" (940). Likewise, the concept of doubling through a mirrored doppelganger in *Anya's Ghost* underscores the fragmented nature of Anya's self-concept.

In this sequence, like the one before it, examining the body is associated with distress, dissatisfaction, and the appearance of the ghost body. This scene shows Anya's private thoughts once again become so excessive that they take up a large amount of space on the page. Anya's imagined self is so large that it takes up just as much space as Anya's actual body does on the page. The reader is yet again forced into a position of viewing Anya's body in a sexualized manner, and in this particular scene the phenomenon is amplified in that the reader views not only the body of the character, but also the internally imagined representation of the character's body alongside it. The reader occupies a voyeuristic position, along with Emily (who once more appears while Anya is smoking a cigarette), in which she must gaze at the body in the private space of the bathroom. The reader is also asked to engage in the evaluation of Anya's body as she simultaneously does the same. The mirror in these panels acts as a lens through which Anya (and the reader) views and critiques her body.

Hillary L. Chute notes that because of its hybrid visual-verbal form, "comics lends itself to expressing stories, especially narratives of development, that present and underscore hybrid subjectivities" (5). Although Chute examines autobiographical comics, her argument can be extended to fictional comics for young readers like *Anya's Ghost*. Chute explains that in comics "the work of (self-)interpretation is literally visualized" (4), and that comics authors "stage dialogues among versions of self" (5). Likewise, as Robert Miles argues, the Gothic novel is "a coherent code for the representation of fragmented subjectivity . . . the Gothic represents the subject in a state of deracination, of the self finding itself dispossessed in its own house, in a condition of rupture, disjunction, fragmentation" (2–3). Brosgol's narrative engages in a similar kind of narrative strategy in terms of interpreting the self, but she does so through the use of her protagonist's thought bubbles and mirrored reflections. These strategies foreground the multiple conflicting versions of the self that Anya experiences. In the previous scenes, Anya examines and thinks about who she is and how (she thinks) she appears to others; she is constantly engaged in the work of self-evaluation, and this work is visually manifested on the page.

### Only in Dreams

In the third instance of braiding, Anya's dream is depicted in a series of panels (111). Structurally, the borders of the panels begin to deviate from the straight lines, becoming fluid and curved. The boy Anya is enamored with, Sean, dances with his girlfriend but then exclaims, "Hark! Who is that stone cold fox before me!" and "I could lose myself forever in that dark hair and those sweet love handles," and finally, "Oh Anya, let's have an intense spiritual relationship for no believable reason!" (111). In this private dreamscape, Anya uses sarcasm as a response to the imagined possibility that she might be able to steal Sean away from his girlfriend. In this instance, Anya's private created narrative projects her dissatisfaction with her body and her desire to be noticed by Sean in a humorous way in order to make clear to the reader that she believes she could never be with Sean in her waking life. Upon waking from her dream, Anya begins to ask Emily questions about whether or not she is being "stupid about Sean" (112), and Emily responds by picking out an outfit that Anna considers too revealing. In this final sequence, Anya's interaction with her ghost occurs as she dresses. Anya puts on a short skirt and a low cut top, and again stands in front of a mirror to observe her body. In this instance, Anya is shocked and then surprised with how she looks, as evident by panels five and six on page 115. Throughout this chapter, Anya is "not too sure" (113) about how she is dressed, worried that she looks too "slutty" (114), "too . . . loose-womany" (114), and that she needs "some industrial tape to hold [her] stomach in" (113). Her ghost, Emily, though, constantly assures Anya that her body will get the attention of men, explaining that she has read magazines, that Anya looks just like a celebrity, and that her body will get her what she wants. Throughout the comic, and in this chapter especially, Anya cracks jokes about her body, and this humor is juxtaposed with the uncanny and ironic prospect of a ghost girl giving her advice about how to use her body to get attention. Concerns about the body are also emphasized by Anya's choice to wear Emily's little finger bone around her neck as a charm on her necklace, again connecting the ghost body with her own physical body. The use of the Gothic in this scene—and throughout the graphic novel—complicates the depiction of gender in general, and adolescent femininity in particular, because like the Gothic body, the teenage body is also often posited as a symbol of excess, deviance, and otherness. Halberstam argues that "the emergence of the monster within Gothic fiction marks a peculiarly modern emphasis upon the horror of particular kinds of bodies" (3), and these new monsters are characterized by their proximity to humans (23). Similarly, the emergence of the ghost that is intimately linked to Anya in Brosgol's narrative, as well as the focus on Anya's body as both sexual and unwieldy, underscores the connection between girlhood and monstrosity. When girlhood intersects with the Gothic, the body of the girl (what it produces, how it moves, and what it might do) is what becomes potentially terrifying.

At the party, Anya receives a great deal of attention from the young men around her, but she becomes so uncomfortable with her newfound status that she leaves the party, much to Emily's distain. As Anya runs away, Emily exclaims, "What is wrong with you?!!?" (126) and "He showed interest in you! . . . And you just leave?!!" (127). Anya rejects the idea that dressing in a way that makes her feel uncomfortable and exposed is the best way to get the attention of men, and ultimately she decides to reject Emily and her ideas about ideal femininity. In the pages that follow, Emily's ghost changes; her hair grows from a short bob into long, flowing locks, and Anya remarks, "You look different. . . . You don't look as much like a dandelion anymore" (130). Emily ignores Anya's rejection of being with Sean, and displays her enthusiasm for her imagined picture of their future together. When Anya refuses to wear Emily's bone on her necklace and take her to school, Emily becomes angry and begins to smoke "a ghost cigarette" (135). It is at this point that Anya becomes suspicious and begins to investigate Emily's death. Once Anya realizes that Emily was not murdered as she claims, but in fact killed an innocent young couple and was chased down by an angry mob, Anya recognizes that she is in danger. It is at this point that Anya begins to disassociate herself from her ghost; Emily represents the monster—the other—against which Anya must define her self. It is in Emily's ghost body that horror is fixed; it is her body and the representations of femininity that she symbolizes that must be dispatched.

Thus far, I have discussed the stylistic use of thought bubbles to portray visceral images and the thematic use of the spectral body of a young girl, but

Brosgol also utilizes the embedded narrative as a structural type of Gothic excess. Two short embedded narratives appear in the comic on pages 90–91 and 153–56; both explain the death of Anya's ghost and are printed with black backgrounds to set them apart from the rest of the comic. The first tale is told from the point of view of Emily, and Anya later discovers that this is a false story created by Emily to deceive Anya about her true motives for helping her. A newspaper article reveals the story of Emily's death, which Anya finds when she does some research in the library (153). The 3-page embedded narrative appears again with a black background, but this time the gutters reveal the background to be black and grey newsprint. The embedded narrative on these pages is told in a series of thirteen images and appears without any narration or dialogue; thus, the reader is forced, like Anya, to piece together the fragments of the narrative of Emily's death. Both embedded narratives, but especially the final one, draw the reader's attention to the life and purpose of Anya's ghost; Emily's concerns and crimes are centralized around her desire for the attention and love of a young man who does not notice her. Once more, excess in the comic takes the form of the seen and the unseen, or the known and the unknown. The uncovered information about Emily's death is horrifying, and Anya's realization that she has been lied to and kept in the dark about the motives of her ghost makes the task ahead of Anya even more frightening. In this moment Emily's living and spectral bodies become inextricably linked to violence, murder, and monstrosity. Anya can no longer see Emily as a part of her self; Emily is instead marked as foreign and Other.

In the final scenes of struggle between Anya and Emily, Emily threatens Anya and her younger brother, Sasha, when they try to take her finger bone away from her. Sasha refers to the ghost as "the monster" (187), and at this reference Emily embodies a conventionally monsterous frame: she expands in size, her teeth become jagged, and her hair flows out around her (194). Moreover, her skeleton materializes in her ghostly body in these final scenes, conflating two prominent monstrosities: the skeleton and the ghost. The connection between subjectivity and the Gothic is useful in reference to Emily's transformation in the final sequences in *Anya's Ghost*. As Halberstam notes, "Gothic fiction is a technology of subjectivity, one which produces the deviant subjectivities opposite which the normal, the healthy, the pure can be known," (2). Thus, while the focus of the comic is on Anya's developing sense of self and identity, in order to Anya to move beyond her struggles with body image, she must destroy the part of herself her ghost represents. Julia Kristeva's explanation of the abject is also useful in underscoring what links Anya to her ghost; Kristeva defines the abject as "the jettisoned object . . . radically excluded" (2) and that which "disturbs identity, system, order" (4). In this schema, Emily represents the abject female adolescent self that is simultaneously within and othered from Anya. Emily is discovered as skeletal remains—a corpse—at the bottom of an old well, and her ghostly form emerges from Anya's own breath. While Emily is the villain, she is also part of Anya. Kristeva argues that the abject "lies there, quite close, but it cannot be assimilated. It beseeches, worries, and fascinates desire" (1). The abject is simultaneously what is rejected and outside of the self, as well as what constitutes and is found within the self. Anya's ghost constantly transforms throughout the narrative—she is cute and innocent, beautiful and aloof, and finally huge and monstrous. Anya's ghost embodies many modes of femininity—both ideal and grotesque—and becomes illustrative of a girlhood and female adolescence of the past that haunts contemporary girlhood.

Ultimately, Anya must return the ghost back into the well in order to emerge from the experience intact. As reviewers of Brosgol's comic have noted, *Anya's Ghost* "invokes the chilling feeling of Neil Gaiman's *Coraline* (2002), though for a decidedly older set" ("Anya's Ghost"). Pointedly, scholars of Gaiman's work have examined a similar abandoned well in Gaiman's *Coraline* as a site of the psychological repression of fears and desires that are brought into consciousness by the protagonist (Parsons et al. 382; Rudd 167; Gooding 403). In *Anya's Ghost*, the abandoned well acts as a space where her unconscious fears and desires specifically, related to her body, emerge and threaten her. Moreover, the well is a Freudian symbol of the female body—a double for the terrifyingly unknown internal space. These fears are made visible through the appearance of her ghost, Emily, and must be banished back to where they came from in order for Anya to move forward. Anya discards the ghost's view of ideal womanhood in order to free herself from body shame, at least for the present. Throughout Brosgol's text, ideas about body shame are intentionally juxtaposed with depictions of both the seen and unseen bodies of the female characters in order to posit disappointment with the body as a social and cultural trauma.

In the aftermath of vanquishing Emily, Anya is shown in the woods where the public safety crew at her school fills in the abandoned well. Anya meets Siobhan, who offers her a cigarette (a potentially phallic referent), which Anya refuses. While this section may appear to be a thoroughly didactic ending to the comic, the rejection of a cigarette by Anya is another pointed connection to her ghost and her concerns with her body. Thus, Anya's rejection of cigarettes in this final chapter represents her self-acceptance regarding her body, her desires, and her sense of self, a fact that is underscored by Siobhan's final comment, "You *may* look normal like everyone else, but you're not. Not on the inside" (220). In *Anya's Ghost*, the reader is asked to enter (through thought bubbles and dream sequences) into the mind of Anya, a girl who is dissatisfied with the way her body appears; the reader is asked to become not only a voyeur, but also a critic of the body; and finally the image of the ghost girl's body is juxtaposed with the "real" girl's body. In her narrative, Brosgol continually draws the reader's attention to the corporeal and ghosted body. Both bodies are viewed as Gothic excess, in that the reader and the protagonist experience the body as too much, too overwhelming, too desirable, an therefore, potentially terrifying.

## Works Cited

"Anya's Ghost." Rev. of *Anya's Ghost*, by Vera Brosgol. *Kirkus Reviews*, 1 May 2011. Print.

Bircher, Katie. "Anya's Ghost." Rev. of *Anya's Ghost*, by Vera Brosgol. *The Horn Book Magazine*, July/Aug. 2011: 142. Print.

Brosgol, Vera. *Anya's Ghost*. New York: First Second, 2011. Print.

Chinn, Mike. *Writing and Illustrating the Graphic Novel: Everything You Need to Know to Create Great Graphic Works*. New York: Barron's Educational Series, 2004. Print.

Chute, Hillary. *Graphic Women: Life Narrative and Contemporary Comics*. New York: Columbia University Press, 2010. Print.

Coats, Karen. "Between Horror, Humour, and Hope: Neil Gaiman and the Psychic Work of the Gothic." *The Gothic in Children's Literature: Haunting the Borders*. Ed. Anna Jackson, Karen Coats, and Roderick McGillis. New York: Routledge, 2008. 77–92. Print.

Freud, Sigmund. "The 'Uncanny.'" *The Norton Anthology of Theory and Criticism*. Ed. Vincent B. Leitch, William E. Cain, Laurie A. Finke, Barbara E. Johnson, John McGowan, and Jeffery J. Williams. New York: W. W. Norton and Company, 2001. 929–52. Print.

Gooding, Richard. "*Something Very Old and Very Slow*: Coraline, Uncanniness, and Narrative Form." *Children's Literature Association Quarterly* 33.4 (2008): 390–407. Print.

Groensteen, Thierry. *The System of Comics*. Trans. Bart Beaty and Nick Nguyen. Jackson, MS: University Press of Mississippi, 2007. Print.

Halberstam, Judith. *Skin Shows: Gothic Horror and the Technology of Monsters*. Durham and London: Duke University Press, 1995. Print.

Hatfield, Charles. *Alternative Comics: An Emerging Literature*. Jackson, MS: University Press of Mississippi, 2005. Print.

Kristeva, Julia. *Powers of Horror: An Essay on Abjection*. Trans. Leon S. Roudiez. New York: Columbia University Press, 1982. Print.

McCloud, Scott. *Understanding Comics: The Invisible Art*. New York: Harper Perennial, 1993. Print.

Miles, Robert. *Gothic Writing 1750–1820: A Genealogy*. Manchester and New York: Manchester University Press, 2002. Print.

Mulvey, Laura. "Visual Pleasure and Narrative Cinema." *The Norton Anthology of Theory and Criticism*. Ed. Vincent B. Leitch, William E. Cain, Laurie A. Finke, Barbara E. Johnson, John McGowan, and Jeffery J. Williams. New York: W. W. Norton and Company, 2001. 2179–92. Print.

Parsons, Elizabeth, Naarah Sawers, and Kate McInally. "The Other Mother: Neil Gaiman's Postfeminist Fairytales." *Children's Literature Association Quarterly* 33.4 (2008): 371–89. Print.

Postema, Barbara. *Narrative Structure in Comics: Making Sense of Fragments*. Rochester: RIT Press, 2013. Print.

Round, Julia. *Gothic in Comics and Graphic Novels: A Critical Approach*. Jefferson, NC: McFarland, 2014. Print.

Rudd, David. "An Eye for an I: Neil Gaiman's *Coraline* and Questions of Identity." *Children's Literature in Education* 39 (2008): 159–68. Print.

Spisak, April. Rev. of *Anya's Ghost*, by Vera Brosgol. *Bulletin of the Center for Children's Books*, June 2011: 459. Print.

Weinstock, Jeffrey Andrew, ed. *Spectral America: Phantoms and the National Imagination.* Madison: University of Wisconsin Press, 2004. Print.

PART FIVE

DRAWING on IDENTITY

HISTORY, POLITICS, CULTURE

# 17

## Graphically/Ubiquitously Separate: The Sanctified Littering of Jack T. Chick's Fundy-Queer Comics

*Lance Weldy*

In *Raising Your Kids Right*, Michelle Ann Abate writes, "Children's literature has a long history of didactic education, socialization, and accultura-
tion among boys and girls" (6). She uses *The New England Primer* as an
example of an early American text "explicitly for children" that incorporated
"strong messages about faith, family, and civic duty," as well as basic literacy
(6–7). In his introductory chapter to *Leaving the Fold: Testimonies of Former
Fundamentalists*, Edward Babinski defines the fundamentalist religious subculture through a series of questions and answers. Specifically, he notes that
"Protestant Christian fundamentalists" believe in "the truthfulness of events
recorded in the Bible, morality prescribed in the Bible, and the Christian doctrines derived from the Bible" (21). But how is the fundamentalist to respond
to those who do not believe these Christian doctrines or who do not believe
them in the same way as fundamentalists? Ernest Pickering, a fundamentalist
pastor, claims that "Biblical separation is the implementation of that scriptural
teaching which demands repudiation of any conscious or continuing fellowship with those who deny the doctrines of the historic Christian faith" (10). For
the fundamentalist child, this separation can become tangible in many forms,
including homeschooling or attending a Christian school instead of a public
school and refraining from mainstream social activities such as rock concerts.

When it comes to morally didactic comics, Jack T. Chick has made a name
for himself by perpetuating fundamentalist (known informally as "fundy"
for short) Christian ideology via numerous religious comic tracts and comic
books. Whatever their specific literary format, these materials preach about
the divine inspiration and inerrancy of the Bible and against a wide range of
topics such as abortion, Catholicism, communism, evolution, homosexuality,
Islam, and rock music. Chick's tracts are well-recognized not just because of
their polarizing content, but also because of their ubiquity. Robert Ito calls
Chick "the world's most published living author" (56), so it should come as

no surprise that Chick Publications provides an annual ordering catalog. As Cynthia Burack has observed about the political rhetoric of the Chick tracts: "For over four decades, millions of believers around the world have evangelized with Chick tracts. In the beginning, the tracts were the product of a social movement that was marginal to mainstream political institutions and leaders" ("From" 178). In her introduction to a special issue of the *Children's Literature Association Quarterly* on religion and children's literature, Jennifer Miskec aptly notes that when authors incorporate theology in texts for children, there is a "potential to be exclusionary" and to receive a "more intense and specific type of critique" (256). Since the very purpose of Chick's comics is to evangelize and to call on the unsaved to separate from the world, this fundamental, exclusionary element makes these texts even more compelling to scrutinize as they fall into the traditional history of didactic literature for children.

## The Queerness of Fundamentalism

To better understand Chick's ideological background, I want to define Christian "fundamentalism" because it plays an important role in the rhetorical strategy of his tracts. As Catherine Pesso-Miquel and Klaus Stierstorfer note in their Introduction, "The word is also applied to very orthodox religious groups characterized by their intransigence toward any form of heterodoxy, and their hostility to the progressive, secularist influences of modernity, in particular where gender and sexuality are concerned" (vi–vii). For Chick, the literalness of the King James Bible is essential, as is evidenced by his free tract, *No Liars in Heaven* (2009), which he insists on his website is "a free promotional message to show Christians they need to check their Bible and make sure nothing is missing" ("*No Liars*"). The aforementioned "hostility" towards progressiveness is also something that this tract addresses, like on page 17,[1] which shows the pastor confused about which Bible to use, surrounded by six people, all clamoring for the pastor's approval. One of the men says, "Here it is, in *today's* language" (17.1). This aversion to progressive mentalities also affects the socio-political arenas as well, as I will point out later through the lens of Abate's argument about widely recognized tenets of the Christian right movement.

Fundies believe that Christianity is about living a life separated from the world, no matter how strange or queer this decision may seem to the unsaved. In fact, it is this queerness that they believe serves as a rhetorical device by which they can attract the attention and consequently convert nonbelievers. Conversely, Chick berates the notion that Christians should blend in with the unsaved. In his out-of-print tract, *Why No Revival?* (1986), Chick discusses ways in which Christians do not exhibit Christian behavior and therefore do not win souls for Christ. For example, near the end of the comic, he shows an embarrassed man who alienated everyone in the workplace because of his laughing at "off-color jokes" and flirting. One woman tells another man, "I thought Christians believed in holiness!" (12.1). As Pesso-Miquel and Stierstorfer write, "Fundamentalists feel they belong to a whole, pure community of beliefs, which strictly excludes the (impure) Other, whatever form that Otherness may take. Fundamentalists are against any form of 'integration' of otherness" (viii). This "Otherness" takes on any form of "worldliness" in general, which could mean anything from drinking, smoking, or wearing immodest clothing.[2]

Because of the varied and politically charged meanings of such a word as "queer," an "intersectional analysis" between Christian fundamentalism and the word "queer" becomes quite useful, especially when focusing on the specific brand of Christianity that prizes a life set apart. In their Introduction to *Over the Rainbow: Queer Children's and Young Adult Literature*, Abate and Kidd note: "The word 'queer,' which first emerged in English in the sixteenth century, has long meant 'strange,' 'unusual,' and 'out of alignment'" (3). Hall and Jagose acknowledge in their introduction to *The Routledge Queer Studies Reader* the rhizomatic features of queer studies, which includes "intersectional analysis"— "the ways in which various categories of [social] difference inflect and transform each other" (xvi). In combining these two terms, "fundy-queer" connotes the proudly self-proclaimed eschewing of anything mainstream, liberal, or "worldly"—such as attending dances or movie theaters or engaging in premarital sex of any kind—through the rhetorical support of Biblical literalism.

"Fundamentalism," like "queer," can be equally politically charged. Scholarship on Christian fundamentalist texts for children, though limited, has given attention to the *Left Behind* series—by writers like Michelle Ann Abate and Melani McAllister—and to Chick's fundamentalist comics from contributors like Cynthia Burack and Anastasia Ulanowicz. While this chapter follows in their tradition, my scope differs because I investigate the queerness of Chick's fundamentalist message, including its dissemination, specifically through a fundy-queer approach that highlights the fundamentalist's desire to be separate from the world's negative influences. My unique use of "fundy" itself adds to this tradition. While many fundamentalist outsiders might agree with renowned linguist Roger W. Shuy's argument that using the -ie suffix, especially about religious denominations, is derogatory (81), I contend for a wider range of connotations. The *Oxford English Dictionary* neutrally defines "fundie" as "A religious fundamentalist, esp. an evangelical Christian," and I, as a former fundamentalist, believe "fundy" can serve as a convenient, vernacularized abbreviation without a negative slant. Nevertheless, fundamentalist insiders can perceive "fundy" as humorous and benign, can proudly accept the label as a badge of persecution from and queerness to the world, or can vigorously debate this term as an evangelistic vehicle. Likewise, ex-fundamentalists share a variety of conflicted feelings about this term—nostalgia, indifference, and resentment—all of which can be fueled by reading Darrell Dow's popular website, *Stuff Fundies Like*. From an academic perspective, a thorough database search shows that neither abbreviated term ("fundy" or "fundie") has been used or analyzed in scholarly essays this way before. Despite this lack, "fundy-queer" intends to distance itself from any potentially distracting connotations associated with fundamentalism, while still calling attention to its queerness.

Children themselves are queer, too, especially in how they are situated within the power structure of adults. As Steven Bruhm and Natasha Hurley note in their anthology introduction, "The authors (ourselves included) use the term *queer* in its more traditional sense, to indicate a deviation from the 'normal.' In this sense the queer child is, generally, both defined by and outside of what is 'normal'" (x).[3] Indeed, Kathryn Bond Stockton's essay in Bruhm and Hurley's anthology argues that "the child, from the standpoint of 'normal' adults, is always queer: either 'homosexual' (an interesting problem in itself) or 'not-yet-straight,' merely approaching the official destination of straight couplehood" ("Growing" 283). In light of both of these statements, the fundy-queer child resides not only on the margins of the adult power structure, but also on that of mainstream, progressive ideology. In this essay, I provide a brief overview of Jack Chick before offering a critical examination of his prolific body of comics tracts. This exploration considers Chick tracts primarily through the lens of what Abate identifies in *Raising Your Kids Right* as the three commonly identified tenets of "postwar American conservatism" (12)—libertarianism, traditionalism, anticommunism/antiterrorism—to demonstrate how Chick's fundy-queer comics rhetorically indoctrinate children through visual literacy while serving a political purpose by means of categorical religious xenophobia.

## Who Is Jack Chick and What Are Chick Tracts?

Ironically, while many people do not recognize the name Jack Chick, he has been called "likely the most widely distributed comics creator in the world" (Orcutt 93). Born on April 13, 1924, Chick's official biography is posted at Chick. com, where visitors can learn about his irreligious life during high school in California and then his stint in World War II stationed in the Pacific. Upon returning home and getting married, he converted to Christianity after hearing a radio program ("Biography"). In the years that followed, Chick began using his drawing skills to complete his first "soul-winning" tract, *A Demon's Nightmare,* in 1962 (Kuersteiner 14). His next tract in 1964 is arguably his most well-known by researchers and mainstream audiences alike: *This Was Your Life!* The 2014 Chick Publications ordering catalog calls it the "#1 All-Time Best Seller!" with "Over 146 million copies in 100 languages" (*Chick Tracts* 4). Since then, he has published hundreds of tracts and over twenty full-color comics. Aside from the biographical information given about him on his website, Jack Chick the artist has a rather mysterious, elusive persona. With the exception of one article that appeared in the August/September issue of Chick's newsletter *Battle Cry* in 1984, he has refused to be interviewed since 1975 (Chick, Dittmer 281). Even so, researchers like Kurt Kuersteiner and others have been able to piece together a timeline of Chick and his work. Such elusiveness, especially from someone who is simultaneously so ubiquitous, further underscores the queerness of Chick and his separatist rhetoric.

While the *Oxford English Dictionary* finds instances of the word "tract" as early as the fifteenth century, the third definition of this word is more aligned to how we think of them today: "a short pamphlet on some religious, political, or other topic, suitable for distribution or for purposes of propaganda." "Tract" falls under the umbrella term "pamphlet," which, according to Joad Raymond, by the 1580s in England meant "a short, vernacular work, generally printed in quarto format, costing no more than a few pennies, of topical interest or engaged with social, political or ecclesiastical issues" (8). Raymond explains how in early modern printing, "Size influenced status," meaning pamphlets were considered "less prestigious formats" (5) because of its folding into such a small book. Chick's tracts follow in this same tradition inasmuch as they are published in a cheap format (16 cents a tract) and folded to such a small size to be given away for evangelical purposes (*Chick Tracts* 2014).

While Chick's early tracts were "slightly larger than 5 × 8 inches" (Kuersteiner 14), the format of his tracts soon changed to what they would be easily identified as today: "three-by five-inch, 22-page, staple-bound" (Roth 150). Chick's tracts contain one to two panels per page, which, in terms of Thierry Groensteen's theories of page layout, would classify it as having less density: "the variability in the number of panels that make up the page" (44). Moreover, Chick's tracts would likely fall into Groensteen's first degree of regularity because each page only contains one strip of panels (43).[4] Drawing on Benoît Peeters's use of the term "rhetorical" as a "technique that molds the shape or size of the panel to the action that it encloses," Groensteen's first, and less complex, rhetorical group, simple rhetoric, aptly describes Chick tracts (46)—which provide a visual narrative about various topics with the overarching purpose of converting the lost to Christianity—because all are done essentially through the same amount and width of panels throughout the text, with little deviation. In this way, as figures like Laurence Roth and Cynthia Burack have noted, Chick tracts share both formatting features and didactic aims with Tijuana Bibles (Roth 151, Burack Sin 37)[5]. As Art Spiegelman explains, Tijuana Bibles were "clandestinely produced and distributed small booklets that chronicled the explicit sexual adventures of America's beloved

comic-strip characters, celebrities, and folk heroes. The standard format consisted of eight poorly printed 4"-wide by 3"-high black (or blue) and white
pages with one panel per page and covers of a heavier colored stock" (6).
Furthermore, Spiegelman notes that "The books were apparently ubiquitous
in their heyday, a true mass medium" (6). Chick tracts are equally omnipresent. The standard mantra on their website is that "Chick tracts *get read!*" and
that they have been "Equipping [Christians] for evangelism for over 50 years"
(Chick.com). The 2014 Chick Publications ordering catalog also boasts having
"over 1,000 non-English titles in over 140 languages" (*Chick Tracts* 60), and
Kuersteiner documents that Chick's company has produced "over half a billion
copies" (Table of Contents). "Witnessing made easy" is the motto that adorns
the top of their website, which is reinforced by a section under "Information"
called "How to Witness" that suggests many ways to partake in stress-free witnessing. Within this section, the website recommends ways to witness in many
different scenarios, such as giving one to a cashier or someone in an elevator,
or leaving one in store shelves, dressing rooms, and clothes pockets. Outside
of stores, they recommend placing them "next to the handrail on the escala-
tor" or "under the windshield wiper on the cars in the parking lot" ("While
Shopping"). Interestingly enough, all but two of the suggestions do not require
social interaction; instead a process that I call "sanctified littering" is encouraged: passive witnessing by leaving a tract where someone else will hopefully
find it. As the 2014 Chick Publications catalog suggests, the number one reason Christians need to employ the tracts in their evangelizing efforts is the
"Cartoon Format: Nobody can resist cartoons" (*Chick Tracts* 2). Apparently,
one of the most persuasive components of these tracts is that they are comics
first. In the words of the Chick Catalog once again, this time from 2013: "Chick
gospel tracts GRAB the reader, with cartoons to make them CHUCKLE, and
soon they're HOOKED! Then they get the GOSPEL" (*Chick Tracts* 3). It would
seem that the recognized page layout of comics serves as a rhetorical device
for Chick, serving to lower the critical-thinking defenses of unwitting readers
who will not even realize they have been proselytized until they have finished
reading the brief tract found left under their windshield wiper.[6]

## My Experience with Chick Tracts

Growing up in a Christian fundamentalist household, I was very aware
of Chick tracts. As a child in the mid-1980s, I spent $5.00 to buy an assort-
ment of Chick tracts and became educated in the art of religious xenophobia, which included an unfeigned superiority over such religious groups as
Catholics, Jehovah's Witnesses, and Mormons. During the process of reading
the tracts as a child, I encountered one that did not simply give me pause: it

shook my still-developing sense of personal identity. Other tracts I had read covered topics I had never faced: dealing with an alcoholic, abusive parent (*Happy Hour* [1976]), the problems of partaking in role-playing games (*Dark Dungeons* [1984]), or even the perils of listening to rock music (*Angels?* [1986]). But *Wounded Children* (1983) spoke to me because it was a narrative about a queer boy who grew up to be gay[7] but then became disillusioned with the gay life and was saved from it.[8] Instead of being instilled with the healthy level of fear that happened with most tracts, I was oddly intrigued in ways I could not explain in my prepubescent mentality. I understood even then that this was not the intended effect Jack Chick wanted it to have on me; it was exactly the opposite (Weldy).[9] Burack recounts a similar experience with reading another tract about homosexuality called *The Gay Blade* (1972): "These cartoon gay blades only made me more curious about their real-life counterparts" (*Sin* 34). The irony becomes even more profound when Burack argues that "Chick's antigay Christian comics violate the standards of the Comics Code Authority, standards put in place to protect youthful consumers from encountering the immoral shenanigans of the adult world" (39). Specifically, she cites two points under the Code's heading, "Marriage and Sex," including number 7: "sex perversion or any inference to same is strictly forbidden" ("Comics Code"). We both eventually reached a point where we realized that Chick's representations of characters and topics were misinformed and heavy-handed, not only for those about homosexuality, but also about others that did not coalesce with the fundy ideology. Until recently, I lived my life as a fundy-queer who was supposed to refrain from being affiliated with the world. But over the past few years, I realized that I was queer in the gay sense, too. In so doing, I became the "Other" from a fundy perspective. Now, almost twenty years after I bought my first assortment of Chick tracts, I find myself reexamining them through a different lens, one of an academic awareness of different kinds of rhetorical strategies employed to maintain a hegemonic control—especially over children—through emotional manipulation.

## Chick and the Right

The introductory chapter of Abate's *Raising Your Kids Right* offers a lens through which I want to consider Chick's publishing legacy, specifically with his tracts. Abate's focus in her book is on "conservative-themed narratives for young readers that have been released since the early 1990s" (3), and she argues that this "new crop of books for young readers that began appearing in the early 1990s did so in a new and far more overt way" (4). Additionally, she says that these texts "form a powerfully influential part of contemporary literature for children and a highly visible aspect of the nation's millennial popular culture" (Abate 4). Having pondered how Abate describes these texts, I vacillate between thinking Chick tracts occupy a similar space as the *Left Behind* series (which she discusses in chapter 3 of her book) or an obscure space relegated to a peripheral religious subculture of didactic texts. Perhaps the Chick tracts reside in a liminal space because, while they are ubiquitous and boast sales in the millions, they do not immediately instill product recognition or connection between author and product in the mainstream audience. Whatever category Chick tracts fall under, I follow the same goals as Abate when she says she wants to "move the growing crop of conservative-themed narratives for children from the edge of mainstream intellectual inquiry and political consciousness to its forefront" (5). Setting aside the uncertain, liminal standing Chick tracts may have alongside the rest of the narratives that she analyzes and the fact that Chick's tracts predate the scope of her focus because they developed in the 1960s, my focus on these tracts follow in the same tradition as her book.

In her Introduction, Abate gives an excellent historical overview of the conservative movement, which is widely regarded as being comprised of three tenets. I want to use these three political categories as a way of contextualizing Chick's tracts. She says "The modern conservative movement coalesced around three main issues: anticommunism, libertarianism, and traditionalism" and that "By far, the most powerful force among these [issues] was anticommunism" (11). Before I give several examples, it is important to talk about how Chick's anticommunism served as a catalyst for his tract empire. Burack examines Chick's "semiautobiographical tract" *Who, Me?* from 1969: "In the story, Chinese communist agents discover the ideological potential of comic books from observing their popularity with American children. . . . Chick, in his turn, takes back the genre to use in winning souls to Christ" (*Sin* 37). One can easily find two examples of Chick's tracts devoted to communism by clicking "Communism" on the categories of tracts online: *The Poor Revolutionist* and *Fat Cats*. Kuersteiner notes that *The Poor Revolutionist* (1972) came out at a time when "Woodstock and the anti-war movement were current events and there were any number of Fundie preachers making their money by going around to Fundie churches and showing the undeniable links between the Hippies and the secret agenda of the Communists" (105). This tract was updated in 2010, and, in it, Chick forges a connection between Catholicism and communism: a priest kills hippies because he worries that they will start a revolution (19.1–2). The other communist-themed Chick tract, *Fat Cats*, which was published in 1989, makes the same connection. In the narrative, Father Dominic is instrumental in an execution.

Abate notes that since the decline of communism, 9/11 helped push "anti-Islamic sentiments and questions concerning religious difference . . . from the margin to the mainstream" (19). The 2014 Chick Publications catalog spends half of page nineteen devoted to eight tracts against Islam (*Chick Tracts*), and their website shows six out-of-print tracts about Islam and seven in-print titles. The main rhetorical strategy of *Who Is Allah?*, an out-of-print tract from 2006, consists of Christian apologetics through the historical debunking of the integrity of Muhammed, while inciting fear of a possible Islamic totalitarian state in the USA in the process. Through the course of the dialogue between an African American fundamentalist Christian and a devout Muslim, the Muslim says, "Islam is the second largest, and fastest growing religion in America! And you people should FEAR US! We expect a Muslim flag to fly over the White House in the near future. It will be the end of Christianity in America" (4.2–5.1).[10] *Camel's in the Tent* (2012), a tract still in print, takes a similar scare-tactic about the infiltration of Islam into America. While recounting the history of Islam, this tract describes the Islamic "pattern of conquest" in five steps: "Infiltrate, Populate, Legislate, Decimate, Eliminate" (12.2). On this same panel is a picture of an armed terrorist wearing a balaclava who says, "America's next" (12.2). Clearly, Chick's tracts are designed to instill a religious and ideological xenophobia.

Libertarianism forms another important pillar of American conservatism. As Abate explains about both the linguistic meaning of this term and its cultural ascendency, conservatives were concerned "that the United States is rapidly drifting toward socialism and that the size and strength of government is infringing on individual freedoms" (11). Consequently, Libertarians "advocate for a drastic reduction in federalism" (Abate 11). In other words, conservatives were displeased and even alarmed by what they saw as the intrusion of big government on the everyday lives of Americans. Once again, a Chick tract speaks to this exact issue. In language that closely mirrors the Libertarian platform, a passage from *The Poor Revolutionist* asserts: "When we destroy this oppressive and unfair free market system, one new world order will rise out of its ashes" (8.2). Originally published in 1972, Chick believes this is still a contemporary issue, which is why he says he reissued *The Poor Revolutionist* in 2010 ("Message").[11] Chick also discusses another aspect of Libertarianism in his March/April 2013 edition of his newsletter *Battle Cry*, when he says that the government ideologically influences children through public schools: "One defense that Christian parents have long used against the influences of a pagan culture is home schooling their children. This allowed them to channel their formative years toward a heart for God and delayed the lying influences of the culture until they were mature enough to deal with them" ("Department"). The rest of the article discusses the plight of the Romeike family who sought asylum in America in 2008 "after the German government threatened them with legal action for homeschooling their children, which has been banned in Germany since 1918," according to Ben Waldron of *ABC News*.[12] Clearly, Chick

Publications is concerned that the minds of children will be brainwashed in the secular public school setting. Homeschooling, in their estimation, allows for better content control.

Finally, a phenomenon united under the broad umbrella of "Traditionalism" forms the third powerful facet to American political conservatism. Abate notes that Traditionalists "fought to preserve conventional gender and sexual roles, long-standing and often religious-based notions of morality, and existing hierarchies of race, ethnicity, and class" (12). This concern permeates nearly every Chick tract, past and present. Indeed, one need look only at the category list online to see that tract topics about abortion, drugs/alcohol/STDs, evolution, global warming, and homosexuality all reinforce Chick's subscription to traditional values and his accompanying resistance to social change.

Burack spends the second chapter of her book *Sin, Sex, and Democracy: Antigay Rhetoric and the Christian Right* discussing the antigay rhetoric present in Chick tracts, used both as a primary and secondary theme. Since the publication of her study, there have been two more primary LGBTQ-themed Chick tracts published, bringing that total to seven.[13] The first one, called *Uninvited*, released in 2011, depicts the main character Clara, who is the nurse, witnessing to a group of men who have AIDS. She tells them that they all became infected with this disease because they were gay. After one of the men accepts Christ, Clara says that "the gay community fulfills Christ's prophecy by terrifying politicians, strong-arming the media, and creating little sodomites in our school systems" (21.2). The second queer-related Chick tract, *Home Alone?*, published in 2014, takes a page from Anita Bryant's conflation of homosexuality and child abuse. In the story, Charlie is babysat by his popular coach from school, who molests him after the coach tells him, "Being gay is cool" (5.2). Clearly, Chick believes that the growing tolerance of homosexuality is an epidemic, as he narrates: "To oppose the coach would be 'intolerant.' This made it easy for [him] to destroy [Charlie's] innocence" (7.2). An article from the July/August 2014 edition of *Battle Cry* promotes the newly published *Home Alone?* as a way of dispelling the trend of sexual tolerance in the twenty-first century for the safety of children (Daniels).

## Saving the Children (and the World) through Tract Proliferation

While synthesizing Burack's five categories of Chick's political expression (*Sin* 53–56) with Abate's three conservative issues is beyond the scope of this chapter, I do want to close by applying Burack's political commentary concerning Chick to Abate's commentary about the Conservative Right as an indication of the additional work that needs to be done on this topic. Burack contends that "the relationship between Chick and the Christian right isn't so much a divorce as it is an affair. . . . As such, Chick's views can still help us decipher the theology and politics of the Christian right" (*Sin* 50). Essentially, she argues that "Chick's views do not lie outside the boundaries of polite Christian right politics"; rather, "Chick's politics line up with the core agenda of the Christian right without remainder" (*Sin* 52). As such, the fundy-queer child who reads Chick tracts will be thoroughly educated in the widely recognized three conservative issues that Abate describes in her opening chapter.

As Douglas Rushkoff says in the foreword of a scholarly anthology about religion and comics, "Religious experience, for human beings, consists of a shift in awareness from the particular to the universal—from the mundane to the mythic or, even more precisely, from the moment to the infinite" (xii). For Jack Chick, this shift from particular to universal and "the moment to the infinite" indicate a dire need to prepare his audience for eternity, a place that is without time, a phenomenon he reminds us of in numerous tracts that conclude with a human soul being condemned to hell. While Chick may believe in the traditionalist sense (as Burack reminds us the Comics Code Authority of 1954 did) that images of the world and worldly pleasures can be detrimental to the child's soul, he also recognizes that the medium of comics can have the didactic power to bring the child to salvation.

The attraction for believers to participate in the sanctified littering of Chick tracts comes not only from avoiding any personal contact while witnessing (and any potential conflict from resistant listeners), but also from having the thrill of never knowing the full extent of the spiritual blessings such littering will have on children and adults alike. On page 8 of his 2014 Chick Publications catalog, Chick shows a picture of a little girl holding a tract and gives an important message: "When passing out Chick tracts . . . don't forget children. . . . Here are 3 Reasons Why . . . . 1) Children are far more likely to get saved than adults. 2) They have their entire lives to serve God and enjoy his blessing. 3) Kids usually take the tracts home, where parents often read them, too." Bruhm and Hurley rightly assert that "The child is the product of physical reproduction, but functions just as surely as a figure of cultural reproduction" (xiii). Clearly, Chick believes that his comics are not the only material, ideological, or rhetorical element at play here. For the author-illustrator, children serve not only as an eager audience for his message, but they also embody powerful, personal conduits whereby Chick's message of fundy-queer religious xenophobia and the impure, unsaved Others of the world can be disseminated to family members and adults for maximum effect.

# Notes

1. All of Chick's online tracts are unpaginated. The anchor first page is always the cover page.

2. Michael Warner makes a good point when he says that fundamentalists "consider themselves an oppressed minority. In their view the dominant culture is one of worldliness they have rejected, and bucking that trend comes, in some very real ways, with social stigmatization" (222).

3. Of course, as their book title suggests, their anthology is concerned specifically with *queer* as it pertains to the "gender and sexual roles" of children (x).

4. This kind of design is not unusual in the comics world. Lynda Barry's *One Hundred Demons* and Jacques Tardi's *It Was the War of the Trenches* contain similar layouts.

5. They both credit Daniel K. Raeburn with calling Chick tracts "*hardcore Protestant pornography*" because they are "spiritual porn, pure sadomasochistic fantasy with an emphasis on the rhetorical foreplay leading up to the inevitable seduction and submission to Jesus Christ. The money shot, when it comes, is a close-up of the humiliated but grateful sinner gasping, sobbing, and quaking with passion as the salty body fluid of tears coat his or her smooth, round cheeks" (7–8).

6. Ulanowicz argues that the Chick Tracts distributors "subscribe to a culturally dominant view of comics. . . . According to this view, comics possess the ability to indoctrinate audiences in ways that verbally specific narratives may not, since their illustrations directly elucidate written content otherwise left open to interpretation" (par. 6).

7. In rereading this draft for revisions, I found myself guilty of reinforcing the very phenomenon Stockton eloquently exposes in her book when she notes that "certain linguistic markers for its queerness arrive only after it exits its childhood, after it is shown not to be straight" (*Queer* 6). She calls this adult identification of a childhood past as a "kind of backward birthing mechanism" (*Queer* 7).

8. Stockton argues that one of the ways children are queer is through their innocence, specifically by "refiguring the Romantic child as queer in its estrangement from adult experience. Innocence, Stockton argues, makes children strange" and also complicated when "these same characters are depicted as knowing, sexualized, or violent children, depictions that disrupt the assumed division between child and adult" (Owen 103). Stockton uses *Lolita* as an example of a knowing or sexualized child (*Queer* 122). Likewise, when a fundy-queer child reads Chick tracts, he or she learns about sins to avoid, and can arguably be labeled as "knowing." For example, David in *Wounded Children* reads his father's porn stash and becomes aware of sexual acts. See next note for more thoughts about the meta-literacy phenomenon of being exposed to the very vice the tract eschews.

9. Ulanowicz articulates this phenomenon when she notes that a Chick tract "permits its reader to gaze upon forbidden acts precisely because doing so might eventually allow her to internalize the tract's final message." She argues this gives "converted readers the license to view characters engaged in licentious behavior so they might reaffirm their righteous *separation* from them" and that "Chick Tracts sanction the very illicit pleasure they claim to disavow" (par. 33, my emphasis).

10. This is out of print, but its in-print equivalent, *Allah Had No Son* (1994), features the same dialogue, plot, and characters, only the Christian character is white instead of African American.

11. He also sells other materials that can be placed in dialogue with Libertarian views on his website. Under the DVD section one can find *Agenda: Grinding America Down*, produced by Curtis Bowers, which argues in its description that "a nation that follows God and His laws will naturally enjoy a free society with limited government. But a people that rejects God and His laws will not be capable of governing themselves, and Big Government will be all too happy to take His place" (*Agenda*).

12. The family's case was resolved in 2014 with their being allowed to remain, but not before they had experienced legal setbacks that included their asylum being repealed.

13. Burack also counts and discusses eleven tracts that "include some treatment of the subject in passing" (*Sin* 47).

# Works Cited

Abate, Michelle Ann. "From Christian Conversion to Children's Crusade: The *Left Behind* Series for Kids and the Changing Nature of Evangelical Juvenile Fiction." *Jeunesse: Young People, Texts, Culture* 2.1 (Summer 2010): 84–112. Print.

––––––. *Raising Your Kids Right: Children's Literature and American Political Conservatism*. New Brunswick, NJ: Rutgers UP, 2011. Print.

Abate, Michelle Ann, and Kenneth Kidd, eds. *Over the Rainbow: Queer Children's and Young Adult Literature*. Ann Arbor: University of Michigan Press, 2011. Print.

*Agenda: Grinding America Down*. Chick.com. Chick Publications, n.d. Web. 6 June 2014.

*Allah Had No Son*. Chick.com. Chick Publications, 2014. Web. 6 June 2014.

*Angels?* Chick.com. Chick Publications, 2014. Web. 6 June 2014.

Babinski, Edward T. *Leaving the Fold: Testimonies of Former Fundamentalists*. Amherst, NY: Prometheus, 1995. Print.

"Biography of Jack Chick." Chick.com. Chick Publications, n.d. Web. 10 June 2014.

Bruhm, Steven, and Natasha Hurley. "Curiouser: On the Queerness of Children." *Curiouser: On the Queerness of Children*. Ed. Steven Bruhm and Natasha Hurley. Minneapolis: University of Minnesota Press, 2004. ix–xxxviii. Print.

Burack, Cynthia. "From Doom Town to Sin City: Chick Tracts and Anti-gay Political Rhetoric." *New Political Science* 28.2 (June 2006): 163–79. Print.

––––––. *Sin, Sex, and Democracy: Antigay Rhetoric and the Christian Right*. Albany, NY: SUNY P, 2008. Print.

*Camel's in the Tent*. Chick.com. Chick Publications, 2014. Web. 6 June 2014.

Chick, Jack. "How Chick Ministry Began." Interview with George Collins. *Battle Cry*, Aug.–Sep. 1984. Web. 6 June 2014. <http://www.Chick.com/bc/1984/chickbeginning.asp>

Chick.com. Chick Publications, 2014. Web. 6 June 2014.

*Chick Tracts Get Read!* Ontario: Chick Publications, 2013. Print.

––––––. Ontario: Chick Publications, 2014. Print.

"The Comics Code Authority." Comicartville.com, n.d. Web. 10 June 2014.

Daniels, David W. "They're After Your Children!" *Battle Cry*, July–Aug. 2014. Web. 6 August 2014. <http://www.Chick.com/bc/2014/after_your_children.asp>.

*Dark Dungeons*. Chick.com. Chick Publications, 2014. Web. 6 June 2014.

"Department of Justice: 'Home Schooling Not a Right in America.'" *Battle Cry*, March–April 2013. Web. 6 June 2014. <http://www.Chick.com/bc/2013/home_schooling.asp>.

Dittmer, Jason. "Of Gog and Magog: The Geopolitical Visions of Jack Chick and Premillennial Dispensationalism." *ACME: An International E-Journal for Critical Geographies* 6.2 (2007): 278–303. Print.

Dow, Darrell. *Stuff Fundies Like*. WordPress 2015. Web. 12 April 2016. <http://www.stufffundieslike.com/>.

*English Stock Titles*. Chick.com. Chick Publications, 2014. Web. 6 June 2014.

*Fat Cats*. Chick.com. Chick Publications, 2014. Web. 6 June 2014.

"Fundie, n.1." *Oxford English Dictionary Online*. Oxford University Press, March 2016. Web. 8 April 2016.

*The Gay Blade*. Chick.com. Chick Publications, 2014. Web. 6 June 2014.

Groensteen, Thierry. *Comics and Narration*. Trans. Ann Miller. Jackson, MS: University Press of Mississippi, 2013. Print.

Hall, Donald E., and Annamarie Jagose. "Introduction: The Queer Turn." *The Routledge Queer Studies Reader*. Ed. Donald E. Hall, et al. New York: Routledge, 2013. xiv–xx. Print.

*Happy Hour*. Chick.com. Chick Publications, 2014. Web. 6 June 2014.

*Home Alone?* Chick.com. Chick Publications, 2014. Web. 6 June 2014.

Ito, Robert. "Fear Factor: Jack Chick Is the World's Most Published Author—And One of the Strangest." *Los Angeles Magazine*, May 2003: 56–63. PDF. 10 June 2014. <http://robert-ito .com/FearFactorO.pdf>.

Kuersteiner, Kurt. *The Unofficial Guide to: The Art of Jack T. Chick: Chick Tracts, Crusader Comics, & Battle Cry Newspapers*. Atglen, PA: Schiffer Publishing, 2004. Print.

McAlister, Melani. "Prophecy, Politics, and the Popular: The *Left Behind* Series and Christian Fundamentalism's New World Order." *South Atlantic Quarterly* 102.4 (Fall 2003): 773–98. Print.

"Message about *The Poor Revolutionist*." Chick.com. Chick Publications, n.d. Web. 6 June 2014. <http://www.Chick.com/jtcmessage_7_1.asp>.

Miskec, Jennifer. "Religion and Children's Literature: A Decennial Examination." *Children's Literature Association Quarterly* 36.3 (Fall 2011): 255–58. Print.

*No Liars*. Chick.com. Chick Publications, 2014. Web. 6 June 2014.

Orcutt, Darby. "Comics and Religion: Theoretical Connections." *Graven Images: Religion in Comic Books and Graphic Novels*. Ed. A. David Lewis and Christine Hoff Kraemer. New York: Continuum, 2010. Print.

Owen, Gabrielle. Rev. of *The Queer Child: or, Growing Sideways in the Twentieth Century*, Kathryn Bond Stockton. *The Lion and the Unicorn* 35.1 (Jan 2011): 101–6. Print.

Pesso-Miquel, Catherine, and Klaus Stierstorfer. Introduction. *Burning Books: Negotiations between Fundamentalism and Literature*. New York: AMS Press, 2012. Print.

Pickering, Ernest. *Biblical Separation: The Struggle for a Pure Church*. 1979. Schaumburg, IL: Regular Baptist Press, 1995. Print.

*The Poor Revolutionist*. Chick.com. Chick Publications, 2014. Web. 6 June 2014.

Raeburn, Daniel K. *The Holy Book of Chick with the Apocrypha and Dictionary-Concordance. King Imp Edition*. Chicago, IL: Imp Publications, 1998. PDF. 8 March 2015. <http://danielraeburn .com/The_Imp,_by_Daniel_Raeburn_files/Imp_JTC.pdf>.

Raymond, Joad. *Pamphlets and Pamphleteering in Early Modern Britain*. Cambridge: Cambridge UP, 2003. Print.

Roth, Laurence. "Innovation and Orthodox Comic Books: The Case of Mahrwood Press." *MELUS* 37.2 (Summer 2012): 131–56. Print.

Rushkoff, Douglas. "Looking for God in the Gutter." *Graven Images: Religion in Comic Books and Graphic Novels*. Ed. A. David Lewis and Christine Hoff Kraemer. New York: Continuum, 2010. ix–xii. Print.

Shuy, Roger W. *The Language of Defamation Cases*. Oxford: Oxford UP, 2010. Print.

Spiegelman, Art. "Those Dirty Little Comics." *Tijuana Bibles: Art and Wit in America's Forbidden Funnies, 1930s–1950s*. By Bob Adelman. New York: Simon & Schuster, 1997. 5–10. Print.

Stockton, Kathryn Bond. "Growing Sideways, or Versions of the Queer Child: The Ghost, the Homosexual, the Freudian, the Innocent, and the Interval of Animal." *Curiouser: On the Queerness of Children*. Ed. Steven Bruhm and Natasha Hurley. Minneapolis: University of Minnesota Press, 2004. 277–315. Print.

———. *The Queer Child: or, Growing Sideways in the Twentieth Century*. Durham, NC: Duke UP, 2009. Print.

"Tract, n.1." *Oxford English Dictionary Online*. Oxford University Press. March 2015. Web. 10 May 2015.

Ulanowicz, Anastasia. "Chick Tracts, Monstrosity, and Pornography." *ImageTexT* 8.1 (2015). 15 July 2015. Web.

*Uninvited*. Chick.com. Chick Publications, 2014. Web. 6 June 2014.

Waldron, Ben. "Home Schooling German Family Allowed to Stay in US." ABCNews.go.com, 5 March 2014. Web. 5 May 2015.

Warner, Michael. "Tongues Untied: Memoirs of a Pentecostal Boyhood." *Curiouser: On the Queerness of Children*. Ed. Steven Bruhm and Natasha Hurley. Minneapolis: University of Minnesota Press, 2004. 215–24. Print.

Weldy, Lance. "Part 1: Wounded Children?" BJUnity.org. 1 October 2012. Web. 6 June 2014. <http://bjunity.org/who-we-are/lance-weldy-part-one/>.

*While Shopping*. Chick.com. Chick Publications, 2014. Web. 6 June 2014.

*Who, Me?* Chick.com. Chick Publications, 2014. Web. 6 June 2014.

*Who Is Allah?* Chick.com. Chick Publications, 2014. Web. 6 June 2014.

*Why No Revival?* Chick.com. Chick Publications, 2014. Web. 6 June 2014.

*Wounded Children*. Waycoolart.angelfire.com, n.d. Web. 6 June 2014.

# 18

## Waiting for Spider-Man: Representations of Urban School "Reform" in Marvel Comics' Miles Morales Series

*David E. Low*

### Charter Schools in Children's Media

In the spring of 2012, the Scantron Corporation was criticized by an activist group in Chicago for including items on a standardized test that exposed an audience of public school students to pro-charter school propaganda. Julie Woestehof, executive director of *Parents United for Responsible Education*, indicated that the reading comprehension passages, which Scantron claimed were designed to test the "critical thinking skills of seventh-grade-level students," were so biased in favor of charter schools that the test's use amounted to an attempt to brainwash the thousands of students who took the test over two years in over 600 schools (Rossi). Written in a nonfiction style, the passage stated that charter schools are "open to all students," that they are "showing improvements in student achievement," and that the fictitious children of a fictitious multimillionaire attend a charter school because their father "believes that charter schools deliver the highest quality education" (Hyde Park Johnny). During *PURE*'s dispute with Scantron, Woestehoff wrote that "students taking a test should not be subjected to false claims about charter schools which could cause them to feel humiliated, second-class, or dumb because they do not attend a '*better*' charter school. . . . They are brainwashing our kids to make them think they should be in a charter school" (quoted in Rossi). Scantron ultimately dropped the passage from future tests and issued an apology.

In the United States, debates about school "reform" in the twenty-first century have been frequent, divisive, and well-covered in mainstream media intended for an adult audience. It is important to note that even when this politically and ideologically charged issue appears lopsided depending on the leanings of a particular media outlet, in the world of adult-geared media, there are typically opportunities to encounter a range of counterpoints. As evidenced by the Scantron incident, however, these opportunities do not as often exist in media intended for young people. After a thorough search, I was able to locate only a few examples of children's media (one novel, one comic book series, and one issue of *Time Magazine for Kids*[1]) in which charter schools are treated as a pertinent topic. The near invisibility of an issue that is salient to the lives of so many young people begs the question: when it appears at all, how is school "reform" represented in media intended for children and youth, and what narratives around this complex issue are coming to the fore?

This chapter examines representations of an urban charter school lottery in Marvel's *Ultimate Comics Spider-Man* (Bendis and Pichelli), a comic book series that is popular with young readers, regularly selling 35,000 to 50,000 single issues in a month, and considerably more once anthologized in hard and softcover editions (Fraser).[2] The critically acclaimed title, which began in September 2011, features Miles Morales, a young Afro-Latino protagonist from a working-class community in Brooklyn, who takes on the iconic role of Spider-Man. Since the title's launch, Miles has proven especially popular with readers from racial and ethnic minority groups who have felt under- and misrepresented in mainstream superhero comics (see Cavna; Foster; Nama). For some fans, Miles functions as a cypher for young Black masculinity within print and other visual media (Fu; McWilliams). Indeed, when I asked a group of Black fifth-grade participants in my Philadelphia-based research project (see Low and Campano for an overview of the project) which actor they imagined playing Miles in a hypothetical movie adaptation, several of the boys emphatically replied, "Me!!!" Miles is, by a wide margin, the comic book character with whom my male students (grades 4–8 in an urban Catholic school) most claim to identify. In the series's first issue, Miles is bitten by a radioactive spider and endowed with the superpowers of Peter Parker, the original (and recently deceased) Spider-Man. Miles also gains the not-so-subtly symbolic ability to turn invisible. Much of the subsequent series focuses on Miles learning to balance his new existence, including fighting crime, attending to family obligations, and beginning school at the Brooklyn Visions Academy, an urban charter school outside his immediate neighborhood. In the series's first issue, Miles wins a lottery to attend the school. It is this three-page sequence on which this chapter will focus.

## Critical Multicultural and Multimodal Analysis

Marjorie Siegel and Carolyn P. Panofsky write, "There is no ready-made toolkit for analyzing multimodal [texts]," so "researchers have turned to a range of theories . . . which can be productively blended" (101). For the purpose of this chapter, I blend critical multicultural analysis of children's literature (Botelho and Rudman) with forms of critical visual analysis (Aiello; Connors; Schieble) in order to examine how urban education "reform" is represented in Marvel's *Ultimate Comics Spider-Man*. I also use terms from comics and multimodalities researchers to assist in my visual analysis.

Critical multicultural analysis of children's literature (CMA), an approach advanced by Maria José Botelho and Masha Kabakow Rudman, maintains that because all literature is an historical product, it is inscribed at multiple levels with implicit and explicit ideologies—"a product of culture as well as evidence of power relationships" (72). This is true even, and perhaps especially, of ideologies that are not deliberately invoked by authors. As Robert D. Sutherland contends,

> Works written especially for children are informed and shaped by the authors' respective value systems, their notions of how the world *is* or *ought to be* . . . To publish books which express one's ideology is in essence to promulgate one's values. To promulgate one's values by sending a potentially influential book into public arenas already bristling with divergent, competing, and sometimes violently opposed ideologies is a political act. (143)

Employing CMA as an analytic framework attempts to surface the ideological and political underpinnings of authored texts, particularly as they relate to the institutional organization of knowledge and power along raced, classed, and gendered lines. Hilary Janks writes that texts "entice us into their way of seeing and understanding the world—into their version of reality," and adds that "language, together with other signs, works to construct reality" (61). This is to say that in children's literature, ideologies are frequently manifested multimodally, within intersections of images, words, and other textual features.

Because children's literature "remains a primary vehicle for intellectual and imaginative maturation" (Ghiso, Campano, and Hall 15), CMA posits that children's identities and realities are constructed—at least to some degree—through their dialogic interactions with literary texts, contexts, and ideologies. In that vein, Perry Nodelman and Mavis Reimer write: "People are not always conscious of the ideologies that affect them. Or, to put it another way, they are not always conscious that the ideas *are* ideologies, and just assume them to be the way things obviously are . . . Ideology works best by disappearing, so that people simply take their ideological assumptions for granted as the only, whole, and unquestionable truth" (80). By focusing my analysis on a specific text and the particular sociopolitical issues that are enacted within it, I aim to explore how its ideologies may be taken up by young readers in the process of constructing identities and realities. This pursuit is assisted in the knowledge that there are very few popular children's texts which deal with the divisive topic of school charterization. In spite of the "divergent, competing, and sometimes violently opposed ideologies" (Sutherland 143) that characterize school "reform" in the twenty-first century, young readers of *Ultimate Comics Spider-Man* are unlikely to encounter the subject in other children's media.

Over the past several decades, literacy scholars and educators have increasingly looked beyond word-centric print texts to consider multiple genres, modes, media, and a wider range of lived experiences within which children, youth, and adults make and express meanings (e.g., Hull and Nelson; New London Group) and perform hybrid identities (e.g., Cowan; Simon). Building from this research, a growing body of scholarship has emerged that is devoted to comics in the field of literacy education (e.g., Low; Pantaleo; Schwarz; Versaci). As Brian Tucker notes, the medium of comics forces readers to attend "not only to the stories but also to their discourse, to how comics constitute meaning in a way that is different from those of other media" (28). Comics is a uniquely visuo-textual medium existing somewhere "between telling and showing on the one hand, and concealing on the other" (Ghiso and Low 28), making it particularly rich for understanding children's multimodal enactments of literacy.

As polysemic texts which require readers to "marry print and visual representations in order to read in ways that are deeply meaningful" (Cromer and Clark 589), neither the visual nor the verbal mode may be given short shrift when analyzing inclusions and exclusions in comics texts. Thus, in looking at visuo-textual representations in *Ultimate Comics Spider-Man*, I will be using an assortment of analytic tools, drawing from picture book scholars, comics scholars, and multimodalities scholars—all through a critical lens—to assist in my meaning-making of Sara Pichelli's images. Critical visual analysis is concerned with how "visual resources are and can be mobilized to *act* and work on the viewer," and attempts to reveal images' "culturally and historically situated ideological implications" (Aiello 101). It is through this framework that I will undertake a close reading of Sara Pichelli's artwork and the ways in which it represents people, objects, and institutions. Additionally, I will apply critical discourse analysis to examine "the social and political significance" of Brian Michael Bendis's written dialogue (Fairclough 135).

The comics scholar Hillary L. Chute argues for the importance of placing images within a chapter "as the chapter unfolds," writing that in order to analyze comics, "one needs to be able to quote an image, just as in analyzing poetry one needs to be able to quote lines from a poem" (*Graphic Women* ix). I have similarly come to the decision—not lightly—that for the purpose of this analysis, I will isolate Bendis and Pichelli's panels from their original layout. Certainly, this decision sacrifices the "gestalt" of the page (Beaty and Nguyen 8;

Versaci 102) by overlooking panel design and spatial features (as well as margins and gutters), but the panel-by-panel nature of my analysis necessitates such fragmentation. Further, Pichelli's artwork is presented here in grayscale, having been stripped of Justin Ponsor's colors. Readers interested in viewing the three-page sequence in its original form are encouraged to seek out *Ultimate Comics Spider-Man* #1 or an anthologized edition of the title.

### Spider-Man Waits for Superman

In a host of cities across the United States, charter schools have become an increasingly contentious topic during the past two decades. The march of urban charterization, as part of a larger market-driven neoliberal "reform" movement (LeBlanc 300) backed by the likes of Michelle Rhee, Geoffrey Canada, Bill Gates, and Michael Bloomberg, has won many followers while igniting pockets of fierce resistance. Proponents of charter schools laud greater school choice and a non-unionized teaching force as panaceas for educational iniquities (see Kirst for an overview), while critics see charterization as an essential ingredient—along with standardized testing tied to punitive school and teacher accountability measures—in the systematic dismantlement of public education (e.g., Karp; Ravitch, "Reign of Error"). The narrative perpetuated by pro-charter advocates is that "public schools, especially those in urban areas, are uniformly failing" and that "charter schools are the best solution to this problem" (Darling-Hammond and Lieberman 31). It has become a narrative that is well-trod in adult media to the point that the story of America's failing urban public schools has largely entered the realm of "common sense." As many scholars and educators draw attention to, however, the story is a fiction, or at least an exaggeration, "framed by half-truths and distortions" (Darling-Hammong and Lieberman 32).

Many Americans became aware of the controversies surrounding the charter school movement with the wide release of the film *Waiting for "Superman"* in 2010, and its subsequent media frenzy. Davis Guggenheim's documentary tells the story of five families who are attempting to escape the "failed enterprise" of American public education (Ravitch, "Myth of Charter Schools" 19) and win lottery spots for their children in charter schools. The film purports to address issues of race in America—four of the five families featured are Black or Latin@—but without examining larger issues such as endemic poverty or inadequate school funding (Darling-Hammond and Lieberman 32). It has thus been argued that the pro-charter film "offers solutions that are simplified, ignore research evidence, and are built on false assumptions" (Dutro). Indeed, in a national study of 5,000 charter schools conducted by Stanford University's Hoover Institution, it was found that fewer than 17 percent achieved better results than matched public schools, while 37 percent yielded worse results and 46 percent showed no significant difference (Lubienski and Lubienski). These statistics have not seemed to slow the onslaught of new charters, however, nor have they significantly altered the perception that public schools are underperforming (Gallup). One wonders if the Superman of comic books and film rescued only 17 percent of people falling from Metropolis skyscrapers, how much longer he would retain the title of Superman. (And what if the numbers of fallers had been greatly exaggerated in the first place?)

It is a different iconic superhero to whom I now turn. If Superman is known as the defender of "truth, justice, and the American way," then Spider-Man is just as celebrated for his mantra that "with great power comes great responsibility," which feels uncannily appropriate for the enterprise of American education. In the pages that follow, I present a panel-by-panel critical visual analysis of the three-page sequence in *Ultimate Comics Spider-Man* #1 depicting the Brooklyn Visions Academy lottery.

In the first issue of *Ultimate Comics Spider-Man*, before 11-year-old Miles Morales is bitten by the spider that will give him superpowers, he is taken by his parents to a charter school lottery not unlike those portrayed in *Waiting for "Superman."* The scene opens with an establishing shot of a bustling street in Brooklyn that is depicted as robustly multiracial and multigenerational.

Miles's family, introduced to the reader as they move from the background into the foreground, is similarly multiracial; his father, the puzzlingly named Jefferson Davis, is Black,[3] and his mother, Rio Morales, is Puerto Rican. The White writer of the comic book series, Brian Michael Bendis,[4] explained in an interview that his goal in creating Miles's family was to "write people outside of [his own] experience" in a way that readers would "recognize as the world around [them]" (Riesman). Certainly, a family walking down the street while arguing is not terribly difficult to identify with, irrespective of class, race, or ethnicity. Miles, wearing the number 2 on his shirt (i.e., the second Spider-Man), is the object of his parents' argument, but he is not provided his own voice in the initial panel.

In the second panel the focus shifts to Miles, pushing his parents and their surroundings momentarily outside the story world (Uspensky 137). The reader meets Miles at eye level, and his slightly turned gaze makes this, in effect, a child-centric "offer" image (Kress and van Leeuwen 381), directing the reader to enter into an empathetic kinship with him. Not incidentally, such kinship is a touchstone of quality children's literature. Miles's position in the panel suggests his centrality to the narrative and his parents' roles as supporting characters (Mikkonen), while his facial features convey a sense of quiet frustration. Although we do not see Rio and Jefferson's faces, the combative tone of the scene lingers from the previous panel and is conveyed via their clashing

Fig. 18.1. *Ultimate Comics Spider-Man* #1 by Bendis, Pichelli, and Ponsor (2011) 10.1.
© MARVEL. All rights reserved.

Fig. 18.2. *Ultimate Comics Spider-Man* #1 by Bendis, Pichelli, and Ponsor (2011) 10.2.
© MARVEL. All rights reserved.

wardrobes. Caught between his mother in unyielding monochrome and his camouflage-clad father, Miles wears an athletic jersey, a player in a figurative game. As his father's camouflage fatigues suggest, Miles has entered the battleground of education "reform."

In panels 3 and 4 of the sequence (figure 18.3), Miles's mother lowers herself nearly to his level to explain the purpose of their day out. There is extensive visual and spatial information conveyed by Pichelli's figural placements within the panels: first, mother and son in profile, and then another "offer" image of Miles looking uncomfortable. Across the two panels, Pichelli employs several levels of contradictory focalization. The comics theorist Kai Mikkonen describes focalization (as it pertains to graphic narrative) as the set of visual and verbal elements which come together on a comics page—i.e., written language, speech balloons, illustrated characters, frames and gutters, etc.—that "interpenetrate each other and thus allow a multiplication of perspectives." Mikkonen explains that these interwoven elements, while inherently multiperspectival, may also "suggest a particular perspective in the story" (71). Thus, in spite of the fact that Rio's voice dominates Miles's in these panels (sixty-six words to his fifteen), Miles remains the focal point due to his being centered in

Fig. 18.3. *Ultimate Comics Spider-Man* #1 by Bendis, Pichelli, and Ponsor (2011) 10.3–4.
© MARVEL. All rights reserved.

the right-hand panel. The reader is visually instructed to experience the scene first through Miles's perspective, then through Rio's. This focalization makes quite a bit of sense considering the comic book's intended audience of young readers.

In spite of Miles's visual prominence in figure 18.3, the text-heavy panels nevertheless direct the reader to construct a great deal of meaning from Rio's and Miles's actual dialogue (Golden and Gerber). Indeed, there is much exposition here. We learn what Jefferson had earlier referred to as "a damn circus": the school lottery event. Rio tells her son that it is unlikely he'll win admission to a charter school that denies roughly 94 percent of applicants from their neighborhood. This is a far cry from the Scantron test item's "open to all students" claim, and more in line with the 7 percent, 5 percent, and 4.5 percent chances that students had of winning a lottery spot in *Waiting for "Superman."* Still, neither Guggenheim's documentary nor *Ultimate Comics Spider-Man* seem to find fault with exclusionary tactics which, through structured admissions, are designed to keep test scores up by keeping "low-achieving," typically marginalized, students out (Bonastia; Darling-Hammond and Lieberman 35). Rather, the lottery is portrayed as a necessary if imperfect instrument for lucky families who are desperate to escape the perceived ruin of public education.

Through both her words and hand gestures, Rio attempts to mollify Miles by reassuring him that his rejection would not be reflective of him "as a person." The implication is that, should Miles fail to win a lottery spot and be forced to remain at his neighborhood school, it would not be a mark against him at an individual level. With only a few words, Rio indicates that

Miles is better than his surroundings, reinforcing "an idea of community decay" (Campano 3) and Miles as the mythical "rose that grew from concrete" (Kirkland 74). The dialogue Bendis has written for Rio is indicative of the "culture of poverty" framework that has infiltrated popular discourses about urban schooling and which draws "from a longstanding U.S. tradition of viewing the poor from a deficit perspective" (Bomer, et al. 2500). This pervasive framework places the onus of poverty on the poor and connects class mobility with individual achievement that is rewarded through infusions of economic and social capital. It is the overarching "American dream" of freedom, meritocracy, and "rugged individualism . . . which is part of our 'can do' national character" (Parini 53)—not too far off, as far as mythologies go, from Superman's commitment to American "truth" and "justice."

As Robert LeBlanc writes about how families are portrayed in *Waiting for "Superman,"* the film's protagonists figure largely as "representations of the capitalist ideal: rugged, hardworking individuals who only wish to make a life for themselves." LeBlanc adds that such representations "perpetuate that fantasy that schools operate as islands from society, untouched by larger structural forces of inequality" (302). Indeed, nowhere in Rio's reassurance of her son does she suggest that poverty and inadequate funding of urban neighborhood schools are part of a larger systemic problem they should organize against, or that their community is a wonderful place to live, full of cultural and epistemological resources (Campano; González, Moll, and Amanti; Neill). Instead, Rio treats their community's perceived circumstances—deficient in comparison to some implicit "benchmark" of excellence (Spencer)—as a given, but not one that should make claims on Miles's identity. In Rio's words, Miles's community is "not a reflection" on him, and in fact, has "nothing to do" with him. In effect, Bendis's dialogue in figure 18.3 exemplifies Joyce E. King's concept of "dysconscous racism," or the perceptions, attitudes, and beliefs which reify inequality by "tacitly [accepting] dominant White norms" and overlaying them onto communities of color (135). In a bit of comic relief, Miles begs his father to "please make this stop."

In the sixth panel of the sequence (figure 18.4), the scene shifts in time and place to the auditorium holding the lottery event itself, which is nearly at its end. The auditorium is decorated as if for a joyous occasion—balloons in the shape of bell curves line the periphery—but tensions are high. With roughly 650 children vying for three remaining spots, it is surprising that anyone is able to remain seated at all. Pichelli's mise-en-scène, paired with Bendis's dialogue, establishes the relative distance between the conveners of the lottery and its contestants.

In the eighth overall panel of the sequence (top-right of figure 18.5), as Katie Hague wins the third-to-last spot at Brooklyn Visions Academy, Jefferson

Fig. 18.4. *Ultimate Comics Spider-Man* #1 by Bendis, Pichelli, and Ponsor (2011) 11.1.
© MARVEL. All rights reserved.

Fig. 18.5. *Ultimate Comics Spider-Man* #1 by Bendis, Pichelli, and Ponsor (2011) 11.2–5.
© MARVEL. All rights reserved.

maintains the criticality he has held from the beginning of the scene. In saying that "the world's gone insane," Jefferson seems to understand how absurd this lottery ceremony truly is. It is unclear whether Jefferson's critique extends to the absurdity of school charterization itself—which, as some critics maintain, may actually widen gaps and reproduce inequalities between middle class and poor students (e.g., Bonastia; Cooper and Jordan; Darder)—or if it refers only to the lottery event and the fervor it has fomented. Surely, there is some visual cruelty in employing a gaming device (*"Bingo!"*) to determine the opportunities of children.

Fig. 18.6. *Ultimate Comics Spider-Man* #1 by Bendis, Pichelli, and Ponsor (2011) 11.6–8.
© MARVEL. All rights reserved.

Behind the Morales family, the Hagues celebrate their good fortune by invoking a higher power and leaping from their seats. Rio looks discernibly uncomfortable, asking Jefferson to shelve his cynicism, while Miles wordlessly stares at the floor. Panels 9 and 10 of the lottery sequence (the bottom two panels of figure 18.5) mainly reiterate what's preceded them. Visually, panel 9's close-up of Miles from a slight overhead view reemphasizes his dejection and powerlessness as Andy London's name is called (Sipe 71). Verbally, Jefferson reiterates his critique while Rio again implores him to stop. To this point, Miles's parents' disagreement about attending the lottery has been one of the consistent narrative through-lines of the sequence.

Near the bottom of the lottery sequence's second page, the moment arrives, delivering the final ball that will, to some degree, determine Miles Morales's future. The panels in figure 18.6 are visually quite interesting without containing a single word. In the first panel, the ball of destiny rolls along its track, building up narrative tension as it does. In the next panel, the ball—emphasized in extreme close-up for dramatic effect (Schieble 50)—seems to be illuminated from above, as if by some celestial force, not unlike the child on the movie poster for *Waiting for "Superman."* I am reminded of an episode of *The Simpsons* in which Homer looks to the heavens and beseeches, "I'm not normally a praying man, but if you're up there, please save me, Superman!" The third panel shows that Rio is in fact praying as Miles looks bored and Jefferson looks irritated. But back to Miles, and his "wait for Superman." Call it luck, destiny, or divine intervention. Whatever the case may be, the Morales family will be sending their son to Brooklyn Visions Academy in the fall. But they do not know it yet.

Fig. 18.7. *Ultimate Comics Spider-Man* #1 by Bendis, Pichelli, and Ponsor (2011) 12.1–2.
© MARVEL. All rights reserved.

The color palette used to illustrate these scenes further augments a message of deliverance. Pichelli's lottery ball operates as a white orb held aloft in a sea of blackness, which could certainly be read to take on racial overtones (Schieble 50). In this vein, the number 42 is itself interesting for several culturally specific reasons. At the surface level of the story, there is a parallel between the lottery ball and the arachnid (specimen #42) that will eventually envenomate Miles. Beyond the interior world of the story, the number 42 likely alludes to the jersey number worn by Jackie Robinson, who, as a member of the Brooklyn Dodgers, became the first African American man to play Major League Baseball in the twentieth century. The number 42 has been reverentially retired by every MLB team and holds special meaning at the intersection of race and popular culture. While Miles is not the first mainstream comic book character to have broken the "color barrier," he is among the most high-profile (Fu). Having a mixed-race child take on the mantle of Marvel's most recognizable character, while not a perfect analogy to Jackie Robinson, feels like an apt homage to both Brooklyn and #42.[5]

Atop a new page, Miles's name is announced, and for the first time, Jefferson cracks a smile. It is interesting how quickly his affect changes once his son's name is called. No longer visibly irritated, it seems Jefferson ceases to reject the lottery once his family has benefited from it. Rio, meanwhile, invokes the deity she had prayed to in the previous panel. In the right-hand panel of figure 18.7, secure in her knowledge that Miles will be attending a charter school, Rio tells her son that now *he has a chance*. The disturbing implication of this utterance is that had Miles *not* won a lottery spot, he would not have had a chance, presumably, to succeed in life; that an urban public education is tantamount to utter catastrophe. It is more or less the story told by *Waiting for "Superman"*

Fig. 18.8. *Ultimate Comics Spider-Man* #1 by Bendis, Pichelli, and Ponsor (2011) 12.3–5.
© MARVEL. All rights reserved.

and a host of corporate education "reformers." And in spite of being both factually inaccurate and effectively pathologizing communities of color, it is a story that persists in the world outside of comics.

Following Miles's lottery win, Pichelli curates a powerful visual sequence, wordlessly illustrating some of the "losers" of the day below Miles's remorseful gaze. Through three "offer images," the reader feels the gravity of the events which, while ostensibly benefiting Miles, are necessarily harming others. Pichelli's images express the social injustice that is perpetuated when not every student's education is equitably funded. Simultaneously, and keeping with the undercurrent of the entire sequence, Pichelli's drawings also serve to re-inscribe the popular opinion that public schools are failing their "at-risk" students, while charter schools are the rescuer of America's poor urban children. The tears of the girl on the bottom-left echo Geoffrey Canada's opening narration from *Waiting for "Superman"*: "One of the saddest days of my life was when my mother told me Superman did not exist. . . . [I cried] because no one was coming with enough power to save us" (Guggenheim). Unexamined here is that "Superman" is a facile symbol for the type of savior complex which "supports brutal policies in the morning, founds charities in the afternoon, and receives awards in the evening" (Cole).

The nineteenth and final panel of the school lottery sequence (figure 18.9) reemphasizes the themes of neoliberal "reform" that have been undergirding the entire scene. Foremost, the tenet of individualism rises to the surface

Fig. 18.9. *Ultimate Comics Spider-Man* #1 by Bendis, Pichelli, and Ponsor (2011) 12.6.
© MARVEL. All rights reserved.

with Rio's counsel to "just focus on you," in spite of Miles's feelings of guilt. Miles, thinking of the "other kids" who were not as lucky as him, and asking "Should it be like this?" seems to endorse a communitarian ethos of inter-dependence, of mutuality (Ghiso)—that nobody wins unless everybody wins. Rio, on the other hand, endorses the competitive ethos of capitalism that is concomitant with a neoliberal ideology: individual advancement is placed above the well-being of community. In *Analysing Discourse*, Norman Fairclough writes that the "textual process of meaning-making is an impor-tant element in the political process of [achieving] hegemony for neoliberal-ism in so far [sic] as it contributes to building up a vision of the 'new age'" (101). That is, Rio's words (i.e., Bendis's dialogue) matter. They contribute to the construction of Miles's (i.e., readers') reality (Janks 61). The message in this three-page sequence is clear: In order to attend a "better" school and to succeed in life, children, and especially urban children of color, must escape their neighborhood schools and focus on competitive individual achieve-ment (defined by White middleclass knowledge norms) at the expense of community commitments. This message has been disseminated by corporate "reformers" for the past two decades as their programs drain public funds from public schools and channel the money into private for-profit institu-tions. While Miles, through Bendis, questions this hegemonic message, it is ineffectual; his ultimate matriculation at Brooklyn Visions Academy does not sufficiently challenge the juggernaut of market-based education "reform" nor question its "common sense" assumptions. As Nodelman and Reimer warn us (vis-à-vis the messages in children's literature): "Ideology works best by disappearing, so that people simply take their ideological assumptions for granted as the only, whole, and unquestionable truth" (80).

Assessment researcher Jamal Abedi, responding to the pro-charter Scantron test item which opened this chapter, argued that without offering an opposing viewpoint, "Poor kids might feel bad when reading it. Kids not in charters may feel bad . . . Taking the side of charter schools is not appropriate" (quoted in Rossi). Herein lies the danger of a popular text like *Ultimate Comics Spider-Man*'s portrayal of a charter school lottery in an urban neighborhood. It is the danger of perpetuating for children only a single story of education "reform" in the United States. As Chimamanda Ngozi Adichie argues in her 2009 TED Talk, we are "impressionable and vulnerable in the face of a story, particularly as children" (Adichie). Without access to multiple stories and a plenitude of counterpoints, children must make do with limited quantities of literature and other media dealing with the contemporary political issues that affect them most intimately. Patricia Enciso writes that children often "have only main-stream culture to refer to as a source of explanation for the fictional and actual events they encounter," and adds that, as readers, how young people "make sense of fictional encounters has a significant bearing on how [they] learn to make sense of the real world" (527). The authors of fictional encounters must therefore recognize their great power and take responsibility for it.

American children and youth in the early twenty-first century—and urban students of color in particular—are forced to navigate an ideological battlefield while attending school. The field has been drawn and is mediated by adults coming from a range of political camps, but young people are the ones pushed into the trenches. As I argue at the beginning of this chapter, contemporary education "reform," as an issue that affects the lives of so many students, should not be elided as a topic in which children are afforded agency and critical-ity. Rather, young readers should be provided many opportunities to engage a range of views, words, and images about the schooling systems to which they are part and parcel. This is one of the central goals and responsibilities of high-quality children's literature. As my late professor Larry Sipe was fond of saying, a chief purpose of literature is to de-familiarize life, to challenge our comfort-able assumptions, and to jar us awake.

Through the medium's inherent multiperspectivity, comics have the poten-tial to destabilize "common sense" ideologies and single-story narratives (e.g., Horstkotte and Pedri; Mikkonen). The creators of comics for young readers should thus emphasize their medium's historically "countercultural function that rebuffs adult efforts to shape children's memories, identities, and tastes" (Hatfield and Svonkin 434) by creating work that stimulates critical multi-modal readings. In order to do this, comics texts produced for an audience of young people should represent a robust diversity of identities, opinions, and experiences (e.g., Mohanty). To paraphrase Beverly Slapin, "issues-based" children's literature does not have to present a "sociological treatise" in order to be of high quality. Simply put, literature "should be honest in its depictions" and invite readers to critically engage topics from a variety of perspectives (Slapin). This is not accomplished when inaccuracies and half-truths are presented as fact. The multimodal medium of comics, which is "structurally equipped to challenge dominant modes of storytelling" (Chute, "Comics as Literature" 456), is ideal for encouraging critical engagement around contested political topics (Carleton). And because comics and graphic novels are currently so popular with young readers in and out of school (Low and Campano; Simon), they should absolutely be employed to invite children to think more deeply, in more complicated and nuanced ways, about contemporary issues such as education "reform."

Employing a hybrid approach to critical multicultural analysis and critical multimodal analysis, I have attempted to make visible the ways in which Bendis's writing and Pichelli's illustration—as part of a three-page sequence on urban school charterization—contribute to dominant education "reform" discourses that have been ubiquitous in America during the opening decades of the twenty-first century.[6] Their discursive ubiquity, as I have previously mentioned, is mostly limited to adult media, which tend to provide a wider range of counterpoints. Children's media do not typically match adult-geared media in this commitment to balance, leaving young readers a narrower spectrum through which to engage contemporary topics like school "reform." As Kathleen O'Neil writes, children's literature today "continues to be a vehicle for cultural reproduction" (41), and the messages in it thus have the potential to profoundly influence the lives of young readers. For this reason, we simply cannot allow a debate as controversial and important as the one currently ripping through America's education system to become so one-sided in its children's media portrayals that it amounts to an invisible, an uncritical—and perhaps most catastrophically, an inevitable—ideology.

## Notes

1. The young adult novel featuring a charter school is Lauren Barnholdt's *Four Truths and a Lie* from 2008. The issue of *Time Magazine for Kids* dealing with charter schools—credited to author Melanie Kletter—was released on September 13, 2013.

2. In May 2014, *Ultimate Comics Spider-Man* was relaunched as *Miles Morales: The Ultimate Spider-Man*. The book's continuity was unaffected by the title change, and Bendis continued as author. In February 2016, Miles joined the "mainstream" Marvel universe in *Spider-Man* #1, which reunited the original creative team of Bendis, Pichelli, and Ponsor. Under the three titles, over forty issues of Miles's story have gone to press since 2011.

3. It is unclear why Bendis would name a Black character "Jefferson Davis" (i.e., the White, slave-owning president of the Confederacy during the American Civil War). It is certainly an

odd symbol for a title that touches on issues of race and opportunity, and I am unable to locate any source in which Bendis explains his decision.

4. Brian Michael Bendis is one of the most prolific and popular writers working in the comics industry today. In addition to *Ultimate Spider-Man* (which he has been writing consistently since 2000), Bendis has worked on Marvel's *X-Men, Daredevil,* and *Avengers* properties. He is also known for creator-owned series such as *Powers* and *Torso.*

5. In addition to Jackie Robinson's jersey, to fans of Douglas Adams's *The Hitchhiker's Guide to the Galaxy,* the number 42 refers to "the Answer to the Ultimate Question of Life, the Universe, and Everything." Unfortunately, as with school reform, no one quite knows what the question is.

6. Moving ahead in the series, Miles's educational experiences at Brooklyn Visions Academy are not a major element of *Ultimate Comics Spider-Man,* which, in general, is a very good comic book series. Nevertheless, the three-page sequence reviewed in this chapter is important to parse in order to understand Bendis's outlook toward his characters and their setting. It helps situate the series within hegemonic "culture of poverty" discourses, even when Bendis is critical of certain institutions that emerge from within those discourses.

## Works Cited

Adichie, Chimamanda Ngozi. "The Danger of a Single Story." *TED Global.* Oxford, UK. July 2009. Web.

Aiello, Giorgia. "Theoretical Advances in Critical Visual Analysis: Perception, Ideology, Mythologies, and Social Semiotics." *Journal of Visual Literacy* 26.2 (2006): 89–102. Print.

Beaty, Bart, and Nick Nguyen. "Foreword." *The System of Comics.* Thierry Groensteen. Trans. Bart Beaty and Nick Nguyen. Jackson, MS: University Press of Mississippi, 2007. vii–x. Print.

Bendis, Brian Michael, and Sara Pichelli. *Ultimate Comics Spider-Man.* Vol. 1. New York: Marvel, 2012. Print.

Bomer, Randy, Joel E. Dworin, Laura May, and Peggy Semingson. "Miseducating Teachers About the Poor: A Critical Analysis of Ruby Payne's Claims about Poverty." *Teachers College Record* 110.12 (2008): 2497–531. Print.

Bonastia, Christopher. "Why the Racist History of the Charter School Movement Is Never Discussed." *National Public Voice,* 9 March 2012. Web.

Botelho, Maria José, and Masha Kabakow Rudman. *Critical Multicultural Analysis of Children's Literature: Mirrors, Windows, and Doors.* New York: Routledge, 2009. Print.

Campano, Gerald. *Immigrant Students and Literacy: Reading, Writing, and Remembering.* New York: Teachers College Press, 2007. Print.

Carleton, Sean. "Drawn to Change: Comics and Critical Consciousness." *Labour/Le Travail* 73 (2014): 151–77. Web.

Cavna, Michael. "Miles Morales and Me: Why the New Biracial Spider-Man Matters." *The Washington Post,* 4 August 2011. Web.

Chute, Hillary, L. "Comics as Literature? Reading Graphic Narrative." *PMLA* 123.2 (2008): 452–65. Print.

———. *Graphic Women: Life Narrative and Contemporary Comics.* New York: Columbia University Press, 2010. Print.

Cole, Teju. "The White-Savior Industrial Complex." *The Atlantic,* 21 March 2012. Web.

Connors, Sean P. "Toward a Shared Vocabulary for Visual Analysis: An Analytic Toolkit for Deconstructing the Visual Design of Graphic Novels." *Journal of Visual Literacy* 31.1 (2012): 71–92.

Cooper, Robert, and Will J. Jordan. "Cultural Issues in Comprehensive School Reform." *Educating Black Males: Voices from the Field.* Ed. Olatokunbo S. Fashola. Washington DC: Brookings Institution Press, 2005. 1–18. Print.

Cowan, Peter. "'Drawn' into the Community: Re-Considering the Artwork of Latino Adolescents." *Visual Sociology* 14 (1999): 91–107. Print.

Cromer, Michael, and Penney Clark. "Getting Graphic with the Past: Graphic Novels and the Teaching of History." *Theory and Research in Social Education* 35.4 (2007): 574–91.

Darder, Antonia. "Racism and the Charter School Movement: Unveiling the Myths." *TruthOut,* 30 November 2014. Web.

Darling-Hammond, Linda, and Ann Lieberman. "Educating Superman." *Finding Superman: Debating the Future of Public Education in America.* Ed. Watson Scott Swail. New York: Teachers College Press, 2012. 31–45. Print.

Dutro, Elizabeth. "Review of *Waiting for 'Superman.'"* National Education Policy Center. 24 January 2011. Web.

Enciso, Patricia. "Cultural Identity and Response to Literature: Running Lessons from *Maniac Magee.*" *Language Arts* 71.6 (1994): 524–33. Print.

Fairclough, Norman. *Analysing Discourse: Textual Analysis for Social Research.* London: Routledge, 2003. Print.

Foster III, William H. *Looking for a Face Like Mine: The History of African Americans in Comics.* Waterbury CT: Fine Tooth Press, 2005. Print.

Fraser, Ryn. "Ultimate Comics Spider-Man Sales Figures." *World of Black Heroes.* 11 February 2012. Web.

Fu, Albert S. "Fear of a Black Spider-Man: Racebending and the Colour-Line in Superhero (Re) casting." *Journal of Graphic Novels and Comics* 6.3 (2015): 269–83. Print.

Gallup Poll of Historical Trends in Education. Gallup, 2013. Web.

Ghiso, María Paula. "The Laundromat as the Transnational Local: Young Children's Literacies of Interdependence." *Teachers College Record* 118.1 (2016): 1–46. Print.

Ghiso, María Paula, and David E. Low. "Students Using Multimodal Literacies to Surface Micronarratives of United States Immigration." *Literacy* 47.1 (2013): 26–34. Print.

Ghiso, María Paula, Gerald Campano, and Ted Hall. "Braided Histories and Experiences in Literature for Children and Adolescents." *Journal of Children's Literature* 38.2 (2012): 14–22. Print.

Golden, Joanne M., and Annyce Gerber. "A Semiotic Perspective of Text: The Picture Story Book Event." *Journal of Reading Behavior* 22.3 (1990): 203–19. Print.

González, Norma, Luis C. Moll, and Cathy Amanti. *Funds of Knowledge: Theorizing Practices in Households, Communities, and Classrooms.* Mahwah NJ: Lawrence Erlbaum Associates, 2005. Print.

Hatfield, Charles, and Craig Svonkin. "Why Comics Are and Are Not Picture Books: Introduction." *Children's Literature Association Quarterly* 37.4 (2012): 429–35. Print.

Horstkotte, Silke, and Nancy Pedri. "Focalization in Graphic Narrative." *Narrative* 19.3 (2011): 330–57. Print.

Hull, Glynda A., and Mark Nelson. "Locating the Semiotic Power of Multimodality." *Written Communication* 22.2 (2005): 224–61. Print.

Hyde Park Johnny. "Chicago Schools Caught Brainwashing Students." *Daily Kos.* 27 May 2012. Web.

Janks, Hilary. *Literacy and Power.* New York: Routledge, 2010. Print.

Karp, Stan. "Charter Schools and the Future of Public Education." *Rethinking Schools* 28.1 (2013): 42–47. Print.

King, Joyce E. "Dysconscious Racism: Ideology, Identity, and the Miseducation of Teachers." *Journal of Negro Education* 60.2 (1991): 133–46. Print.

Kirkland, D. E. "'The Rose That Grew from Concrete': Postmodern Blackness and New English Education. *English Journal* 97.5 (2008): 69–75. Print.

Kirst, Michael W. "Politics of Charter Schools: Competing National Advocacy Coalitions Meet Local Politics." *Peabody Journal of Education* 82.2–3 (2007): 184–203. Print.

Kress, Gunther, and Theo van Leeuwen. "Representation and Interaction: Designing the Position of the Viewer." *The Discourse Reader.* Ed. Adam Jaworski and Nikolas Coupland. London and New York: Routledge, 1999. Print.

LeBlanc, Robert. "Reform, Ideology and the Politics of *Waiting for 'Superman.'*" *Power and Education* 2.3 (2010): 300–308. Web.

Low, David E. "'Spaces Invested with Content': Crossing the 'Gaps' in Comics with Readers in Schools." *Children's Literature in Education* 43.4 (2012): 368–85. Print.

Low, David E., and Gerald Campano. "The Image Becomes the Weapon: New Literacies and Canonical Legacies." *Voices from the Middle* 21.1 (2013): 26–31. Print.

Lubienski, Sarah Theule, and Christopher Lubienski. "School Sector and Academic Achievement: A Multi-Level Analysis of NAEP Mathematics Data." *American Educational Research Journal* 43.4 (2006): 651–98. Print.

McWilliams, Ora C. "Who Is Afraid of a Black Spider(-Man)?" *Transformative Works and Cultures* 13 (2013): n.p. Web.

Mikkonen, Kai. "Focalisation in Comics: From the Specificities of the Medium to Conceptual Reformulation." *Scandinavian Journal of Comic Art* 1.1 (2012): 69–95. Print.

Mohanty, Satya P. "The Epistemic Status of Cultural Identity: On *Beloved* and the Postcolonial Condition." *Reclaiming Identity: Realist Theory and the Predicament of Postmodernism.* Ed. Paula M. L. Moya and Michael R. Hames-García. Berkeley: University of California Press, 2000. 29–66. Print.

Nama, Adilfu. *Super Black: American Pop Culture and Black Superheroes.* Austin: University of Texas Press, 2011. Print.

Neill, Monty. "Don't Mourn, Organize!" *Rethinking Schools* 18.1 (2003). Web.

New London Group. "A Pedagogy of Multi-Literacies: Designing Social Futures." *Harvard Educational Review* 66.1 (1996): 60–92. Print.

Nodelman, Perry, and Mavis Reimer. *The Pleasures of Children's Literature.* 3rd ed. Boston: Allyn and Bacon, 2003. Print.

O'Neil, Kathleen. "Once Upon Today: Teaching for Social Justice with Postmodern Picturebooks." *Children's Literature in Education* 41.1 (2010): 40–51. Print.

Pantaleo, Sylvia. "Reading Images in Graphic Novels: Taking Students to a 'Greater Thinking Level.'" *English in Australia* 49.1 (2014): 38–51. Web.

Parini, Jay. "The American Mythos." *Daedalus* 141.1 (2012): 52–60. Print.

Ravitch, Diane. "The Myth of Charter Schools." *Finding Superman: Debating the Future of Public Education in America.* Ed. Watson Scott Swail. New York: Teachers College Press, 2012. 19–30. Print.

———. *Reign of Error: The Hoax of the Privatization Movement and the Danger to America's Public Schools.* New York: Alfred A. Knopf, 2013. Print.

Riesman, Abraham. "Sexism and Making a Nonwhite Spider-Man." *Vulture,* 1 May 2014. Web.

Rossi, Rosalind. "Question Criticized as Charter-School 'Propaganda' Pulled from CPS Tests." *Chicago Sun-Times,* 25 May 2012. Web.

Schieble, Melissa. "Reading Images in *American Born Chinese* through Critical Visual Literacy." *English Journal* 103.5 (2014): 47–52. Print.

Schwarz, Gretchen. "Expanding Literacies through Graphic Novels." *English Journal* 95.6 (2006): 58–64. Print.

Siegel, Marjorie, and Carolyn P. Panofsky. "Designs for Multimodality in Literacy Studies: Explorations in Analysis." *National Reading Conference Yearbook* 58.1 (2009): 99–111. Print.

Simon, Rob. "'Without Comic Books, There Would Be No Me': Teachers as Connoisseurs of Adolescents' Literate Lives." *Journal of Adolescent & Adult Literacy* 55.6 (2012): 516–26. Print.

Sipe, Lawrence R. "Learning the Language of Picturebooks." *Journal of Children's Literature* 24.2 (1998): 66–75. Print.

Slapin, Beverly, with Allyson Criner Brown. "*Smoky Night* by Eve Bunting: Misguided Effort to Help Kids Understand Rodney King Events." *Teaching for Change*, 17 May 2012. Web.

Spencer, Tamara. "Learning to Read in the Wake of Reform: Young Children's Experiences with Scientifically Based Reading Curriculum." *Perspectives on Urban Education* 8.2 (2011): 41–50. Web.

Sutherland, Robert D. "Hidden Persuaders: Political Ideologies in Literature for Children." *Children's Literature in Education* 16.3 (1985): 143–57. Print.

Tucker, Brian. "Gotthold Ephraim Lessing's *Laocoön* and the Lessons of Comics." *Teaching the Graphic Novel.* Ed. Stephen E. Tabachnik. New York: The Modern Language Association of America, 2009. 28–35. Print.

Uspensky, Boris. *A Poetics of Composition: The Structure of the Artistic Text and Typology of a Compositional Form.* Trans. Valentina Zavarin and Susan Wittig. Berkeley and Los Angeles: University of California Press, 1973. Print.

Versaci, Rocco. "'Literary Literacy' and the Role of the Comic Book: Or, 'You Teach a Class on What?'" *Teaching Visual Literacy: Using Comic Books, Graphic Novels, Anime, Cartoons, and More to Develop Comprehension and Thinking Skills.* Ed. Nancy Frey and Douglas Fisher. Thousand Oaks, CA: Corwin Press, 2008. 91–111. Print.

*Waiting for "Superman."* Dir. Davis Guggenheim. Paramount Vantage, 2010. Film.

# 19

## "Walk Together, Children": The Function and Interplay of Comics, History, and Memory in *Martin Luther King and the Montgomery Story* and John Lewis's *March: Book One*

*Joanna C. Davis-McElligatt*

In *Walking with the Wind: A Memoir of the Movement*, Congressman John Lewis (D-GA 5th District) recalls that by the fall of his sophomore year of college in 1958, he had become significantly involved in the burgeoning civil rights movement. Lewis explains that he was inspired by speakers he heard at Fisk University, such as Thurgood Marshall, Fred Shuttlesworth, W. E. B. Du Bois, and the Rev. Kelly Miller Smith, a man he credits as being "an inspiration to me, a model, someone we all looked up to" (74). Yet Lewis explains that "it wasn't Kelly Miller Smith's teaching . . . that had as much of an impact on my life as a visitor he brought into his church one Sunday that fall" (74). That man was James Lawson. At the time, Lawson was a member of both the Congress of Racial Equality (CORE) and the pacifist-activist group the Fellowship of Reconciliation (FOR). Lawson first introduced Lewis to the strategy of nonviolent direct action, the method that would become the modus operandi of the civil rights movement. Lewis attended a workshop led by Lawson on the principles of nonviolence at First Baptist Church in downtown Nashville, Tennessee. As he recounts in *March: Book One*, the workshop left a lasting impression on him:

> Jim talked about the Montgomery Bus Boycott, about war resistance, about nonviolence. He spoke of Gandhi, this little brown man from India using the way of nonviolence to free an entire nation of people. And how we could apply nonviolence, just as Dr. King did in Montgomery, all across America—South AND North—to eradicate some of the evils we all faced: the evil of racism, the evil of poverty, the evil of war. Jim Lawson conveyed the urgency of developing our philosophy, our discipline, our understanding. His words liberated me. I thought, this is it . . . this is the way out. (77–78)

In addition to numerous workshops and lectures, Lewis notes in *Walking with the Wind* that FOR "had published the wildly popular comic book-style pamphlet title *Martin Luther King and the Montgomery Story*, which explained the basics of passive resistance and nonviolence as tools for desegregation. The pamphlet wound up being devoured by black college students across the South. I'd read a copy of it myself" (74). The centrality of this comic book to the promulgation of what came to be known as the Montgomery Method of direct action has been largely lost to history, as has the integral role child and young adult demonstrators played in the movement. Lewis's graphic memoir *March: Book One*, co-written by Andrew Aydin and drawn by Nate Powell, has been chiefly responsible for making known the importance of the FOR comic and its impact on young adults and children during the movement. Indeed, so central to his understanding of the methods of nonviolence that Powell incorporates an illustrated version of cover of the comic in *March: Book One*, and, with Chris Ross, designed the cover as an homage to *The Montgomery Story* (Powell). Furthermore, Lewis and Aydin clarify in *March: Book One* the genre to which *The Montgomery Story* belongs; they refer to the text as a "popular comic book" rather than a "comic book-style pamphlet."

A 2013 episode of the radio program *On Point with Tom Ashbrook* coincided with the 50th anniversary of the March on Washington for Jobs and Freedom and with the release of *March: Book One*. During his appearance on the program, John Lewis explained how the participants in Nashville Student Movement came to understand the process and value of staged nonviolent sit-ins: "Many of the students . . . had read the same [FOR] comic book. [ . . . ] That's one of the reasons we worked on this comic book called March, because we wanted to inspire another generation of young people. See, I was told over and over again by people, 'Don't get in trouble! Don't go to jail!' But we got in good trouble. Necessary trouble" ("John Lewis and the 50th Anniversary"). The leadership of FOR intended *The Montgomery Story* to be an instructional tool for children and young adults who were preparing to participate in a frequently violent and potentially deadly social movement. Consequently, they intended for the comic book to be accessible and straightforward in both content and style. To that end, the text included specific directives for young people who hoped to participate in sit-ins and protests. Unlike *The Montgomery Story*, *March* is autobiographical, focused on re-constructing the past of Lewis's childhood and early involvement in the civil rights movement. *March* explores the harrowing social conditions of the segregated South, the effect of racial violence, and the accepted social use of racist language. Lewis's memoir, then, is designed to introduce young people to the historical circumstances that precipitated the movement, the material conditions of African Americans prior to the successful legislation that followed the movement, and the central tenets of passive resistance. Drawing as it does on *The Montgomery Story*, *March* is also a critical response to arguments that Obama's presidency marks a new postracial era in America in which the efforts and struggles of the civil rights movement are no longer important.

In this chapter, I argue that *March* serves three interlocking purposes. First, by working within the comics medium, Lewis, Aydin, and Powell acknowledge the historical centrality of the medium in the dissemination of information to children and young adults not only during the civil rights movement, as in the case of *The Montgomery Story*, but in the present moment as well. Second, by bringing *The Montgomery Story* out of obscurity through direct visual and narrative references to the comic, Lewis, Aydin, and Powell not only remind readers of the unique ability of comic art to reach readers in ways that other narrative forms cannot, but simultaneously make the case that the medium played a role in the success of the movement itself.

On a related note, in highlighting the significance of *The Montgomery Story*, Lewis, Aydin, and Powell draw our attention to the important role that children and young adults played in the movement. From its opening pages, the first book of Lewis's memoir is focused on children, both in its broad narrative structure and in its attention to the details of Lewis's own childhood, adolescence, and young adulthood. The comic takes seriously the contributions of children to the civil rights movement, and it makes a strong case that contemporary young readers are instrumental in continuing that legacy. Though *March: Book One* has enjoyed adult readership and has been both a literary and commercial success, Lewis, Aydin, and Powell's text is widely read by and taught to child and young adult readers. The comic has been adopted as school curriculum in thirty states—which has generated a number of teaching guides for children and young adults—and has been selected for the first-year reading programs at Michigan State University, Marquette University, and Georgia State University (Reid). In addition to being named Coretta Scott King Honor book, as well as numerous other awards, the comic was also listed as one of YALSA's Top 10 Great Graphic Novels for Teens, and one of YALSA's Outstanding Books for the College Bound.

Third and finally, by participating in a long-standing tradition of African American autobiography, Lewis's memoir highlights the particularity of his experience in order to explore the relationship between the past and the present. Readers are able, through a consideration of his work, to see how far African Americans have come from the days of his youth, but to understand the importance of preserving those freedoms for themselves and for future generations. As Michael A. Chaney has argued, Lewis's comic shares with other graphic narratives written by African Americans an emphasis on "strategies for revising the boundaries between black and white, past and present, performance and history, and a range of other binary formulations central the maintenance of Western culture" (175). Chaney suggests "works such as *March* explicitly thematize . . . the burden of history within particular registers of an African American context and milieu. Rather than reflect the putative facts of history from some transparent or bounded notion of a 'black' perspective, these texts question institutions of recollection . . . upon whose premises any such thing as the past is produced for scrutiny in the first place" (175–76).

Indeed, by blending Lewis's recollections of the past with the contemporary moment of Obama's first term in office, readers are encouraged to forge connections between the late twentieth century and the opening decade of the new millennium, between the spectacle of the inauguration and the disenfranchisement of African Americans during Lewis's youth and early adulthood, and between black and white Americans. In sum, in this chapter, I explore the importance of the comics form to the civil rights movement by way of the inception, dissemination, and reception of *Martin Luther King and the Montgomery Story*, the attendant importance of children to the success of the civil rights movement, and the function of *March* as a syncretic document which blends past and present not only in a traditional African American autobiographical form, but also in keeping with the increasing number of, as Patrick Rosencrantz has described them, "autobiographix." In the end, I make the case that Lewis, Aydin, and Powell's comic memoir is a powerful contribution to work on the civil rights movement, and to the history of comic art.

### "Don't Worry about Your Children": The Birmingham Children's Crusade and the Role of Children and Young People in the Civil Rights Movement

During the 1950s, FOR was focused, in part, on lending support to the burgeoning civil rights movement. According to Claudia Rowe, FOR "provided speakers in churches, synagogues and schools, held workshops, raised money for bombed churches and produced films and literature" (Rowe). Led by A. J. Muste, and in concert with CORE, FOR sponsored the first interracial sit-in in 1943, over a decade before the commonly recognized beginnings of the civil rights movement. As noted in the introduction, FOR staff member James Lawson, who was based in Nashville, led a number of important workshops on the ethics of nonviolence, and was responsible for training not only John Lewis, but other notable activists, such as Bernard Lafayette and James Bevel. Among FOR's most significant contributions to the movement, however, was their publication of the *Martin Luther King and the Montgomery Story*, a text aimed at informing children about the earliest history of the movement in Montgomery, Alabama, and encouraging them to follow the path of passive resistance by providing them with a step-by-step guide for the process of direct action. It is worth noting, however, that in spite of their lack of concrete numbers, FOR estimates on their website that hundreds of thousands of copies of the comic have been sold, both in the United States and abroad.

Children in primary and secondary schools, as well as college students, played a pivotal role in demonstrations, protests, and marches, even though many of the goals of the movement, such as the elimination of obstacles to voting and the hiring of African American police offers, were not necessarily child-centered. As part of their training, all protesters, including children, were required to sign pledges acknowledging their adherence to "The 10 Commandments of Nonviolence," which included, among other things, an obligation to "seek regular service for others and for the world," "refrain from the violence of fist, tongue, or heart," and "meditate daily on the teachings and life of Jesus" (Levinson 34). The 10 Commandments of Nonviolence were difficult imperatives even for adults. Yet hundreds of children, teenagers, and young adults willingly signed the pledge, determined to march and be jailed, should that be required of them.

In the early part of 1963, Rev. Dr. Martin Luther King, Jr. and the Rev. Fred Shuttlesworth launched Project C, the object of which was to fill the jails of Birmingham with demonstrators, and in doing so force Eugene "Bull" Connor, the chief of police of Birmingham, into a position to renege on the city's policies of segregation. If the prison occupants reached a critical mass as the protests continued, King and Shuttlesworth reasoned, city officials would find themselves unable to resist the demands of the demonstrators if they wanted to return order to the city. King and Shuttlesworth, however, quickly discovered that adults were largely unwilling to put themselves in danger, no matter how important the cause. After several rounds of scheduled protests, insufficient numbers of adults had volunteered to be detained, fearing that incarceration would threaten their jobs or, more seriously, put their lives at risk. African American adults were beaten and murdered as a matter of course, and homes were frequently bombed—in fact, there were so many bombings in the early-1960s in Birmingham the city earned the nickname "Bombingham" (66).

James Bevel, then the Director of Direct Action and Director of Nonviolent Education of the Southern Christian Leadership Conference (SCLC), approached King and Shuttlesworth with a radical idea: "Fill the jails with school children" (66). Given that hundreds of children had already been trained in methods of nonviolence, it made sense to enlist children, teenagers, and college students to do the work that their parents were unable to do. King initially resisted the idea that children should be put in harm's way. Bevel, however, made the case that the age of the protestor was of no concern so long as "the child made a conscious decision" (68), and King, somewhat reluctantly, agreed. Indeed, as Gwen Cook, a teenage activist, told it, "[a] lot of people were worried we were going to get hurt. The reality of it was we were born black in Alabama. And we were going to get hurt if we didn't do something" (68). On Friday, May 3, described by Bevel as "Double D-Day" (81), nearly two thousand children in both elementary and high schools—as well as some students from nearby Miles College—walked out of classrooms in order to participate in a march that they knew would, if successful, end with their incarceration. The police were armed with vicious attack dogs and fire hoses, which they turned on the crowd. Children were bitten, slammed into walls, and were lifted into the air by streams of water; one young girl, Carolyn Maull, had an entire side of her hair sheared by the power of the fire hose (82).

In the first four days of what came to be known as the Birmingham Children's Crusade, nearly 2,500 young people had been arrested. On the night of May 6, Dr. King spoke to crowd of worried parents, encouraging them to believe in the work that their children were doing: "Never in the history of this nation have so many people been arrested for the cause of freedom and human dignity. Don't worry about your children. Don't hold them back if they want to go to jail. For they are doing a job for not only themselves but for all of America and for all of mankind" (115). Children as young as nine spent as many as ten days in jail. In order to survive and keep their minds and bodies strong, incarcerated children relied on toys, snacks, and games that their parents had packed for them, as well as the occasional candy bar distributed by other adults in the jail, and whatever food (however meager and even inedible) the city offered them. All told, the Children's Crusade was the first successful large-scale event of the era. Children and young adults effectively shut down the city, flooded the jails with peaceful participants, drew national attention to the cause of the civil rights movement, and bolstered King's reputation as a leader.

Crucial to the success of this protest was its representation in the media. Katharine Capshaw has argued that photographic evidence of the maltreatment of children, in particular, resulted in the movement's most recognizable images: "We witness the Little Rock Nine entering Central High School in 1957, thronged by angry crowds; we see young people attacked by police dogs and fire hoses during the 1963 Birmingham "Children's Crusade"; we see dozens of girls imprisoned in Birmingham after the protests" (x). These images, collected in photoboooks, published in newspapers, and aired on television, made the forceful case to observers both white and black that even youthfulness was not a protection against the injuries of Jim Crow. Capshaw suggests that it was

photographic coverage of the Children's Crusade [which] helped turn the tide of national sympathies and ignited support for the Civil Rights Act of 1964.

> Picturing childhood became a powerful instrument of civil rights activism, because children carry an important aura of human value and potential, and threats to young people made the stakes of the movement palpable to individuals and to the nation. Undoubtedly, images of children under seige had generative effects for the civil rights campaign. (x–xi)

In the racist South, black children's bodies were always already under threat, and consequently open to acts of racial violence. In the decision to use child and young adult protestors, and to make available to the public evidence of the bruality against them, the organizers of the movement made the forceful case that the purveyors of violence did not discriminate in their targets. The refusal to take a stand against Jim Crow was a tacit acceptance of the destruction of the innocent.

I want to make it clear that I offer this detailed explication of the 1963 Birmingham Children's Crusade for two reasons. First, I want to draw attention to one of the most important contributions that young people made to the civil rights movement, which I argue has not received enough critical attention. Second, I seek to explore the ways in which the recruitment of children to the movement necessitated the production of child-specific materials capable of informing children and young adults of the important role they had to play. In the remainder of this chapter, I examine a selection of those materials and their influence in greater depth.

## "*YOU* Can Do Something": *Martin Luther King and the Montgomery Story* as an Instructional Tool for Children

In addition to regular workshops, meetings, and organized protests, SCLC, CORE, and FOR published and widely circulated a variety of written materials, such as fliers, booklets, essays, articles, and letters—and a ten-cent comic book printed on inexpensive newsprint. According to Ethan Vesely-Flad, *Martin Luther King and the Montgomery Story*, published in 1958, was the brainchild of Alfred Hassler, a former FOR executive director. The comic was written by Benton Resnick, and drawn by an unknown artist who was at that time working in the Al Capp Studios. Though *Martin Luther King and the Montgomery Story* is a complex text that opens itself up to a number of readings, I highlight the comic's narrative structure and style, which I argue are fundamental to understanding the ways in which the comic instructs children about their important role in the movement.

The style of *The Montgomery Story* would have been familiar to readers of history or romance comics marketed to children and teens in the 1950s, such as those published by Atlas Comics or Fawcett Comics. As is typical in those genres, the comic art is realistic—buildings, structures, and objects are meticulously reproduced. Characters are likewise drawn with an eye for realism and authenticity—the artist makes certain that readers will immediately recognize Rosa Parks and King upon sight. The structure of the panels—six panels per page in groups of two—is basic and fixed throughout, only deviating in the final section entitled "How the Montgomery Method Works." The cartoonist took very few creative liberties in the construction of either the art or narrative structure of *The Montgomery Story*. Robert Kirby contends that the art is uncomplicatedly weak: "Factual historical comics are often produced with professionally rendered but characterless drawings. *Martin Luther King and the Montgomery Story* itself, though certainly important as an inspiration to Lewis and other activists of the civil rights era, featured technically proficient but generic art, devoid of personality, the message itself obviously being more than the (comics) medium"[1] (Kirby). I claim that the comic's seemingly "generic art" performed an important function for young African American readers at the time. Given the long history in American comics of racist caricatures of African Americans in the comics medium—a history I do not have time to explore even in brief here—*The Montgomery Story* would likely have been one of the only titles that young African Americans would have encountered that did not represent them as simian primitives living in the jungle, or with the embellishments of thick red lips, and unreasonably black skin. In fact, prior to the publication of *The Montgomery Story*, there were only two comics marketed exclusively to African American children and teenagers. All-Negro Comics published a single issue of *All-Negro Comics* in 1947, and Fawcett comics published three issues *Negro Romance* in 1950. Though these comics worked to eschew racist stereotypes of African Americans, their shorts runs indicate that readership was limited. Simply put, young African Americans in the 1950s had very few opportunities to see themselves positively—and humanely—represented in comic strips and books.

Scott McCloud, in a process he defines as "amplification through simplification," has argued that reader identification with comics characters requires that figures be drawn blankly and minimally: "When we abstract an image through cartooning, we're not so much eliminating details as we are focusing on specific details. By stripping down an image to its essential 'meaning,' an artist can amplify meaning in a way that realistic art can't" (30). In other words, McCloud claims that the more rudimentary a character's face is drawn, the more easily readers will be able to identify themselves both with and as it. Conversely, the more realistic a character is, the more readers are encouraged to read that figure as Other. Though McCloud's formulation may work in some cases—such as in *March*, which I will delve into later in this chapter—in the case of *The Montgomery Story* I argue that the opposite is true. By encountering African American characters who are drawn realistically, and in the same manner as their white counterparts, African American readers were encouraged to see themselves not only as human, but as possessing as much humanity as white Americans—a progressive and even radical social statement for this time. For example, on the first page of *The Montgomery Story*, we see Martin Luther King seated at a table "with both white and colored students"—all of the characters are drawn in the same realistic manner, and, aside from the difference in skin color, are each recognizably human in exactly the same way. To that end, the generic, straightforward, and relatively unembellished style of the comic could be seen as visual rhetorical cues prompting young African Americans, unaccustomed to seeing nonracist images of themselves in any media, to an understanding of themselves as human as white Americans. This invocation to self-understanding was key for young activists.

The narrative style of *The Montgomery Story* likewise pushes African American readers to see themselves as a potentially vital part of the movement. The comic is narrated by an African American man who lives in Montgomery, Alabama, works as a mechanic, and has a wife and child. He introduces himself as Jones, but in the same sentence insists that his name "doesn't matter"—rather, he argues, his "story's important for you as well as for me. We're ALL caught up in it one way or another!" (2). Though Jones is likely older than the average audience for the comic, he nevertheless serves as a narrative blank slate who invites readers to see themselves, their friends, and their parents in him. Jones explains to readers that "a Negro anywhere in the Deep South has a hard time. JIM CROW sits mighty heavy on a man's spirit. People live scared under Jim Crow. You never know when something might bust out" (2). By addressing specific incidents of violence under Jim Crow, such as Ku Klux Klan parades, cross burnings, home and church bombings, and shootings, readers can see the ways in which white supremacy affects all African Americans by creating a culture of fear and intimidation. Jones's emphasis on the greater plight of African Americans under Jim Crow at the expense of his own personal identity, and his emphasis on the collective suffering of African Americans rather than his own personal difficulties, can be read as tacit encouragement for young readers who were learning about the ways in which their own personal suffering at the hands of Jim Crow was related to the suffering of all other African Americans. Indeed, participation in the civil rights movement required African Americans, in the words of Gayatri Spivak, to "strategically essentialize," or to temporarily set aside their very real differences in class, gender, and sexual orientation in favor of underscoring the ways in which their racial classification marked them as Other (205).

*The Montgomery Story*'s treatment of the historical circumstances of the early stages of the movement are bound up in the events leading up to the

Montgomery bus boycott, and the ways in which African Americans successfully employed the tactics of passive resistance to desegregate the public
transportation system. To that end, when the actions of specific individuals
are depicted in the comic, such as Rosa Parks's decision to remain seated at the
front of the bus, they are always placed in the broader context of the movement. Readers are therefore instructed that the self must be sublimated, and
that individual suffering must always be situated within the broader goal of
freedom for all African Americans. For example, following the arrest of Rosa
Parks, Jones realizes that he must do something proactive to protect himself
and his family, and his first impulse is to "talk to some of [his] friends," who
immediately produce a "mimeographed sheet protesting what had happened
to Rosa Parks and calling for a one-day boycott of the buses" (4). The language
that Jones selects repeatedly emphasizes collectivity: "everyone walked"; "our
protest is a success"; "we formed a committee"; "we walked and walked and
walked"; "we weren't going to give up"; and "we began to make preparations
for what we would do" (4–6). Jones's conflation of his efforts with those of the
group serves as an important lesson for young people. Although their particu-
larized personalities, goals, expectations, and experiences were important, the
success of the movement was contingent upon their unified action.

The final section of *The Montgomery Story* is also its most stylistically inven-
tive. "How the Montgomery Method Works" provides readers with a list of
important instructions for employing this approach, ranging from deeply personal commands, such as admonitions to "see *him* [your enemy] as a human
being" (12; italics in original), to practical orders, such as the directive to "practice situations as we did in Montgomery" in order to "make sure you can face
any opposition without *hitting back, or running away, or hating*" (14; italics in
original). This section of the comic abandons the use of panels in favor of a
more complex composition: pictures accompany text throughout the page in a
flowing list-like structure. The lack of panels exhorts readers to forge their own
connections between the text and the images, which are set side-by-side in a
loose relation. In this structure, the disembodied text is given equal weight on
the page as the images, which encourages readers to examine the words more
carefully and to read them more slowly. In this section, readers are addressed
as "you," which can be read as an individual address or as a group address. The
first sentence prompts readers to "remember that *you* can do something about
the situation. Not just the government, or some big organization. God says
*you* are important. He needs *you* to change things" (12; italics in original). The
illustration here is telling: a large, dark-skinned and disembodied hand points
emphatically at a group of five African American busts. The hand, pointing
towards the middle of the group, can be read as signalling either one figure
independently or all of them together. It is this clever rhetorical interrelation

of the individual and the collective that made *The Montgomery Story* such a powerful resource for the recruitment of youth to the movement.

### "Let the Spirit of History Be Our Guide": The Interplay of Narration, Style, History, and Memory in *March: Book One*

From its very first page, *March: Book One* is concerned with the relationship between the past and present, the function of memory, and the role of children in the movement. The graphic memoir begins in the past, specifically on March 7, 1965, otherwise known as "Bloody Sunday." John Lewis, chairman of the Student Nonviolent Coordinating Committee (SNCC), planned to lead several hundred activists across the Edmund Pettus Bridge during the Selma-to-Montgomery March. Just short of the bridge, the protestors were met by a wall of state troopers who savagely beat and gassed the demonstrators. *March* depicts these events *in medias res*, without any narrative context. In the first three pages, readers are presented with images of terrified African American demonstrators juxtaposed with those of outraged troopers in gas masks, military-grade helmets, and rifles. Readers who are unfamiliar with Bloody Sunday may initially be confused as to why the comic begins this way. However, these images help to contextualize the bucolic title page featuring a long shot of a pre-dawn Washington Monument from the steps of the Lincoln Memorial. In the pages immediately following the title page John Lewis is shown readying himself to attend President Barack Obama's inauguration in January of 2009. In this way, *March* immediately forges powerful visual and narrative connections between the violent and difficult past of the movement and the present moment of Inauguration Day, in which Americans, as the newscaster on Lewis's television exclaims, "reaffirm our commitment to democracy by bearing witness to the peaceful transfer of power" (14).

The structure of *March* is split in two sections of uneven length, in which the present moment of Inauguration Day is interspersed with Lewis's childhood and young adulthood. In the present moments of the comic, we witness Lewis meet in his Capitol Hill office with two young African American boys, Jacob and Esau, who have traveled from Atlanta with their mother, one of Lewis's constituents, to attend the Inauguration. Lewis takes the boys— always narrated in his own voice—through the story of his life, beginning with his earliest days as a child preaching to chickens on his parents' 110-acre Alabama farm, to his days as a college student who staged sit-ins and participated in demonstrations. Unlike *The Montgomery Story*, the narrative of *March* is entirely focused the experiences of children and young adults. Despite the fact that the comic is narrated from the perspective of an older man reflecting back on his youth, the stories are geared to a youth readership. As a result, the narrative is a circular motion, moving fluidly between the present and Lewis's past. In so doing, *March* not only underscores the powerful relationship between these two time periods, but it also counters arguments that the past has little or even no bearing on our present.

*March* is far more free in its layout than *The Montgomery Story*, often ignoring the structure of panels altogether in favor of long-shots and close-ups. Robert Kirby has described Nate Powell's art in *March* as "expressionistic realism," which effectively describes the way in which the characters are portrayed in a realistic, though cartoony, style. Powell does not capture Lewis's image exactly. As discussed above in the context of *The Montgomery Story*, I would argue that in this case the cartoony features of the characters *do* function according to McCloud's conception of amplification through simplification. Because *March* is a memoir, focused on representing the truth of certain historical events, by destabilizing Lewis's narrative authority the cartoony characters urge young readers to identify themselves with Lewis as a child in the past, and with Jacob and Esau in the present. The panel structure in *March* evokes this temporal connection. As the narrative itself moves back and forth between Lewis's conversation in his office with Jacob and Esau and his childhood on the farm, the panels visually signal the process of memory, as the edges of the panels themselves give way, often by becoming blurry and tattered around the edges. In other instances, one particular aspect of an event in the present moment shiftsoutside the boundaries of a panel. For example, at the end of *March: Book One*, a sound bubble containing the noise of a ringing phone in Lewis's Capitol Hill office breaks through the far right side of the panel, which is visually linked to the subsequent panel in which Lewis answers a ringing phone in the distant past. The transition between past and present happens at the level of the narrative as well. In one instance, Jacob and Esau ask Lewis whether or not his desire to study when he was young was motivated by the fact that he was a weak student, and Lewis informs him that even though he "wasn't the best," "school was important to me, and it was ultimately the reason I got involved in the Civil Rights Movement" (35). Following these words, the narrative immediately reverts back to Lewis's childhood. This shift in temporal perspective is indicated by a portion of Lewis's body appearing outside of the panel.

Ultimately, the way in which *March: Book One* cycles back and forth between the mid-twentieth century and the opening decade of the new millennium impresses upon readers that history and memory are essential to understanding current conditions. In this regard, the use of history as a literary device in *March* is vastly different from its use in *The Montgomery Story*. Whereas FOR leadership felt that young African American readers needed to be able to see themselves as connected to one another and to the suffering of all African

Americans in order to become part of the movement, Lewis and Aydin suggest that young people are, in the present moment, connected to America's past, no matter how tenuous that link may seem. *March* makes the case that the senseless death of Emmett Till, the suffering of peaceful protestors on the Edmund Pettus Bridge, and sacrifice of Rosa Parks—or, Claudette Colvin, a teenage girl who refused to give up her seat in Montgomery, Alabama, a full nine months before Parks—are inextricably linked to the contemporary moment. Lewis, Aydin, and Powell make plain that the significance of a historical event is not truly in the past if reverberations of it continue to be felt in the present.

## "Walk Together, Children": A Conclusion

*March: Book One* and *Martin Luther King and the Montgomery Story* might best be described as autobiographical comics, or "autobiographix," though *March* is more obviously so. In writing about the function of autobiography, Julia Swindells has argued that the genre "has the potential to be the text of the oppressed and the culturally displaced, forging a right to speak both for and beyond the individual. People in a position of powerlessness—women, black people, working-class people—have more than begun to insert themselves into the culture via autobiography, via the assertion of 'personal' voice, which speaks beyond itself" (229). *March* and *The Montgomery Story*, through the voices of Jones and Lewis, speak to as well as for a broader African American community. In this way, both comics also participate in the African American autobiographical tradition. These narratives, as Magnus O. Bassey has explained, are focused on group consciousness. They "give blacks an understanding of their predicament, of the social order of which they are a part and their place in relation to it . . . which cannot be separated from their long history of suffering" (214). Fredrick Harris has argued that especially for civil rights activists, group consciousness is fostered through the cultivation of collective memories: "Collective memories of past injustices inspired activism during the movement. . . . By 'keeping the story before' succeeding generations, narratives of resistance provided a historical framework for activists in their struggle against white supremacy" (22). More importantly, the stories of "elders . . . connected past grievances with present struggles" (22). By providing young readers with the stories of "past grievances," stories that connect them to narratives of struggle, Aydin, Lewis, and Resnick invite children to share in the glory and pain of the collective memories of the civil rights crusade for freedom. Both *March* and *The Montgomery Story* make a strong case that the suffering of African Americans facilitated social progress possible. It is this history of peaceful suffering as a response to violence, on both an individual and group level, that readers must reconcile if they hope to understand their contemporary moment.

*March* is dedicated to "the past and future children of the movement," so it is fitting that these words are echoed at the end of the comic. In the final two pages of *March*, Martin Luther King, Jr. reminds a group of Nashville activists that "no lie can live forever. Let us not despair. The universe is with us. Walk together, children. Don't get weary" (120–21). Ultimately, it is these ideas of solidarity and activism that *March* and *The Montgomery Story* emphasize for readers. Through joint action and shared memory, these two powerful comics demonstrate that if young people "walk together," in solidarity with one another, refusing to "weary," they too will be able to effect constructive change in their world.

## Notes

1. For more work on the history of African American caricature in comics art, see Sheena Howard and Ronald Jackson, eds., *Black Comics: Politics of Race and Representation*, New York: Bloomsbury Academic, 2013; Derek Royal, ed., *Coloring America: MultiEthnic Engagements with Graphic Narrative*, Spec. issue of *MELUS* 32.3 (2007); and Marc Singer, "'Black Skins' and White Masks: Comic Books and the Secret of Race," *African American Review* 36.1 (2002): 107–19.

## Works Cited

Bassey, Magnus O. "The Place of Group Consciousness in Black Autobiographical Narratives." *Journal of African American Studies* 11 (2007): 214–24. Print.

Chaney, Michael A. "Drawing on History in Recent African American Graphic Novels. *MELUS* 32.3 (2007): 175–200. Print.

Harris, Frederick. "It Takes a Tragedy to Arouse Them: Collective Memory and Collective Action during the Civil Rights Movement." *Social Movement Studies* 5.1 (2006): 19–43. Print.

Kirby, Robert. "Review of *March: Book One*." *Comics Journal*. 23 October 2013. Web. 1 July 2014.

"John Lewis and the 50th Anniversary of the March on Washington." *On Point with Tom Ashbrook*. WBUR, Boston. 21 August 2013. Radio.

Levinson, Cynthia. *We've Got a Job: The 1963 Birmingham Children's March*. Atlanta: Peachtree Publishers, 2012. Print.

Lewis, John, Andrew Aydin, and Nate Powell. *March: Book One*. Marietta, GA: Top Shelf Productions, 2013. Print.

Lewis, John. *Walking with the Wind: A Memoir of the Movement*. New York: Harcourt Brace & Company, 1998. Print.

McCloud, Scott. *Understanding Comics: The Invisible Art*. New York: HarperCollins, 1993. Print.

Powell, Nate. Personal Interview. 11 March 2015.

Reid, Calvin. "Rep. John Lewis' *March: Book Two* Coming in 2015." *Publisher's Weekly*. 14 July 2014. Web. 19 April 2016.

Resnick, Benton, et al. *Martin Luther King and the Montgomery Story*. Nyack, NY: Fellowship of Reconciliation, 1958. Print.

Rowe, Claudia. "The Good Fight." *Fellowship of Reconciliation*. Fellowship of Reconciliation, 4 August 1999. Web. 1 July 2014.

Spivak, Gayatri Chakravorty. "Subaltern Studies: Deconstructing Historiography." *In Other Worlds: Essays in Cultural Politics*. New York: Metheun, 1987. Print.

Swindells, Julia. *Victorian Writing and Working Women*. Cambridge: Polity Press, 1985. Print.

*Top Shelf Productions. March: Book One*, June 2013. Web. 19 April 2016.

# 20

## *Sita's Ramayana*'s Negotiation with an Indian Epic Picture Storytelling Tradition

### *Anuja Madan*

The two main Indian epics, *Ramayana* and *Mahabharata*, have had a decisive and wide-ranging influence on the oral traditions, art, architecture, theatre, and literature of the Indian subcontinent and Southeast Asia over many centuries.[1] The epic tradition in India is characterized by a rich multiplicity and fluidity. Countless versions of the *Ramayana* exist in a range of languages and media, and across countries and regions. Valmiki's *Ramayana*, a highly ornate Sanskrit epic poem (*kavya*) consisting of twenty-four thousand verses and some fifty thousand lines, is recognized as the oldest extant literary rendition of *Ramakatha* (Rama's story). The poem is believed to have expanded over time, with a core dating back maybe to the fourth or fifth century BCE, but crystallized in its current form by the second century CE (Pauwels 30). While the Valmiki version is recognized as one of the authoritative versions of the epic, on which many other retellings draw, Ramayana studies scholars have resisted viewing it as the "Ur-text."

This essay analyzes *Sita's Ramayana*, a graphic novel published in 2011 by the Indian publisher Tara Books in partnership with Groundwood Books in the United States and Canada. Illustrated by Moyna Chitrakar, a female folk artist from West Bengal, and written by Samhita Arni, a young, cosmopolitan female Indian author, *Sita's Ramayana* has been marketed as a feminist retelling of the epic. It has been primarily targeted at a young adult readership (though the publishers and author have maintained that the audience is not restricted to any particular age group) and has been critically acclaimed as well as commercially successful both in India and abroad (Wolf). In the US, it won recognition as a 2012 USBBY Outstanding International Book, an American Library Association Notable Children's Book (2012), and a South Asia Book Award Honor Book (2012).[2] Reviews of the book in *Booklist*, *Publishers' Weekly*, *Kirkus Reviews*, and *School Library Journal* have been very positive. NCTE and Primary Source have recommended *Sita's Ramayana* under the category of global children's literature. This chapter discusses the text's incorporation of the *patua* art form, paying special attention to moments of dissonance and consonance engendered by the experiment of creating a graphic novel based on a picture storytelling epic tradition. It also investigates the graphic novel's negotiation with the women's folk tradition and explores the conceptions of Sita that emerge in this dialogic exchange.

Valmiki's story revolves around King Dasarath's eldest son, the virtuous and dutiful prince Rama, who is heir to the throne of Ayodhya. Dasarath's youngest queen contrives to have Rama sent into exile for fourteen years, and have her own son crowned as the king instead. Rama proceeds to the forest, accompanied by his wife Sita and devoted step brother Lakshmana. One day, a demoness named Surpanakha falls in love with Rama and proposes to him. When Rama refuses, she perceives Sita as the impediment in her plan and prepares to eat her. In response, Lakshmana mutilates Surpanakha, prompting her to urge her brother, Ravana, the immensely powerful king of *rakshasas*, to take revenge.[3] She also tells him about Sita's extraordinary beauty, which arouses in Ravana a passionate desire for Sita. Soon after, Ravana abducts Sita and imprisons her in his island kingdom of Lanka. Ravana continually attempts to persuade Sita to marry him, but she adamantly refuses him, remaining steadfast in her devotion to Rama.

While searching for Sita, Rama and Lakshmana make an alliance with a dispossessed monkey king, Sugriva, whose advisor, Hanuman, becomes Rama's chief ally. Rama, Lakshmana and their monkey allies build a bridge over the ocean, and fight a war with the *rakshasas*, in which Rama kills Ravana in a one-to-one combat. However, Rama refuses to take Sita back with him, accusing her of having becoming tainted by living under another man's roof. After Sita successfully undergoes a trial by fire (*agnipariksha*), he accepts her and they return to Ayodhya, where Rama reclaims the throne. Persistent rumors questioning his wife's chastity lead Rama to banish the now pregnant Sita from his kingdom. Sita finds refuge with the revered sage Valmiki, the author of the Sanskrit epic. In the forest, Sita gives birth to twin sons, Lava and Kusa. When they have grown up, Valmiki arranges for Rama to meet them. Rama asks Sita to become his queen after she has performed another truth test so that the public may see her stalwart virtue. In a counter move, Sita asks her mother, the earth-goddess,[4] to open up and take her back into her womb if she has been pure in thought and deed. The earth cracks open, and Sita descends into it. Heartbroken by the loss of his wife (and subsequently, Lakshmana), Rama eventually ascends to heaven with a large gathering of followers.

Throughout Valmiki's epic, Rama is glorified as the embodiment of compassion, justice, generosity, valor, and dutifulness. However, as Paula Richman observes, "Despite the widespread belief that Rama acts as the embodiment of righteous action, certain deeds that he performs have troubled various authors of *Ramayana* texts over the centuries" (*Many Ramayanas* 10). These episodes have also created discomfort among devotees who worship Rama as an avatar of the Hindu god Vishnu. One is the episode in which Rama shoots Vali in the back while the latter is engaged in battle, which goes against the warrior code. Another is the mutilation of Surpanakha by Rama and Lakshmana. Even more controversial has been Rama's rejection of Sita after the war, and her eventual banishment (Sattar liii). Scholars suggest that the diversity and questioning that is inbuilt into the Ramayana tradition can be partly accounted for by the countless attempts to resolve the moral ambiguities of this tale (Richman, *Many Ramayanas* 10–11; Sattar liii). A wide variety of retellings are oppositional, and interrogate different aspects of authoritative versions of the epic,[5] such as its patriarchal values, caste hierarchy, and idealization of Rama as the upholder of *dharma* (or righteousness). Sita's fate mirrors that of a huge number of Indian women who are victimized in a deeply patriarchal society. Thus, creative representations of Sita abound; in some way or another, they all grapple with the injustice faced by her. Many of these versions are radically feminist in tone.[6]

As Tara Books editor V. Geetha notes, *Sita's Ramayana* testifies to the diversity of the Ramayana tradition at a time when the Hindu Right is invested in ossifying hegemonic versions of the *Ramayana* and violently protesting oppositional versions that are deemed to be "sacriliegeous" ("*Sita's Ramayana*: the Many Lives of a Text"). The graphic novel draws on several *Ramakathas*[7]: the Valmiki epic; the *Krittibasi Ramayan*, composed by fifteenth-century Bengali poet Krittibas Ojha; the *Ramayana* sung and drawn by the *patuas* of Mednipur, scroll-painters from West Bengal; and the female oral epic tradition that has been prevalent among rural women in India since many centuries. Visually, *Sita's Ramayana* comes across as a strikingly different adaptation when compared to the vast majority of picturebook/comic book adaptations of the epic for children because of its basis in *patua* art. Chitrakar's paintings were made with vegetable and mineral dyes and use rich, earthy hues. Like other Tara Books publications, the hand-made book is a visual treat and succeeds in the publisher's aim of elevating the book to the status of a cultural object while also reinforcing the shift in value that *patua* art has undergone, from performance to art object (Chatterji 44).

The *patua* folk art form is a centuries-old picture storytelling tradition that has many regional variants in India (Chatterji 63). The Chitrakar performer displays the *pata* (scroll) "to the accompaniment of a song that serves as a commentary on the images painted in the scroll" (62). Stories from the *Ramayana* and *Mahabharata* are popular themes, but contemporary Chitrakar artists have expanded their repertoire to include current events, both local and global. Folklore scholar Roma Chatterji suggests that, unlike many other similar performative traditions that are becoming extinct, "the *patua* tradition has survived largely because the painted scroll has acquired a status independent of the performative context and can circulate on its own" (63). In fact, the painted scrolls have become exotic artefacts for sale for urban buyers in the country and abroad (Singh 66). Chatterji argues that reflexivity and innovation is a part of folk tradition and destabilizes the association of folk art with timeless tradition.

*Sita's Ramayana* originated at a workshop organized by Tara Books inviting five *patua* artists to experiment with the graphic novel format. Moyna Chitrakar was one of these artists. Chennai-based Tara Books, an independent, internationally renowned and award-winning publishing house, has released many handmade picturebooks in collaboration with folk artists from different parts of India. This particular venture was facilitated by Chitrakar artists' enthusiasm about embracing new modes of circulation for their work. According to Gita Wolf, the founder of Tara Books, transforming *patua* art into a graphic novel format was aided by the Chitrakar artists' prolificity and flexibility as well as the shared features of both genres. Moyna Chitrakar provided her images first, and Arni's script was based on the artwork.

Chatterji points out that graphic novels and *patua* art share some similarities. Significantly, both "are used to depict sequential narratives and both are cross-discursive" (181). Moreover, *patua* art allows for iconic interplay between song and image. Thus, in both the medium of *patua* art and comics, "the images are not merely illustrations of the story as it is told in a text. Instead they tell a separate story using the verbal or textual story as 'diegetical horizon'" (181). However, she observes that there are also striking differences between both genres: "Unlike the graphic novel mode in which each story is broken down into many incidents, the action sequences are abbreviated with only the start and climax of the sequence being depicted, often in the same frame." *Patua* art renders events in a synoptic fashion or as a tableau, with several episodes coexisting in one frame or line of song (181). Furthermore, while comics creators who develop original works would pay attention to the episodic structure, since the plot of their works will be new to readers, the Chitrakar artist narrating the *Ramayana* is "not constrained by the demands of a fixed episodic structure as her audience is already familiar with the plot." The artist "can select specific events for elaboration depending on her performance style and the emotions (*rasa*) that she wants to convey to her audience" (184). The *patua* form lacks narrative devices and features common to the comics form such as suspense, the development of characters, and the attribution of agency (187).

Chatterji's discussion makes evident that each of these mediums is characterized by divergent visual registers, modes and objectives of narration. The transformation of *patua* art into a graphic novel not only entails a shift from a synoptic multimedia narrative to an episodic printed narrative but also in the texts' relationships with audiences. In the translation of *patua* art into the comics medium, what tensions arise? Which discursive modes take precedence over others? The paratext offers us some clues. The blurb describes *Sita's Ramayana* as "a gripping, fast-paced graphic novel," and the afterword highlights this orientation: "Patua artist Moyna Chitrakar, from Bengal in eastern India, adapted her scroll-version to the form of a fast-paced graphic narrative. . . . It starts in the middle of the action, as it were. . . . And, before we know it, we are in the thick of an uncertain and intriguing tale of sorcery, abduction and kingly pride" (Arni 150). *Sita's Ramayana* conforms to generic expectations that young adults may have about graphic novels being action-packed and fast-paced. Rama's rescue mission and the war between Rama and the *rakshasas* are an important focus of the graphic novel, occupying half the narrative. The publisher's aim to provide readers with a thrilling narrative full of plot twists is in sharp contrast to the *patua Ramakathas*, in which artists focus on a few episodes of the epic to generate the play of emotions or moods (Chatterji 185).

The battle scenes and war strategies are represented in detail, and are broken down into smaller moments, often in multiple panels on one double spread. Yet the adjustment of scale from larger sized *patas* (scrolls) to multiple-panel sequences may occasionally cause some visual confusion, for instance in the episode when Hanuman steals Ravana's crown (70.1–71.3; figure 20.1). The problem of difference in scale becomes especially noticeable and disorienting when the protagonist's body is fragmented (Arni 104; 110–11). In other instances, this issue is worked around by representing the action metonymically, such as when Hanuman and Sita exchange Rama's tokens (Arni 49). In these scenes, the text becomes crucial to explain the image.

Moreover, for a reader unfamiliar with the *patua* art form, the unchanging expressions of the characters may become an impediment to the suspense. Moyna Chitrakar portrays all the characters in accordance with conventions of *patua* art rather than realistically. The calm faces of Rama and Lakshmana as they are in the tight hold of massive snakes (figure 20.2) or the placid expression of Sita as she chastises Rama can be disconcerting, especially for those unfamiliar with the art form. The boldface and capital font used at crucial moments seems to overcompensate for the static expressions of characters. Since Sita narrates most of the epic, the graphic novel has many long voiceover narration boxes and some pages come across as text-heavy. Often, the narration and dialogue boxes are placed on the body of the characters, in another point of divergence from many Western graphic novels.

Fig. 20.1. Hanuman steals Ravana's crown. Samhita Arni and Moyna Chitrakar, *Sita's Ramayana*, Tara Books and Groundwood Books. 70. Image courtesy of Tara Books.

Fig. 20.2. Rama and Lakshmana in the death grip of snakes. Samhita Arni and Moyna Chitrakar, *Sita's Ramayana*, Tara Books and Groundwood Books . 79. Image courtesy of Tara Books.

The text's emphasis on action is also a pronounced deviation from the female oral epic tradition that the text draws on, which has been prevalent in India for centuries. Editor V. Geetha asserts in her note on the "Female Re-Tellings of the Ramayana" that *Sita's Ramayana* belongs to "a distinctive female narrative tradition" that "continues to leaven the epic world of heroes and war with the virtues of nurture, compassion and tolerance." She writes that Arni "builds on the feminist possibilities of Chandrabati's *Ramayana*" (Arni 151). The sixteenth-century female Bengali poet Chandrabati collected many rural women's songs about Sita to write the epic from Sita's point of view in an anti-canonical way (Sen, "Rewriting the *Ramayana*" 175).

However, unlike the extended focus on the battle scenes in *Sita's Ramayana*, the war is completely elided in the women's oral tradition. Nabaneeta Dev Sen observes that Chandrabati dismisses the epic battle in one line, "And then Rama killed Ravana in a single combat," showing how little importance it has for her story. Women's retellings spurn the Great Tradition and epic values, replacing epic themes with female concerns ("Rewriting the *Ramayana*" 170). Women's songs (often called *Sitayanas*) often do not mention some familiar *Ramayana* themes such as Dasaratha's glory, Rama's friendship with Sugriva, the killing of Valin, the search for Sita, and so on, many of which are recounted in the graphic novel. On the other hand, events of interest to women receive detailed attention in folk songs, such as childbirth, pregnancy and weddings (Sen 169-170; Rao 119). It is Sita who takes center stage—her experiences, emotions and hardships are foregrounded, and her sorrows sympathized with. In the graphic novel, the detailed treatment of Rama's rescue mission and the war shifts the focus from Sita to Rama and limits the feminist potential of the graphic novel.

The differing contexts and audiences of the oral tradition and the graphic novel play a crucial role in their varying orientations. As a mass-mediated cultural form, *Sita's Ramayana*'s aim is to present the epic in a way that has a broad-based appeal for its transnational audience, especially since many readers would be unfamiliar with the plot. In contrast, much like the audience of the *patua* performers, the listeners of women's folk songs are highly conversant with the epic, which allows for selective episodes to be narrated. Moreover, the women singers and listeners identify deeply with Sita due to her vast suffering. Rural women sing songs of Sita to narrate their own woes and critique patriarchy in their own fashion: "All the songs complain about neglect and denial of their rights" (Sen, "When Women Tell the *Ramayana*" 20).

Though multiple levels of narration are an important feature of the Indian epic tradition, Sita's mediated narration of Rama's actions and the battle scenes serve to reinforce her confined position on the margins of the action, and position *Sita's Ramayana* as Rama's story more than Sita's. Since Sita is

Fig. 20.3. Sita as second-hand witness. Samhita Arni and Moyna Chitrakar, *Sita's Ramayana*,
Tara Books and Groundwood Books. 41. Image courtesy of Tara Books.

imprisoned and has no first-hand information of these events, she relies on other narrators for information. For example, when Hanuman comes to visit her in Lanka as an emissary of Rama, he tells her about Rama's actions following her abduction. In contrast, in some women's folk songs, Hanuman's visit becomes an opportunity for Sita to recount to him her memories of an idyllic life with Rama (Rao 118), thus foregrounding her experiences. Ravana's kind-hearted brother, Vibhishana, and the prescient *rakshasi* Trijatha become Sita's other informants. Sita's role as second-hand narrator is visually represented in an inset (Arni 41.1), which shows the top half of her face encased in a small frame that represents Lanka (figure 20.3). This image is drawn in a way that makes Sita appear segmented and imprisoned within the screen. While the inset is symbolic of Sita's role as witness and her physical confinement in Lanka, it is also indicative of her marginalization within the diegetic universe, which is further reinforced by her visual absence from the majority of the book.

This elision is especially noticeable in the episodes that revolve around her. Though she mentions her refusal to marry Ravana (Arni 29), she is not shown speaking with Ravana. A little later, Sita expresses her anger at Ravana's stubborn belief that she would change her mind about his proposal, saying, "I felt sick with rage. But I was helpless" (Arni 57). The accompanying illustration is a full-length, frontal image of Ravana; here, as in several other panels, Sita's voice assumes a disembodied quality (figure 20.4). Sita's repeated rebuffs of Ravana's proposals and her castigation of Ravana for his arrogance and unethical behavior are very significant moments in authoritative as well as oppositional versions, since she exercises her agency in these episodes. They also reflect her strength of character and unflinching devotion to Rama. In excluding Sita's dialogues with Ravana at the level of image and text, *Sita's Ramayana* loses a crucial opportunity to showcase Sita's agency and courage and to reinforce her position as the moral center of the epic. Sita's internal monologues allow readers to get a glimpse into her subjectivity, her anguish, sorrow and grief. However, for some readers, the absence of Sita's image at various points in the book may be an impediment in their ability to relate to her.

These structural choices reflect the differences between the graphic novel and *patua* modes of narration. In the *patua* art form, first and third person voices coexist such that there is no dominant voice. None of the *Ramayana* songs focus on the point of view of a single character, though formulaic utterances are placed in the mouths of Sita, Lakshman, Hanuman and other characters (Chatterji). Moreover, Chatterji observes that "the song that accompanies the display of the scroll completes the picture narrative, drawing the viewers' attention to specific details in the painted scene but also supplementing the scene by presenting verbal images that are not depicted in the pictorial scene unfolding before the viewers" (215). The frequent elision of Sita's images may in

Fig. 20.4. Ravana. Samhita Arni and Moyna Chitrakar, *Sita's Ramayana*,
Tara Books and Groundwood Books. 57. Image courtesy of Tara Books.

part emerge from the fundamentally synoptic mode of narration in the *patua* art form, and the absence of a single dominant point of view.

Nevertheless, the graphic novel succeeds in highlighting Sita's suffering and is informed by a female-centred ethos. A particularly effective narrative strategy is to start the text with Sita's abandonment, which positions readers to read the story as the testimony of a woman who has been wronged. The book begins with a tearful Sita entering the Dandaka forest where Lakshmana has left her on Rama's orders, and pleading with the forest to let her stay there (Arni 8). The woods urge her, "Tell us, sister, how you came here" (Arni 9). As she tells her story, the flowers cry—a powerful image that is reprised later in the text as well (figure 20.5). Sita's communion with the forest is emphasized and tied to Sita's identity as daughter of the Earth (Arni 8), which is an important aspect of the women's oral epic tradition. Just as in women's folk songs, the forest in the graphic novel takes on a nurturing, protective role, imbuing the text with an ecofeminist ethos. When Sita finishes her retrospective narrative, "Her tale was passed from tree to tree, leaf to leaf," and the animals "swore to leave her in peace" (Arni 128). Moyna's art in these panels foregrounds the emotive sensibility that is crucial to the female oral *Ramayana* tradition as well as the *patua* Ramakatha tradition, and displays the organic connections between women and nature in both folk forms.

Moyna Chitrakar's evocative art also powerfully depicts Sita's grief at being kidnapped. In an arresting double-spread, we see a full-length image of Sita crying while reclining against a tree in Ashok Vatika (32.1). The adjacent page is left almost entirely blank and painted dark black, representing her despair powerfully. In another panel, the full-length image of a crying Sita is dissected by multiple gutters symbolizing her fragmented mental state during her imprisonment and innovatively representing the impact of the passage of time on her consciousness (Arni 56.1). These are instances where image and text work in tandem to develop Sita's interiority.

Yet the book portrays Sita as more than a grieving wife. Her intervention in the narrative is routinely critical of Rama's morally questionable actions in different episodes. Her compassionate, questioning voice critiques the martial values and hierarchical power structure of the epic. The text begins with the episode in which Lakshmana cuts the nose of the *rakshasi* Surpanakha, which, as we noted earlier, has been widely critiqued. Lakshmana's mutilation of the *rakshasi* has been read as the display of a male supremacist ethos that punishes the expression of carnal desire in women (Erndl 82). Sita's comment casts Surpanakha as a victim: "Violence breeds violence, and an unjust act only begets greater injustice. Rama should have stopped him [Lakshmana]. Instead, he spurred him on. . . . I can never forget that scream. It still echoes in my ears" (Arni 16). Moyna's art gives us no visual cue that Surpanakha is a *rakshasi*

Fig. 20.5. The Dandaka forest hears Sita's tale. Samhita Arni and Moyna Chitrakar, *Sita's Ramayana*, Tara Books and Groundwood Books. 129. Image courtesy of Tara Books.

even after her true identity is revealed; she looks almost exactly like Sita, with the same figure, attire, and ornaments.[8] Unlike the Valmiki version, *Sita's Ramayana* does not depict Surpanakha threatening to devour Sita. Through both image and text, *Sita's Ramayana* resists demonizing Surpanakha—this is in contrast to some other retellings which portray Surpanakha as a monstrous, dehumanized, ethnic "other," including Campfire's *Sita: Daughter of the Earth*. When Rama kills Vali from behind as the latter is engaged in battle, Sita's empathy towards his widow constitutes a subtle critique of the power imbalances between Rama and his *vanara* allies. Tara's grief and indignant response to Sugriva when he claims her as his wife (47) highlights the status of *vanara* women as the property of their husbands, while Sita's guilt about whether she is responsible for Tara's fate[9] reflects the text's commitment to forging connections between the female characters of the epic, especially as victims of the patriarchal values that pervade their world.

Sita's inclusion of the epic's subalterns in her humanistic vision is most evident in the section in which Rama refuses to take her back because he doubts her chastity. As is the case in the Valmiki *Ramayana*, Rama states that "he had fought [the war] to redeem his honour" (Arni 117). Asserting that "his honour had exacted a bloody price," Sita reminds him of the deceit used to win the war, and speaks of the grieving *rakhsasi* widows, stunning Rama into silence. Her pithy indictment of the masculinist values of war (120) transcends the specificities of time and location. It is apparent from Sita's monologue that the author is invested in constituting for her a political, feminist, and socially interventionist subjectivity. The double spread in which Sita rebukes Rama show him receding to the margins (116.1–2) while she gains a central position visually (117.1), drawing the reader's attention to her, and symbolizing the shifting power dynamics. Yet the panels simultaneously crowd her in, imprisoning her yet again, and reflecting her trapped position (figure 20.6). What further underlines Sita's limited power in the scene is that she does not chastise Rama for his cruelty in doubting and rejecting her, which is in contrast not only to a range of feminist retellings, but also to the more conservative Valmiki version.

Sita's representation in the graphic novel is informed by a contested field of debate about her. The central character is a highly influential role model for millions of Indian girls and women—educated and uneducated, rural and urban, young and old (Kishwar 20). However, many feminists believe that she is a harmful role model; they point out that patriarchy has upheld the stereotype of Sita as a self-sacrificing, submissive, extremely dutiful and devoted wife (*pativrata*) to impose on Indian wives an ideal of unquestioning submissiveness. Not only scholars and feminists, but ordinary Indian women too have been part of the protests against the Sita role model (Pauwels 9).[10]

The editors and author of *Sita's Ramayana* partake of this discomfort with the stereotype of Sita as a submissive wife, as is evidenced in their media statements. According to V. Geetha, "The *Ramayana* is an over-interpreted epic where Sita is usually a stereotype of a perfect Indian wife. Everyone has positioned her character in that manner. We asked ourselves if there was something else we can do with Sita's character" (quoted in Parthasarathy). Samhita

He then told me he hadn't fought the war for
me. He had fought it to redeem his honour.

HIS HONOUR HAD EXACTED A BLOODY PRICE.

VALIN AND
INDRAJIT DEAD,
BOTH KILLED BY
DECEIT. TARA AND
MANDODARI ARE
WIDOWS, AND SO ARE
THE WOMEN OF LANKA.
THEIR CHILDREN,
AND THE CHILDREN
OF LANKA ARE
ORPHANS.

THE
BATTLEFIELD
IS DRENCHED
WITH BLOOD
AND
CORPSES.

Rama was silent.

Fig. 20.6. Sita rebukes Rama. Samhita Arni and Moyna Chitrakar, *Sita's Ramayana*, Tara Books and
Groundwood Books. 117. Image courtesy of Tara Books.

Arni observes, "Many people I talked to shared some of the discomfort I felt
with the treatment of Sita. I think my book expresses it and recasts Sita not as
an ideal, suffering woman but as a woman who discovers great courage and
strength, a woman who voices critical thoughts. I think this Sita is one we
can find more in common with, and this changes our relationship with the
*Ramayana*" (quoted in Bagchi). The editors' and author's desire to recast Sita is

part of a laudable feminist agenda to counter representations of her that serve patriarchy and masculinist-nationalist ideologies. Their statements also reflect the desire to contemporize this role model such that she is a relatable figure for their audience—urban, middle and upper-middle class, and elite children and adults in the country and abroad—presumably the "we" that Arni refers to. However, as the women's folk traditions shows, the image of a strong, courageous Sita is not one that appeals only to certain classes or generations but to the vast majority of Indian women.

Madhu Kishwar has been a very influential voice in countering negative evaluations of the Sita role model, and deconstructing her appeal for the majority of Indian women. She writes:

> My interviews indicate that Indian women are not endorsing female slavery when they mention Sita as their ideal. Sita is not perceived as being a mindless creature who meekly suffers maltreatment at the hands of her husband without complaining. . . . She is seen as a person whose sense of *dharma* is superior to and more awe-inspiring than that of Ram—someone who puts even *maryadapurushottam*[11] Ram—the most perfect of men—to shame. (22–23)

In the crucial *agnipariksha* episode, which probably posed a representational dilemma for the Tara Books team, the image-text dissonance seems to emerge from contested views of Sita. Sita's trial by fire has been criticized by scholars, artists, and even sections of the general public since it upholds the expectation of extreme chastity from women, and ties a woman's right to existence to her husband's faith in her purity. Madhu Kishwar, however, highlights Sita's agency in this scene. She writes:

> Sita's offer of *agnipariksha* (trial by fire) and her coming out of it unscathed is by and large seen not as an act of supine surrender to the whims of an unreasonable husband but as an act of defiance that challenges her husband's aspersions, as a means of showing him to be so flawed in his judgment that the gods have to come and pull him up for his foolishness. (306)

Moyna's artwork seems to be informed by this perspective on Sita. Moyna does not show her crying as she enters the fire, in contrast to many other panels that show a tearful Sita (figure 20.7). We see a dignified, calm Sita praying to the gods for protection in the flames (Arni 121.1). However, Arni chooses not to articulate Sita's prayer, despite the visual cue. Sita's words instead highlight her helplessness and portray her decision as that of committing suicide: "I thought the end of the war had meant freedom for me. I had hoped for love, I had hoped for justice . . . Instead of love, I found suspicion. Instead of justice,

I met with false accusation and distrust. *Where could I go? What could I do?* I stepped into the flames of the tall pyre that Lakshmana had built" (Arni 121; italics added). The dissonance between image and text here is similar to an earlier panel in which Moyna portrays Sita praying for her rescue, but articulates her anxieties instead (Arni 56.1). These panels suggest that, for the author, the modernization of tradition entails its secularization. In the *agnipariksha* episode, the rural folk artist's vision may be more subversive than that of the cosmopolitan author's, insofar as it seems to partake of the prevalent belief that Sita acted out of faith and defiance rather than helplessness, and thus discourages us from seeing her solely as a victim in this episode.

An interesting moment of consonance between the various visions that inform the graphic novel occurs towards the end, when Sita starts living in the forest with her sons. We learn that "In time, Sita found peace and happiness in the forest, loving her sons. She tried to forget her past, forget Rama and Ravana, Ayodhya and Lanka. She was no longer Sita, the queen. She was Sita, the simple forest woman" (Arni 135). Sita's casting away of her marital identity is a part of the women's oral tradition and a few modern feminist retellings as well, and is predicated on the role of the forest in providing Sita with a community more nurturing than "the world of men" (Arni 9). The protagonist's dissociation from Rama allows us to read her ritual suicide in subsequent panels as an act of defiance against her husband.

Carol A. Breckenridge and Arjun Appadurai point out that at the very heart of public modernity in India are the tensions between national sites and transnational cultural processes, as well as the contestations between national, mass, and folk culture (5). Such negotiations are, Breckenridge and Appadurai imply, inevitable byproducts of overlapping, disjunctive, and polymorphous global flows of information, capital, and cultural trends (44–46). *Sita's Ramayana* is a space where the local and the global, as well as the traditional, the modern, and the contemporary negotiate and contest with each other in complex ways, and in doing so, place into relief varying notions of tradition and modernity. This essay has attempted to show that the incorporation of *patua* art form and the women's oral tradition is instrumental in constituting the oppositional vision of *Sita's Ramayana*, highlighting for readers the need to complicate the hierarchy that is often created between contemporary and traditional art forms with regard to the issue of modernity.

In the final analysis, the transformation of *patua* art into a graphic novel is a productive one, since the inter-genre shift does not entail a loss of the emotive sensibility that is at the heart of the *patua* tradition. Despite the significant shift in aims and modes of narration, Tara Books succeeds in creating an engaging, visually rich retelling for young readers across three countries. Some structural choices limit the feminist potential of the graphic novel, and *Sita's Ramayana*'s critique of Rama or the epic's patriarchal values are not radical

Fig. 20.7. Sita's trial by fire. Samhita Arni and Moyna Chitrakar, *Sita's Ramayana*,
Tara Books and Groundwood Books. 121. Image courtesy of Tara Books.

when compared to some other interrogative retellings. Nevertheless, the text's
questioning of martial values and its female-centered sensibility provides a
much needed counternarrative to more conservative retellings (including popular TV adaptations of *Ramayana* and *Campfire's Sita: Daughter of the Earth*).
Chitrakar and Arni create an empathetic, courageous, and multidimensional
Sita whose power derives not from her self-sacrificing nature, but from her
critical agency and her connections with nature.

# Notes

1. I am very grateful to the editors of this anthology and Dr. Roma Chatterji for their helpful comments on previous drafts of this essay, as well as to Ms. Gita Wolf for her input on my research. The interview with Ms. Gita Wolf was conducted during a fieldwork trip made possible by the Hannah Beiter Graduate Student Research Grant awarded by the Children's Literature Association in 2013.

2. *Sita's Ramayana* is one of two graphic novels that retell the *Ramayana* from Sita's perspective. The other is Saraswati Nagpal and Manikandan's *Sita: Daughter of Earth*, published by Campfire Graphic Novels in 2011.

3. The word *rakshasa* is translated as "demon," and *rakshasi* as "demoness." The terms signify malevolent creatures of the night.

4. In the epic, Sita is found in a furrow by King Janaka. The name Sita means "furrow."

5. Paula Richman defines authoritative versions as those that "have achieved a level of acceptance and legitimacy greater than most other tellings of Rama's story" (*Questioning Ramayanas* 8).

6. See Chaudhuri (2013); Gokhale and Lal (2009); Hess (1999); Richman (2008).

7. "*Ramakathas*" translates as "stories of Rama."

8. This may not necessarily be a deliberate choice, however. According to Roma Chatterji, some *patua* artists highlight Surpanakha's demonic transformations, while others present her almost as a doppelgänger of Sita (personal communication). Later on in *Sita's Ramayana*, Moyna paints some *rakhsasis* with claws and fangs to emphasize their demonic nature.

9. This is because Rama killed Vali in exchange for his brother Sugriva's help in finding Sita.

10. Some mainstream *Ramayana* retellings have been instrumental in perpetuating this stereotype of Sita. A highly influential version of the epic in recent times has been Ramanand Sagar's TV *Ramayana* (1987–1988). Scholars such as Purnima Mankekar and Heidi Pauwels have discussed how it served to reinforce the image of a self-sacrificing, pious, submissive, passive wife. Campfire's graphic novel, *Sita: Daughter of the Earth*, also reinforces this image.

11. Translated as the "epitome of social propriety."

# Works Cited

Appadurai, Arjun. *Modernity at Large: Cultural Dimensions of Globalization*. Minneapolis: University of Minnesota Press, 1996. Print.

Arni, Samhita, and Moyna Chitrakar. *Sita's Ramayana*. Chennai: Tara Books; Berkeley and Toronto: Groundwood Books, 2011. Print.

Bagchi, Shrabonti. "We Need to Reclaim the Various Sitas." *Times of India*. 30 October 2011: np. Web. 15 July 2013.

Breckenridge, Carol A., and Arjun Appadurai. "Public Modernity in India." *Consuming Modernity: Public Culture in a South Asian World*. Ed. Carol A. Breckenridge. Minneapolis: University of Minnesota Press, 1995. 1–20. Print.

Chatterji, Roma. *Speaking with Pictures: Folk Art and the Narrative Tradition in India*. New Delhi: Routledge, 2012.

———. Personal Interview. 5 June 2013.

Chaudhuri, Sutapa. "Revisiting Sita: the Subversive Myths of Womanhood in Contemporary South Asian Writers." *The Asian Conference on Literature and Librarianship 2013: Exchanges and Encounters*. April 4–7, 2013, Osaka Japan.

Erndl, Kathleen. "The Mutilation of Surpanakha." *Many Ramayanas: The Diversity of a Narrative Tradition in South Asia*. Ed. Paula Richman. Berkeley: University of California Press, 1991. 67–85. Print.

Geetha, V. "*Sita's Ramayana*: The Many Lives of a Text." *Tara Books Blog*. 5 December 2011. Web. 29 April 2013.

Gokhale, Namita, and Malashri Lal, eds. *In Search of Sita: Revisiting Mythology*. New York: Viking Press, 2009.

Hess, Linda. "Rejecting Sita: Indian Responses to the Ideal Man's Cruel Treatment of His Ideal Wife." *Journal of the American Academy of Religion 67.1* (1999): 1–32. Web. 21 February 2012.

Kishwar, Madhu. "Yes to Sita, No to Ram: the Continuing Popularity of Sita in India." *Manushi* 98 (1997): 20–31. Web. 20 May 2013.

Parthasarathy, Anusha. "A Different Perspective." *The Hindu*. 4 August 2011. The Hindu Group. Web. 16 April 2013.

Pauwels, Heidi R. M. *The Goddess as Role Model: Sita and Radha in Scripture and on Screen*. Oxford: Oxford University Press, 2008. Print.

Ramanujan, A. K. "Three Hundred Ramayanas: Five Examples and Three Thoughts on Translation." *Many Ramayanas: The Diversity of a Narrative Tradition in South Asia*. Ed. Paula Richman. Berkeley: University of California Press, 1991. 1–21. Print.

Rao, Velcheru Narayana. "A Ramayana of Their Own: Women's Oral Tradition in Telugu." *Many Ramayanas: The Diversity of a Narrative Tradition in South Asia*. Ed. Paula Richman. Berkeley: University of California Press, 1991. Print.

Richman, Paula. "Introduction: the Diversity of the Ramayana Tradition." *Many Ramayanas: The Diversity of a Narrative Tradition in South Asia*. Ed. Paula Richman. Berkeley: University of California Press, 1991. 3–16. Print.

———. "Questioning and Multiplicity within the Ramayana Tradition." *Questioning Ramayanas: A South Asian Tradition*. Ed. Richman. Berkeley: University of California Press, 2000. 1–21. Print.

———. *Ramayana Stories in Modern South India: an Anthology*. Bloomington, Ind.: Indiana University Press, 2008. Print.

Sattar, Arshia. Introduction. *The Ramayana* by Valmiki. New York: Penguin Books, 1996. xvii–lviii. Print.

Sen, Nabaneeta Dev. "Rewriting the *Ramayana*: Chandrabati and Molla." *India International Centre Quarterly* 24.3 (1997): 163–77. Web. 21 May 2012.

———. "When Women Retell the Ramayana." *Manushi* 108 (Sept.–Oct 1998): 18–27. Web. 15 April 2012.

Singh, Kavita. "What's New in *Pata* Paintings?" *Indian Painting: the Lesser Known Traditions*, Ed. Anna Dallapiccolla. New Delhi: Niyogi Books, 2011. 64–69. Print.

Wolf, Gita. Personal Interview. 20 June 2013.

# CODA

## Whether We Want Them or Not:
## Building an Aesthetic of Children's Digital Comics

*Joe Sutliff Sanders*

At first, we weren't even really sure that we *wanted* digital comics.

The century opened with a flurry of high-profile position pieces, the most visible of which was surely Scott McCloud's 2000 *Reinventing Comics*, a book-length follow-up to his massively successful *Understanding Comics*. Here, McCloud spells out the extraordinary artistic and financial potential of comics in a paperless marketplace. *Reinventing Comics* was, famously, followed by Gary Groth's two-part review—tellingly titled "McCloud Cuckoo-Land"—in the *Comics Journal*, and McCloud replied in the subsequent issue of *TCJ*. After the dust settled, McCloud wrote, "I remain convinced that the digital delivery of comics has the potential to revolutionize the industry, and that the aesthetic opportunities of digital comics are enormous" ("Print Comics: Reinventing Comics"). Scott Bukatman followed by arguing that Groth's objections amounted to another iteration of defending "'pure' comics" against "the barbarian at the gate" (138), but Sean Fenty, Trena Houp, and Laurie Taylor echoed many of Groth's complaints in their 2005 essay on digital comics, demonstrating that Groth's objections still remain. And Roger Sabin, in an essay drawn from a conference presentation that pre-dates all of these, concludes that "comics are a unique medium. The net is a unique medium, too. Let's hope they stay that way" (57). These views have, I am almost certain, softened in the years since they were first expressed,[1] but when critics and professionals first started talking about digital comics, just about the only point of consensus was that they were worth arguing about.[2]

Today, however, digital comics enjoy considerably more acceptance. Since 2005, the Eisner Awards—the North American industry's highest award—have included a category for digital comics. In 2012, Mark Waid lent his considerable name recognition to the form with the release of *Insufferable*, a comic designed in a 4 × 3 landscape orientation ill-suited to paper comics but excellent for computer, tablet, and cell phone screens. In the same year, Marvel unveiled the imprint "Infinite Comics" for its comics designed to be read on screens rather than in print. But most of the progress has been made in comics for older readers. The first Eisner for digital comics, for example, went to Brian Fies's story *Mom's Cancer*, a tale in the tradition, narrowly, of Joyce Brabner and Harvey Pekar's *Our Cancer Year* or, more broadly, the genre of autobiographical comics that traces most obviously back to the underground comix movement. *Insufferable* helped launch Waid's online imprint Thrillbent, which still supports various titles, but only a few of them are for younger readers. Of the new wave of successful digital comics, only the Infinite Comics stories have shown a commitment to readers under the age of eighteen, and I do promise to look closer at those at the end of this chapter, but considering that the Infinite Comics fit easily into the mainstream universe of Marvel superheroes (indeed, *Avengers vs. X-Men: Infinite*, the first of the Infinite Comics, was a lead-in to the print series *Avengers vs. X-Men*), its suitability for the audience might be regarded more as an accident than any artistically theorized dedication to digital comics for young readers.[3]

This chapter will provide an overview of the state of the field of digital comics for young readers today, especially in the context of the critical and aesthetic fears and hopes offered in the first reactions to the potential of the field. Although I find that in general, creators have made little attempt to seize the artistic potential of digital comics when writing for children, there is impressive reason to hope that the future holds promise.

A great deal of my analysis will, of necessity, be subjective, but the main tool by which I will be measuring the current crop of digital comics for children is hardly uncommon. My central question is simply whether these comics take advantage of the available artistic tools to help their books succeed in their artistic goals or whether they produce stories that might as well have been told in the familiar boxes of paper comics. McCloud memorably asked this question when he prophesied that "Once released from that box, some [cartoonists] will take the shape of the box with them—but gradually, comics creators will stretch their limbs and start to explore the design opportunities of an infinite canvas" (222). In the transition from paper to digital formats, McCloud argued, the real breakthrough will come when digital comics "embrace the digital environment as their native soil—and at best . . . plant in that soil what could never grow anywhere else" (206). This point is one that Groth mocks in his review (35), but it is a point that had already been prepared for in 1999 (though not translated into English until 2007), when Thierry Groensteen argued that the only reason traditional comics pages tend to feature multiple tiers per page instead of one long continuous strip is that paper pages require them to do so. After praising the sequential storytelling of the Bayeux Tapestry, Emakimono, and "the two hundred-meter frieze that

decorates Trajan's Column," Groensteen complains that "this imaginary ribbon must be placed into the mold that forms the publishing format, into the
page," and that the resulting layout "has all the appearance of a violent surgical intervention, of an aggression." He goes on to concede that this violence is
necessary, lest the sprawling series of panels be compressed "and thus made
illegible" (58), but in digital comics, the limitations imposed by paper are *not*
necessary. One frequently loses the sense in reading *Reinventing Comics* that
digital comics have *other* limitations, and those are certainly worth quantify-
ing. Still, despite Groth's protests, the only reasonable way to judge the success
of digital comics is whether they take full advantage of the medium in which
they appear—just like paper comics. Using this standard, it is easy to be disap-
pointed in most children's digital comics.

At the very least, one might argue, digital comics have over paper comics
the virtue of being more accessible: one can reproduce them almost without
limitation, and distribution can be all but universal. Sabin provided the most
important rebuttal to this argument in 2000: digital comics' claim to acces-
sibility effectively accepts a gap in access dictated by household income: once
one has a device capable of connecting to the internet—a not-insignificant
economic investment—one still must pay for admittance to the information
superhighway (50–51).[4] Further, given the size of files rich with images, the
internet access necessary for downloading comics must be robust, which
is another way of saying expensive. Still, the absolute minimum that digital
comics can offer, apparently, would be their widespread distribution.

The current crop of digital comics for children does live up to that criterion, if only barely. As Daniel Merlin Goodbrey, writing about the largest online distributor of digital comics, has put it, most children's comics
available through digital media are little more than "straightforward digital
remediations of comics originally designed for the printed page" (188).[5] In
some cases, these can be forgiven and even applauded, as in the example of
*The Big Blog of Kids' Comics*, an online repository of scanned pages from
classic children's comics. In others, though, such as the case of Paul Tobin
and Colleen Coover's *Bandette*, the lack of artistic investment in the digital format is frustrating. *Bandette* is the winner of the 2013 Eisner for Best
Digital Comic, and although the story and art are outstanding (and well
within the conventions of stories for young readers), each page directly
mimics the orientation and dimensions of a comics page. Indeed, when
the print version of *Bandette* appeared in 2013, its pages matched the pages
of the digital version exactly. Again, *Bandette* is an excellent comic, but it
makes no attempt to use any of the artistic potential of its medium except
for the increased distribution available online[6]—and this is, at least according to the award, the *best* digital comic of its calendar year. So most of the

existing digital comics for children manage to clear the very low bar of wider distribution, but that criterion is almost immediately unsatisfying.

In fact, when the burgeoning catalog of digital comics includes remediated paper comics, there is a pointed lack of interest in revising those comics to take advantage of their new medium. Many digital comics for young readers feature, it should be no surprise, intellectual properties previously distributed through film and video, but even these—*Annoying Orange, Batman Adventures, Transformers Animated, Young Justice*—are presented in portrait orientation and with the dimensions of pages from a paper comic book. Other titles fumble basic aspects of reading on mobile devices. *Aladdin: Legacy of the Lost*, for example, is a 44-page story, and all but two of those pages are in portrait orientation. The other pages fit nicely onto the screen when the device is rotated into a landscape orientation, but there is no aesthetic reason for readers to turn the device on these pages apart from the fact that if they fail to do so, the font is so small as to be indecipherable.[7] *Peanutbutter & Jeremy's Best Book Ever*, another title available in Comixology's "Children's" genre section, contains an especially egregious example of a remediated comic in which insufficient effort has been put into adaptation. After the cover art, the first page features Peanutbutter, a cat, commenting to Jeremy, a bird, that "This book has flaps." "Of course it does," replies Jeremy, "You know why? 'Cause I LOVE flapping!" Here, the paper comics mindset remains in the electronic version, opening the book with a joke that only makes sense in a paper context. All of these are titles that have the air of appearing in digital format reluctantly, with sensibilities obviously derived from print. And perhaps it is unfair to criticize these titles, originally designed for print media, for failing to be good digital comics. Indeed, *Batman Adventures* was an extraordinary paper comic, often matching the artistic excellence of the Emmy-winning animated show that inspired it, even collecting multiple Eisner awards beginning in 1994 and 2004. Still, these examples demonstrate that the great majority of publishers, who make as little investment as possible in adapting their print comics to the new medium, aren equally unsure of whether they want digital comics.

In these and so many other disappointing examples of digital comics, the books ignore an obvious rule of artistic design, one that is simple to address. In Sabin's early protests against digital comics, he correctly argues that even mediocre cartoonists "tend to use the page as a structural unit," and when electronic screens fail to present the entire page at once, they lose the benefits of that common technique (53). But Jakob F. Dittmar contends that "The unifying aspect of all digital comics, whether download-only or online-readable, is perhaps simply that they can define their own format. Unrestricted by print, these comics are no longer bound to a uniform page format, even within a narrative that stretches over several (digital) pages" (87). Sabin's point is that a page conceived at certain dimensions ought to be presented in those dimensions, and Dittmar's point runs parallel: creators of digital comics can and should take advantage of the new page format offered by digital comics. Indeed, although I earlier suggested that the least a comic could do in order to take advantage of the digital medium is make use of the new modes of distribution available to digital comics, I think that Dittmar justifies us in raising the bar a little higher: at the very least, a digital comic ought to take advantage of the unique "canvas," to borrow McCloud's term, on which it appears, whether that canvas allows for an infinitely unspooling ribbon or simply a canvas that matches the size of the screen on which it appears. Happily, some digital comics make at least this minimal effort. *Celadore* and *The First Daughter*, two digital comics from smaller publishers, use a landscape orientation that fits electronic screens well. Too, the entire Thrillbent line of digital comics—most of which are, alas, for adults—uses a similar presentation. These comics show that with minimal effort, digital comics can be presented in a way that embraces the format and thinks about the digital page in ways that allow for the same sort of artistic unity as a print page, though these are all examples of comics created for the screen, not remediated from paper.

One aspect of digital comics that first appears to be a limitation on the form is actually one in which some recent digital comics for young readers have excelled. Writing in the days before widespread Western adoption of smart phones, Sabin complains that the limitations of computer screens wrest control of pacing from readings. "By scrolling up and down a page in order to see different panels," he explains, "you are at the mercy of your computer, and the fact of how fast it can scroll. This, again, can be very frustrating." Conversely, when reading print comics, he points out, "You are in total control of the pace at which you read" (53). Elsewhere, I have argued that this control has been overstated ("*Valentine*"), but I want to take Sabin's complaint at face value: some of the agency traditionally in the hands of comics readers is certainly removed to the electronic devices mediating the sequential narratives. I think, in fact, that this is a necessity of the form, but the fact that this limitation exists is does not necessarily damn the medium. After all, print comics arrive in our hands with a finite amount of space per page, which is to say that the medium of print comics itself has limitations—it can only present a page or, at most, a spread's worth of information at a time—and no one has complained about that limitation (apart from Groensteen's "violent surgical intervention"). On the contrary, one of the great delights of paper comics is the page turn, which is nothing more than an expression of cartoonists making a virtue of the limitation of paper comics. I have praised this aspect of paper comics in Hergé's work ("Hergé's Occupations") myself, and Sabin hints that he has a similar opinion in his comments about "the page as a structural unit." Therefore, I understand the frustration of losing some of the control to the electronic interface, but I want to work from the assumption that the fact that (like paper) an electronic screen mediates the rate of display provides us with another aesthetic dimension to evaluate, not something that disqualifies digital comics as an art form.

In fact, it seems to me that many of digital comics' greatest successes have to do with exactly the willingness to control pacing in a way that pays artistic dividends for the story, and a few comics for children illustrate that success well. One example is the "Along Came a Tyrantula" issue of *Atomic Robo: Two-Fisted Tales*, by Scott Wegener and Brian Clevinger. The paper version of *Atomic Robo* first appeared in 2007, and its clean yet atmospheric art combined with snappy dialog won instant fans, leading to an Eisner nomination in its first year of eligibility. "Tyrantula," however, was released in 2013 as a "first-ever digital exclusive" for the Emerald City Comicon. Wegener and Clevinger told fans that "This is not a paper comic adapted to digital. It was a from-scratch ground-up experiment with the boundaries of the comic reading experience" (quoted in "Atomic Robo in First Ever Digital Comic Convention Exclusive"). The phrase "experiment with the boundaries" fits with the argument I have been making that the limitations of the form might yield aesthetic rewards, and "Tyrantula" carries the promise well, in some places perhaps even soothing concerns over the problems inherent in digital comics. One of the issue's most common techniques, for example, is that although it does reveal the panels within a page one at a time, it leaves the old panels in place to allow for comparison between panels within a page, something that Sabin points out is threatened by the pacing imposed by the electronic interface. An especially clear example appears on pages 64–65 (figures 1–3). Here, the first panel of what will eventually be a three-panel landscape page shows Robo and Tyrantula rushing toward each other. A swipe of the finger moves this panel to the top of the page, and a second panel, in which Tyrantula blocks a punch, appears below the first. A third swipe leaves the two panels in place and shows Tyrantula fending off yet another blow. By presenting the three panels alongside one another, the comic allows for the kind of comparison between panels that has typified well-unified page compositions in paper comics. Further, the contrast between the size of the panels reinforces the subtle zoom that takes place between the first and second panels: the size of the panels becomes more cramped as the combatants close. "Tyrantula" uses a version of this technique a dozen different times, and in each case the comic's manipulation of the pacing helps rather than harms the artistic execution.

Even more impressive is a related technique, this one used less often but with greater effect. On pages 30–32 (figures 4–6), the camera shows Robo dodging from left to right as Tyrantula fires a series of blasts at him. The first page shows a panel tucked in the upper-left corner, and the second shows not precisely a new panel, but an extended version of the original that now stretches two-thirds of the way across the top of the screen. The background of the first panel remains, now with a scar on the brick wall from Tyrantula's first blast. Another swipe reveals a panel that now runs across the entire top half of the screen, with the progress of the panel expansion following Robo's progress across the screen, this time with another scar where Tyrantula's second blast marked the wall behind him. The comic uses this same technique on pages 56–58—tracing a vertical rather than horizontal progression—and in both cases, the action sequence is enhanced by the carefully apportioned reveal of the extended panels. That this technique is made possible by the pacing controlled by the digital text is obvious, but it also bears pointing out that this technique is one that a paper comic could *not* achieve. I make that claim not to argue for the superiority of digital comics—part of my point throughout this essay is that we should be asking how *all* comics thrive within their limitations, something that good paper comics also do—but to point out that this approach is evidence that "Tyrantula" may have, ha, sprung from origins in paper comics, but it uses techniques that cannot have been born there. "Tyrantula" is a book that makes use of its form—and its form's limitations—rather than trying to be a paper comic in a digital format.

Elsewhere, the techniques developed by Yves Bigerel have resulted in effective digital comics marketed for young readers, especially the Infinite Comics imprint from Marvel. Two of Bigerel's personal online comics came to wide attention when, in 2009, McCloud praised them in a blog post ("About"). Both the first comic ("About Digital Comics") and the second ("About 'About Digital Comics'") experimented with Flash to provide sequential narratives that appeared panel by panel, with each panel taking the place of the last rather than appearing beside it. This approach—taking for granted a rectangle of a given size and filling that space with panels revealed at the reader's touch—is the one that has since become popular for comics designed to be read on electronic devices: it is true not only of *Atomic Robo*'s one digital comic, but also of the titles offered in the Thrillbent and Infinite Comics lines. Mark Waid (the creator most closely associated with Thrillbent) and Stuart Immonen brought this sensibility to Marvel with the first Infinite Comic, a prelude to the print *Avengers vs. X-Men* limited series and crossover event. Later, *Ultimate Spider-Man: Final Exam* brought Bigerel into collaboration with Matt Kindt, who had already won impressive acclaim for the print comics *Pistolwhip*, *Super Spy*, and *Revolver*. In a very short period of time, the technique that came to broad attention following McCloud's blog post has spread to other well-conceived digital comics.

Perhaps the most impressive use of this approach is in *Wolverine: Japan's Most Wanted Infinite Comic*, which premiered digitally in thirteen parts in

2013 and then was released again as both a digital collection (with 848 pages) and a print collection (with 158 pages) in 2014.[8] The similarities between this book and others by Bigerel, to whom the "storyboards" are credited in the digital edition and the "layouts" are credited in the paper edition, are many, and the fact that he was involved in both editions offers a rare opportunity to compare two comics intent on telling the same story while making the most of the print and digital media. Early in the story, Wolverine kills Councilor Fujita, who, we later discover, is a clandestine member of an evil organization. Page 12 of the print edition shows Wolverine dispatching a bodyguard and then interrupting Fujita, who is in the process of praising the hero when Wolverine kills him. Panel two (see figure 7) shows Fujita in mid-compliment, and panel three presents Wolverine choking him. The sequence is supposed to be dramatic, and Wolverine's attack is supposed to be surprising, but because panel two is on the top tier and panel three on the middle tier, the contrast between the two scenes is weakened: the two panels are separated from each other, making the moment less startling. Compare this example with pages 69–71 in the digital version (figures 8–10). Here, the moments captured in two panels in the paper version can be spread into three panels, allowing the second page to quote Fujita closer to the moment in which he is choked, giving more focus to the moment of interruption. Even more importantly, the digital version is able to leave the illustration of the middle page in place following the transition to the third page. On the screen, page 71 takes the place of page 70, and the reveal of Wolverine's hand at Fujita's throat is more immediate, allowing for a comparison between panels that could not be achieved in the paper version. Paper comics, of course, *can* achieve a similar effect, and in fact, the paper version of the comic does so on the next page, when it shows a sushi roll in one panel and then, immediately to the right of that panel, the same roll being quickly sliced (figure 11). As this example demonstrates, paper comics certainly have the ability to encourage close comparison of two neighboring panels, but what the example of the murdered councilman demonstrates is that there are times when paper comics cannot place two panels next to each other even though those panels would benefit from the proximity. This limitation comes about because—think of Groensteen's "violent surgical intervention"—no space remains on the page where the artist might place the second panel.

This *Wolverine* story also allows me to close by returning to my concession that it might be unfair to criticize paper comics that have been remediated into digital formats without any significant attempt to take advantage of the artistic potentials of the new form. But *Wolverine* is evidence that such an argument is only valid because we have come to ask so little of digital comics, especially digital comics for young readers. After all, *Wolverine* was originally developed as a digital comic, and the publisher invested resources in the adaptation of the book to have the story republished as a quality paper volume. The paper version is not as effective as the digital version, but the images from the first version were thoughtfully redeployed to fit into the paper dimensions, something that cannot be said of the adaptations of paper comics to a digital format. Indeed, the paper version works perfectly well, and in at least one place, the paper version uses an image better than does the digital version.[9] If the publisher could invest in adapting the digital comic into a paper format, why is it that the overwhelming majority of paper comics adapted to a digital format are still so disappointing?

The answer is not that there is something inferior about the new medium, but that most publishers are still anxious about digital comics. And of course, the reason they are so anxious is that those comics have not yet proved themselves as a commodity at least as reliable as paper comics. And that is the case because consumers are not yet committed to reading comics in any medium other than paper. In other words, for all the developments in the field of digital comics, especially digital comics for children, we are still pretty much where we started: not even sure that we really *want* them.

## Notes

1. In fact, a book of five new essays on comics coedited by Sabin and published in 2000 includes one chapter on digital comics, so I suspect that his opinions were already softening even as his essay appeared in print.

2. T. Campbell's *A History of Webcomics v1.0* traces the conversation back even further, to at least 1992, though that conversation had not quite crystallized until the turn of the millennium (7).

3. The phrases "for young readers" and "for children" throughout this chapter are sure to bother many of my readers. First of all, I use both terms interchangeably for no better reason than to avoid redundancy. Second, I use both terms to mean readers who are eighteen or younger. Finally, the preposition itself is problematic: many of the books I am considering may have been classified as "for" children by publishers or distributors (especially Comixology, which offers a genre category of children's comics), but the idea that creators themselves wrote the stories for or even mainly for children is an idea that deserves critique in a venue with more space than I have here.

4. Dirk Deppey has also sketched the very real possibility of the development of an industry standard for digital comics software that would make entry into the market impossible for anyone other than major publishers (48). Thus, the democratization of comics that digital comics are often seen to promise is threatened from the side of both consumers and producers.

5. A complaint McCloud was making more than a decade earlier (*Reinventing* 203), so we see that this is a persistent problem.

6. McCloud continues to complain about comics. For example, see minute 11:00 of "The Visual Magic of Comics," his TED talk from 2005.

7. *Neotopia* and *Globworld* have similar problems (see page 7 in the former and 5 in the latter), demonstrating that problem is not limited to the *Aladdin* series. Further, although the Comixology app offers what is called a "Guided View"—in which panels are presented one at a time, an option that solves the problem of the illegible font and the necessity of rotating

the device, this option magnifies other problems of the comic, as the view zooms in and out, sometimes within the same panel. As a result, illegibility is solved at the cost of pacing. I should concede, though, that a recent essay disagrees with my assessment of Guided View, saying that although Guided View sometimes results in "a careless butchery of the artist's intent," at other times, by delaying the reveal of a panel late on a page, Guided View can actually improve the drama and indeed pacing of a page (Murray).

8. I am grateful to Troy Kristoffer Mayes for helping me understand the fairly convoluted history of this book.

9. Compare pages 222 and 223 of the digital version with pages 28–29 of the print version. In the digital version, a character stands to reveal dramatically that her body is covered in kanji, but the tall panel fails to fit in the space afforded by a landscape orientation, and when the mobile device is rotated to a portrait orientation, the size of the image does not change to fill the available space. In the print version, however, the revelation of her marked skin is delayed until just after a page break, and the image fills the page well. My point is not so much that the print book did a better job as it is that in adapting the story from digital to print, the creators paid attention to how to use the qualities of the new medium (here, page turn and page size) fully.

## Works Cited

Aaron, Jason, Lason Latour, Yves Bigerel, et al. *Wolverine: Japan's Most Wanted Infinite Comic*. 14 issues. 2013.

———. *Wolverine: Japan's Most Wanted*. New York: Marvel Entertainment, 2014. Print.

"Atomic Robo in First Ever Digital Comic Convention Exclusive." Red5comics.com. 25 February 2013. Web. 20 July 2014.

Bigerel, Yves. "About Digital Comics." DeviantArt. 2009. Web. 14 July 2014.

———. "About 'About Digital Comics.'" DeviantArt. 2009. Web. 14 July 2014.

Brabner, Joyce, Harvey Pekar, and Frank Stack. *Our Cancer Year*. Philadelphia: Running Press, 1994. Print.

Bukatman, Scott. "Online Comics and the Reframing of the Moving Image." *The New Media Book*. Ed. Dan Harries. Berkeley: Univ. of California Press, 2002. 133–43. Print.

Campbell, T. *A History of Webcomics v1.0*. San Antonio, TX: Antarctic Press, 2006. Print.

Clevinger, Brian, and Scott Wegener. "Along Came a Tyrantula." *Atomic Robo: Two-Fisted Tales*. 2013.

Deppey, Dirk. "Format Wars: What Cartoonists Can Learn from Other Media in the Digital Age." *Comics Journal* 232.2 (2001): 48–50. Print.

Dittmar, Jakob F. "Digital Comics" *Scandinavian Journal of Comic Art* 1.2 (2012): 83–91. Print.

Edgington, Ian, and Patrick Reilly. *Aladdin: Legacy of the Lost*. Issue 1. 2010.

Fenty, Sean, Trena Houp, and Laurie Taylor. "Webcomics: The Influence and Continuation of the Comix Revolution." *ImageTexT* 1.2 (2005). Web. 14 July 2014.

Fies, Brian. *Mom's Cancer*. 2004. New York: Henry N. Abrams, 2006. Print.

Goodbrey, Daniel Merlin. "Digital comics—new tools and tropes." *Studies in Comics* 4.1 (2013): 185–98. Print.

Grall, Caanan. *Celadore*. 2011.

Groensteen, Thierry. *The System of Comics*. 1999. Trans. Bart Beaty and Nick Nguyen. Jackson: University Press of Mississippi, 2007. Print.

Groth, Gary. "McCloud Cuckoo-Land, Part One" *Comics Journal* 232 (April 2001): 32–40. Print.

———. "McCloud Cuckoo-Land, Part Two." *Comics Journal* 234.3 (2001): 49–52. Print.

Kindt, Matt, Yves Bigerel, and Ramon Bachs. *Ultimate Spider-Man: Final Exam*. 2012.

Kochalka, James. *Peanutbutter & Jeremy's Best Book Ever*. 2013.

Mayes, Troy Kristoffer. "Wolverine: Japan's Most Wanted Infinite Comic." Message to the author. 20 June 2014.

McCloud, Scott. "About 'About '*About Digital Comics*.'" *Scottmccloud.com*. 9 March 2009. Web. 21 July 2014.

———. "McCloud in Stable Condition Following Review, Groth Still at Large." *Comics Journal* 235 (July 2001): 70–79. Print.

———. "Print Comics: Reinventing Comics." *Scottmccloud.com*. 2002. Web. 14 July 2014.

———. *Reinventing Comics*. New York: Harper Collins, 2000. Print.

———. "The Visual Language of Comics." *Ted* 2005. Web. 23 March 2015.

Murray, Noel. "Reading Comics on Cell Phones Changes the Way the Medium Works." *A. V. Club*. 21 July 2015. Web. 29 July 2015.

Rosenzweig, Mike, and Rob Nix. *The First Daughter*. 2009.

Sabin, Roger. "The Crisis in Modern American and British Comics, and the Possibilities of the Internet as a Solution." *Comics & Culture: Analytical and Theoretical Approaches to Comics*. Eds. Anne Magnussen and Hans-Christian Christiansen. Copenhagen: Museum Tusculanum, 2000. 43–57. Print.

Sabin, Roger, and Teal Triggs. *Below Critical Radar: Fanzines and Alternative Comics from 1976 to Now*. Hove, UK: Slab-o-Concrete, 2000. Print.

Sanders, Joe Sutliff. "Hergé's Occupations: How the Creator of *Tintin* Made a Deal with the Devil and Became a Better Cartoonist." *The Comics of Hergé: When the Lines Are Not So Clear*. Jackson, MS: University Press of Mississippi, 2016. Print.

———. "*Valentine*, Comics for Mobile Devices, and the Limits of Empowerment." *On the Edge of the Panel: A Collection of Essays on Comics*. Ed. Esther Claudio Moreno and Julio Cañero. Newcastle Upon Tyne: Cambridge Scholars Publishing, 2015. Print.

Tobin, Paul, and Colleen Coover. *Bandette*. 2012.

———. *Bandette Vol. 1: Presto!* Milwaukie, OR: Dark Horse Comics, 2013. Print.

Waid, Mark, and Peter Krause. *Insufferable*. 2012.

Waid, Mark, and Stuart Immonen. *Avengers vs. X-Men: Infinite*. 1 issue. 2012.

# CONTRIBUTORS

**Michelle Ann Abate** is associate professor of literature for children and young adults at The Ohio State University. Michelle has published articles on comics and graphic novels in *Jeunesse* and the *Journal of Graphic Novels and Comics*. Michelle also serves on the advisory board for the Billy Ireland Cartoon Library and Museum as well as for *Inks*, the official journal of the Comics Studies Society. With Karly Marie Grice, Michelle co-curated the exhibit "'Good Grief!': Children and Comics," which was on display at the Billy Ireland Cartoon Library and Museum in the summer of 2016. The exhibit was accompanied by a collection of catalogue essays, titled "Children's Comics, Past and Present," which Michelle coedited with Joe Sutliff Sanders. Michelle is author of *The Big Smallness: Niche Marketing, the American Culture Wars, and the New Children's Literature*; *Bloody Murder: The Homicide Tradition in Children's Literature*; *Raising Your Kids Right: Children's Literature and American Political Conservatism*; and *Tomboys: A Literary and Cultural History*.

**Eti Berland** is the head librarian at the Saul Silber Memorial Library at Hebrew Theological College, where she teaches courses in children's literature and oral interpretation of literature and storytelling. She volunteers in the youth services department at Evanston Public Library to support its homeschool program, focused on STEM, creative writing, and filmmaking. She was most recently a member of the 2015 John Newbery Committee. She is also the social media coordinator for 90-Second Newbery Film Festival.

**Rebecca A. Brown** received her PhD from the University of Florida and teaches English at North Seattle College. She is coeditor of the monograph *Monsters and Monstrosity from the Fin de Siècle to the Millennium: New Essays*. She has also published essays on children in Hammer films and the evolution of picturebook monsters. Her forthcoming works focus on ghosts in Eva Ibbotson's YA fantasy novels and sea serpents in picturebooks.

**Christiane Buuck** is a senior lecturer in the Department of English at The Ohio State University, where she specializes in teaching developing writers. Her interests include Shaun Tan's visual languages and the power of the image in teaching analysis and composition. Her fiction and nonfiction have appeared in numerous publications, including *Cutthroat*, *Crab Orchard Review*, the *Sun*, and *Glamour*. She is currently finishing her first novel.

**Joanna C. Davis-McElligatt** is assistant professor of ethnic studies at the University of Louisiana at Lafayette. Her work has appeared in the *Comics Journal* online, *The Comics of Chris Ware: Drawing Is a Way of Thinking*, *The Pedagogy of Pop: Theoretical and Practical Strategies for Success*, and *Critical Insights: American Multicultural Identity*. She is currently working on a book-length project entitled *Black and Immigrant: Representations of the New African Diaspora in American Literature*.

**Rachel Dean-Ruzicka** received her PhD in American culture studies from Bowling Green State University. She is author of *Tolerance Discourse and Young Adult Holocaust Literature: Engaging Difference and Identity*. In addition to young adult literature, she has published on the graphic novel *Fun Home: A Family Tragicomedy*, the web comic *Girl Genius*, and the films of director Wes Anderson. She lives and writes in Atlanta, Georgia.

**Karly Marie Grice** is a doctoral student in the Department of Teaching and Learning in the College of Education and Human Ecology at The Ohio State University. She teaches introductory classes of children's literature and multi-cultural children's literature. Her research includes comics, graphic narratology, and visual culture. She has a published article on Sara Varon's graphic novel *Robot Dreams* as graphic medicine and is co-curating the comics exhibit "'Good Grief!': Children and Comics" at the Billy Ireland Cartoon Library and Museum with Michelle Ann Abate.

**Mary Beth Hines** is associate professor and former chair of the Department of Literacy, Culture, and Language Education at Indiana University, where she teaches undergraduate and graduate literacy courses. She has published a number of articles in *English Education, Teacher Development, Curriculum Journal, English Teaching: Practice and Critique*, and a variety of book chapters. Her work focuses on nonmainstream students as they construct texts and identities in the English classroom.

**Krystal Howard** is a doctoral candidate at Western Michigan University, where she teaches children's and young adult literature and writing. Her research interests include children's and young adult literature, comics studies, literary theory and criticism, and contemporary poetry, and she has published scholarship on the history of the American comic book and Neil Gaiman's picture books. The recipient of the Children's Literature Association 2016 Graduate Student Essay Award—PhD level, as well as a WMU Dissertation Completion Fellowship, she is currently working on her dissertation, "The Collage Effect and Participatory Reading in Contemporary Children's and Young Adult Literature."

**Aaron Kashtan** is a lecturer in the University Writing Program at UNC Charlotte. His research interests include comics, material rhetoric, and multimodal composition. He received his PhD in English with an emphasis in comics and visual rhetoric from the University of Florida.

**Michael L. Kersulov** is a graduate student in literacy, culture, and language education at Indiana University, Bloomington. Much of his research focuses on visual and digital literacies, teacher education, and English language arts classrooms in both alternative schools and gifted education. His current work looks at the use of memoir and nonfiction comics in the classroom in an effort to explore new literacy strategies and diverse forms of self-expression.

**Catherine Kyle** holds a PhD in English from Western Michigan University. She teaches at the College of Western Idaho and writes grants for the Cabin, a literary nonprofit. Her writings on comics, manga, video games, and pop culture have appeared in *Heroines of Film and Television*, *Colloquy*, and the *Culture-ist*. Her comics have been published in the *Rumpus*, *Gravel*, and *inkt|art*, among other places.

**David E. Low** is assistant professor of literacy education at California State University, Fresno. His research examines how young people's multimodal reading and composing practices—via the medium of comics, in particular—facilitate their various enactments of critical literacy. David has previously written articles for *Children's Literature in Education*, *Literacy*, *Voices from the Middle*, and *Journal of Early Childhood Literacy*. Aside from his scholarly work, David is a single-panel cartoonist.

**Anuja Madan** is assistant professor in the Department of English at Kansas State University, where she teaches courses in world literature. She received her PhD from University of Florida in 2016. Her coauthored book, *Notes of Running Feet: English in Primary Textbooks*, grew out of a commissioned group study of Indian English-language textbooks. She has also published articles on contemporary picture-book adaptations of the Indian epic *Mahabharata* and Jean-Luc Godard's films.

**Meghann Meeusen** teaches children's and adolescent literature at Western Michigan University, and she earned her PhD from Illinois State University. In addition to her work in comics, she has published on young adult dystopia and critical pedagogy approaches to YA fantasy, and her current research explores ideology and binary patterns in film adaptations of texts for young people.

**Rachel L. Rickard Rebellino** is a doctoral student specializing in literature for children and young adults in the Department of Teaching and Learning at The Ohio State University. She received her MA in Children's Literature from Eastern Michigan University and has taught courses in composition and adolescent literature. Her research interests include multimodality in books for young readers, fan-made responses to literature for children and young adults, and representations of parents in young adult literature.

**Rebecca Rupert** teaches high school English at Monroe County Community School Corporation in Bloomington, Indiana; she is also a Hoosier Writing Project Teacher Consultant and a National Board Certified Teacher.

**Cathy Ryan** teaches composition and visual narrative theory in the Department of English at The Ohio State University. She has coauthored plays and monologues and has published in *James Joyce Quarterly*, *International Journal of Business Communication*, *Business Communication Quarterly*, and *Encyclopedia of Management*. Her current interests include sound mapping animated films with friend and musician Dr. Gail Robertson (University of Central Arkansas), teaching wordless graphic novels, and mucking about in the creative worlds of Shaun Tan.

**Joe Sutliff Sanders** is associate professor of children's literature in the English Department at Kansas State University. His essays on comics (digital and otherwise) have been appearing in Europe and the United States since 2006, and his edited collection *The Comics of Hergé: When the Lines Are Not So Clear* was published in 2016 by the University Press of Mississippi. He and Charles Hatfield delivered the Francelia Butler lecture on comics at the Children's Literature Association Conference in June 2016.

**Marni Stanley** teaches English and women's studies at Vancouver Island University in Nanaimo, British Columbia, Canada. Her academic research and publication areas include graphic narrative, sexualities, nineteenth-century women travellers, and cinema.

**Joseph Michael Sommers** is associate professor in the Department of English at Central Michigan University, where he teaches coursework in children's and young adult literature, comics studies, and popular culture. He has published extensively on comics in his books *Sexual Ideology in the Works of Alan Moore*, *The American Comic Book*, and the forthcoming *Critical Insights: Neil Gaiman*, in addition to numerous articles and chapters on subjects such as posthumanism in *The Walking Dead*, Gaiman's *Hansel and Gretel*, and trauma in the work of Spider-Man.

**Gwen Athene Tarbox** is associate professor in the Department of English at Western Michigan University, where she teaches children's literature and comics studies. In addition to her book *The Clubwomen's Daughters: Collectivist Impulses in Progressive-era Girls' Fiction*, she has published articles on the clear line comics of Hergé and Gene Luen Yang, on the Harry Potter phenomenon, on the history of American children's fiction, and on youth participatory writing communities. She has a monograph on children's and YA comics forthcoming in 2017 from Bloomsbury Publishing.

**Sarah Thaller** is an instructor in the English Department at Washington State University, where she received her PhD in 2015, and currently teaches young adult literature and composition. While working to develop mental illness studies as a unique field of literary study, she has published articles on comics and mental illness, mental illness in young adult literature, and models of representation for depictions of mental illness in children's and YA fiction.

**Annette Wannamaker** is professor of children's literature in the Department of English Language and Literature at Eastern Michigan University, where she teaches courses about illustrated texts, children's media, and criticism of children's literature. She is North American Editor-in-Chief of *Children's Literature in Education*, has edited several collections of academic essays, and is the author of *Boys in Children's Literature and Popular Culture: Masculinity, Abjection, and the Fictional Child*. She is very active in the Children's Literature Association, serving as the 2015–2016 ChLA President.

**Lance Weldy** is associate professor in the Department of English at Francis Marion University, where he teaches composition and children's and young adult literature. He has coedited both the *C. S. Lewis: The Chronicles of Narnia New Casebook* and also a special issue on sexualities and children's culture for the *Children's Literature Association Quarterly*. He is currently finalizing a book chapter submission on child reality TV star Honey Boo Boo.

# INDEX

Made in the USA
Las Vegas, NV
12 January 2022

41228190R00217